KICKING DAFFODILS

Twentieth-Century Women Poets

KICKING DAFFODILS

Twentieth-Century Women Poets

Edited by Vicki Bertram

EDINBURGH UNIVERSITY PRESS

© The contributors, 1997

Edinburgh University Press
22 George Square, Edinburgh

Typeset in Fournier
by Hewer Text Composition Services, Edinburgh, and
printed and bound in Great Britain

A CIP record for this book is available
from the British Library

ISBN 0 7486 0782 X

Contents

Acknowledgements

I would like to thank the co-organisers of the *Kicking Daffodils* festival and conference: Jacqui Mansfield, fundraiser and co-ordinator; Deana Rankin, Manager of the Pegasus Theatre, Oxford; Caroline Jackson-Houlston, my colleague in the English Studies Department at Oxford Brookes, and Joanne Reardon, Literature Development Worker for Oxfordshire County Council. The event could not have taken place without generous funding from the English Arts Council, Southern Arts and Oxfordshire County Council, so on behalf of all the organisers and participants, I would like to thank them for their support. Over fifteen poets from the UK offered their services for very reasonable fees; thank you to all of them for their time, and for such valuable and memorable contributions.

The academics, poetry editors and poets who contributed to discussions and papers during the conference gave their ideas, and the results of painstaking work, for free; thank you for the input that resulted in such a stimulating weekend. Those who have contributed to this volume have met deadlines and dutifully kept me informed of their endless changes-of-address during its (overlong) gestation. Thank you also to Jackie Jones at Edinburgh University Press, for taking on the project when many others felt too constrained by their profit targets to even consider it.

On a personal note, the last few years have not been particularly easy, but I have had the love and support of countless friends, and of course I've drawn on them shamelessly. Without Jacqui's confident support *Kicking Daffodils* would never have happened; but without her love, wisdom and the boldness and energy of her attitude to life, mine would be so much the poorer. Jo Evans has been both mentor and dear friend for the last ten years, and I value her insight and intelligence greatly. My D. Phil. supervisors, Treva Broughton and Nicole Ward

Jouve, from York University, still serve as inspiring role models to me, as well as being supportive friends. With her tremendous skill, kindness and consistency Penny Hill has helped me work myself out. Clare Brant, Helen Bruder, Caroline Morrell, Nigel Messenger, Sarah and Jane O'Brien and Lisi Kunzeman have been 'there for me', with kindness and good humour, through many a crisis.

   And my family: they aren't great ones for poetry, but they make up for it with affection, and through their confidence in me. This book is dedicated to them: my mother Diana, my brother Richard, Nikki his wife, Scarlett her daughter; and to my late father Bob – with much love.

Copyright Permissions

Introduction

These essays have their origins in a simultaneous conference and festival, *Kicking Daffodils*, devoted to 'women and poetry' and held at Oxford Brookes University in April 1994. The title *Kicking Daffodils* is loosely-based on a poem 'Spring' by Grace Nichols in which a woman, newly-arrived in the United Kingdom from far warmer climes, passes her first winter enveloped in scarves and woolly jumpers, nursing the ailments that invariably accompany those endless damp, grey days. She barricades herself inside until finally the weather begins to look slightly kinder:

> with all the courage of an unemerged butterfly
> I unbolted the door and stepped outside
>
> only to have that daffodil baby
> kick me in the eye[1]

Hibernation is obviously a reaction to both literal and metaphorical coldness, and her shock of delighted surprise on encountering such a vivid announcement of new growth and renewal is signalled by the closing lines' lively rhythm. Nichols was born and brought up in Guyana; she is one of the first generation of Caribbean poets to have had some indigenous models to offset the influence of the colonial education syllabus, and her work harnesses the vernacular speech of her homeland. Nevertheless, it is surely not mere chance that makes this harbinger of new life and vitality none other than the daffodil, immortalised in Wordsworth's poem. If the flower represents English poetic tradition (the colonial model), the poem is in no doubt of the enduring potence of that tradition: this is not a dead white patriarch's tradition but one that issues its own challenges to the contemporary post-colonial poet, and to all the women poets discussed in this collection. It is the daffodil –

symbol of English poetic tradition – that is doing the kicking; and it is not a vicious kick but something more mischievous or goading. But the seductive attractions of that tradition also need to be addressed; for such attractions invariably accompany every system that operates to ensure women's oppression. In Nichols' poem, the bright yellow flowers are invitingly beautiful. It is with the responses to that challenging – and sometimes oppressive – kick that contributors to this volume are concerned, as it was in that spirit that the conference was planned. The essays that follow consider the many ways in which twentieth-century women poets have engaged with, questioned, subverted or recast mainstream, overwhelmingly male-authored traditions of 'English' poetry.[2]

The phrase 'Kicking Daffodils' is of course ambiguous. Some interpreted the conference title as a feminist call-to-arms, for women poets to rid themselves once and for all of what Gertrude Stein memorably described as 'patriarchal poetry', and to junk the lot of it. Such wholesale rejection has very rarely formed part of any feminist project in relation to prose or poetry. Rather it is the more insidious, subtle influences that women poets have needed to confront: the myths that hover around poetry and the idea of The Poet; the lack of models for the kind of vision they want to convey. As the poet Eavan Boland has pointed out, such things may exert a profoundly negative psychological influence over the woman who wants to write poetry.[3] Are these then 'feminist readings'? I have always been unhappy with the term, since the potential richness of the word 'feminism' invariably gets reduced to some facile and wildly simplistic slogan. Feminist practitioners are thus accused of narrowness of vision, of being swayed by resentment, and being openly partisan. In my view all criticism partakes of some of these qualities, and may be the better for it. The contributors to this book have certainly been influenced by feminist perspectives on cultural and literary production, though their work does not display these negative characteristics. They all believe that gender is a significant factor both in the reception and potential interpretations of poetry. Far from this implying any uniformity of approach, the variety of positions demonstrated in these essays actually draws attention to the narrow uniformity that characterises the attitudes and aesthetics behind most mainstream accounts of poetry. Feminist insights do, certainly, lead to political analyses – and are valuable for precisely that reason. But it is the poetry, not any (mythical) united feminist project that leads the way in these essays; it is the poetry that does the kicking.

Similarly this anthology is not trying to establish an alternative female canon. Indeed one of the most valuable things to emerge from it is the refreshing shift in criticism away from questions of value. Certainly it does not try to be comprehensive. While Charlotte Mew appears to be the 'oldest' poet under consideration, in reviewing the contemporary situation contributors take a much longer historical perspective, tracing the roots and traditions out of which today's writing grows. In recognition of the exciting work that has appeared during the last twenty years, a majority of the essays do concentrate on the contemporary period, but they situate this recent work in context, and see it – where appropriate – as emerging from dialogue with, or in response to, particular poetic forms and traditions. So, for example, essays on women's poetry in the 1990s devote significant attention to eighteenth-century ballad forms, epic poetry, and the symbolic importance of Sappho. Poetry from the 'peripheries' – as post-colonial theory terms those areas far from the powerhouse of the imperial centre – is also explored: from Scotland, Northern and Southern Ireland, and – though coverage of such a large, heterogeneous area in a book of this nature can be no more than a beginning – the Anglophone Caribbean. It is a pity there is no discussion of the Welsh poetry scene, but there are, inevitably, omissions; this book is only a start, and I hope there will be many more such studies. The famous are represented: Sylvia Plath, Grace Nichols and Jackie Kay, for example, though for the most part the essays are concerned with themes and issues rather than focused on specific poets. In part this is a deliberate attempt to avoid the fêting of one or two individuals, and to place poetry firmly within its social context. Experimental poetry receives long-overdue attention in essays on neglected poets like Lorine Niedecker, Veronica Forrest-Thomson and Denise Riley. While North American poetry has its own very separate tradition, there have been periods of fruitful communication and overlap, and these are represented here in discussions of Niedecker, H.D., Sylvia Plath and Elizabeth Bishop, and in the essays by Romana Huk and Deryn Rees-Jones.

Sometimes the specific geographical location of a poet is treated as less significant; a case in point is Voth Harman's analysis of birth poetry, where the experience of giving birth and writing about it is the unifying theme. In Ward Jouve's exploration of the relation between the Poet and the Mother, uneasiness with this potentially-homogenising approach is made explicit. So while geographical boundaries are significant, it would be inaccurate to imply that nationality is a prime definition-point for these poets. As Eavan Boland comments, the idea of the nation is deeply problematic for women poets.[4] There is evidence in this collection to suggest that women poets are less interested in questions of nationhood than their male counterparts. In her essay on the innovative versions of epic poetry by Derek Walcott and Jean Binta Breeze, Paula Burnett suggests that Breeze envisages a scenario beyond nationalist boundaries. And as Ailbhe Smyth notes in her discussion of (southern) Irish poets, national boundaries, however fiercely contested, do not hold much sway in their work. Instead, poetic emigration is a hallmark; these women have 'looked west' for liberating initiatives and inspiration.

Just as national boundaries prove inadequate alone, so too do other categories that are associated with feminist studies. There is no section on Black poetry, nor Lesbian poetry, but several of the essays discuss work by black and lesbian poets. I hope that my decision to opt for different categories does not erase the significance of these identities; it is not intended to do so. In part I felt that the rigid demarcations such sections would imply would be misleading. Jackie Kay exemplifies the problem: as black Glaswegian Lesbian, it would be unhelpful to squeeze her into one category as opposed to another.

Scepticism of categorisations also characterises the use of theoretical models in the essays. Alison Donnell warns of the reductiveness of applying either a strict post-colonial or feminist theoretical perspective to Una Marson's sonnet sequence, pointing out how much of the text's complexity would thus be lost. Paraskevi Papaleonida displays a similar desire to critique post-colonial theory itself, using the poetry to do so. Indeed, 'dissolution of rigidities' might have been an appropriate subtitle for the volume.

In keeping with the feminist impulse behind this project aspects of women's experience that have previously been ignored are acknowledged and explored. So, too, is the question of sexual identity – for example, heterosexuality, as figured in the love poetry of Una Marson; lesbian poets in Ireland, and H.D.'s struggles towards articulating a bisexual identity. In *Stealing the Language*, Alicia Suskin Ostriker suggested that the problem of establishing an identity was the central theme in women's poetry.[5] The essays in this collection imply that this has begun to change, and offer some explanations as to why. They also urge feminist critics to move forwards accordingly, to tackle some of the uncomfortable areas still largely taboo in feminist criticism (like motherhood and [heterosexual] love) because of their close association with traditionally constricting definitions of 'natural' female roles.

Finally, in keeping with this eclectic inclusivity, a few of the essays consider male poets too – not as straw men to knock down gleefully, but as writers faced with similar challenges, finding different paths. Such work can, I believe, lead to a more profound understanding of the workings of gender.

WOMEN'S POETRY: CRITICAL TRADITIONS

The publication of two anthologies, *The World Split Open: Four Centuries of Women Poets in England and America, 1552–1950* and *The Penguin Book of Women Poets*[6] marked the first major attempts to retrieve and celebrate the wealth of women's poetic productivity. The scope of both was huge, and in its effort to cover the world and all history in one volume, the Penguin collection can now be seen to have been somewhat over-ambitious. Throughout the 1980s many more anthologies appeared: many were small-press productions, often motivated by the excitement of the Women's Movement.[7] Slightly later larger publishing houses realised they had been missing out on a lucrative market, and published their own anthologies, implicitly claiming to offer an authoritative overview of the terrain.

Debate about the justification for women-only anthologies – previously regarded by the editors of the early collections as wholly appropriate in the face of the 'general' anthologies' utter neglect of women – took a new turn. The introductions to these 'authoritative' collections are especially interesting because they reveal the anxiety of the well-respected women poets commissioned to undertake the editing work when faced with the publication of what they regarded as a flood of inferior poetry.[8] Clearly, they were worried that their work would somehow be contaminated by association, and set out to differentiate between quality poetry and that of, in Carol Rumens' phrase, 'the amateurs'. It is hard to imagine male poets fearing contagion by writers for whom they had little respect, and I take this as evidence of the precariousness with which those few women whose work has been accepted by the mainstream occupied their privileged positions.

Little critical discussion accompanied this flurry of anthologies, although the need for some thoughtful discussion of questions of aesthetic criteria was already evident from frequent uneasy asides in reviews of women poets' work. Sally Minogue's essay, 'Prescriptions and Proscriptions: feminist criticism and contemporary poetry'[9] is a fascinating testament to the confusion and anxiety that pervaded the scene of women's poetic productivity. Meanwhile in the US, a couple of studies of twentieth-century women poets appeared.[10] Their approach was thematic: anger, the struggle for self-definition, and a new sensuality were identified as the most prominent hallmarks of women's poetry. It was not until 1987 that the first study was published in Britain (although The Women's Press did bring out an edition of Alicia Suskin Ostriker's *Stealing the Language* in the same year): Jan Montefiore's *Feminism and Poetry: Language, Experience, Identity in Women's Writing*.[11] At last some discussion of the confused terrain was available. Montefiore tackled many angles, including the vexed questions of aesthetics and evaluation, and used the theoretical work of Luce Irigaray to reveal the textual dynamics at work in women's love poetry. The book takes its examples from relatively well-known UK and US poets from the nineteenth and twentieth centuries though, in retrospect, the absence of examples from contemporary UK women poets is surprising. In 1991 Liz Yorke's *Impertinent Voices* appeared,[12] offering a poststructuralist analysis, once again largely of US poets.

Over the last few years mainstream poetry criticism's almost pathological avoidance of theory has been challenged by the appearance of theoretically-informed analyses of the contemporary scene. Alan Robinson's *Instabilities in Contemporary British Poetry* and *English Poetry since 1940* by Neil Corcoran are two such studies:[13] both include only one chapter on women poets, and acknowledge their discomfort and uncertainty in this territory. Many of those interested in poetry and theory seem to have found their ideal subject matter in 'experimental' poetry, long-marginalised in the UK. *Literary Theory and Poetry* and *New British Poetries: the scope of the possible* are both dedicated to this neglected work, and both show interest in the dynamics of race and gender, and how they may be articulated in poetry.[14] Antony Easthope's collection, *Contemporary Poetry meets Modern Theory*,[15] includes several essays on women poets and thus represents a marked departure from tradition in more than its methodology. Perhaps this is a sign that things are changing, but the world of *Poetry Review*, self-styled 'official' voice of poetry in the UK, remains stolidly opposed to the 'nonsense' produced by experimental 'cliques',[16] and to the suggestion that gender, race or class might have any light to shed on the designation of 'good poetry'.

In spite of the signs of interest from these more theoretically-inclined critics, women poets continue to gain little attention in the mainstream. The strategies outlined so wittily by Joanna Russ all those years ago in *How To Suppress Women's Writing*[17] would still seem to be in operation in the esoteric world of poetry criticism. So why have women poets received so little critical attention? There is not space here to do more than outline some of the explanations offered by feminists over the last decade; the interested reader should consult these in full. Louise Bernikow offers a comprehensive and lively overview in her introduction to *The World Split Open*. She writes of the debilitating effect of entrenched ideas about woman as the silent Muse, incubator of male creativity rather than producer of her own; the squeamishness of male critics when faced with 'women's subject matter', and their tendency to be disdainful of women's religious and love poetry, the two themes traditionally considered suitable for their attention. Jeni Couzyn, introducing *The Bloodaxe Book of Contemporary Women Poets*[18] resurrects a submerged female tradition of poetry and song in ballads, lullabies and other predominantly oral forms. She also includes insightful prose contributions from each of the poets represented. Cora Kaplan, grappling with Lacanian theories of the gendering of subjectivity, suggests that poetry, as the most privileged discourse within a society, has been barred to women and reserved for the male élite. She speculates about the effect of that exclusion on women poets who dared to trespass into its hallowed realms.[19] A central barrier still, in my view, is the primacy of liberal humanist approaches wherein poetry is prized for its universality, its transcendence of the personal to offer wisdom and insight, ostensibly to all. I have argued elsewhere[20] that it is the unspoken equation of 'human' with 'male' that renders women's insights partial, merely personal, and lacking in human resonance. As one of the participants at this year's Amnesty Lectures in Oxford observed, Amnesty's own publicity leaflet, 'Women's Rights Are Human Rights' makes clear just how strong resistance remains to the idea that women are fully human. It is sobering to realise that this slogan still needed repeating in 1996.

Several other, more specific explanations for the neglect of women's poetry are proposed in the essays collected here. Kathleen Bell suggests that the shaping of literary history has privileged the work of an educated élite, overlooking that of socially- or educationally-marginalised figures like Charlotte Mew and Lorine Niedecker. The barriers to publication are still immense, and there are still very few women poetry editors. Several contributors comment on the way in which the preferred themes of male anthology editors and critics are implicitly gendered: women's preoccupations do not fit within the same parameters at all comfortably. Hence the notorious exclusion of all but three women from Tom Paulin's *The Faber Book of Political Verse*.[21] 'Politics' means class and national struggles, not women's efforts to win justice and human rights. The essays on 'experimental' poetry comment on the marginality of women even within these already peripheral groups: because women are writing aslant, their work seems to break the rules of the avant-garde. Thus Denise Riley is criticised for being too self-referential; Lorine Niedecker is patronised as a naive nature poet, her commitment to the local collapsed into a preoccupation with the personal. These poets' gendered – and sexed – struggles with language and form are not understood because their male colleagues have their eyes on a different set of obstacles. A couple of the essays link the neglect of women's poetry to a much broader and damaging cultural silencing of women, and this is viewed as particularly pertinent in relation to women's bodies. Karin Voth Harman looks at some of the attempts her contemporaries have made to reclaim the act of giving birth from its co-optation as a (male) metaphor for creativity. Gill Plain argues that female subjectivity, emerging forms of which can be traced in women's war poetry, was – and is? – surplus to patriarchal requirements, and thus dropped out of literary history.

The essays in this collection employ a rich range of methodologies and offer new directions for poetry criticism. They don't chuck out the old methods of exegesis, with their recognition of the importance of the relation between form and content in a poem, and their close reading strategies; but they work by incorporating these techniques within newly politicised and theorised reading methods. Many make use of the work of the poststructuralist 'French feminists' – Julia Kristeva, Hélène Cixous and Luce Irigaray; others offer illuminating juxtapositions of psychological theories of female subjectivity and women's poetic production. But these ideas are integrated with an awareness of the specific context – historical, geographical, cultural and political – in which the poetry was written and published, as well as reflections on the target audience. Perhaps the most exciting development signalled here is in the identification of poetry as a valuable index of cultural change: yielding insights into the placing and construction of women in culture and society, and offering a record, hitherto neglected, of changes and challenges to the status quo. In this schema, women's poems offer not the radical revolution envisaged by Julia Kristeva's semiotic irruptions, but a more socially-grounded and gradual erosion of the resistances of patriarchal hegemony.

The 'Kicking Daffodils' festival aimed to bridge the gulf between poets, critics and readers. To this end, Jackie Kay ran a weekend writing workshop with a group of young women who had recently moved out of local authority care and were living independently for the first time. They then performed the poetry they had created. There were other workshops over the weekend itself, open to conference delegates and to local residents (spaces were reserved for a quota of the latter). There was also an Open Forum each day, where anyone could read their poetry. We wanted to create an environment in which poetry was alive and, indeed, kicking; to ensure that the art we set out to celebrate and explore intellectually was not suffocated in the process. It is my hope that this written record of that event preserves at least some of the atmosphere of excitement and enthusiasm that was so tangible during that weekend.

NOTES

1. Grace Nichols, 'Spring', in *The Fat Black Woman's Poems* (London, Virago, 1984), p.34.
2. I use inverted commas here to highlight the dubiousness of this designation. In keeping with colonialist confidence, the writings of many who would not, as a matter of choice, have called themselves 'English', have been subsumed within the category.
3. 'The Woman Poet: Her Dilemma', *Stand* (Winter 1986–7), p.48.
4. Eavan Boland, 'The Woman Poet in a National Tradition', *Studies* (Dublin), Vol. 76 (1987), pp.148–58; extended version published in *LIP: A Kind Of Scar* (Dublin, Attic Press, 1989).
5. Alicia Suskin Ostriker, *Stealing the Language: the emergence of women's poetry in America* (Boston, Beacon Press, 1986; London, The Women's Press, 1987), pp.59–90.
6. Louise Bernikow, *The World Split Open: Four Centuries of Women Poets in England and America* (New York, Vintage, 1974; London, Women's Press, 1979); *The Penguin Book of Women Poets*, Carol Cosman, Joan Keefe and Kathleen Weaver (eds) (London, Allen Lane, 1978; London, Penguin, 1980).
7. See, for example, *One Foot On The Mountain: an anthology of British Feminist Poetry 1969–79*, ed. Lillian Mohin (London, Onlywomen Press, 1979); *Bread and Roses: women's poetry of the nineteenth and twentieth centuries*, ed Diana Scott (London, Virago, 1982); *In The Pink*, ed The Raving Beauties (London, The Women's Press, 1983); *Purple and Green: Poems by 33 Women Poets* (London and Bradford, Rivelin Grapheme, 1985); *A Dangerous Knowing: Four Black Women Poets* (London, Sheba Feminist Publishers, 1986); *Beautiful Barbarians: Lesbian Feminist Poetry*, ed. Lillian Mohin (London, Onlywomen Press, 1986); *Watchers and Seekers: Creative Writing by Black Women in Britain*, (eds), Rhonda Cobham and Merle Collins (London, The Women's Press, 1987).
8. Here I am thinking of Fleur Adcock, editor of *The Faber Book of Twentieth Century Women's Poetry* (London, Faber and Faber, 1987); and of Carol Rumens, editor of *Making for the Open: the Chatto book of post-feminist poetry 1964–84* (London, Chatto & Windus, 1985).
9. Sally Minogue, 'Prescriptions and Proscriptions: feminist criticism and contemporary poetry', pp.179–236, in *Problems for Feminist Criticism* (London, Routledge, 1990).
10. Suzanne Juhasz, *Naked and Fiery Forms: Modern American Poetry by Women: A New Tradition* (New York, Harper and Row, 1976); Alicia Suskin Ostriker, *Stealing the Language* (London, The Women's Press, 1986, 1987); Mary K. DeShazer, *Inspiring Women: reimagining the muse* (New York and Oxford, Athene/Pergammon Press, 1986).
11. Jan Montefiore, *Feminism and Poetry: Language, Experience, Identity in Women's Writing* (London, Pandora, 1987; revised and republished 1994).
12. Liz Yorke, *Impertinent Voices: subversive strategies in contemporary Women's poetry* (London, Routledge, 1991).
13. Alan Robinson, *Instabilities in Contemporary British Poetry* (London, Macmillan, 1988); Neil Corcoran, *English Poetry since 1940* (Harlow, Essex, Longman, 1993).
14. *Literary Theory and Poetry*, ed. David Murray (London, Batsford, 1989); *New British Poetries: the scope of the possible*, Robert Hampson and Peter Barry (eds), (Manchester, Manchester University Press, 1993). The poetry anthology *the new british poetry*, Gillian Allnutt, Fred D'Aguiar, Ken Edwards and Eric Mottram (eds), (London, Paladin, 1988), is one of the very few to transfer theoretical interest in race

and gender to actual poetry. Each of the editors offers a selection of work: Allnutt's is titled 'Quote Feminist Unquote Poetry', to signal her misgivings about the category; D'Aguiar's provides an invaluable selection of recent black British poets.

15. *Contemporary Poetry meets Modern Theory* Antony Easthope and John O. Thompson (eds), (Hemel Hempstead, Harvester Wheatsheaf, 1991).
16. Peter Forbes, 'How the century lost its poetry', *Poetry Review*, Vol. 86(1) (Spring 1996), pp.3–6. Forbes continues, 'What the theorists of modernism and postmodernism have done is to encourage poetry that needs justification, critical props, excuses for the wilfulness of self-indulgent individuals – as if most needed any further excuse. But self-indulgent art will never last beyond the life of its mutual support coterie system.'
17. Joanna Russ, *How To Suppress Women's Writing* (London, The Women's Press, 1984).
18. Jeni Couzyn, *The Bloodaxe Book of Contemporary Women Poets* (Newcastle-upon-Tyne, Bloodaxe Books, 1985).
19. Cora Kaplan, 'Language and Gender', in *Sea Changes: Essays on Culture and Feminism* (London, Verso, 1986).
20. 'Post-Feminist Poetry? "one more word for balls" ', in *Contemporary British Poetry: essays in theory and criticism*, ed. James Acheson and Romana Huk (Albany, State University of New York Press, 1996).
21. Tom Paulin (ed.), *The Faber Book of Political Verse* (London, Faber and Faber, 1986).

Section One: Oblique Angles: Women Poets and Modernism

During the last decade, feminist scholars have challenged conventional male-centred versions of literary modernism, and begun to redraw the cultural map of the period 1880–1935. The three essays in this section explore the poetry of women who do not fit comfortably into orthodox classifications of modern literature. They place the female poets centre-stage in their analysis, restoring a sense of the contemporary contexts within which they wrote, and applying current theories about sexual identity and female subjectivity to their work.

Kathleen Bell considers the poetry of Charlotte Mew, who has been uncomfortably stranded between 'Victorian' and 'Modern' literary eras. Bell proposes a move away from critics' reliance on the well-known manifestos of the period, since such a starting point inevitably privileges the writings of the educated (and thus largely male) élite. The resulting picture may be less clear (and therefore less attractive to critics), but should yield 'a fuller picture of literary debate, interaction and development'. Bell retrieves evidence of the preoccupations of the journals in which Mew's work was published in order to illuminate the more radical and political angles of her work. Arguing that Mew's modern themes were matched by stylistic innovation recognised by her contemporaries, she goes on to compare Mew with T.S. Eliot and, in a radical conclusion, suggests that she is more of a modernist than the *maestro* himself. Bell claims that, unlike Eliot's, Mew's characters do not shrink from the full implications of fragmentation and incoherence.

Gill Plain's subject is women's poetry of the First World War. Like Bell, she recreates the contemporary context within which these poems were written and published in her effort to move beyond the uneasy reactions that have greeted the recovery of this work. Her essay suggests 'a shift in critical attention from what women wrote to the (f)act of their writing' and, accordingly, she reads the poems as 'grief work', part of the process of mourning. In order to do this she draws on psychological studies of that process by Freud, Julia Kristeva and Colin Murray Parkes. At a time when women had no claim to political subjectivity except through their identification with a man, acts of self-definition in poetry can also be seen to contain a liberating potential; as Plain comments, 'If women, whose identity traditionally derives from that of their menfolk, undergo a loss of attachment to these men, then they can also be seen to be distanced from the symbolic order that would control them.' The poetry records the emergence of new forms of female subjectivity, and Plain explores the potentially subversive nature of such activity.

Megan Lloyd Davies traces how H.D. manoeuvred a way around the 'rules' of Imagism in order to clear space for the articulation of a bisexual identity. Lloyd Davies argues that although H.D. was initially faithful to the movement's precepts, even in the early poems she is experimenting with the subversive effects of desire. This gradually develops into the more overt depiction of a lesbian subject, although here desire is only articulated in parentheses, and through the use of homoerotic myths. The essay concludes with an analysis of 'The Master', H.D.'s critique of Freud's theories about female sexuality, in which she successfully articulates a bisexual self that incorporates both masculine and feminine sides of her personality. Nevertheless, as the author of the essay comments, she faces – and thus anticipates – the difficulties still encountered in any attempt to move beyond the binary opposition of heterosexuality versus homosexuality.

1

Charlotte Mew, T.S. Eliot and Modernism

Kathleen Bell

Critics discussing modernism in Britain have often treated it as a self-defined movement – understandably, given the profusion of manifestos and critical writings produced by certain writers commonly recognized as 'modernist'. However, with modernism as with the majority of literary movements, most of the defining selves are masculine. Thus in Peter Faulkner's *Modernist Reader*,[1] a compilation of pronouncements on and prescriptions for poetry and prose, only two of the fourteen contributors are female and one of these merits inclusion for a single piece which she may not have written.[2]

It may be appropriate to accept that writers can define the movements to which they belong in certain cases; for instance, imagists and vorticists set out manifestos and their work can usefully be related to their stated aims. However, in the case of modernist writing, much of which was defined retrospectively,[3] while the stated aims of later-defined 'modernists' are naturally of interest, it is unhelpful to read these as prescriptive for a movement. The concentration of critics on those writers who have defined and propounded their aims for literature may say more about the relation of critics and writers to the academy than it does about modernism. T.S. Eliot, educated at Harvard and the Sorbonne, was inevitably more likely to adopt the authoritative tones of academe than Charlotte Mew, whose formal education ended when her beloved teacher, Lucy Harrison, left the Gower Street School.

To dispense with the clear distinctions offered by writers' manifestos creates problems for the critic; the definition of movements becomes less manageable and their edges may seem to blur. In the place of clear definitions and rules we must substitute thematic and stylistic congruence and even past public perception. The corresponding benefit may be a fuller picture of literary debate, interaction and development, and the shift of emphasis will place women more plainly within the literary scenario. Women writers were, after all, read and reviewed by both male and female writers while their works were, for the most part, selected for publication by male editors and publishers. Therefore if they wished to resist or influence society they were compelled to do so by interaction with it. If Mew is accepted as a modernist, perception of Mew should change but so should the perception of modernism.

The first difficulty in situating Mew as a modernist is that she is too easily regarded as Victorian. Born in 1869 and first published in the 1890s, she may seem to invite the 'Victorian' tag, although Yeats, born four years earlier, has eluded it while Pound's narrow escape from *The Oxford Book of Victorian Verse*[4] may indicate an overlap between Victorianism and modernism. Recently Angela Leighton has assigned Mew's poetry to the Victorian era by including her in her book, *Victorian Women Poets*. While Leighton acknowledges Mew's stylistic modernism, she concentrates on what she sees as her Victorian themes and sensibility, asserting:

> . . . in spirit Charlotte Mew is one of the last Victorians. Untouched, in life, by the sexual and political emancipations of the twentieth century or, in her art, by the obvious thematic freedoms of modernism, she remained imaginatively tied to the symbols of a past age.[5]

Leighton's perspective does offer some helpful insights (notably into Rossetti's influence on Mew). I shall argue, however, for a different view of Mew's relation to her time, encouraged by reading Mew's poems in the publications in which they first appeared, and relating them to feminist debates both in Mew's time and our own.

Today, Mew's poem 'The Farmer's Bride' offers a chilling picture of a young married woman ('Too young maybe', p.1, 1.12) who lives in fear of marital rape. She is kept prisoner in her husband's house and society actively concurs in her detention. The poem is particularly chilling because of the calm reasonableness with which the farmer speaks, until the poem gives way to his desire at the conclusion:

> What's Christmas-time without there be
> Some other in the house than we!
> She sleeps up in the attic there
> Alone, poor maid. 'Tis but a stair
> Betwixt us. Oh! my God! the down,
> The soft young down of her, the brown,
> The brown of her – her eyes, her hair, her hair!

> (p.2, 11.40–6).

Critics hostile to feminist readings might argue that to view the farmer's voice as 'chilling' demonstrates a contemporary feminist sensibility and that the poem is concerned primarily with the farmer's suffering (although the title proclaims a concern with his bride). It might even be suggested that to read the conclusion as prefiguring rape is to read too much into the poem.[6] After all, the volume of which 'The Farmer's Bride' is the title poem was reviewed in *The Nation* in 1916 when the reviewer plainly took the farmer's side, albeit slightly defensively: 'the farmer is made so sympathetic that a mere man can hardly imagine why the most sensitive woman should run out into the night to avoid him'.[7]

However this conclusion would have been far less probable for *The Nation*'s readers when the poem was first published in 1912. As the Royal Commission on Divorce and Matrimonial Causes approached the end of its deliberations,[8] articles and letters in *The Nation* were debating the proper relations of men and women in marriage on the assumption that the extension of the franchise to women was a foregone conclusion. For example, two weeks before the publication of Mew's poem, an unsigned article in the 'Life and Letters' section of the magazine condemned both inequality in marriage and the requirement that a wife promise to obey her husband. It argued that 'the seeds of despotism are nourished in the closer circle of the family' and that, as long as this despotism was nourished, men would remain 'spiritually [un]fitted for the true civic equality' which would be necessary when women finally achieved the franchise.[9] The controversy is further evidenced by a letter the following week, advocating male leadership and female subordination in marriage.[10] While neither article nor letter deals directly with marital rape, both address the question of socially sanctioned male dominance. Mew's use of an example beyond the book-reading bourgeoisie might well, for middle-class feminist readers, have strengthened the argument against wifely obedience by moving into social circumstances in which abuse of power was frequently reckoned more extreme. The feminist campaigner Margaret Llewellyn-Davies, in a letter to *The Nation* in 1911, had expressed her aim to alleviate the 'hidden suffering and enforced degradation existing among women often termed "the respectable working-class" '.[11]

While 'The Farmer's Bride' seems to have had the greatest impact, many of Mew's poems similarly derive from the context and debates of their time. 'The Fête', first published in *The Egoist* on 1 May 1914 was included in a publication known both for sexual daring and its adherence to the literary avant-garde.[12] According to Mew's biographer Penelope Fitzgerald, it was the novelist May Sinclair who first took Mew's work to Pound;[13] however Mew must have approved of her work appearing (without payment) in a publication notorious for its daring. 'The Fête', seen in this context and placed beside other poems Mew wrote in a male voice, seems to follow the trend of much feminist thought and campaigning of the period in shifting the idea of danger from female to male sexuality. In 'The Fête' the event which is the poem's core, while clearly associated with the speaker's adolescent discovery of sex, is obscured as 'this Thing' and 'the Enchanted Thing' (pp.6–7, ll.108, 115 and 149) and associated with both 'a strange room' and a woodland glade with 'fern', 'black trunks of trees', 'violets' and 'cruelly broken' stalks (ll.104–5 and 150–3). Exactly what has happened is ambiguous. It may be simply a sexual encounter or an act of violence, suggested by the repeated references to death and dust. The boy's voice, in its consciousness of sex and projection of guilt onto women ('Only the hair/Of any woman can belong to God.', ll.151–2), is neurotic and traumatised. In this the poem seems to have something in common with the undeniably modernist work which, at Pound's insistence, was being serialised in *The Egoist* that year, James Joyce's *Portrait of the Artist as a Young Man*.[14]

Much of Leighton's definition of Mew as Victorian takes as its focus her interest in the figure of the Magdalen, the prostitute and the fallen woman. Leighton repeatedly describes such interest as 'out of date', calling 'Madeleine in Church' 'one of the last "fallen women" poems in English'.[15] But while the motifs which Mew uses may be familiar from Victorian writing, they have a particular pertinence in the modernist period. Not only did the re-establishment of the sexual woman as sympathetic character engage directly with the purity campaigning of Christabel Pankhurst and the Women's Social and Political Union[16] but it contradicted the increasingly unsympathetic treatment of the prostitute or fallen woman by male writers from the 1890s onward.[17] Like Mew, T.S. Eliot was fascinated by the image of the fallen woman and he too linked her to past depictions, loading his work with the depiction of unchaste sexual encounters. A recent article by David Newton has even suggested that Eliot was influenced by Mew, adapting a line from 'Madeleine in Church' into the famous declaration in 'The Waste Land', 'I will show you fear in a handful of dust'.[18] The epigraph to 'Portrait of a Lady' (p.18) refers to fornication, suggesting an unstated sexual relationship in the poem. In 'Rhapsody on a Windy Night' the woman 'who hesitated toward you in the light of the door' (p.24, l.17) at half past one in the morning is presumably offering her body for sale while Sweeney in 'Sweeney Erect' seems to have taken up residence in a brothel.[19] Meanwhile 'The Waste Land' is filled with references to all kinds of fallen women. The 'unstoppered perfumes' in 'A Game of Chess' ('The Waste Land' p.64, l.87) recall the inner sanctum of the famous bad woman of Victorian fiction, Lady Audley.[20] Meanwhile the sexual availability of the typist and the passive compliance of the three Thames maidens is set against earlier schemes of fall and retribution, suggested by the poem's cultural frame of reference. Readers are expected to know the original ending to the song from *The Vicar of Wakefield* (p.69, ll.253–6), in which the ruined woman's only end to grief is death, just as they are expected to know the fate of the adulterous lovers, Tristan and Isolde, whose story is recalled in quotations from the Wagner opera (pp.61–2, ll.31–4 and 42). The contrasts Eliot offers suggest a nostalgia for past punishment of fallen women – even a desire on the poet's part for a firm system of guilt and retribution. It may even be suggested that the unpunished female sexuality of the present is held to blame for the emasculating wound of the Fisher King which such critics as Cleanth Brooks and Charles Moorman have identified as central to the poem. Against 'The Waste Land', Mew's slightly earlier 'Madeleine in Church', reads like a defence of female sexual impulsiveness. Madeleine rejects 'Virtue', defining it as the boredom of being owned by husband and child in marriage:

> The temperate, well-worn smile
> The one man gives you, when you are evermore his own:
> And afterwards the child's . . . (p.24, ll.76–8)

In its place she asserts her own sexual identity, which she fears losing as she ages, but which is inextricably bound up with her sense of self:

> I think my body was my soul,
> And when we are made thus
>   Who shall control
> Our hands, our eyes, the wandering passion of our feet . . . (ll.64–7)

The controversy created by 'The Waste Land' is well-documented, even to the point of exaggeration. But Mew's poems, despite the small print-run of 500 for the first edition of *The Farmer's Bride*, created their own, minor controversy. According to one of Alida Monro's memoirs of Mew,[21] the Poetry Bookshop's usual compositor refused to typeset the poem 'Madeleine in Church' on the grounds that it was blasphemous. Monro attributes this to the printer's Methodism; however the law of blasphemous libel may have played its part since it threatened to punish printer and publisher as well as author.[22] The Poetry Bookshop had to find a new printer before the book could be produced.

But contemporary reviewers of *The Farmer's Bride* were, in 1916, more interested in Mew's poetic style and its relation to contemporary or earlier movements than the content of her work. H.D., reviewing in *The Egoist*, compared Mew to Ford Maddox Hueffer (later Ford) and began by suggesting that:

> even the most 'original' among us may take a sort of perverse pleasure in finding a new writer daring to discard his personality to follow, remotely or unconsciously perhaps, the tradition of an earlier generation.[23]

In the context of modernist writing, H.D. is not defining Mew as old-fashioned; the inverted commas around the word 'original' suggest some problems with the term. Her references to discarded personality and the possibility of following an earlier tradition anticipate Eliot's 1919 essay 'Tradition and the Individual Talent' which famously declares that it is only by awareness of tradition that a writer can be conscious of contemporaneity and that poetry is 'an escape from personality'.[24] H.D. continues by praising Mew as 'a new blossom from the seed of Browning's sowing', referring to one of the few writers of the nineteenth century who found a place in Pound's pantheon. In discarding personality and following Browning, Mew could be held to assert her own modernism.

Like H.D., the reviewer in *The Nation* (identified by Penelope Fitzgerald as H.W. Nevinson) praises Mew's suppression of the 'strictly personal' (which suggests that Eliot was, in accordance with his own doctrine, not wholly original in his essay) but relates this to the poet's evident acquaintance with France, the French language and 'the French spirit'.[25] But it is the reviewer in the *Times Literary Supplement* who most clearly, from a 1990s perspective, identifies Mew as a modernist, describing her work in terms which resemble Virginia Woolf's later prescription for modern fiction:[26]

> These compositions, in an irregular but rhymed metre, will often strike the reader as unintelligible. Some of them seem to have all the grotesque inconsequence of a dream. But if we had flashed before us the swiftly changing kaleidoscope of the workings of another's mind under some special impulse or impression it would probably seem unintelligible, at any rate at first. That is what Charlotte Mew attempts; and you cannot get away from the conclusion that when she is at her strangest there is something before you which is true and human, that there is a meaning, a unifying thread running through it all, although you do not quite understand it.
>
> An intense realization of the flow of sensuous impressions, hopes, reflections which go to make the inner drama of a single mind is the mark of most of these poems, and it finds its meaning in what seems to be a native unconscious gift of expression.[27]

This could be a description of Woolf herself, or Joyce or Eliot. The idea of the 'unconscious gift' is here, as in H.D.'s review, at odds with the deliberate decision assumed elsewhere. H.D. attributes conscious agency to Mew in her phrase 'daring to discard' while the *TLS* reviewer suggests a deliberate decision when writing of Mew's 'attempt to show the workings of another's mind'. The uncertainty of reviewers may derive from Mew's gender; it may also be related to her experimentation with both method and technique. Three main features which can be held as characteristic of modernism and which suggest ways in which the works of Mew and Eliot can be compared are tackled in the *TLS* review. These are: gaps (the *TLS* reviewer's 'grotesque inconsequence'), fragmentariness (found in the 'flow of sensuous impressions, hopes, reflections') and underlying coherence (the 'unifying thread').

Eliot's gaps are well known. In 'The Waste Land' the voices in the pub give way to Ophelia's farewell (p.66, l. 172). Cultural references collide in the encounter with Stetson (from Mylae) on London Bridge just as everyday lived experience collides with *grand guignol* in the reference to 'That corpse you planted last year in your garden' (pp.62–3, ll. 69–71). The leap from cultural frame to cultural frame or from one mode of expression to another leaves the reader with an awareness of something not quite said, an incompleteness. In 'The Waste Land' these gaps, while not resolved, tend to lead to a turning to 'higher culture' or spirituality or both. Thus Section 1 ends with Baudelaire, Section 2 with Shakespeare, Section 3 with St Augustine, Section 4 with Phlebas as *memento mori* (in a translation from Eliot's earlier 'Dans Le Restaurant') and Section 5 with the Sanskrit 'Shantih' which Eliot glosses in the notes in Christian terms as 'the peace which passeth understanding' (p.80, note to l. 433). In Eliot we are drawn away from the gaps and the impression of discomfort they tend to produce toward the comfortable effects of high art and religious faith. If the gaps are not, in fact, resolved, the drawing away tends to leave an impression of resolution.

In 'Prufrock', perhaps, the gaps come closer to those offered by Mew. Throughout the poem we are confronted by the speaker's awareness of the unsaid and the unsayable – the 'overwhelming question' (p.13, l. 10). The word 'overwhelming', combined with the question's unsayability, serves to buttress the idea of its importance. The poem seems to be continually on the brink of identifying its concern, only to rush away from the subject in an excess of startling and appalled metaphor:

> Shall I say, I have gone at dusk through narrow streets
> And watched the smoke that rises from the pipes
> Of lonely men in shirtsleeves, leaning out of windows? . . .
>
> I should have been a pair of ragged claws
> Scuttling across the floors of silent seas.
>
> (p.95, ll. 70–4)

Since the excessive reaction of the last two lines cannot follow logically from the previous three, it can only refer to what is not said – to three dots and a line of space.

Mew's 'The Quiet House' offers a similar series of gaps – repeated flights from the ostensible subject. For instance, the narrator moves in a stanza and a half from conversational references to an unhappy family life and the speaker's acquaintance with 'my cousin's friend' (p.19, l. 56) to what appears to be, as in Eliot, an excessive reaction in startling metaphor:

> He frightened me before he smiled —
> He did not ask me if he might —
> He said that he would come one Sunday night.
> He spoke to me as if I were a child.
>
> No year has been like this that has just gone by;
>   It may be that what Father says is true,
> If things are so it does not matter why:
>   But everything has burned, and not quite through,
>   The colours of the world have turned
>   To flame, the blue, the gold has burned
> In what used to be such a leaden sky.
> When you are burned quite through you die.
>
> . . . Red is the strangest pain to bear.

(p.18, ll. 17–29)

Here the frequent gaps in logical progression, heightened by the possible incompleteness of statements ending in dashes, seem to derive largely from assertions referred to but not explained in the poem. The reader wants to know, but is never told, just what Father says as well as what has brought about the transformation of the world indicated in the poem by a shift from naturalism to what seems to be an unclear symbolism ('A rose can stab you across the street/Deeper than any knife.', ll.34–5). Here the gap – the unsayable – places the reader in the position not just of critic but of analyst as it seems that a personality or group of personalities is laid before us for investigation.[28] Yet at the same time the reader must be aware of the futility of analysis. The 'truth' for which analysis strives is not located in the poem while the subject of analysis is a fictive character whose malaise can never be healed by the analyst's art.

While Eliot's poems seem to reach toward a universal solution, which the modernist method might be expected to deny – even the absurd Prufrock's vision is of such importance that he can ask 'Do I dare/Disturb the universe?' (p.14, ll.45–6) – Mew's poems repeatedly retreat from and deny such universal values. In 'The Quiet House' the church spire is 'dead' (p.19, l.56), in 'The Changeling' God belongs to a remote, unreclaimable world of domestic harmony: 'the king who sits on your high church steeple/Has nothing to do with us fairy people' (p.14, ll.55–6); mad Ken, pointing to the figure of Christ, says 'Take it away' (p.16, 1.48) while Madeleine's longing that Christ 'would only speak' (p.28, 1.223) closes the poem with an implication of divine silence.[29]

The fragmentariness of Mew's writing is related to the fragmentariness of the characters who speak in her poems. The bereaved man at the grave of his dead fiancée 'In Nunhead Cemetery' moves through conflicting and opposing states of mind from obsessive concentration on the details of the present ('It is the clay that makes the earth stick to his spade' p.8, 1.1) to alienating generalisations ('There is something horrible about a flower' and 'There is something horrible about a child', 1.16). Much as in 'The Quiet House' the poem shifts between specific recollections ('last week in the Strand', p.9, 1.17) and not quite realised metaphors ('The eyes of the Crystal Palace train', 1.24, and 'The lions in Trafalgar Square/Who'll stand and speak for England when the bell of Judgement tolls', ll.34–5) which seem to derive from a private conversation known only to the speaker and the dead woman. Then, from an allusion to a death-bed scene, the poem turns to threatened violence against the dead and buried woman: 'Now I will burn you back, I will burn you through,/Though I am damned for it we two will lie/And burn . . .' (p.10, ll.54–6). The effect of compressing so many diverse elements into a single poem is to suggest a fragmentary self, incapable of coherence and continually repelling the reader's attempts at understanding or empathy.

This kind of fragmentariness is typical of Mew's characters. She presents a range of alienated people on the margins of society, incoherent in themselves and viewing everyday social interactions as similarly incoherent. The speakers may be alienated by events ('In Nunhead Cemetery') or simply by who they are (a fully sexual woman in 'Madeleine in Church'; a perceptive halfwit in 'Ken' or the lost child in 'The Changeling'). 'The Changeling' presents a double alienation; the ungendered child, stolen by the fairies, is at home in neither the human nor the fairy world. The fairies with whom the child now lives are 'They' ('Why did They bring me here to make me/Not quite bad and not quite good . . .', p.14, ll.61–2) and the child's experience with them is as alienating as its sense of unease with the humans:

> Black and chill are Their nights on the wold
>   And They live so long and They feel no pain:
> I shall grow up, but never grow old,
> I shall always, always be very cold!
>   I shall never come back again!

(ll.69–73)

As elsewhere with Mew, although sympathy is invited, we as readers are left unsure about the nature of the fictive individual to whom it is given.

While Mew's use of fragmentariness is often based on the personal and works to call into question the consistent self and the constraints of the church, the family and society, Eliot's fragmentariness, based on the accumulation of snatches of knowledge and cultural references, functions quite differently. In 'The Waste Land' one of Eliot's 'different voices'[30] declares 'These fragments I have shored against my ruins' (p.75, 1.430). The task Eliot's fragments have is of building and reconstruction. They are to create a new order founded on high art, spirituality and hierarchies – an order which will require for its maintenance its own exclusions and marginalisations. In 'Gerontion' 'the Jew squats on the window-still' (p.77, 1.8); in 'Rhapsody on a Windy Night' the prostitute hovers in the doorway (p.24, 1.17). The woman in 'Portrait of a Lady' has been left behind in 'another country' (p.18, epigraph) while the traveller through 'The Waste Land' achieves a vision of spiritual harmony and fulfilment only after seeing the 'Falling towers' (p.73, 1.373) of cities with the implication of mass destruction.

In the *Drafts and Fragments* of his final cantos, Eliot's mentor, Pound, refers to his universalising project as he admits its failure:

> I have brought the great ball of crystal;
>   who can lift it?
> Can you enter the great acorn of light?
>   But the beauty is not the madness
> Tho' my errors and wrecks lie about me.
> And I am not a demigod,
> I cannot make it cohere.[31]

Eliot, referred to as a fellow modernist innovator in Pound's last work, similarly aimed to create a coherence but he worked through fragmentariness and exclusions to create a tradition in which his own individual talent would shine.

Mew's modernism, by contrast, with its focus on the marginal and states of alienation, investigates more clearly the fragmentation of personal thought and experience. Through the fractured utterances of characters whose lives and nature take them beyond the limits of society's conventions, the inadequacy of conventional coherences is revealed while social norms and values become simultaneously strange and estranging. Her characters' bleak visions often carry the logic of modernism through to its most extreme conclusion by having no end in view but personal annihilation. In the words of 'The Quiet House' they anticipate that 'some day I *shall* not think, I shall not *be*!' (p.19, 1.70)

NOTES

Endnotes and page references refer to the two following editions of Mew and Eliot: Charlotte Mew *Collected Poems and Prose*, ed., Val Warner, (Manchester/London, Carcanet/Virago, 1981); T.S. Eliot, *The Complete Poems and Plays* (London, Faber and Faber, 1969).

1. Peter Faulkner, *A Modernist Reader: Modernism England 1910–30* (London, Batsford, 1986).

2. The two female contributors are Virginia Woolf and Amy Lowell; Lowell is represented solely by the preface to *Some Imagist Poets, 1915*, the authorship of which is uncertain.

3. Stan Smith points out in *The Origins of Modernism: Eliot, Pound, Yeats and the Rhetorics of Renewal* (Hemel Hempstead, Harvester Wheatsheaf, 1994 p.1), that modernism was a movement without a name until it received its 'formal christening' from Laura Riding and Robert Graves in 1927.

4. Noel Stock, *The Life of Ezra Pound* (New York, Pantheon Books, 1970), p.124. Pound considered the proposed inclusion 'no small honour'.

5. Angela Leighton, *Victorian Women Poets: Writing Against the Heart* (Hemel Hempstead, Harvester Wheatsheaf, 1992), p.266.

6. Students (predominantly male students) often argue that the conclusion of the poem is an expression of love and has nothing to do with rape.

7. 'The Lyric', *The Nation*, XIX No. 15 (8 July, 1916), p.444.

8. For further details of feminist debates on marriage see Lucy Bland, *Banishing the Beast: English Feminism and Sexual Morality 1885–1915* (London, Penguin, 1995), particularly Chapter 4.

9. 'The New Wife' *The Nation*, X No. 16 (20 January, 1912), p.651. The argument that it is men's authority that renders them unfit for civic life neatly turns around the popular argument of the day that women's subordination made them unfit – or unready – for the franchise.

10. Honora Twycrosss, 'The New Wife' (letter), *The Nation*, X No. 17 (27 January, 1912), p.696. This declares that 'The instinct of obedience in woman is difficult to uproot, and she does, as a rule, prefer the headship of a man.'

11. Margaret Llewellyn-Davies, 'Of Marriage and Divorce' (letter), *The Nation*, VIII No. 23 (4 March, 1911), p.908.

12. *The Egoist* (1 May, 1914), pp.175–6. As *The Freewoman* and, later, *The New Freewoman*, the magazine had debated questions of sexuality from an avowedly anarchist perspective. When, under the influence of Ezra Pound and Richard Aldington, it changed its name to *The Egoist*, this interest in sexuality remained, indicated, for instance, by a disapproving review of Christabel Pankhurst's book on venereal disease, *The Great Scourge and How to End It* (1913, reviewed in *The Egoist*, 2 February, 1914), pp.44–6 and by letters on such matters as the need for husbands to masturbate their wives to orgasm (*The Egoist*, 16 March, 1914), pp.119–20.

13. Penelope Fitzgerald, *Charlotte Mew and her Friends* (London, Harvill, 1992), pp.119, 124.

14. Serialisation of *Portrait of the Artist* began in *The Egoist* on 2 February, 1914.

15. Leighton, *Victorian Women Poets.*, particularly pp.283–7.

16. The cover of Bland's *Banishing the Beast* (cit. supra) shows a seller of *The Suffragette* wearing a shield advertising Christabel Pankhurst's *The Great Scourge and How to End It* which also bears the slogan 'Wear the white flower of a blameless life'. Against this public insistence that women wear white for purity (this was the implication of white in the suffragette colours), Mew's return to the fallen-women colours of scarlet and gold may have a political as well as a historical relevance.

17. See, for instance, Oscar Wilde's 'The Harlot's House' and D.H. Lawrence's 'Fooled'. The latter was published in *The Egoist* (1 April, 1914), p.135.

18. John Newton, 'Another Handful of Dust', *The Times Literary Supplement*, No.4804 (28 April, 1995), p.18, further discussed in the correspondence columns on 12, 19 and 26 May.

19. Note particularly the reference to 'the house' (1.40).

20. M. E. Braddon, *Lady Audley's Secret* (Oxford, Oxford World's Classics, 1987; first published 1860–3), particularly p.69.

21. Typescript memoir deposited in the British Library.

22. The precise focus of the printer's objections is unclear; however possible causes may be found in Madeleine's reiteration of Christ's silence, her statement that 'His arms are full of broken things' (*Mew, Collected Poems and Prose*, p.26, 1.129) or, most probably, her emphasis on Mary Magdalen's recognizably sexual passion for Christ. (The suggestion that Jesus might have considered and rejected marriage with Mary Magdalen – including sex and children – as an alternative to crucifixion was sufficient to generate more than 1,500 complaints to the BBC when Martin Scorsese's film *The Last Temptation of Christ* was shown on television in 1995.)

23. *The Egoist* (September, 1916), p.135.

24. T.S. Eliot, 'Tradition and the Individual Talent', in *Selected Prose* by T.S. Eliot (ed. Frank Kermode, London: Faber and Faber, 1975), pp.38, 43.

25. 'The Lyric,' *The Nation*, XIX No. 15 (8 July, 1916), p.444.

26. 'Let us record the atoms as they fall, let us trace the patterns, however disconnected and incoherent in

appearance, which each sight of incident scores upon the consciousness.' From Virginia Woolf, 'Modern Fiction' (1919), included in Woolf, *The Common Reader* (London, Hogarth, 1951), p.189.

27. *The Times Literary Supplement*, No.766 (21 September, 1916), p.455.
28. The analyst's role may be further indicated by the probable sexual allusions in such images as the scarlet flower and the pain which stabs but is 'deadly sweet' (*Mew, Collected Poems and Prose*, pp.18–19, 11.38–45).
29. However, the final poem of the first edition of *The Farmer's Bride*, which immediately follows 'Madeleine in Church', is 'Exspecto Resurrectionem', which it is possible to read as an assertion of Christian faith.
30. The original title for the first two sections of 'The Waste Land' was 'He Do The Police In Different Voices'. T.S. Eliot, *The Waste Land: A Facsimile and Transcript* (London, Faber and Faber, 1971), pp.4, 5, 17, 18.
31. Canto CXVI (11.23–9) in Ezra Pound, *Cantos* (London, Faber and Faber, 1981), pp.795–6.

FURTHER READING

Bland, Lucy, *Banishing the Beast: English Feminism and Sexual Morality 1885–1914* (London, Penguin, 1995).

Eliot, T.S, *The Complete Poems and Plays* (London, Faber and Faber, 1969).

Faulkner, Peter, *A Modernist Reader: Modernism in England 1910–30* (London, Batsford, 1986).

Fitzgerald, Penelope, *Charlotte Mew and her Friends* (London, Harvill, 1992).

Leighton, Angela, *Victorian Women Poets: Writing Against the Heart* (Hemel Hempstead, Harvester Wheatsheaf, 1992).

Mew, Charlotte, *Collected Poems and Prose*, ed. Val Warner (Manchester/London, Carcanet/Virago, 1981).

2

Great Expectations: Rehabilitating the Recalcitrant War Poets*

Gill Plain

> . . . a distinction should be made between two groups – those who themselves risk their lives in battle, and those who have stayed at home and have only to wait for the loss of one of their dear ones by wounds, disease or infection.[1]

The rediscovery of women's poetry of the First World War has been greeted more with alarm than with enthusiasm. The work of over 500 disparate women constitutes a considerable body of writing, but it is one that resists any easy categorization.[2] These, then, are troublesome poets. As a group they lack the 'authenticity' of trench experience, and their poetry cannot provide a single, coherent vision of life on the home front. The result of this indeterminacy has been a critical tension between the excitement of discovering women's writing and the disappointment that can follow when it does not quite turn out as hoped. Even positive responses are followed by confusion over what to do with a body of literature that refuses to conform to any coherent literary or political framework.[3] Perhaps the problem presented by these poets is the same one that haunts Susan Schweik in her study of Marianne Moore. Schweik challenges the fluctuating cultural criteria that determine literary worth and asks how a war poem can survive the imposition of 'a familiar set of post-war aesthetic values'? Discussing Moore's 'In Distrust of Merits', Schweik ironically suggests that the poem has fallen victim to attempts at a definition of aesthetic merit:

* A longer version of this essay first appeared in *Feminist Review* 51, October 1995.

> A good poem ... will be cleanly universal and timeless, where 'In Distrust'
> bears too obviously the imprints of an immediate historical and cultural
> context; it will be neutral, where 'In Distrust' is polemical; it will enact
> poetically, where 'In Distrust' spouts off oratorically; it will address an
> elite readership, where 'In Distrust' invites the same kind of attention as
> the *Saturday Evening Post*.[4]

Women's war poetry, like Moore's later poem, fails to conform to a cultural
demand for ahistorical, transcendent, and 'difficult' writing. The penalty for
this perceived popularism is exclusion from the literary canon – a sentence
from which much war poetry is yet to be released. These poets deserve to be
rehabilitated, but this will not be possible until we revise the frames of reference
within which their work is considered. One way of achieving this is through a
change of critical focus.

In war the act of writing is potentially as significant as what is actually written.
A poem's explicit content, the form that conveys that content, and the tensions that
may exist between the two, create an arena for the articulation of a plethora of implicit
possibilities. The writing and publishing of poetry constitutes an engagement with
the act and ideology of war that is not private but public. It is all too easy to
forget that in the years of the First World War, poetry had an audience.[5] It was
produced and consumed by a voracious public who both shaped and were shaped
by the verse they read. In consequence I would like to suggest a shift in critical
attention from what women wrote to the (f)act of their writing.[6] This transition
raises two significant questions. Why did women write in wartime and why was
this writing effaced from the record of war? To the first question I would answer
that many wrote as a part of the work of mourning; they produced a poetry
of grief that encodes not just the pain of personal loss but also the politics of
personal identity. The second question is both a mystery and a case of *déjà vu*
that this essay cannot hope to resolve. Nonetheless I believe that a consideration
of women's mourning as a subversive act may cast helpful light upon the case of
the recalcitrant war poets, and that by connecting theories of women's subjectivity
with the psychological study of grief and bereavement, we can see these diverse
poetic fragments as complex articulations of war's paradoxical emancipation and
repression of women.

The dominant images of the First World War into which this poetry refuses
to fit are founded on a particular version of masculine experience, just as the
literary categories it eludes have been defined by men. The social, political, legal
and economic status of women in 1914 was such as to leave them almost no grounds
for connection with the masculine arena. The energetic suffrage activity that preceded
the conflict was not something that could be translated into a single unified female

response to the fact of war. These poems, like the enormously diverse range of male voices from the period, are the products of an intellectual and emotional economy of war, and in war nothing is ever quite the same. Daily life was transformed by absences, shortages, and above all by the rhetoric of patriotism, which effectively legitimises the repression of internal debate and dissent in the name of national security – the claim that 'we must all pull together for the duration'.

Historians and literary critics have debated the extent of the transformation war wrought on British society. Amongst those analysing women's writing, Sandra Gilbert has argued that a remarkable sense of female liberation emerged from the conflict, while Sharon Ouditt offers a more restrained reading that suggests simply an element of emancipation in the wartime work experiences of women.[7] Historians, meanwhile, have debated the idea of a 'lost generation' and the associated perception of a somehow impoverished postwar world. Although J.M. Winter has convincingly argued that the lost generation was more of a myth than a reality, other historians, including A.J.P. Taylor and David Cannadine, contend that whether there was a 'demographic disaster' or not, the important fact was that people believed in one.[8] It would be a mistake to underestimate the power of such myths in shaping responses to the war. Taylor also observes that '[c]asualties were about three times heavier in proportion among junior officers than with common soldiers', a factor which cannot be ignored in the study of a body of women's poetry which is almost exclusively middle class. Irrespective of statistics for the country as a whole, for the middle-class women who struggled to write war poetry in this period, both the perception and the actuality of loss would have been significant.

Early twentieth-century gender politics add an extra dimension to this dislocation. Ouditt observes that war is 'isolating and annihilating for women who live their lives through their men and who then lose their entire investment',[9] a comment which raises significant questions about the precarious nature of female subjectivity. If women are encouraged to live their lives through and for their men, what happens when those men are removed? Are the women who stay behind left to exist in a vacuum? Do they go into some form of existential cold storage until their plucky soldier boys come marching back? Or do they begin the slow process of formulating an identity in which the absence of the subject to which they are Other gives them an unprecedented degree of mobility within the constraints of the symbolic order? These questions beg others. The impact of war on women's lives is inevitably mediated through the ideologies and institutions of English class society. The opportunities open to women for a public redefinition of their subjectivity were controlled by the demands not only of the war machine, but also of a class hierarchy determined to maintain the status quo. To a large extent the public father of institutional organisation, be it in the ranks of the Voluntary Aid

Detachment (VAD) or in the munitions factories, took over the role left vacant by the absence of the domestic male.

The arena of women's public redefinition was, then, necessarily constrained. But these limitations could not apply to the same extent to women's private exploration of a new subjectivity – however much the women's magazines of the period fought to impose upon their readership the moral duty of uncomplaining self-sacrifice. Within the fragmentary and diffuse body of women's war poetry there is an articulation of these changes in women's sense of self, and these changes gained access to the margins of the public sphere through the act of publication. The extent of the poetry's readership is hard to gauge, but whether these works were ignored or applauded, they provide fascinating information for a study of the ways in which women survive war. In order to explore women's relation to the contending logics of war, I will be using Julia Kristeva's terminology of the semiotic and the symbolic, by which I understand a distinction between the dominant order of language that constructs our identity (the symbolic) and the elements that must be repressed in order to maintain or enter that order (the semiotic). 'Semiotic' refers to the pre-Oedipal stage of child development, the period in which the child knows no boundaries and has no sense of itself as an independent social or gendered being, and Kristeva theorises a revolutionary potential within this chora of repressed drives. These constantly fluctuating forces are never fully silenced by the symbolic order, but exist in parallel, or beneath the surface, to return as irruptions and dislocations that have the power to destabilise and disrupt that order. Women are marginal to the symbolic order. They exist on the periphery and are faced with a choice between a masculine identification, which includes that deriving of a sense of self through a husband or father (as described above) or a feminine identification that leaves them outside the arena of power – if not without a voice, then certainly without an audience!

What, then, is the connection between an exploration of female subjectivity and the study of grief? Ironically, it seems that the socially legitimate articulation of grief creates a space in which the more radical articulation of a new female subjectivity becomes a possibility. Grief can be described as the manifestation of loss. Usually considered as the affect of a private trauma, it also has the potential to assume a public dimension. This wider significance becomes evident in Sharon Ouditt's examination of the reactionary ideology that characterised many women's magazines of the period, from which she draws a disturbing conclusion:

> In one of *Woman's World's* 'Heart to Heart Chats' the editress replies rather impatiently to a reader who has already lost three children and whose husband has now gone to France:

> Dear sister, I am so sorry to hear of your unhappiness. But, dearie, you
> must really try to be more cheerful, and face the separation from your
> husband a little more bravely ... (1915)

The appellation 'dearie' creates an atmosphere of (false) intimacy, within which
it can be clearly intimated that revealing one's unhappiness is unpatriotic.[10]

Revealing one's unhappiness is unpatriotic.[11] And yet, whether it is manifested
in an 'ecstacy' of sacrifice, or in religious sublimation, or a total revulsion from
the futility of war, grief and loss form the dominant tone of Catherine Reilly's
anthology *Scars Upon My Heart*. If misery is unpatriotic, then the collected grief
within this work has the potential to form a revolutionary text!

This suggestion is not as improbable as it may at first sound. Individual grief
may be powerless to effect political change, but collective grief would seem to
have embodied a sufficiently threatening force to intimidate Britain's postwar
government. In a fascinating article on the changing patterns of mourning
in Britain, David Cannadine describes the government's reluctance to institute
both the ritual of Armistice Day and the Cenotaph monument. Lord Curzon's
committee, established to organise the national postwar rejoicing, proved to be
'distinctly unenthusiastic' about Lloyd George's proposal for a war memorial, and
in their response Cannadine discerns a genuine fear of the extent of public grief, and
of the potential force of its expression. These anxieties were not without foundation.
Much of Cannadine's article is concerned with the difficulty of maintaining pre-war
standards of outward mourning in the face of such an unprecedented excess of death.
He observes that the conditions of the battlefield exacerbated the impossibility of
paying due respect, resulting often in the adoption of a protective cynicism, which
would have contributed to the more general perception of a postwar breakdown
in traditional patterns of deference based on age and class.

Nonetheless, the plans for both Cenotaph and Armistice Day went ahead and
proved to be enormously popular, which ensured that they became permanent
rather than temporary legacies of the nation's loss. The extent of the public
response suggests that there existed a huge desire for the legitimisation of their
individual and collective grief. However, the government need not have worried
that these monuments would become sites of disaffection. Cannadine concludes that
the popularity of the rituals lay in their capacity to make 'public and corporate
those unassuageable feelings of grief and sorrow which otherwise must remain
forever private and individual'[12]. The idea of incorporation ultimately suggests a
ritual appropriated by patriarchal authority rather than a show of opposition or
resistance to that authority, but it is nonetheless interesting to note that momentary
hesitation on the part of those in power.

How, then, does this body of poetry engage with grief? Psychoanalytic theorists from Freud to Kristeva, in an attempt to explore the melancholic condition, have given considerable thought to defining its close relation, the so-called 'normal' process of mourning. In 'Mourning and Melancholia' Freud describes the relation between the two conditions:

> Profound mourning, the reaction to the loss of someone who is loved, contains the same painful frame of mind, the same loss of interest in the outside world – in so far as it does not recall him – the same loss of capacity to adopt any new object of love (which would mean replacing him) and the same turning away from any activity that is not connected with thoughts of him [as is witnessed in melancholia].[13]

In this state, the ego is inhibited and circumscribed by its 'exclusive devotion to mourning', and the gradual recovery from this position is achieved through a process described by Freud as 'reality-testing'. The memories of the past are juxtaposed against the actuality of the present until it becomes possible for the bereaved to acknowledge the absence of the loved object:

> This demand arouses understandable opposition . . . [which] . . . can be so intense that a turning away from reality takes place and a clinging to the object through the medium of a hallucinatory wishful psychosis. Normally, respect for reality gains the day. Nevertheless its orders cannot be obeyed at once. They are carried out bit by bit, at great expense of time and cathectic energy, and in the meantime the existence of the lost object is psychically prolonged.[14]

This process is evident in the considerable number of wartime and postwar poems that revisit places previously shared with a lost lover, or which focus on an activity or ideal associated with the lost person. Eileen Newton's poem 'Revision (For November 11th)', for example, reveals a refusal of reality. Newton will not dwell on 'the untimely slain', preferring instead to let her thoughts seek 'a hallowed place-/The little, leafy wood where you and I/Spent the last hour together'.[15] Alternatively, Anna Gordon Keown's 'Reported Missing' operates within a state of limbo that could be described as pre-bereavement. Keown's sonnet redirects the operation of reality-testing, turning it into an act of defiance, a statement of presence that covers the unacknowledgable fact of absence: 'Of these familiar things I have no dread/Being so very sure you are not dead'.[16]

  The work of mourning is a burden, its painfulness evident in the tension between the desire to remember and the instinct to survive that demands that we forget. Yet, as the work of Vera Brittain reveals, it is not easy to free oneself, even from a past that imprisons. In Brittain's poetry the immensity of her loss gives rise to a sense of total, debilitating exhaustion:

> SIC TRANSIT –
>
> *(V. R., Died of Wounds, 2nd London General Hospital, Chelsea, June 9th, 1917)*
>
> I am so tired.
>
>   The dying sun incarnadines the west,
>
> And every window with its gold is fired;
>
>   And all I loved the best
>
> Is gone, and every good that I desired
>
>   Passes away, an idle hopeless quest;
>
> Even the highest whereto I aspired
>
>   Has vanished with the rest.
>
> I am so tired.
>
> *London,*
>
>   *June, 1917*[17]

Brittain, like many of the poets in Reilly's anthology, juxtaposes short monosyllabic lines against heavier Latinate syntax in what can be seen as an attempt, through formal experiment, to augment the sense of fragmentation and dislocation already contained within the content of the poems. The opening of 'Sic Transit', however, achieves considerable impact through its extreme simplicity, and the repetition of this line at the end of the poem reinforces the contrast between the poem's central 'elevated' or poetic diction, and the reality of exhaustion. The polysyllabic outburst within the frame is laden with images of death and finality. 'Incarnadines', apart from meaning to dye flesh-coloured or crimson, has its roots in *Macbeth*:

> Will all great Neptune's ocean wash this blood
> Clean from my hand? No; this my hand will rather
> The multitudinous seas incarnadine,
> Making the green one red.

> (II, ii, 59–62)

Brittain's imagery evokes blood and wholesale, gratuitous slaughter from motives of greed and ambition. The window which is fired with gold not only represents the closure of sunset, symbolic of an end to youth, hope, and life; it also evokes an image of 'stained' glass.

   The irregularity of the poem's stress pattern also works to create the overriding impression of weariness and despair. The contextually hopeful open-ended line 'And all I loved the best' rises in pitch before receiving its sense conclusion in the flat beginning of the next line with the simple words 'Is gone'. The rhythm that is created in this phrase is echoed in the following four lines, gradually and inexorably turning this short poem into one in which hopes and happiness are destroyed with an exhausting regularity before the reader is returned to the concluding and inevitable statement, 'I am so tired'.

Brittain's alternation in this poem between exhaustion and intensity can be related to the psychologist Colin Murray Parkes' anatomy of the process of grief. Parkes describes alternating patterns of anger and passivity as a characteristic phase of grief, alongside avoidance, postponement, searching, self-reproach and 'the gradual building-up of a fresh identity'[18]. Instances of searching, which Parkes believes to be unique to the experience of bereavement, are particularly prevalent in women's poetry. Vera Brittain's poem 'Roundel' provides an example:

> Because you died, I shall not rest again,
>   But wander ever through the lone world wide,
> Seeking the shadow of a dream grown vain
>   Because you died.[19]

But searching is more complex than this restlessness might suggest. Parkes observes that the bereaved often develop a fresh attachment to items or people of whom the deceased was particularly fond – a phenomenon that can do much to explain why so many women were able to maintain a belief in the war that had killed their husbands, sons or lovers. Particularly in the early years of the conflict, women whose menfolk departed for battle imbued with a noble spirit of love for their country, continued to believe in the necessity of the war. Aside from the obvious need to give a purpose to an otherwise futile death (the process of 'making sense' that Freud terms 'grief work'), this can be seen as a desire to 'keep faith' with the dead, which in turn enables the preservation or restoration of some part of the person who has been lost. May Wedderburn Cannan's poem 'After' encapsulates this dynamic:

> Dear, since it was for England that you died
> Who so adored her, I will love her still;[20]

Cannan is more self-conscious than most, but her comment is typical of a need for belief, or for explanation, that accompanied the moral vacuum of war. At its worst this need for some sort of answer is manifested in the prescription poetry of Katharine Tynan, who dispensed the consolation of her religion to readers in need of comfort. Her poem 'To The Others' reveals her tendency to view the war as some form of religious crusade in which all those participating will receive an indulgence:

> Your son and my son, clean as new swords,
> Your man and my man and now the lord's!
> Your son and my son for the great crusade,
> With the banner of Christ over them – our knights, new-made.

Tynan believed that the war was being fought in a good cause, and that all soldiers, particularly dead ones, were necessarily heroic.[21] This belief was accompanied by the idea that those who sacrificed a loved one to the cause were equally heroic. Acceptance of this dubious consolation was perhaps one of the more conservative strategies that women employed in the process of surviving grief.

However, not all the poems which manifest religion as a coping strategy are as straightforward as those of Katharine Tynan. Violet Spender's 'Forever and Forever' provides an example of this complexity. The poem reinforces the association of unhappiness with treachery by suggesting despair to be the devil incarnate. What is curious about Spender's poems is not the patriotic line that they ultimately take, but the time and effort she devotes to the delineation of doubt, anxiety and the very 'unpatriotic' feelings she protests to abhor. Far removed as her poetry is from that of Milton, she suffers, it would seem, from a tendency to make the devil's part the more convincing:

> But when his friends had bidden her farewell
> And all the letters had been laid aside,
> She heard a voice that whispered in her ear:
> 'He was a hero; but he lives no more!
> You may now listen, listen for his tread,
> But he will never, never come again! . . .
>
> But he will never, never come again
> Your daily plans and pleasures! Never more!
> The dreams, the hopes, the visions! Faded! Fled!
> The Future? Music ended! Lights put out!
> And is there any sound in all the world
> But Never! Never! Never any more?'[22]

The constant repetition of 'never', while not a sophisticated expression of her emotions, nonetheless contains considerably more vigour than the pallid expression of piety that follows it:

> I know that he will never come again;
> But God be praised because he came at all!

This can be read, as Jan Montefiore reads Macaulay's 'Picnic', more as a defence against emotional collapse than a genuine belief in the clichéd consolation that it is better to have loved and lost than never to have loved at all.[23]

Grief, then, is an integral component of this body of poetry; but what psychological function does the creative process serve? Freud's idea of 'grief work' can perhaps provide an answer. In *Testament of Youth*, Vera Brittain describes an almost physical need to write poetry: 'and all at once the impulse to put what I felt into verse – a new impulse which had recently begun to fascinate and torment me – sprang up with overwhelming compulsion.'[24] The act of writing a grief poem involves the transforming of a painful amorphous emotion into a concrete form, with a solid, repeatable shape. The poem metamorphoses the grief into a more finite entity – in effect it creates a monument. As a monument the poem can bear witness to both the loss and the grief, while at the same time placing it outside, at a distance from the poet. By providing at least a temporary detachment from the emotion that provoked the urge to write, the poem assumes a cathartic function. Eleanor Farjeon's poem 'The Outlet' embodies this idea:

> Grief struck me. I so shook in heart and wit
> I thought I must speak of it or die of it.
>
> A certain friend I had with strength to lend,
> When mine was spent I went to find my friend,
>
> Who, rising up with eyes wild for relief,
> Hung on my neck and spoke to me of grief.
>
> I raked the ashes of my burned-out strength
> And found one coal to warm her with at length.
>
> I sat with her till I was icy cold.
> At last I went away, my grief untold.[25]

Perhaps the most significant element of Farjeon's deceptively simple poem is the title. On one level 'The Outlet' refers to the source of comfort which fails, that is, the friend. On another it refers to the poet herself who forms the outlet for her friend's grief. Finally, though, the title is self-referential: it is the poem itself that forms the real and only outlet for her grief. Within this context both the surface conformity and the inarticulable subtext of this poetry, its 'symbolic' and its 'semiotic' inscriptions, become what Julia Kristeva has described as the 'communicable marks of an affective reality, present, palpable to the reader (I like this book because sadness – or anxiety or joy – is communicated to me by it) and nevertheless dominated, kept at a distance, vanquished'. Creative discourse, she argues, performs a significant function within grief work, possessing 'a real and imaginary efficacy that, cathartic more than of the order of elaboration, is a therapeutic method utilised in all societies throughout the ages'.[26]

If, then, poetry enables women to assume a distance from grief, it can also be seen to place them beyond the identity of 'the bereaved'. 'When the work of mourning is completed' observes Freud, 'the ego becomes free and uninhibited again'.[27] The poem frees the writer from obligations to the past, it provides an end to the search, and facilitates the formation of a new identity. Here, perhaps, is the first stage of a transition from wife, to widow, to woman.

Yet there is another dimension to the grief process. Kristeva suggests that '[a]ccording to classical psychoanalytical theory ... depression, like mourning, hides an aggression against the lost object and thereby reveals the ambivalence on the part of the afflicted with respect to the object of his mourning.'[28] In the particular socio-historic context of the First World War, what form might such an ambivalence take? If women, whose identity traditionally derives from that of their menfolk, undergo a loss of attachment to these men, then they can also be seen to be distanced from the symbolic order that would control them. In consequence, the co-existent contradictions of attachment and aggression create in mourning a double-edged phenomenon with the capacity to shift the parameters of conflict into the arena of sexual politics, a battleground thought to be safely buried by the 'higher' priority of prosecuting the war.

An awareness of the ambivalence that exists within the condition of mourning certainly puts a different perspective on one of the poems I considered earlier. Vera Brittain's 'Roundel', on one level symbolic of the relentless search for the lost love object, can also be seen to contain an element of resentment. 'Because you died', *because* the loved one has left her, she has been abandoned to 'brief and idle hours' beside 'lesser loves', in an empty world where 'disillusion's slow corroding stain/will creep upon each quest but newly tried'. The love object is hated and resented for the crime of abandonment at the same time as it is cherished and mourned. This paradox is integral to the mourning process, and it also suggests why women's mourning must also possess a political dimension. In *Thoughts for the Times on War and Death*, Freud comments:

> These loved ones are on the one hand an inner possession, components of our own ego; but on the other hand they are partly strangers, even enemies. With the exception of only a very few situations, there adheres to the tenderest and most intimate of our love-relations a small portion of hostility which can excite an unconscious death-wish.[29]

The man who is the object of Brittain's desire simultaneously represents the enemy – the patriarch who would deny her political subjectivity.[30]

The tension within Brittain's poem, and indeed among many of the poets examined by Khan and Montefiore, suggests another side to the loss created by the carnage of the First World War, and it seems important to ask what does the lost object (man) symbolise for these wartime women? The woman war poet, observes Jan

Montefiore, 'asserts the melancholy privilege of a poetic voice predicated on the absence and – possibly – death of the loved one'[31] – and, without denying the attachments that existed, the loss of the man must also be seen as the potential liberation of the woman.

Yet, the problem remains that the act of finding a voice only temporarily disassociates women from their appropriation by the patriarchal war machine, and poetry as an individual response seems powerless to disturb the symbolic order. However, although the expression of grief is not in itself a necessarily radical act, the writing process can be seen to symbolise the stronger new identity that Parkes has identified as a frequent outcome of the grieving process. For many women there could be no return to the deadly romantic myth of identification through their man as the men, either temporarily or permanently, had gone. Women's war poetry is a testament to the ways in which women changed during the First World War, and to the sometimes radical – and sometimes not so radical – new identities that they formed in the fracture of war's dislocation.

There is however a coda to this picture of the interaction between war, women and creativity. At the end of the war women's poetry suddenly and mysteriously disappeared from the literary record, and this postwar disappearance gives the poetry a political cohesion that its presence could never achieve.[32] Sharon Ouditt observes that '[t]he war generation is not wanted by its more hard-headed, sybaritic successors: war-grief is unwelcome, reconstruction and forgetting are prioritized':[33] perhaps a reason for the government's reluctance to institute the Armistice Day ritual of remembrance? May Cannan's autobiography emphasises the gender specific nature of this rejection:

> The census for 1921 had found there was a surplus of women who, inconsiderately, had not died in the war, and now there was an outcry and someone christened them 'The Surplus Two Million'. *The Times* suggested they might seek work abroad; the unemployment figures were swollen with these unnecessary and unwanted persons: and the name stuck.[34]

Women formulate a new identity in wartime, but it would seem to be an identity that nobody wants. Single women, women without husbands, are categorised as socially useless objects by those institutions that define public opinion (the press, the pulpit and parliament). They become the 'surplus two million', a blatant acknowledgement that female subjectivity is surplus to requirements.

Grief, then, is a problem: unpatriotic in wartime and unwelcome in the brave new world of postwar reconstruction. And because the symbolic order chooses to situate it in this oppositional position, it develops the potential to become a site of resistance. I think it is possible to see grief, and the poetic monuments it erects, in opposition to and in excess of the dominant patriarchal logic of war.

The poetry forms a leftover residue that resists assimilation into the history of war, and which must in consequence be repressed. Hence in the aftermath of war these monuments, these calls to the dead, remain as semiotic irruptions within a symbolic order fundamentally unchanged by the ravages of war. In this context it is no surprise that these poems disappeared from the anthologies of war verse. They told a story that was 'other' to the official record, and as such constituted a threat. Real or imagined, or indeed, made real *because* so imagined, the threat was neutralised by marginalising it. The poems were silenced because they could not be read – just as the outcry of their male authored counterparts was ultimately dismissed through their literary promotion from the voices of protest to the well wrought urns of art. Siegfried Sassoon makes an ironic acknowledgement of this assimilation when he undermines his own claims to political influence in a letter to Lady Ottoline Morrell (21 November 1917): 'But the poets will get the upper hand of them – some day (when bound in half-calf, suitable for wedding presents).'[35] The protests of men, it would seem, are deflected through assimilation and incorporation into the very establishment whose hegemony they challenged, while women's voices can be rendered safe through the strategies of exclusion, omission and expulsion. Women's mourning was briefly recognised as a complex and subversive embodiment of anger, desire and nascent subjectivity, and in the completeness of its annihilation lies the greatest testimony to its power.

NOTES

1. Sigmund Freud, 'Thoughts for the Times on War and Death', in *The Standard Edition of the Complete Psychological Works* (Vol. XIV), ed. James Strachey (London, Hogarth, 1978), p.291.
2. The major work of recovering these poets was undertaken by Catherine Reilly, and a good selection is available in her anthology, *Scars Upon My Heart* (London, Virago, 1981).
3. For example, Nosheen Khan's *Women's Poetry of the First World War* (Brighton, Harvester, 1989).
4. Susan Schweik, 'Writing War Poetry Like a Woman', in *Speaking of Gender*, ed. Elaine Showalter (London, Routledge, 1989), pp.312–13.
5. The particularly literary climate of the First World War is discussed by Paul Fussell in *The Great War and Modern Memory* (Oxford, Oxford University Press, 1975). Fussell suggests that an enduring belief in the value of literature, combined with the peak of liberal ideas about popular education and 'self improvement', resulted in 'an atmosphere of public respect for literature unique in modern times' (p.157). In a chapter appropriately entitled 'Oh What a Literary War' Fussell argues that in 1914 'language formally arranged' was almost the only available form of amusement, and concludes that '[i]t is hard for us to recover imaginatively such a world, but we must imagine it if we are to understand the way "literature" dominated the war from beginning to end' (p.158).
6. Jan Montefiore in particular has articulated the problem of evaluating this poetry, and confesses that her first response to the patriotic content and technical crudities of some of the verse was to label women's war poetry as bad. When faced with the misguided romanticism and religious rhetoric of writers such as Katherine Tynan it is hard not to share such a feeling of repulsion. The poetry could be said to move from the sublime to the distressing, but I would like to try and move away from this question of qualitative analysis to think instead about the function of writing within the social context of war.
7. Sandra Gilbert, 'Soldier's Heart: Literary Men, Literary Women, and the Great War', in *Behind the Lines: Gender and the Two World Wars*, eds Margaret Randolph Higonnet et al., (New Haven, Yale University Press, 1987), p.200. Sharon Ouditt, *Fighting Forces, Writing Women* (London, Routledge, 1994).
8. J.M. Winter, *The Great War and the British People* (Basingstoke, Macmillan, 1981), pp.256–63. A.J.P. Taylor, *English History 1914–1945* (Oxford, Oxford University Press, 1965; reprinted 1992), pp.120–1.

David Cannadine, 'War and Death, Grief and Mourning in Modern Britain', in *Mirrors of Mortality: Studies in the Social History of Death*, ed. Joachim Whaley (London, Europa, 1981), pp.200–1.

9. Ouditt, *Fighting Forces*, p.125.

10. Ibid., p.95.

11. In this context it is interesting to note Julia Kristeva's observation in her article 'On the Melancholic Imaginary' that 'for the Catholic West, sadness is a sin and the wretched citizens of the "abode of woe" are placed by Dante in the circles of Inferno'. From *Discourse in Psychoanalysis and Literature*, ed. Shlomith Rimmon-Kenan (London, Methuen, 1987), p.105.

12. Cannadine, 'War and Death', p.222.

13. Sigmund Freud, 'Mourning and Melancholia', in *The Standard Edition of the Complete Psychological Works* (Vol. XIV), ed. James Strachey (London, Hogarth, 1978), p.244.

14. Freud, 'Mourning and Melancholia', pp.244–5.

15. Reilly, *Scars Upon My Heart*, pp.81–2.

16. Ibid., p.58.

17. Vera Brittain, *Verses of a VAD* (London, Macdonald, 1918), p.34.

18. Colin Murray Parkes, *Bereavement* (Harmondsworth, Penguin, 1975; reprinted 1986), p.12.

19. Brittain, *Verses of a VAD*, p.28.

20. May Wedderburn Cannan, *The Splendid Days* (Oxford, Blackwell, 1919), p.33.

21. Katharine Tynan, *The Holy War* (London, Sidgwick & Jackson, 1916), p.16. In some of Tynan's most distressing poems, the 'common' soldier, a sinner awaiting redemption, is elevated to heroism through a mutilating salvation. The translation of physical injury into symbolic stigmata supposedly gives spiritual satisfaction to the unfortunate 'Private Flynn' (Tynan, 1916) and 'The Broken Soldier' (Tynan, 1916, reprinted in Reilly, *Scars Upon My Heart*, 1981).

22. Violet Spender, *The Path to Caister and Other Poems* (London, Sidgwick & Jackson, 1922), p.47.

23. Jan Montefiore, 'Shining Pins and Wailing Shells: Women Poets and the Great War', in *Women and World War I: The Written Response*, ed. Dorothy Goldman (Basingstoke, Macmillan, 1993), p.61.

24. Vera Brittain, *Testament of Youth* (London, Gollancz, 1933; reprinted Virago, 1978), p.268.

25. Eleanor Farjeon, *Sonnets and Poems* (Oxford, Blackwell, 1918), p.45.

26. Julia Kristeva, 'On the Melancholic Imaginary', in *Discourse in Psychoanalysis and Literature*, ed. Shlomith Rimmon-Kenan (London, Methuen, 1987), pp.108–9, 110.

27. Freud, 'Mourning and Melancholia', p.145.

28. Kristeva, 'On the Melancholic Imaginary', p.106.

29. Freud, 'Thoughts for the Times on War and Death', p.298.

30. The vulnerable male soldier co-exists with his symbolic counterpart the repressive patriarch – a paradox that is further complicated by the observations of Sandra Gilbert. Although her image seems rather overstated, Gilbert does make a valid point when she suggests that 'the sexual gloom expressed by so many men as well as the sexual glee experienced by so many women ultimately triggered profound feelings of guilt in a number of women' (p.201). The guilt of the survivor is combined with grief's integral components of resentment and aggression to further complicate women's emotional and creative responses to war.

31. Montefiore, 'Shining Pins', p.62.

32. To reinforce this observation I undertook a brief survey of anthologies across the century. I began at the end of the war with G.H. Clarke's *A Treasury of War Poetry* (London, Hodder & Stoughton, 2nd edn, 1919) and Bertram Lloyd's *Poems Written during the Great War 1914–18* (London, George, Allen & Unwin, 1918). Of Clarke's 183 poets, thirty-nine were clearly identifiable as women (approximately twenty-one per cent), while amongst Lloyd's twenty-nine writers, there were five women (seventeen per cent). By 1930, women's representation had dropped to five per cent (three out of sixty) in Frederick Brereton's *An Anthology of War Poems* (London, Collins), and by the 1960s the dominant perception of war poetry had become totally synonymous with combat experience. *Poetry of the First World War*, ed. Maurice Hussey (London, Longman, 1967) has one woman amongst fifty-five poets, while Brian Gardner's *Up the Line to Death* (London, Methuen, 1964) takes the prize for having no women at all amongst its seventy-two poets – in spite of boasting a section entitled 'Home Front'.

33. Ouditt, *Fighting Forces*, p.123.

34. May Wedderburn Cannan, *Grey Ghosts and Voices* (Kineton, The Roundwood Press, 1976), p.175.

35. *Siegfried Sassoon Diaries 1915–1918*, ed. Rupert Hart-Davies (London, Faber & Faber, 1983), p.194.

3

H. D. Imagiste? Bisexuality: Identity: Imagism

Megan Lloyd Davies

H.D.'s work has been the subject of extensive discussion as a result of her problematic position within the Imagist movement. Her relationship with Ezra Pound has cast him as her mentor, even though she provided him with invaluable intellectual support. I shall argue that her assessment as an Imagist needs to focus on the ways in which she transgresses the 'rules' set by Imagism. Tracing the development of these transgressive tactics, looking first at *Sea Garden*[1], then 'I Said' and the title poem of *Hymen*[2], I shall show how H.D. tries out various strategies to probe questions of gender and the possibility of an unlocalised desire, thus undercutting the central tenets of Imagist form. In the latter poems, a specific homosexual or heterosexual object choice is made and, in contrast to the shifting, unlocatable authorial presence found in *Sea Garden*, the speaker becomes unified when engaging with a single-sex desire. I conclude with a brief discussion of 'The Master', in which H.D. uses insights drawn from her analysis with Freud in order to attempt expression of a bisexual identity.

In March 1913 F.S. Flint set down the three central tenets of Imagism: direct treatment of the thing whether subjective or objective; use of no excess word; and composition in the rhythm of the musical phrase. Pound, whose brief involvement with the movement resulted in his 'A Few Don'ts by an Imagiste', added that 'the natural object is always the adequate symbol'.[3] In reaction to the excess and 'femininity' of Victorian poetic form, the Imagist poets were attempting to create a new aesthetic that was based on the strict control of form rather than the nebulous expression of emotion.

The Imagist idea of language was based upon a primitive model: language is that which can directly represent, rather than mediate thought into words. Language was not seen as organic, culturally and socially specific, but unchanging. Thus the Imagist poet was able 'directly' to treat his subject matter with no thought of the processes that structure language because it was a pre-ordained entity, able to represent a transcendent truth which the poet was to reveal. Thus the role of sexual difference in structuring the relationship to words and writing was denied; the poet revealed truth rather than creating his or her personal view of it. The male imagist was able to assume unchallenged the male 'I' that governs language.

Male Imagists were also at pains to draw clear boundaries around the self. They wanted the separation of subject from object, in order to remove the threat of absolute creative autonomy being compromised by narcissistic identification with an other. The fixing of sexual difference was a prerequisite to such absolute division, and woman was figured as that which would overwhelm the poet in the mire of emotion which had so ruined Victorian poetry. An insistence on visual form aided this objectification, for if the poet's job was to create a structured, controlled and visually-based form with which to reveal the image then he was able to maintain a contemplative distance from emotion. As T.S. Eliot later wrote, 'Poetry is not the turning loose of emotion but an escape from emotion; it is not the expression of personality, but an escape from personality.'[4] This aesthetic coincidentally but precisely typifies the Imagist preoccupation with form and control of emotion; the subjective was given attention only if objectified through distance. The poet, given his unproblematic relationship to language, is able to reveal the image to his reader.[5]

H.D.'s Imagist volume *Sea Garden* superficially adheres to these criteria: the poems are centred on the image, concise language is used, and a distance between the author and the subject for contemplation is thus superficially created. But the overt control of form allows the woman author to explore the transgressive subtextually; formal adherence enables a radical subversion of the central precepts of this masculine-orientated style. H.D. constantly challenges Imagism's philosophical premises while adopting its formal style. The authorial subject is not a detached omnipotent force conveying the image; she becomes a shifting, uncertain presence. Read as a whole the volume consistently subverts traditional images; gender and desire are portrayed in flux; the perspective and value judgements inherent in the authorial position are revealed and questioned; and the stable authorial 'I' is challenged.

The title *Sea Garden* immediately locates the image as that which unites seemingly opposing elements – the land and sea: the sheltered, cultivated space and an elemental libidinal force. This image of dual reality is central to the subtextual thematics of the volume, for H.D. is attempting to articulate an alternative that many would mark as dissident. The first poem, 'Sea Rose' (*H.D. Collected Poems*, p.5)[6] is indicative of the Imagist style: the authorial 'I' observes from a distance the central image of the rose. No metaphor is utilised, the syntax is clipped and short phrases build up the image. The garden rose had been extensively used in Victorian literature and painting as the ideal image of feminine delicacy and vulnerability; this sea rose is its alter ego, a seemingly 'meagre flower' in comparison. Suddenly, though, in the second stanza the rose is hailed as:

> more precious
> than a wet rose
> single on a stem

(p.5)

An alternative perspective is offered, there is no longer a single, unified image that the poet can reveal to the reader: the rose is both hideous and beautiful, powerless to resist the might of the seascape ('you are flung . . . you are lifted') but celebrated, for, unlike the 'spice rose', its 'acrid fragrance' has been achieved in the face of such adversity. The Imagist accumulation of detail is imbued with the author as presence – a consciousness is at work which offers different views on the image, the reality, and validates the sparse rose which has achieved fruition within the harsh seascape.

'Sea Rose' is the first of five sea flower poems scattered enticingly throughout the volume, suggesting the presence of a cohesive theme. Sexual difference is exposed as an issue: the flowers, as symbols of femininity, are dislocated from the traditional view of them as meagre. In these poems the flowers are often seen as passive in relation to the might of the sea, but this passivity is not on a continuum with powerlessness: they do not flourish as they would in the protected garden, but they survive in the elemental and harsh seascape, and thus achieve a nobility, an autonomy which would not be realisable in the oppressive luxuriance of the garden. Using the backdrop of Victorian associations of femininity, floweriness and vulnerability, H.D. makes a plea for freedom and elementality in an adverse yet liberating imaginary place. In this environment female triumph is powerful because based upon withstanding of adversity, not sheltered fruition. Thus the leaf is able to compact fragrance, brightness, multiplicity:

> what meadow yields
> so fragrant a leaf
> as your bright leaf?

('Sea Poppies,' *CP*, p.21)

Linked to the sea flower poems are 'Sheltered Garden' and 'Garden'. These poems expand on the associations of the garden and its implications for female creativity. 'Sheltered Garden' (pp.19–21) explores the sense of entrapment found in the cultivated space: 'I have had enough./I gasp for breath.' exclaims the speaker in the opening lines. The fruits are 'protected from the frost', 'coaxed' into a 'bitter' enripement (CP, p.20); but better that they grow unprotected, says the speaker, for:

> it is better to taste of frost –
> the exquisite frost –
> than of wadding and of dead grass.

(p.20)

In the penultimate stanza the speaker envisions the violent destruction of the garden, and cries:

> O to blot out this garden
> to forget, to find a new beauty
> in some terrible
> wind-tortured place.

(p.21)

The sea flowers intersperse the volume as images which mediate the reversal of traditional values. 'Sheltered Garden' explores the protected space in terms of fruition and production, but bitterness and frustration are the real 'fruits' of this garden, which result in its violent rejection in favour of the stark seascape.

In 'Garden' (pp.24–25) there is, as Claire Buck asserts, 'a problem of interpretation for the reader'.[7] H.D., in being faithful to Imagist techniques, offers no explanation of the speaker's violence towards the rose – the reader must refer to 'Sheltered Garden' in order to interpret the implications of the cultivated space, and this creates problems with Pound's assertion, noted above, that 'the natural object is always the adequate symbol.' The image of the rose cannot effectively contain the speaker's feelings towards it; only a cross-reference to the earlier poem can explain this. But this is one of the crucial ways in which H.D. deconstructs Imagism in *Sea Garden*: it is a *volume*, not a collection of individual poems. The repetition of themes and the overt use of a classical background indicate an orderliness, a specific authorial aim, that Imagism disavows. Read alone 'Garden' creates a gap between the actual contents of the poem and the sentiments expressed by the speaker; understanding comes only when it is read as part of a volume which consistently engages with specific themes and questions. I would suggest that H.D. intended *Sea Garden* to be read as a body of work which goes beyond the exposition of images and engages the reader in a cohesive set of themes, and a complex destabilisation of perspective and authorial cohesion. 'Garden', 'Sheltered Garden' and the sea flower poems form one thematic strand of the web: underlying the subversion of traditionally gendered symbols is an interrogation of the act of writing and creation, and the specific meanings it has for the woman writer.

Throughout *Sea Garden* H.D. also attempts to subvert many of the reader's expectations of poetry and the author through her use of language. 'Garden' provides a backdrop to this interrogation. Interestingly, it is one of the most 'Imagist' of the poems in *Sea Garden*. In the first section the rose is centralised, 'cut in rock':

> I could scrape the colour
> from the petals
> like spilt die from a rock.
>
> If I could break you
> I could break a tree.
>
> If I could stir
> I could break a tree –
> I could break you.

> (pp.24–5)

The rose becomes a rock which the speaker wishes to destroy but cannot – 'If I could break you' becomes 'If I could stir' – the slightest action is impossible in response to this implacable image, suggesting an uneasiness with the very foundations of Imagist practice. Thus in the second section, echoing 'Sheltered Garden', the speaker calls for the wind to 'rend open the heat' which has become, like the rose, so solid that 'Fruit cannot drop' (p.25). The author as an active presence, whose 'I' dominates the first half of the poem, is literally barred entry to the Imagist garden in the second half, describing it from a distance, denied even pronominal presence in the oppressive stasis of this stultifyingly 'thick air'. As Gary Burnett states, ' "Garden" situates itself firmly within Imagist definitions and finds itself stuck'[8]: strict adherence to its formal aims leaves H.D. trapped.

The poems in *Sea Garden* which explore desire highlight the problem of locating the authorial subject: 'The Helmsman' (pp.5–7) typifies this shifting, fluxing authorial presence in relation to desire. The poem opens:

> O be swift –
> we have always known you wanted us.
>
> We fled inland with our flocks

> (p.5)

There is an invocation to, and immediate fleeing from, that which desires: and the main part of the poem is preoccupied with the attempted escape from this desire by retreating to the safety of the inland forest. Finally, though, such attempts at escape are futile even though 'we loved all this' (p.6). The last stanza asserts powerlessness to resist desire:

> But now, our boat climbs – hesitates – drops –
> climbs – hesitates – crawls back –
> climbs – hesitates –
> O be swift –
> we have always known you wanted us.

(p.7)

In contrast to the descriptive passages of the flight to the forest, the verse is now literally marked by urgency in the form of dashes: formal punctuation, which would accord the sentence some containment, is foregone. Breathless propulsion towards desire forces the reader to engage in its inexorability and urgency which, paradoxically, the reciprocator is unable either to escape or fulfil.

The poem is also free of gender-specific pronouns – only the helmsman of the title is identifiable in this respect, and the speaker is also impossible to locate: the speaker could be a part of the 'we' who attempts to escape; the whole of the 'we'; or the helmsman of the title who is unable to guide his boat away from the pull of that which wants to engulf it. Thus when desire enters the text it precipitates a destabilising of the speaking subject – where are the voices, between whom is the desire felt, and what is the nature of this desire? It is not sexualised in the poem: it is figured as a driving, elusive, yet unrealisable force.

This paradox is reworked consistently throughout the volume: 'The Cliff Temple' (pp.26–8) and 'Pursuit' (pp.11–12) have as their central image the chase of the object of desire. In both these poems the speaker's attempt at satisfaction is coupled with a retreat inland, but is frustrated – for as the very nature of the *Sea Garden* stresses, such fulfilment is only to be found on the boundaries between sea and land 'where sea-grass tangles with/shore-grass' ('Hermes of the Ways', p.39). This recurring preoccupation with the merging of the boundaries between two elements, and the inability to fulfil desire, are the first attempts at circumventing conventional heterosexual binary schemas: but H.D. is doomed for the object of desire is unattainable in *Sea Garden*.

Two poems specifically centralise woman's interaction with the seascape. In these poems perspective and value become specifically gendered with reference to the speaker (in contrast to the sexless speaker of the sea flower poems who offers us different views). In 'The Shrine' (pp.7–10) the speaker is located as female by their view of the shrine contrasting directly with that of 'the quiet men', 'the landsmen', 'the men in ships'. Gary Burnett has suggested that the epigram 'She watches over the sea' creates a multiplicity of possible identifications: 'she' may be the goddess of the shrine, the shrine itself, or the speaker looking down to the sea: but I would suggest that as the speaker is specifically feminised through their alternative perspective to the landsmen, so the shrine is by the epigram. The speaker is set in an oppositional (I/you) relationship with the shrine:

> You are useless
> O grave, O beautiful,
> the landsmen tell it – I have heard –
> you are useless.

> (p.8)

A complicity is evoked between the shrine and the narrator though, and thus I would conclude that the epigram, rather than throwing doubt on the speaking source, feminises the shrine along with the female speaker.[9]

The men, 'tempted' to shelter in the shrine, meet only destruction and death, and warn the speaker:

> there are wrecks on the fore-beach,
> wind will beat your ship,
> there is no shelter in that headland,
> it is useless waste, that edge,
> that front of rock

> (p.9)

In the reported speech of the men the adjective 'useless' is repeatedly associated with the shrine: this jarringly passive adjective to describe that which violently destroys boats and lives illustrates the reductivity of the male viewpoint in the face of a feminine power. In direct contrast to this the speaker experiences the shrine as a source of beauty and security. Flowers are again mobilised as specifically feminine: 'we spread throat on throat of freesia/for your shelf' (p.8), and the speaker persists in the attempt to reach the shrine despite the warning of the fishermen. Finally it is reached and shelters the speaker: 'your eyes have pardoned our faults,/your hands have touched us' (p.10). The desire to attain a specifically feminine, maternal embrace is realised, and with it comes security and peace. With female-orientated desire a sense of authorial stability emerges, unlike the unspecified desire of 'The Helmsman' which produces a fragmented identity.

In 'The Gift' (pp.15–18) the text itself is offered as the 'gift' of the title, placing the poem in the tradition of the love lyric, designed to seduce the receiver who will wonder 'what is left, what phrase/after last night?' (p.16). The receiver is identified as female by the 'comb', 'gold tassel', and pearl 'necklace' that she wears. The gender of the speaker is unspecified as it describes the woman's garden, full of flowers and 'over-sweet', yet Sappho and her female community are invoked by the references to 'the initiates', 'their inmost rites', 'the moment of ritual' (p.17). That Sappho provides a backdrop to *Sea Garden* has been convincingly argued by Eileen Gregory,[10] and the Sapphic community is evoked in the woman-centred space of the garden. Finally, though, the speaker finds the woman's garden and the life to be had there too restrictive for it is centred within the traditionally flowered perfection of the garden, and yet again a plea is made for escape to the seascape, for in its relentlessness there will be 'some hideousness to stamp beauty . . . on our hearts' (p.18). Again female desire is contained within an I/you schema, but to realise it within the confines of traditional society, in the garden, is unsatisfactory; an escape needs to be made to the sea garden, and the liberation it offers.

Thus *Sea Garden* is a volume which explores gender and value: the conventional poetic construction of – and resulting restrictions placed upon – the female; the plea for a violent liberation; desire as a disparate force; and a female-orientated fulfilment of desire in the seascape. Working within the confines of Imagism, H.D. was attempting to subvert the early twentieth-century's expectations of the woman poet and challenge the accepted vision of woman and heterosexual paradigms based upon the subject/object model of desire. Ultimately, though, she was forced to seek out a poetic form which could convey her themes more satisfactorily, and this she began to do in 'Hymen' and 'I Said'.

The poem 'I Said' (pp.322–25), although written in 1919 and published posthumously, illuminates an important aspect of H.D.'s development. The largely unfocused desire of *Sea Garden* becomes eroticised, and lesbian desire becomes the central textual dynamic. It was headed 'To W.B.' – Winifred Bryher, H.D.'s lifelong companion, and written in response to Bryher's suicide threat, at the end of a year when both women had consulted the sexologist Havelock Ellis about their sexuality.

The speaker of the poem rallies their beloved by mobilising Greek notions of the soldier's heroism in the face of adversity, and thus implicitly locates the speaker and subject as masculine. This is reinforced in the second section by the use of male pronouns, as the speaker states that there is a heroism to be found in the contemplation of death:

anyone to-day who can contemplate
the idea of death, abstract death,
(romantic though he be,
young without doubt, mad perhaps)
anyone to-day who can die for beauty,
(even though it be mere romance
or a youthful geste)
is and must be my brother.

(p.323)

Until this point gender and identity have been fluid, but they are now firmly located
as filial, based on the admiration to be found in the male bond of comradeship.
Such a device is a familiar displacement of lesbianism onto a culturally acceptable
homosocial model, and is also in accordance with Havelock Ellis' theory on the
homosexual as an 'invert' – literally a person trapped in the opposite sex's body,
who thus displays the 'natural' desire of their gender despite their outward sex.
But this device also enables the subtextual exploration of the social oppression
which forces lesbianism into silence.

As Diana Collecott has so incisively demonstrated, lesbianism is encoded both
through signs and subject matter:

I said:
"think how Hymettus pours divine honey,
think how dawn vies
in the shelter of Hymettus,
with clusters of field-violet,
(rill on rill of violets!
parted and crested fire!)
think of Hymettus
and the tufted spire of thyme,
hyacinth, wild wind-flower

(p.322)

'I Said' resonates with hidden allusions and intertexts: these bracketed clauses are
infused within the lesbian subtext with an urgent eroticism, confirmed by the
allusion to the hyacinth. Read as a proper noun, Hyacinth evokes the homoerotic
legend in which Apollo, grieving at the death of his beloved, turned Hyacinth's
blood into a flower. In this poem, then, the feminine flower imagery of the *Sea
Garden* becomes eroticised, the bracketed clauses that end with exclamation marks

of delight, mapping the female body – 'parted and crested fire' – suggest a breaking free from earlier formal constraint.[11]

Perspective and value are again centralised: lies become truth in 'I Said' because the beloved is unable to express personal truth for fear of ostracism. The lie inherent in outward conformity to convention mediates inner personal truth:

> But it seems to me Greek rather
> to live as you lived,
> outwardly telling lies,
> inwardly without swerving or doubt –
> "if I cannot have beauty about me
> and people of my own sort,
> I will not live,
> I will not compromise" –

(p.323)

Active lesbian desire is not shown as ultimately liberating: rather it seems to intensify the restrictions placed upon the individual by society. If the beloved attempts, 'in a crude speech' (p.325), to express their desire, the speaker warns them that they 'must count (them)self now, *now* amongst the dead' (p.325). Thus H.D. was forced to textualise her desire for women obliquely: veiling it under the homosocial bond, mobilising homoerotic legends, and ultimately not publishing this poem in her lifetime.

The eponymous poem of the *Hymen* volume (pp.101–10) textualises heterosexual desire, and specifically the problems it represents for the woman writer, within the framework of the Sapphic marriage song (elsewhere in this and in *Heliodora* the 'Fragment' poems similarly form an intertext to the fragmented remains of Sapphic manuscripts).[12] The verse is interspersed with extensive prose sections, giving detailed 'stage directions' and creating a visual context in which the poem is to be read. A woman-centred community is evoked, which laments the loss of a maiden due to her impending marriage. Again flower imagery is crucially associated with femininity: the bride is a flower, while her husband is portrayed as an invasive bee, which comes to imbibe the vital nutrition that woman provides for him:

> There with his honey-seeking lips
> The bee clings close and warmly sips,
> And clings with honey-thighs to sway
> And drink the very flower away.

(Ah, stern the petals drawing back;
Ah rare, ah virginal her breath!)

Crimson with honey-seeking lips,
The sun lies hot across his back,
The gold is flecked across his wings.
Quivering he sways and quivering clings
(Ah, rare her shoulders drawing back!)
One moment then the plunderer slips
Between the purple flower-lips

(p.109)

Heterosexual relations threaten to efface woman; the male 'plunderer' will 'drink the very flower away', and this image is reinforced in the final section of the poem for 'Before his fiery lips/ Our lips are mute and dumb' (p.110). Unlike the social sanctions of 'I Said' which render the women lovers speechless, the heterosexual bond in 'Hymen', so publicly celebrated and formalised, effaces woman, and she is literally consumed and made mute (actually and creatively) by the male.

Working in contrast to this central theme, the bracketed clauses in 'Hymen' challenge the assessment of heterosexual desire as totally self-effacing: as those bracketed clauses in 'I Said' map the female body, so those in 'Hymen' hint at a complicity, an openness towards receiving the copulatory bee ('Ah, rare her shoulders drawing back' p.109). Thus an ambivalence towards heterosexuality is created: the overt lament for the loss of the maiden is juxtaposed with a stifled attraction towards heterosexual relations, and the fear of this is rooted in the fear of the male/female bond as self-effacing for the woman artist.

'The Master' (pp.451–61), written in 1933, during H.D.'s consultations with Freud, marks a watershed in her work, for it provides a conclusion to the thematics of gender and desire that had so far characterised her poetry. After this point she was to centre her epic poems decisively on the figure of the mother, as prophetess and poet. A large part of her analysis with Freud centred upon sexuality, and 'The Master' is a testament to these discussions. The anxiety of gender and desire that infused *Sea Garden*, the exploration of heterosexual and homosexual desire in 'I Said' and 'Hymen', give way to an overt textualisation of bisexual desire, and an engagement with – and critique of – Freud's theories of woman's sexuality.

As has been so well documented by feminist critics, these theories were predicated upon male, phallic sexuality as the universal human model, while woman could only be defined as lack and absence within this schema. The male child's Oedipus complex results in anxiety focused on the perceived castration of the mother, and the threat of his own castration by the father in response to the boy's incestuous desire for the mother; thus he represses this desire and later in life transfers it onto a heterosexual object. In contrast the female child's complex is characterised by penis envy – she is lacking that most potent of signifiers – and angrily she abandons her mother as a love object, transfers her feelings to her father, and sublimates her desire for a penis into the longing for a baby.

Freud also characterised the healthy, 'normal' female child as passive in relation to men; only the 'masculine' girl sublimates her penis envy in her desire for achievement in a masculine vocation – the creation of art and literature being one such example. The female homosexual displayed the most extreme characteristics of the 'masculine' woman: penis envy, and the failure to transfer affection from the mother during the Oedipus complex, resulted in lesbian tendencies. Despite his belief in the bisexual basis of the psyche, Freud still maintained that 'normal' development resulted in the repression of such tendencies, and an adult heterosexual object choice.[13]

Of course, Freud's theories were far more complex than this schematic outline, and it is within the gaps and contradictions repeatedly registered by Freud that H.D. was able, in 'The Master', to create an empowered vision of the bisexual woman as perfect and whole, no longer predicated on lack. H.D. as both the creator of the text and enunciating 'I' is registered in the first section by the use of the personal pronoun and the autobiographical reference to her analysis with Freud through which she found 'wisdom' and 'measureless truth' (p.451): the intellectual tools with which to write the poem.

For the first time in her work bisexuality is specifically referred to:

> I had two loves separate;
> God who loves all mountains,
> alone knew why
> and understood
> and told the old man
> to explain
>
> the impossible,
>
> which he did.

(p.453)

Bisexuality within 'The Master' is defined as the merging of both masculine and feminine characteristics in the individual: physically explicit descriptions of both men and women are given, but the specific connection between bisexuality and the active choice of sexual partner is never made. The central aim of the poem is to create a vision of woman, reclaimed from Freudian lack, with bisexuality as the basis of her perfection: for such a woman holds both the masculine and the feminine within her.

Echoing the dual reality which was repeatedly negotiated in *Sea Garden*, woman is figured in the poem by the use of oxymoron:

> for a woman
> breathes fire
> and is cold,
> a woman sheds snow from ankles
> and is warm

(p.454)

The perfect woman, the bisexual woman, is she who contains both genders within her – 'the delicate pulse of the narcissus bud' (p.455) and 'that dart and pulse of the male' (p.456). But the Utopia that H.D. is attempting to define in 'The Master', rooted in the concept of the bisexual woman as perfect and whole, is challenged by the dependency of bisexuality upon the very categories it seeks to transcend. Bisexuality within 'The Master' is not synonymous with an androgynous third sex, it is the incorporation of both genders within woman; but the truly empowered, perfect, bisexual woman is still dependent upon the phallus, the Freudian economy, for definition, and is thus, in part, forever lacking.[14]

Despite this, H.D.'s vision is an exuberant one. The flower becomes an overt vulvic image, previously hinted at in 'I Said', and worship and dance become specifically feminine forms of empowerment:

> there is a rose flower
> parted wide,
> as her limbs fling wide in dance
> ecstatic
> Aphrodite . . .
> we were together
> we were one;
> sun-worshippers

(pp.456, 460)

The rhythms of speech, so rigorously controlled in H.D.'s Imagist poetry, are freed: woman is centralised, assigned erotic and creative agency, and delivered from the conflict that has permeated earlier texts. A sense of release is conveyed as 'her limbs fling wide in dance', 'ecstatic' satiation is realised through the acceptance and worship of the perfect bisexual woman.

After the uncertainty that marks *Sea Garden*, and the textualisation of exclusively lesbian or heterosexual desire in 'I Said' and 'Hymen', comes the bisexual desire of 'The Master', and the resolution of these themes. Through Freud, H.D. found the vocabulary with which to express bisexual desire and signify woman as whole. This aim is in some senses doomed to failure, for in attempting to free woman from Freudian lack, H.D. is forced to use the terms of the economy that she seeks to move beyond. This problem of definition affects us even today: sexual identities are constantly in the process of negotiation and definition both culturally and academically.[15] Bisexuality as both a term and an identity is particularly pertinent to this discussion. Do we define it as actual sexual contact, or use it to signify a mental incorporation of masculine and feminine attitudes? How do we define gender and implicated identity? At the level of the text what are the terms with which we critique the bisexual author? Is there a need to develop a theory of the bisexual reader? In researching this article I was struck by the lack of bisexual critical work: all too often the critic is forced into the reductive stance of either/or.[16] H.D.'s work stands as an invaluable testament to the creation of a bisexual identity, the problems faced, and the possibilities it offered. Desire is diffuse, subversive, and ultimately ecstatic: it is tantalising, consistently repudiating the attempt to classify, and thus totalise it. Through her poetry H.D. found a method of textualising this desire: albeit problematic, it nevertheless exposed the identifications inherent in the supposedly static classifications of gender and sexual identity, their dependency on the individual's complicity with such categories, and the possibilities to be glimpsed in manipulating the positions of identity we adopt. Today feminist theory is recognising the importance of bisexuality as a space in which to move beyond the categories with which it first engaged. Hélène Cixous heralded this shift in her seminal article 'The Laugh of the Medusa'.[17] In this she attempted to articulate the need to move beyond a neutered vision of bisexuality to:

> the *other bisexuality* on which every subject not enclosed in the false theatre of phallocentric representationalism has founded his/her erotic universe. Bisexuality: that is, each one's location in self (repérage en soi) of the presence – variously manifest and insistent according to each person, male or female – of both sexes[18]

H.D. attempted to do this half a century earlier. Her work moves far beyond Imagism to question the fundamental precepts of gender and identity, and provides us with valuable material with which to continue our own debate.

NOTES

1. Published in 1916, included in *H.D. Collected Poems 1912–1944*, ed. Louis L. Martz (New York, New Directions, 1983).
2. 'I Said', first published in 1982, is thought to have been written in 1919; 'Hymen' was published in 1921. Both are included in *H.D. Collected Poems*.
3. These first definitions of Imagism were published in *Poetry*, 1, 6 (March, 1913).
4. Eliot, *Selected Prose* (London, Penguin, 1965), p.43.
5. Information on Imagism taken from Claire Buck, *H.D. and Freud, Bisexuality and a Feminine Discourse* (New York and London, Harvester Wheatsheaf, 1991), pp.18–23; Peter Nicholls, *Modernisms, A Literary Guide* (Bassingstoke, Macmillan, 1995), pp.187–97; and Natan Zach, 'Imagism and Vorticism', in Malcolm Bradbury and James McFarlane (eds), *Modernism 1880–1930* (Bassingstoke, Macmillan, 1995), pp.228–42. I must here also acknowledge my debt to Buck's study of H.D. which provided me with an original and thought-provoking basis for the direction of my research, and I would direct the reader to her work for a more complex and detailed analysis of many of the themes that I have considered.
6. All page references will be to *H.D. Collected Poems 1912–1944*, ed. Louis L. Martz (New York, New Directions, 1983).
7. Claire Buck, *H.D. and Freud*, p.31.
8. Gary Burnett, 'The Identity of 'H': Imagism and H.D.'s Sea Garden', *Sagetrieb*, 8, 3 (Winter 1989), pp.55–75.
9. Gary Burnett, 'The Identity of "H" ', p.67.
10. Eileen Gregory, 'Rose Cut in Rock: Sappho and H.D.'s Sea Garden', *Contemporary Literature*, 27, 4, pp.525–52. Gregory asserts that the central images of Sappho's poetry are: the spatial image of a 'private space', which accords emotional openness between women in a setting apart from that of everyday life; the image of the bride/nymph as a figure of passage and erotic potential; and the flower image. All of these are repeatedly utilised by H.D. in *Sea Garden*.
11. Diana Collecott 'What is not said: a study in textual inversion', in J. Bristow (ed.), *Sexual Sameness: Textual differences in lesbian and gay writing* (London, Routledge, 1992), is an incisive decoding of 'I Said' and other lesbian texts, and the textual inversion which allows the lesbian writer to express what has so long been suppressed.
12. Susan Gubar in 'Sapphistries', *Signs* 10–11 (Autumn 1984), pp.43–62, discusses the importance of Sappho in the work of H.D. and other women writers, suggesting that the fragmentary nature of the Sapphic manuscripts allows the modernist woman writer to quell the anxiety of authorship and create a literary inheritance 'which holds out the promise of excavating a long-lost ecstatic lyricism that inscribes female desire as the ancient source of song' (p.47).
13. All information on Freud taken from Susan Stanford Friedman, *Psyche Reborn: The Emergence of H.D.* (Bloomington, Indiana University Press, 1981), pp.121–30.
14. For a more detailed analysis of H.D.'s attempts to articulate a bisexual self and the fundamental problems she has in doing this within Freudian theory see Claire Buck, *H.D. and Freud*, pp.78–92.
15. The term lesbian has come to signify a vast range of meanings, practices and ideologies: Monique Wittig asserts that 'Lesbians are not women', in *The Straight Mind and Other Essays*: (New York and London, Harvester Wheastsheaf, 1992), p.32, because the term 'woman' only has meaning within heterosexual systems of thought and economy. Rich identifies a 'lesbian continuum' (in 'Compulsory Heterosexuality and Lesbian Existence', in *Signs: Journal of Women in Culture and Society*, 5, 4 (Summer 1980), p.548), which is not limited to woman/woman sexual, genital contact, but expands the term lesbian to 'embrace many more forms of primary intensity between and among women' (ibid.).
16. Gubar's assessment is indicative of this problem: she asserts that 'lesbianism furnishes her [H.D.] with a refuge from the pain of heterosexuality and with the courage necessary to articulate that pain' in 'Sapphistries', *Signs*, 10:1 p.53. Implicitly she opposes lesbianism to heterosexuality in a manner that denotes it as an inferior method of escape, denying it status as a positive personal and creative identity.
17. Hélène Cixous, 'The Laugh of the Medusa', *Signs*, 1,4 (Summer 1976) pp.875–93.
18. Ibid, p.884.

FURTHER READING

Agenda Special Issue no.25 (1987–8).

Bristow, Joseph (ed), *Sexual Sameness: Textual Differences in lesbian and gay writing* (London, Routledge, 1992).

Buck, Claire, *H.D. and Freud: Bisexuality and a Feminine Discourse* (New York and London, Harvester Wheatsheaf, 1991).

Burnett, Gary, 'The Identity of "H": Imagism and H.D.'s Sea Garden', *Sagetrieb*, 8:3 (Winter 1989), pp.55–75.

Cixous, Hélène, 'The Laugh of the Medusa', *Signs: Journal of Women and in Culture and Society*, 1:4 (Summer 1976), pp.875–93.

Doolittle, Hilda, *H.D. Collected Poems: 1912–1944*, ed. Louis L. Martz (New York, New Directions Books, 1983).

Farwell, Marilyn R., 'Toward A Definition of the Lesbian Literary Imagination', *Signs*, 14:1 (1988).

Friedman, Susan Stanford, *Psyche Reborn: The Emergence of H.D.* (Bloomington, Indiana University Press, 1981).

Friedman, Susan Stanford, *Penelope's Web: Gender, Modernity, H.D.'s fiction* (Cambridge, Cambridge University Press, 1990).

Friedman, Susan Stanford, and DuPlessis, Rachel, *Signets: Reading H.D.* (Madison, University of Wisconsin Press, 1990).

Gubar, Susan, 'Sapphistries', *Signs* 10:1 (1984).

Laity, Cassandra, 'H.D.'s Romantic Landscapes: The Sexual Politics of the Garden', *Sagetrieb*, 6 (1987).

Nicholls, Peter, *Modernisms: A Literary Guide* (Basingstoke, Macmillan, 1995).

Rich, Adrienne, 'Compulsory Heterosexuality and Lesbian Existence', *Signs*, 5:4 (Summer 1980), pp.631–60.

Wittig, Monique, *The Straight Mind and Other Essays* (New York and London, Harvester Wheatsheaf, 1992).

Section Two: The Politics of Place

The essays in this section take as their theme the complex relationships between poet and place – in terms of geography, location, language, culture and politics. Two of the essays consider poets from Ireland (North and South); the third looks at the work of contemporary Scottish women poets, and their relationship both to indigenous traditions and to their female predecessors.

Ailbhe Smyth suggests that Irish literary criticism is dominated by a narrow (and gendered) agenda: a preoccupation with questions of 'Irishness', nationhood, myth and history. Many women poets, she argues, do not fit this template of the 'Irish poet', but are concerned with women's lives: topics like childhood, sexuality and motherhood. The Irish context is inevitably relevant, but is approached from an oblique angle and thus overlooked by male critics. Sex, she argues, is entirely missing from Irish critics' agendas, and yet the poetry is not so recalcitrant; despite the censoring effects of Catholicism, sex – including lesbian sex – is a common topic in contemporary Irish women's poetry. Interweaving her own meditations with excerpts from the poems, Smyth examines this material and mischievously suggests that literary critics are operating like the law, intervening to constrain or outlaw the transgressive excesses of poets' sexual behaviour.

Declan Long explores the absence of women poets from the lively literary scene of Northern Ireland. Showing how the nationalist question has fissured women's solidarity in the North, he suggests that the very specific political and cultural climate there may partly account for this silence. While Medbh McGuckian is the only woman to appear in both Irish and British anthologies, there is evidence that poetry writing is important to many Northern women. Long examines a lone anthology, *The Female Line: Northern Irish Women Writers*, and finds that these poems are often preoccupied with questions of gendered identity. He confesses himself uneasy with what he sees as their presentation of an almost ahistorical uniformity of female experience. This homogenised approach parallels the essentialism of the impossibly pure versions of Irishness and Englishness created by 'The Troubles'. A more radical poetry, he implies, would subvert the specious uniformity of both perspectives, without denying the place of gender: after all, 'a female line may not need to be a straight one'.

Helen Kidd considers the ways in which contemporary Scottish women poets articulate a sense of place in their writings. She emphasises the importance of regionality and the diversity of tongues which their work preserves, arguing that they are more alert to such heterogeneity than their male counterparts. She shows how Liz Lochhead, Jackie Kay, Sheena Blackhall and Catriona Nic Gumeraid, among others, work with their foremothers' ballad tradition, harnessing the opportunities offered by orality in order to celebrate the many contemporary forms of the vernacular. Delivering canny ripostes to the pronouncements of Hugh MacDiarmid, and focusing on the lives and contributions of women in Scotland, they offer a spirited defence against the ongoing threat of literary and cultural standardisation.

4

Dodging Around the Grand Piano: Sex, Politics and Contemporary Irish Women's Poetry

Ailbhe Smyth

Spaces Between

All things are hard: man cannot explain them by word. The eye is not filled with seeing, neither is the ear filled with hearing.

(Ecclesiastes 1:8)

I am making separate entries in the whole world. Always from here because I am where I am, cannot too be elsewhere, now and not forever.

I am not all-seeing, all-hearing, all-knowing. I am not god.

I know enough to know that these knowings cannot be enough. That each separate entry is a partial fulfilment for the requirements of wholeness.

I want the whole. To see it all, hear it all, laid out in all its richness, before me, around me, within me. Ordered, patterned, making sense, extricated from its chaos.

But I'll deny the lures of godness. Not unknowing, but not owning. Entering here and there. Taking what I find and leaving it for those beside and after. God-dodging.

> She told the one
> who was beyond saving
> to have a nice day
> (she said it twice for effect)

> I will, she assured,
> I'll have a bastarding ball
> dodging the Gods
> around the grand piano
> that isn't really there at all.[1]

They say we have no 'I' or cannot know the 'I' we have. How can they know, ungodly, what I may or may not have? How can they know if they, like me, ungodly, have no eye to see, no ear to hear, no self to know? What is their present talk about my absence?

Knowledge is limited by the scope of the eye, the acuity of the ear, the accuracy of memory. Human, not godly. Even interpreters, explicators, extricators. What can I know if I do not look, if I do not listen, if I do not remember?

Entrée en matiere: how to enter without breaking? We are locked and barred against entries of all kinds. Or maybe just we who have lost our innocence. Who has not? Lost, stolen, aged away. What is the matter of sex, of poetry, of sex and poetry and the spaces between?

> Some things insist on becoming lost,
> like the be-ribboned straw hat
> the girl waved over the bridge
> to me.
>
> How ridiculous it looked,
> floating on the water
> between two swans
> who were coaxing
> one another to love.
>
> Although I tried to reach it,
> it was swept away.
> 'Sit still in the boat, you fool',
> she called, 'sit still
> or you'll fall into the river.'[2]

Silences

Looking for sex in Irish poems, even in poems by Irish women, could make you believe in the un-thereness of grand pianos. First time around. It's only on your second coming that you begin to notice the effect.[3]

And I did go looking for it, sex, purposefully, in poems, and in the writing about the poems, to help me notice the effect. But cruising (Irish) poems is still, apparently, a private pursuit. There has been very little written about it (sex-and-poetry) critically, theoretically, historically, or in any way at all.[4] Now, it is absolutely not the case that there is nothing on what Irish women poets are on about (in Irish poems). There are essays and articles, journal special issues and multiple theses on Irish women's poetry and on Irish women poets. Not enough yet, and not necessarily in all the best places. But that's another debate, and another day. Men critics say very little about women's poetry, and when they do, they still say remarkably little, although often at length and damagingly. Women critics, and often poets, make the running and the openings, not always to loud acclaim (or any at all). But the important thing is, the great conspiracy of silence around the *fact* of Irish women's poetry has been exposed, and broken. Which does not mean, however, that we are free to enter how and where we will.

There seems to be an agreed terrain within which Irish poetry criticism – including, perhaps ironically, the very lately included feminist kind – can be exercised. I am not saying it's a fixed terrain, once and for all, because in the last decade or so its borders have been shifted in more ways than one, and by feminists more than most. But it isn't entirely open either. There is an agenda of acceptable *topoi*, of critical and discursive priorities, beyond which you venture at your own risk. The risk being oblivion, no-critics land.[5] To be sure, it is difficult, given the political geography and socio-historical circumstances, to write outside the terrain of Ireland and Irishness – because that, I think, is what it is. Irish poetry criticism is (still) hyper-concerned with questions of myth and history, with national and cultural identity.[6]

This preoccupation with Irishness as the primary terrain of criticism has disturbing repercussions for poetry, because *poems* which do not nourish these critical concerns are considered as either not really Irish, or not really poems; or remain entirely unconsidered. Clair Wills, for example, in her study of politics and sexuality in Northern Irish poetry, devotes a chapter to a discussion of contemporary Irish women's poetry, which she specifically construes as questioning 'current definitions of cultural and national identity in Ireland, in particular the repeated association of the use of myth and the writer's attempt to link himself with, to repossess, a history and a community' (see Note 4 at the end of this chapter). Her analysis is instructive, but given her definition, I wonder if it doesn't keep out a good deal more than it allows in?[7] What about poems not determined by 'debates over the figure of the motherland'? What about poems which explore areas of experience expressly suppressed by the myth-makers and law-makers of the motherland?

Certainly, I agree with Eavan Boland (and thus with Clair Wills) that 'a "nation" is a potent, important image'.[8] But however powerful/disempowering an image Mother Ireland has been for many Irish women poets, it is not the only one and some have chosen to disregard/discard it through poetic re-location (from 'contemporary Irish poetry' to the 'women's poetry movement', in the

English-speaking West). Poetic emigration moves in much the same direction as the economic kind ('go West, young woman'), and is likewise not always experienced (or represented) as negative. It can be an experience of opening up where, liberated from the particular burdens and boundaries of the 'nation', the world becomes a bigger place and can be, may be, differently phrased. Irish critics need to acknowledge that Irish poets – especially women – do not necessarily write 'Irish' poems, given the strength of the pressures to discard tradition and the marked opportunities for poetic and political migration to a more welcomingly open terrain.

'In the City of Boston' is the opening poem in Mary Dorcey's collection *Moving into the Space Cleared by Our Mothers*. This is terrain unmarked by history or tradition, trans-national, open, spacious. But movement towards implies at the same time movement away from: the collection title, and the title and positioning of the first poem, decisively accentuate a self-conscious distancing from Ireland and the man-made canonical Irish poem. 'In the City of Boston' cuts us loose from what we know too well to see clearly, places us in a new relation to both lived experience and poetic vision: it re-locates us:

> I have seen mad women in my time,
> I have seen them waiting row on row,
> I have seen the stripped flesh,
> the abandoned eye,
> I have seen the frothing mouth
> and heard the cries,
> I have seen mad women in my time
> – I have never seen them mad enough.
>
> In the city of Boston I once saw a woman
> and she was mad – as mad as they come
> (and oh do they come, mad women,
> as often as the rest?)
> She walked the street in broad daylight,
> neat as a pin – a lady no doubt
> in blue coat, blue hat, blue purse
> blue shoes – the only note
> out of place in it all
> was her face – the peculiar angle
> of her head; thrown back, jaws wide
> and a scream so shrill poured out
> it lifted birds from her feet.[9]

This magnificently angry poem strips away, line by incantatory line, the layers of decorum which, sealed tightly in place, keep the world neatly in order, *in sanity*. It exposes, in broad daylight, the agonising irony and literally maddening dislocation of women in a world which defines as sane what is experienced as mad, and as mad what is necessary for survival. The edge defines the centre: the edge is where you go when there is nowhere else to be. It is at least in part about the eccentricity of women's symbolic place, and the physical and psychic cost of that displacement. But it is not a victim poem. There is no resignation here. The 'peculiar angle of the head', in principle antithetical to both sanity and poetry, is here re-positioned to become a different angle of sight and of hearing, enabling us to make sense of the cries, the shrill screams of a mad woman in Boston, not as 'other', but as connected with our selves:

> I have seen the abandoned faces
> row on row,
> I have seen mad women in my time
> – I have never seen us mad enough.

We can never say it often enough: the repetition with its strategic replacing of the pronoun makes this clear: survival requires that we refuse to be ordered, that we creatively embrace the madness of our anger, even though there is not, anywhere, any guarantee that it will be enough. For a poem is a delicate instrument and may not, after all, be able to provide us with either a sense of (erotic) connection or an answer to our futures:

> (and oh do they come, mad women,
> as often as the rest?)

Irish women's poetry is no more confined to, within or by national/historical borders than sexuality within motherhood, or sex by love, or Irish women within the jurisdiction of Ireland by legal prohibitions against abortion. This is part of my point: poems by Irish writers continue to be read through narrow-gauge tracks of convention and tradition where lesser (or no) value is accorded to poems not in thrall to the nation. When I read many Irish critics, I am depressed by their introversion, by the limited range of their interests, and I am bothered by the absence of sex on their critical agenda.[10] This bothers me, among other critical silences, because it is certainly in the poems, at least in poems by women, although not always where, when or how you might expect:

> My wild hills come stalking
> Did I perhaps after all, in spite of all
> try to cast them off,
> my dark blue hills,

a denunciation no less real
for all its refinement?
have I dissembled,
cast myself in the role of a discerning mountain lover,
my acceptance of these as optimal hills
being based upon the most impeccable of aesthetic criteria?
Have I stooped so low
as to lyricise about heather,
adjusting my love
to fit elegantly
within the terms of disinterested discourse?

Who do I think I'm fooling?
I know these hills better than that.
I know them blue, like delicate shoulders,
I know the red grass that grows in high boglands
and the passionate brightnesses and darknesses
of high bog lakes
and I know too how
in the murk of winter,
these wet hills will come howling through my blood
like wolves.[11]

It is low-minded and not quite 'lit.crit.' to seek out sex in poems. This has partly to do with the current bent of literary theory, partly with notions of poetic decorum, and also of course with the historical and socio-political regulation of sex and sexuality. Women are so much more amenable to control in the lowlands. But silences echo one another, howling through our lives, like wolves. The social conventions of sex-talk and the aesthetic conventions of poem-talk place each in frigidly separate spaces and we are, mostly, governed by strict rules of propriety in their observance, rarely broken.[12] There is no denying that Irish society has a highly dishonourable history of sexual repression, which continues to reverberate in the present. Sex is unspeakable in scholarly company in Ireland.[13] More significantly and not at all surprisingly, the unspeakability of sex has been constructed (can you construct a silence? most assuredly) through the control of women's sexuality, unthinkable because unspeakable (or vice versa), outside the domain of reproduction. It is equally undeniable that contemporary Irish women's refusal to be regulated out of mind and body, our insistence on the right to sexual autonomy, are crucial elements in the social, political and cultural disruptions which are re-defining Irish society and culture.[14] The audibility of women's breaking of sexual silences – literally and symbolically, politically and culturally – is resounding. Although it continues to be ignored.

But contradictions and double-talk (ambiguous and ambivalent) seem almost inevitable the moment you step on sex. Even in godly Ireland, we *do* talk and write about sex, not always euphemistically, in private and in public, in bed and in the media, in pornography (which circulates, despite its regulation), in medical and educational materials (although not in school curricula), in church and parliament and law and fiction.[15] Indeed, we (i.e., Irish) talk so much about the silence about sex in Ireland, that there comes a point when you realise that talking about the silence is a crucial way of actually talking about sex.

> I've already had my fill of sermons against sex. In the Belfast mission-halls of my youth, I remember the sex-haters with their needy wrathful eyes and anoraked bumptiousness.

> I have a theory of my own: fleeing from sex is just another way of being caught by it.[16]

So, when sex occurs in a poem, we flee, turning a critically coy blind eye, as if the poetic solecism had never happened. As if the poem simply did not exist.[17]

The odd thing is that so many of the poems I have been reading really are so much braver and bolder, venturing into territories untouched by criticism. Or is it so odd? Perhaps the relation between poetry and criticism is not unlike that between sexual behaviour and the law: at odds with one another much of the time, the law restraining and containing what transgresses the boundaries, the limits set by convention, demanded by decorum. Whatever. Mary O'Donnell (see Note 8) comments:

> It's difficult to talk about them [my erotic poems], because they're about the zones between what is acceptable socially and what is not. It's not a favourite topic in this country.

Yet a giddily ungodly reading of poems by Irish women turns up far more of 'alla this foolishness', in Ntozake Shange's memorable (and quite un-Irish) phrase, than lurks within the terms of (disinterested) critical discourse.[18] Eithne Strong (see Note 8) says:

> Women talk about sexual things much more. This is something very new in Irish poetry. You would have been excommunicated for masturbation at one time. Now it's much broader and more honest, not before time.

Yes, although forms of critical excommunication still operate. And you do have to go looking for the grand piano. Which means clearly identifying the silencers, reading beyond the academic criticism, beyond the reviews, beyond the mainstream anthologies of 'Irish Poetry'. Now, with less than half a dozen exceptions which prove this general rule, you have to do this anyway to know anything about what women are writing.[19] Women poets who write about sex, for specific example, rarely get reviewed, or if and when they do, the sexy poems are politely not mentioned. Rita Ann Higgins is a stunning case in point, as is Maighread Medbh, in another idiom. Mary Dorcey received the Rooney Prize for her short stories, but not the least little award for either of her two poetry collections. You won't find much in the line of sexual explicitness in the poems by women included in anthologies of 'new Irish poetry'. You will need to go to anthologies edited by women,[20] to the collections by women, in which women choose not to un-sex themselves.

Which is not to say the sexing (of the writing) is easy.[21]

> She was important enough
> to be left out
> powerful enough
> to be hidden away
> alive enough
> to be killed
> poet enough
> to be censored[22]

Shadows and Secrets

> I believed that in the dark place
> beneath the stairs, I would be safe
> until the game turned sour
> and I heard their laughter
> after they locked me in
>
> Over and over I am still the one
> who crouched down there
> long enough to feel
> water seeping down my legs.
>
> I remember nothing of our play
> but the sound of everyone running away,
> and the empty house echoing my cries
> and the heat
> in the glory-hole
> stifling,
>
> the smell of musty clothes
> old shoes
> the buzz
> of a single trapped wasp.[23]

For a woman to write about sex, she must come boldly out into the broad daylight; she must emerge from the glory-hole, the double-edged protection of anonymity and the long shadows cast by the socio-cultural denial of her self. This is true, of course, for women in any patriarchal society, not just mine (or yours). But the coming out is not everywhere, for each one, the same, because shadows are everywhere differently inflected, because they lie with more or less emphasis on this sin or that, on this secret or the other.

In Ireland, shadowed by a particularly puritanical form of catholicism for so many centuries, the conflation of sex-as-sin and, therefore, of sex-as-secret is especially marked. Sex is a negative construction, with particular and still inescapable reverberations in women's lives, materially and psychically, as Ruth Hooley makes clear:

> Self-sacrifice and selflessness have been elevated by the Catholic Church (and many other institutions) to a level of female sanctity, epitomised in the image of the Virgin Mother. In reality, that self, so neglected and exploited, so denied, often sinks invisible, under-developed, frustrated, warped and parasitic. But sometimes, out of a desperate need to survive ... that self can summon up a sense of itself/herself ... out of such a struggle the startling, painful, personal identification 'I' is born. This is the coming of age of the sexual self as I perceive it.[24]

In *Flesh the Greatest Sin*, her long narrative poem, Eithne Strong recounts the tragedy of those taught to despise the flesh, deny the body, fear sex, and hate themselves; those refused the right to question, to experience, to live; those condemned to shame, self-mortification, self-denial:

> The Terrible Sins are those against purity;
> the vilest. Remember the sixth commandment
> Thou shalt not commit adultery.
> What is adultery? Hold your tongue
> and learn obedience. Mortify the flesh,
> that is the enemy;
> scourge it that you may not fall into eternal fire.
> Remember what it is like to be burned. Imagine
> your whole body burning and never ending.[25]

Flesh the Greatest Sin is an indictment of the women-erasing sins of catholicism. Strong narrates the history of Ellen, moving from childhood, through marriage and childbirth/childraising to her death. But has her life ever been more than an apprenticeship for her death?

Long since terrorised to non-response, flesh
of Ellen could not accommodate to this unwelcome licence
called Conjugal Right; it established her bewilderment,
recoil, hate, but never joy.

'Never joy': the story of women's de-sexualisation in Irish society. And the story
of women's silence in culture: 'Hold your Tongue!/Do what you're told!'. Women
are seduced, threatened, blackmailed, bullied, beaten into purity, than which there
is no more honourable calling, and no bleaker destiny: 'to be virgin/there is nothing
higher for a woman.'[26] What is it, Clair Wills wonders, 'about the Catholic ideal
of femininity, the virginal-maternal, which enables it to become something which
women are willing to identify with?' (see Note 2). But what choice was there, I
ask myself? What social and economic alternatives? What symbols and words at
hand to overwhelm the 'Voices of Authority'?

The old voices sounded always
unrelentingly in her life. Do not indulge. Punish.
Crucify self.

How many of my generation, *a fortiori* that of my mother or grandmother, could
find a way out of 'the valley of the shadow'?

Guilt grew with Nance,
outgrowing her, going through and all about her.
The Voices, active in Ellen, mother,
continued in the child,
sounding the maxims, endorsing.

Yet Nance, daughter, does find a way. 'No galvanic revelation . . . No dazzling
vision'. But a slow knowing:

. . . a beginning of belief
in the great importance
of believing, hoping, loving
– against odds.[27]

Flesh the Greatest Sin is an exorcism rather than a catharsis: we require rites capable
of banishing the deadly purity imposed by history, culture, religion, which prevents
our living. We need a clear space where self-knowing can begin, where a 'fusion
of flesh and spirit' may become possible:

and the space between now
and then must be filled

>   carefully
>   with ritual[28]

But if 'now is moveable', as Anne Le Marquand puts it, there is still the question
of how we came to inhabit it. Curiously, although we are willing and able to
talk about Irish women poets' exploration of the meanings of motherhood (in
relation, for example, to the writing of Medbh McGuckian, Nuala Ní Dhomhnaill
and Eavan Boland), the significance of women writers' retrieval of childhood has
not been noted at all, as far as I am aware. I don't know how widely this applies
elsewhere, but the evocation of childhood – its 'gratuitous, accidental joys', in
Moya Cannon's words [29], as well as its residue of fear and secrets – figures
strongly in contemporary Irish women's poetry.[30] This may not seem to have
much to do with sexuality, first time round, but of course it does.

We do not come to a negative sense of sexuality 'naturally' or fully formed.
We learn the prohibitions in the beginning, from the beginnings, and we learn
them well for they are embedded and emblazoned everywhere in our culture. We
can't miss them, even before we have any clear idea of what it is we might be
missing.

>   Before that buckle fell away forever
>   The habit of concealment laced the soul,
>   Left yellowing and tidy in the drawer.
>   Outside I'm raking the loose gravel still
>   Over the scrunch of tumbrils.[31]

We encounter sex through the codes of concealment which mark it off as forbidden
terrain. Language conceals it, and the same language perversely reveals it. To
decipher its enigma, if we ever can, we must expose the sly rhetoric as adroitly
as we identify the duplicitous practices. We must learn to break the language
which represents sex as forbidden, which expressly refuses it expression:

>   The neighbour's daughter is painting her toenails
>   bright red in the afternoon sun
>
>   and the room is dark and cool
>   where her mother is dusting the photograph
>
>   of a girl in a white dress on a swing
>   with her legs near the sky
>
>   Her father stands at the other side
>   of the gate squinting and averting his eyes.[32]

Making sense of what we see is another matter. All is given, but nothing is clear.
What we thought we saw and what we make of it in review are not one and the

same thing. Poetry works in the space between the darkness and the light, ascribing meaning to both: sometimes in contradiction, sometimes glimpsing connection in the side glances, the discrete gestures, the reflections. It enables us to catch sight of ourselves at crucial moments, personal and communal. Understanding requires double vision – of the moment and of re-view (or 're-vision' in Adrienne Rich's phrase), of the here and the then. If we can review the secrets of our childish visions, re-vert our gaze to the 'dark place' in which we have been forced to abandon them, we will find not innocence but perhaps the questions which we needed then even as the answers played out their enigmatic patterns before our very eyes:

> Burnt incense at my throat,
> the flicker of a brightening candle,
>
> I watched the priest
> raise a scrupulous hand,
>
> to swing the silver thurible.
> A row of heads bowed.
>
> And going home in the car
> my father dipped headlights
>
> and slowed to enter our gate
> past a black Morris Minor
>
> backed to the grassy river –
> Reilly's hand ventured under tweed
>
> all the way up nylon stockings,
> coming to grips with
>
> the fluid inside of thighs,
> her head thrown back,
>
> she inhaled a Sweet Afton –
> unaware of a passing car,
>
> the wide eyes of a girl
> in darkness closing a gate
>
> held by the red light
> of a cigarette.[33]

In these (and many other) poems by Irish women, childhood is not at all the idyllic repository of lost goodness. Nostalgia and the 'rapt romanticism' of childhood innocence, which convention imposes on reminiscence, are cut right back to the root. The remembering of childhood springs from a need both to name the sources of those silences which will continue to burn our throats if we cannot find words to give them meaning and to make sense of the secrets we have kept, or that have kept us, for so long in the glory-hole. Eavan Boland in *A Kind of Scar* (see Further Reading) believes: 'There are certain areas that are degraded because they are silent. They need to be re-experienced and re-examined. Their darker energies need to be looked at.'

Subversions

The dark silences and half-understood secrets of childhood are not the only ones, to be sure, in need of exposure. If the representation of women's heterosexual experience can be 'outed' only with difficulty from the shadows and secrecy surrounding it, consider how much more powerfully the prohibitions apply to lesbian sexuality. It is not that lesbianism is forbidden, as a practice, by Irish law. But that it is not is a sign of its absolute unthinkability. When male homosexuality was effectively defined as unlawful under the (British) Offences Against the Persons Act of 1861, lesbianism was so utterly taboo that legislative measures to prevent its occurrence were simply unnecessary.

> When and where did your lesbianism last occur? Last month? Last year? At home? In bed? At school? In front of the neighbours? Please write clearly, preferably in bold, to make yourself as conspicuously different as possible.[34]

Yet outbreaks of lesbianism have been occurring, even in Ireland, with astonishing continuity for a considerable time,[35] although Irish lesbians' struggle for rights, freedom and social and cultural visibility has been arduous and fraught with humiliation and silent pain:

> Have you ever made love
> with the TV on
> – to spare the neighbours
> landlady, lord –
> the embarrassment;
> the joy undisguised
> of two people;
> especially women
> (imagine the uproar!)
> coming together?
>
> Come quietly
> or the neighbours will hear.[36]

Mary Dorcey was the first Irish poet to make no secret of the fact that she is lesbian. She was the first to use women-embracing pronouns and nouns, and one of the first women poets to write explicitly about sex, certainly the first to name and to brave the 'uproar' about lesbian sex, though where her work was concerned it was more a roaring silence of dismissal and disregard for many years. Her first collection of poems was published in 1982, in Britain; her short stories appeared in 1989. In 1991, Salmon Publishing became the first Irish press to publish a collection by Mary Dorcey.[37]

Her poems do not deal with questions of 'national identity', although they do indeed explore other aspects of identity, relations to place and to myriad 'others'. It strikes me that, ironically, one of the greatest dangers facing a lesbian poet writing in a milieu where such work is exceptional, is the insidious expectation that her work will always be sexual (even 'sexy'), and always centered on 'lesbian issues', however defined. An Irish poet is always and ever (still) defined by (his) 'Irishness', but a lesbian poet in Ireland does not fit within the given meanings of 'Irishness' and her work thus cannot be categorised as anything other than lesbian.

Mary Dorcey is no longer the only 'out' Irish lesbian writer, although there are still extraordinarily few such poets. Nuala Archer's work has been published in the USA and in Ireland, and since she is only partly Irish, different standards are applied, sexually and canonically. Cherry Smyth writes explicitly and sensuously about lesbian desire and pleasure (*inter alia*), but her work rarely appears in Irish publications. Smyth, who was brought up in Northern Ireland and now lives in London, inflects the ambivalence of emigration with a powerfully sexual intensity:

> I unpack clothes smelling of London,
> Lulled by the tease of familiar voices
> I still yearn for the anonymity of city.
> Peace to read, think, eat, not eat, to sweat,
> Clutter, clatter, stay in bed all day
> With the one I love
> And talk about her openly.
> There is no forgiveness
> For escaping the rite of match 'n hatch.
> 'No sign of a wee wedding ring
> slipping on your finger?' they ask.
> The spinster is come home with her fancy airs
> And graces and new-fangled ideas.[38]

There is then no 'tradition' of lesbian poetry-making in Ireland at this stage – although the trail-blazing of Dorcey, Archer and Smyth, in their very different ways, is crucial in diversifying the mono-directional assumptions of heterosexual

writers and readers, and in giving voice to truths and visions for lesbians in Ireland. Perhaps the wonder is not that there is so little, but that it is there at all.
So much subversion is needed to shake Ireland by the roots of its orthodoxies.[39] There is the vast domain of women's privatised sexual pain which urgently needs to be spoken about. Irish women poets are doing so, not because anger has become 'almost an axiom of feminist poetry',[40] proof of one's *bona fides* as a woman poet, but quite simply because women, who may or may not be poets, are angry. Because there are events so shocking that we cannot afford, for our own survival and that of countless other women, to remain silent. This is an ethical and political imperative (why would we separate the two?) as well as a personal and communal one. Now, while I am as wary as the next (white academic) woman of metonymy, of presuming that my part is women's whole, I am not prepared to be so separated from other women that solidarity becomes a functional impossibility. Division is a strategy of the powerful, and connection still seems to me a more effective way of thwarting it than any other (what other is there?). Making and maintaining the connections is about wanting to do so, about imagining how they can solder what has been torn wilfully asunder, about finding the delicate language to meld the tenuous links.

An activist directs her anger towards actions whose objective is to eradicate the source of women's oppression, to change the system that allows, or at the very least does not formally prohibit, sex and gender-based exploitation and abuse. An activist poet[41] may direct her anger towards realising an intensity and clarity of vision which enables articulation of women's unspeakable sexuality – publicly in perpetration and/or privately in annihilation. Feminist activism speaks and acts out of the need, passionately experienced because cruelly denied, to inhabit our bodies, minds, souls, lives. All activism is not poetry, but it does not follow that poetry cannot (must not) be political, nor that anger dilutes the aesthetic.[42]

I do not accept that rage is *definitionally* irrational, and therefore aesthetically disabling. Poetry which finds the words to speak what has been stifled by history and culture is bound to seem different, because it is. It *minds* the anger, in every sense, giving it its due weight of passion, alongside reflection, analysis and vision. Passionate conviction is never *enough* to make a 'good' poem, but it is absurd to assume it is therefore an impediment. Nor do I think that 'anger poems' (which are not, in any case, a genre apart) were merely a transitional moment in women's poetry, now redundant. There is nothing *passé* about violence in women's lives and outrage seems to me to be an entirely reasonable response to the fact of the continuing oppression of millions of people for no reason other than that of their sex. Anger is not a phase you work through (whatever therapy may tell us) or grow out of if its source remains painfully alive. If outrageous oppression continues, why should it be *poetically* necessary to 'move on' – and to what? Yes, we may be blinded by rage, but even that – especially that – can be a powerful focus of vision, raising us up and off the 'yes, but' fences erected by patriarchal versions of rationality, which construct women, women's pain, women's anger as unspeakable. Why, we must constantly ask, is anger disallowed? Whose interests does the prohibition serve? Reason can blind us to the necessity of passion: 'I have never seen us mad enough.'

The poems which deliberately intervene in and gloss the grosser attempts by state and society to control women's sexuality are important. Powered by indignation, they speak out of rational rage. In their very utterance, these poems defy the interdiction against women's entry into the *polis*; they refuse to accept as 'private' practices which demean and, worse, destroy the personhood of women. In so doing, they launch a crucial challenge to the powers that keep women in silence and in place: such poems are properly and necessarily political.

Paula Meehan's superb poem, 'The Statue of the Virgin of Granard Speaks', evokes an especially shameful occurrence in recent Irish social history: the death of Ann Lovett. It is at once a meditation on the disempowerment of all women, the difficulty of speech in a world where public silence about sex is a commandment, and a condemnation of the silences we agree to keep through convention, cowardice, or fear of reprisals:

> On a night like this I remember the child
> who came with fifteen summers to her name,
> and she lay down alone at my feet
> without midwife or doctor or friend to hold her hand
> and she pushed her secret out into the night,
> far from the town tucked up in little scandals,
> bargains struck, words broken, prayers, promises,
> and though she cried out to me in extremis
> I did not move,
> I didn't lift a finger to help her,
> I didn't intercede with heaven,
> nor whisper the charmed word in God's ear.[43]

Ann Lovett died giving birth, and her baby too. Alone, Christianity notwithstanding. There was no formal public inquiry, and no major changes in social policy or sex education in the wake of these deaths. In the poem, the statue of the Virgin speaks her solitary confinement in the profound silence of her plaster virginity, speaks her grief, isolation and shame: 'My being/cries out to be incarnate, incarnate,/maculate and tousled in a honeyed bed'. She keens the death of a young girl – 'a cacophony of bone imploring sky for judgement/and release from being the conscience of the town'. There is no release for those who choose silence over life.

> There are our streets.
> If you are a woman you must break the mould,

> smash the flashy screen
> that makes us meat for pricks
> and not for joy.
> If you are a woman you must fight
> to choose to work, to dress, to fuck,
> to look straight in the eye,
> to stroll and not
> Walk faster.[44]

Street-walking with the new meaning of freedom, means straight-talking and new ways of naming and claiming what we have never been allowed to own. Maighread Medbh fights the mould of tradition with her flashy rap-rhythms, attention-grabbing 'un-literary' language and gloriously undecorous imagery. It is indeed poetry of and for 'everyday use'.

For many Irish women poets, writing up and through the darkness, the secrecy which shrouds and shapes their/our sexuality is almost too painful. There are moments when it seems as if the poem must collapse, or altogether disappear, under the weight of prohibition and fear:

> There was reason
>   WHY
>   I
> Went back
> Into that
> House
> My home,
> Picked up, in a flurry,
> And left
> With a few WORDS
> SCULLED
> On paper
> TESTIFYING
>   Testifying,
>   Testifying
> My Life
>   My Love
>   My Art
>
> I have Known
> a red hot
>   PoKer
>
> Ta-p-p-i-n-gout

                                    burns

                          on
                          my Spine -----

                          Booo oring holes

                          Burning sin
                                into the knuckles of my spine[45]

Scanlan's 'Terrorfull Return' self-knowingly seeks a space outside and beyond the
possibilities of its material existence – its pain is too hot for the page which would
bore it into place. The 'Irish poem' contained, in the most conventional sense,
the given meaning of Virgin-Mother-Ireland; through exclusion and silence, it
constrained the complexity, the polyvalence, the painful/pleasurable confusion
of women's sexuality.[46] Breaking up that singular form, finding the words, the
rhythms, the patterns capable of carrying, shaping, sounding women's experiences
and understandings of their sexuality is a mind-, spirit- and body-consuming struggle,
fraught with personal dangers and technical risks: 'You could die for this. The gods
could make you blind.'[47] Or dumb.

   But the power of the gods is not what it used to be. It is being thwarted and
undermined by the strategic subversions of coolly targeted, hotly expressed anger,
by the sharp truths of irony, by the incisive derision of wit and humour. The diktats
of those with clay feet are not long for this world.

                          Hey Missus,
                          you're the poet,
                          write a poem about me,

                          about the time
                          I lived
                          in a toilet
                          for six months,
                          no shit girlie.

                          Nothing to whine
                          home about
                          but it was dry
                          and beggars can't be choosers.

                          You're the poet,
                          the one with
                          the fancy words,
                          I'm the one

> with the toilet –
> they call me
> the space invader.
>
> A toilet, a toilet
> my kingdom is a toilet –
> give us a poem
> or piss off missus.[48]

Nothing is safe. Hallelujah!

The willing ability to mock poetry, and everything else, is one of the most powerful marks contemporary Irish women poets are making, with transformative intentions and effects, on the world – of poetry and everything else. There is an invigorating and regenerative boldness about much of the writing, a delicious impropriety which subverts our understandings of the 'proper' means and matter of poems:

> She sat on the lip
> Of events.
>
> Waiting
> for some new mouth
> to open.
>
> Offering
> An original sin.[49]

History, myth and icon are turned on their heads: the effects are heretical, ludic, provocative:[50]

> Alone in the room
> with the statue of Venus
> I couldn't resist
> cupping her breast.
>
> It was cool
> and heavy in my hand
> like an apple.[51]

Romance and its flowery growth are given short, ironic shrift, which the speaker turns against herself, with a sidelong glance of rueful complicity to her reader:

> Because she carried flowers:
> Lilac and wild red poppies
> When she first came to my bed,
> I loved her.

> Because she carried flowers:
> Marigold and lilies
> To another woman's bed,
> I left her.[52]

And the tales they tell, oh how they can sting with malice aforethought, providing occasions of multiple pleasure:

> That man
> Is an occasion of some sin
> Against a number of commandments
> Committed in haste,
> to be repented at great leisure.
>
> He is like a whole box
> Of very rich chocolates
> With a hint of mint in the tail,
> The kind that only tantalise the lips
> Linger on the tongue
> And slowly settle on the hips.[53]

These poems have a sharpness which comes from their tight control and a line pared down so far it reaches the quick of sensibility and sensuality. Their extreme brevity mockingly counters patriarchal designations of women as 'essentially' garrulous. It is no accident that so many of these 'quick notes' take sex as their centre of gravity:

> Platonic my eye,
>
> I yearn
> for the fullness
> of your tongue
> making me
> burst forth
> pleasure after pleasure
> after dark,
>
> soaking all my dreams.[54]

'She is Embodied Now'

In Her Own Image, the 1980 suite of poems by Eavan Boland, explores the relationship between identity, sexuality and representation. Rising defiantly above 'the hubbub and the shriek of daily grief/that seeks asylum behind suburb walls', the poems passionately reject the violent acts of physical, sexual and symbolic annihilation done to women, exposing the lie of patriarchal definition:

> He splits my lip with his fist,
> shadows my eye with a blow,
> knuckles my neck to its proper angle.
> What a perfectionist![55]

Flattened, brutalised, denied until nothing remains but the image, less than a shadow – 'I was not myself, myself' – the poet yet mazes her way to womanhood, through her 'nightly, shifty, bookish craft', cunningly retrieving the elements of her fragmented self, her dis-re-membered sex:

> I wake to dark,
> a window slime of dew.
> Time to start
>
> working
> from the text,
> making
>
> from this trash
> and gimmickry
> of sex
> my aesthetic . . .[56]

In Her Own Image contributed powerfully to the articulation of new myths and grammar, a new poetics and a new politics. The poems do not so much indicate as sear – 'from spark to blaze' – a way towards re-embodiment and the sexualisation of our 'woman selves'. Essentialist, some will say. But that is not right. These poems do not posit the body or sexuality as the sole source of truth, the essence of our 'selves'. I read them as insisting that to excise bodily and sexual experience from the body of our (self)-knowledge is to deny a vital part of what we need to know in order to live. The specialist, 'freshing death across his desk', the surgeon, 'blade-handed', the sculptor, god-like, summoning 'form from the void' produce sterile perfection, the antithesis of 'the fledged and edgy mix' which is the only uncertain truth of our living. 'I want to tell her she can rest. She is embodied now.'[57]

The process of symbolic embodiment was initiated by *In Her Own Image*, which thus marked a crucial moment in the development of a feminist aesthetic for Irish poets. It articulated what was shrouded – 'dulsed' – in shadows, secrets and silence, tore women's sexuality out of the realm of the tacit and exposed it, angrily, in words and in public. One of the most remarkable and ground-breaking aspects of the collection is its rejection of either romanticism or domestification as solutions

for living or understanding. The excision of traditional (and canonical) versions of
women's sexuality undertaken here by Boland is a necessary basis for the achievement
of self-representation which, in turn, is a crucial moment in the strategic process of
self-realisation.

But inscription – the scripting of realities – is not universal prescription:

> The truth of this
>
> wave-raiding
> sea-heaving
> made-up
> tale
> of a face
> from the source of the morning
> is my own.[58]

Savouring

> Weird little wordless words
> like fresh-scented breath,
> soft lips, pagan clits
>
> responding to memory's tongue
> transforming the debris
> of incest into living flesh,
>
> cascaded down the domes of my breath.
> They balanced on the brink
> of my blood then somersaulted
>
> into the blue vaults of lightning
> where passion's way of talking
> woke me up to a trace of
>
> irretrievable years
> & these moments now
> mine to embody and savor.[59]

In those 'irretrievable years', when sex was unspeakable for a woman, and pleasure
inadmissible, how were women to write about sexual experience? Where the range
of sexual destinies for a woman was limited to virginity, maternity or – the
paradox is only apparent – commercial availability, how was a woman to admit
publicly to sexual experience in non-designated categories? Where lesbians were
(are still) social and cultural outcasts, how was (is) a lesbian to talk, or write, at

all? How, indeed, was (is) a lesbian to exist? Where women's sexual pleasure is still never directly spoken in public discourse (church, medicine, law, education), but everywhere regulated out of sight and out of mind; where there is no available tradition of women's erotic/sexual writing; where smutty talk is a male prerogative and common pursuit (still); where sex may figure explicitly in 'boys' own' fiction (I'm thinking of James Joyce, among others) but only on the tip of the boys' own poetic tongue; given all of this (and more), what was (is) a woman, what was (is) a woman poet to do?

> Question:
> Can you tell me
> the way to the maternity?
>
> Answer:
> Walk on the beach
> in the West of Ireland
> at four in the morning
> in the middle of summer
> with a man who's six foot two
> and you'll get there
> sooner or later.[60]

Like women elsewhere, Irish women have fought long and hard for the right to disconnect sexuality and maternity. This is often misunderstood (wilfully?) as a denial of the value and eroticism of motherhood, which it is not. It is rather the assertion that sexuality and/or eroticism are not limited to/by/within maternity. I chose not to discuss the erotics of motherhood here because the two have been for so long tied together in the Irish context. The laws of patriarchal logic and reason and history and culture and, simply, the law, prescribe that women should make babies, not poems, and have families, not sexual pleasure. Notwithstanding and nevertheless, Irish women are making far fewer babies and a lot more poems. Informed speculation, based on a reading of the poems, indicates that there is considerable pleasure in the having of the sex and the making of the poems. There is an increasingly rich abundance of sex in poems by Irish women: lesbian and heterosexual, complicated and direct, explicit and subtle, straight-talking and visionary, solitary, singular and plural, exploratory, interrogative, analytical, descriptive, subversive, political, playful, ironic, funny and celebratory.

Where does it all come from?

I do not think that sexuality is at the 'core' of our selves (if we have such an unfashionable thing as a core, or even a self, any more). Nor do I think that sexuality is the fundamental source of imagination and creativity (if, likewise, there be such a thing). But sexuality – and simply, sex – is *also* part of experience and it *also* touches the imagination. It is thus *also*, like politics, part of the matter of poetry.

Of course, I don't know exactly where it all comes from, any more than I know how or why we experience sex as variously as we do. Analysis and explanation seem peculiarly inadequate when they try to explain these things. I do, however, know a grand piano when I see one – or an abundance of them. And I know for certain that poems by contemporary Irish women have been important to me in sighting, naming and exploring 'my wild hills':

> . . . the red grass that grows in high boglands
> and the passionate brightnesses and darknesses
> of high bog lakes[61]

NOTES

1. Rita Ann Higgins, 'God Dodgers Anonymous', in *Philomena's Revenge* (Galway, Salmon Publishing, 1992).
2. Joan McBreen, 'The Straw Hat', in *The Wind Beyond the Wall* (Brownsville, Oregon, Storyline Press, 1991).
3. The echo here is Ruth Hooley's brilliantly impertinent poem, 'Cut the Cake', itself an ironic echo of Yeats' 'The Second Coming'.
4. Notable exceptions are Clair Wills, *Improprieties: Politics and Sexuality in Northern Irish Poetry* (Oxford, Clarendon Press, 1993). and Jacqueline McCurry, ' "Our Lady Dispossessed": Female Ulster Poets and Sexual Politics', *Colby Quarterly*, (1991) Vol. XXVII, No.1, pp.4–8.
5. I do know who sets the agenda and how they do it, and what happens to those who venture too far, too soon. To be sure, I am not alone in the 'knowledge', but that is not my point here.
6. Edna Longley talks about the 'narrow and doctrinaire perspective' on Irish literature, culture and politics of the Field Day analysis in a recent interview. (*Krino*, No.15, 1994).
7. Medbh McGuckian, on whom Wills focuses significantly, has said that she is 'sexless' (as a poet) and claimed that there is 'no such thing as an *Irish* poet' (in Gillian Somerville-Arjat and Rebecca Wilson (eds), *Sleeping With Monsters: Conversations with Scottish and Irish Women Poets*, Dublin, Wolfhound Press, 1990; Edinburgh, Polygon 1990, p.5). Which seems a high price to have to pay for being a woman, a poet – and Irish.
8. In Somerville-Arjat and Wilson (eds), *Sleeping with Monsters* (1990), p.84.
9. Mary Dorcey, from 'In the City of Boston', in *Moving Into the Space Cleared by Our Mothers*, (Galway, Salmon Publishing, 1991.
10. I am also bothered by how indirectly sexuality bears on sex, in literary critical or theoretical terms (even feminist). I do not even try to sort out sex, sexuality and the erotic here, but see Marilyn Frye's witty and pertinent discussion in 'Lesbian "Sex" ', in *Willful Virgin: Essays in Feminism* (Freedom, California, The Crossing Press, 1992).
11. Moya Cannon, 'Hills', in *Oar* (Galway, Salmon Publishing, 1990).
12. There is no anthology of Irish Erotica (it sounds like an oxymoronic joke). This signifies more about 'our' image of Irish Literature (and of Ireland) than its realities. Soul and spirit are, of course, more high-minded (and Catholic).
13. There are just two references to sex in the index of J.J. Lee's *Ireland: 1912–1985*: to the Censorship of Publications Act and to Contraception/Abortion. The discussions of these in-text are ultra-brief. There is no discussion at all of the impact of feminism and the women's movement on changes in sexual practice or on the regulation of sexuality.
14. See Smyth (1995a) for a discussion of these 'disruptions'.
15. *In Dublin*, a fortnightly event guide, contains several pages of advertising for what are coyly called 'Personal Services', offering 'everything a man's heart desires' in 'leather and lace' from 'beautiful new young girls' to 'elegant ladies from 18 years upwards.'
16. Linda Anderson, 'Private Dancer' (n.d.), *Fortnight*, Supplement, No.292, p.5.

17. The only poem I have come across (i.e. in a contemporary publication) by an Irish woman poet from an earlier period (writing in English) that talks about sex at all does so in just such terms of negative fascination:

> Let them not listen to her fatal song
> Nor trust her pictures, nor believe her tongue.
> Contentment blooms not on her flowing ground,
> and round her splendid shrine no peace is found.
>
> (Mary Tighe (1172–1810) from 'Dissipation', in *Kelly, Pillars of the House: An Anthology of Verse by Irish Women from 1690 to the present* (Dublin, Wolfhound Press, 1987)

18. Alicia Ostriker, in *Stealing the Language: The Emergence of Women's Poetry in America* (London, The Women's Press, 1987) uses the phrase 'giddy glee' to describe women poets' ludic and irreverent desolemnisation of the body and sex.

19. Richard Hayes (*Poetry Ireland*, No. 36, Autumn 1992) notes that 'only one-fifth of the three hundred and thirty or so contributors [to *Poetry Ireland*] have been women in the journal's first 21 issues' (p.62). A survey carried out by *The Steeple* (Three Spires Press, Cork, June 1992, pp.56–57) found that women writers now account for five per cent of poets published by Daedalus Press, sixteen per cent by Gallery Press, eleven per cent by Raven Arts Press and forty-five per cent by Salmon Publishing (the only poetry press headed by a woman). See also Dennis J. Hannan and Nancy Means Wright, 'Irish Women Poets: Breaking the Silence' (1990), in *Canadian Journal of Women's Studies*, vol.16, no.2, pp.57–65; Patricia Boyle Haberstroh, 'Literary Politics: Mainstream and Margin' (1992), in *Canadian Journal of Irish Studies*, vol.18, no.1, pp.181–91; Mary O'Connor, 'The Thieves of Language in Gaol?' (1994), in *Krino*, No.15, pp.30–42.

20. See, for example, Ruth Hooley (ed.), *The Female Line: Northern Irish Women Writers* (Belfast, NIWRM, 1985); Nuala Archer (ed.), Special Issue: *Irish Women's Writing, Midland Review*, No. 3 (1986); A.A. Kelly (ed.), *Pillars of the House: An Anthology of Verse by Irish Women from 1690 to the Present* (Dublin, Wolfhound Press, 1987); Ailbhe Smythe (ed.), *Wildish Things: An Anthology of New Irish Women's Writing* (Dublin, Attic Press, 1989).

21. I don't think it is for men poets either. The silencing of men poets who write 'off the agenda' is also ferocious.

22. Nuala Archer, from 'Sheela ˜Na˜ Gigging Around', (1994), *Poetry Ireland Review*, No. 41.

23. Joan McBreen, 'The Glory-Hole', in *The Wind Beyond the Wall*.

24. Ruth Hooley, in *Fortnight*, 292, Supplement, n.d.

25. Eithne Strong, from *Flesh the Greatest Sin*, (Dublin, Attic Press, 1993).

26. Ibid.

27. Ibid.

28. Anne Le Marquand Hartigan, from *Now is a Moveable Feast* (Galway, Salmon Publishing, 1991). The only other sustained narrative poems I am aware of in contemporary Irish women's work are Anne Le Marquand Hartigan's *Corbieres* (which is more precisely a poetic drama than a narrative) and her *Now is a Moveable Feast* which, among other themes, explores the imaginative interplay of diverse voices, 'in the past, now and in a possible future'. No one voice prevails, not that of God nor of man, for their words cannot reach beyond the limits and edges of being:

> Words were shut in his head
> He was not trained in the art of touching,
> To fondle bodies or words;
> Was only easy with horses.

29. Moya Cannon, *Oar* (Galway, Salmon Publishing, 1990)

30. I don't know of any study of the theme of childhood in women's poetry – or even of adolescence. The indexes of major studies of women's poetry generally list 'childbirth', and 'children' in the context of 'motherhood'/'maternity', but nothing about growing up. Where did they all come from, these poets? Two recent Irish poetry collections with especially powerful evocations/explorations of childhood are Joan McBreen, *A Walled Garden in Moylough* (Galway, Salmon Press, 1991) and Catherine Phil McCarthy, *This Hour of the Tide* (Galway, Salmon Publishing, 1994). See also various poems in *Senecca Review* (1993). For Irish women writers' accounts of childhood, see John Quinn, *A Portrait of the Artist as a Young Girl* (London, Methuen, 1986).

31. Mairide Woods, from 'Covering the Traces – A Convent Education' (1986 *Midland Review*, No. 3).

32. Joan McBeen, 'The Neighbour's Daughter', in *The Wind Beyond the Wall*.

33. Catherine Phil McCarthy, 'Sweet Afton', in *This Hour of the Tide* (Galway, Salmon Publishing, 1994).

34. Ailbhe Smyth, 'Outings, Guilt Trips and Other Kinds of Excursions' (forthcoming)

35. See Emma Donoghue, *Passions Between Women: British Lesbian Culture, 1668–1801* (London, Scarlet Press, 1993). Despite the title, many Irish women are included.

36. Mary Dorcey, from 'Come quietly or the neighbours will hear', in *Moving into the Space Cleared by Our Mothers* (Galway, Salmon Publishing, 1991).

37. Mary Dorcey's poetry has never been reviewed, for example, in the influential, USA-published *Irish Literary Supplement*. I am not suggesting that this is deliberate, but the omission is revelatory of the prevailing values and priorities.

38. Cherry Smyth, from 'Coming Home', (1995), *Feminist Review*, No. 5

39. Eavan Boland, discussing the choice between 'separatism' and 'subversion', comments: 'I want to subvert the old forms. I think where those elements of the Irish experience are repressive, I would rather subvert them than throw the baby out with the bathwater', Dennis J. Hannan and Nancy Means Wright, 'Irish Women Poets: Breaking the Silence.' (1990), *Canadian Journal of Women's Studies*, vol.16, No.2, pp.57–65. Subversion, of course, may also lead in extrovert directions where baths no longer seem relevant at all.

40. This is Ostriker's phrase – not entirely positive. (Ostriker, *Stealing the Language*, 1987, p.126)

41. 'Poetic activist' is a term missing from our vocabulary. Its very absence is significant.

42. Ruth Hooley encountered the hostility of 'poetry' to 'politics' in concrete form: 'I recently selected a poem on incest for *H.U.* [*The Honest Ulsterman*]. It was challenged as having been chosen for its political content: I was told I wanted the poem because of its subject and that had coloured my judgement about it ... The other editor's block to the subject prevented him from seeing the poem objectively, as a careful, intelligent piece.' (Cited in Mary O'Connor, 'The Thieves of Language in Gaol?' (1994), *Krino*, No.15, p.36)

43. Paula Meehan, from 'The Statue of the Virgin of Granard Speaks', in *The Man Who Was Marked By Winter* (Oldcastle, Gallery Press, 1991).

44. Maighread Medbh, from 'Our Streets', in *The Making of a Pagan* (Belfast, Blackstaff Press, 1990).

45. Patricia Scanlan, *Three Dimensional Sin* (Cork, Ink Sculpters, 1988).

46. See Eavan Boland, *A Kind of Scar: The Woman Poet in a National Tradition.* (Dublin, Attic Press, LIP Pamphlet, 1989) at Gerardine Meaney *Sex and Nations: Women in Irish Culture and Politics* (Dublin, Attic Press, LIP Pamphlet, 1991).

47. Eavan Boland, from 'Solitary', in *In Her Own Image* (Dublin, Arlen House, 1980).

48. Rita Ann Higgins, from 'Space Invader', in *Philomena's Revenge* (Galway, Salmon Publishing, 1992).

49. Anne Le Marquand Hartigan, 'Eve - New Mouth', in *Immortal Sins* (Galway, Salmon Publishing, 1993).

50. 'If it will be difficult for the serious critic to determine exactly how seriously such playful poetry asks to be taken, there can be no question of the widespread tendency among women poets to promote a yeasty triumph of life over the exhaustion and annihilation that always threaten it.' (Ostriker, *Stealing the Language*, 1987, p.201) Since I have never experienced this difficulty, I infer – with relief – that I am not a serious critic. Can play (or pleasure) exist only in a relation of opposition to 'seriousness'? Like poetry and politics? For a discussion of the 'iconic feminine', see Lia Mills', ' "I won't go back to it": Irish Women Poets and the Iconic Feminine' (1995), *Feminist Review*, no.50, pp.69–88.

51. Paula Meehan, 'Secret', in *The Man Who Was Marked By Winter*.

52. Mary Dorcey, 'Because she carried flowers', in *Moving into the Space*.

53. Mary O'Malley, 'Gluttony', in *A Consideration of Silk* (Galway, Salmon Publishing, 1990).

54. Rita Ann Higgins, 'It's Platonic', in *Philomena's Revenge*.

55. Eavan Boland, from 'In His Own Image', in *In Her Own Image*.

56. Eavan Boland, from 'Exhibitionist', ibid.

57. Eavan Boland, from 'False Spring', ibid.

58. Eavan Boland, from 'Making Up', ibid.

59. Nuala Archer, from 'Weird Little Wordless Words', *The Hour of Pan/ama* (Galway, Salmon Publishing, 1992).

60. Rita Ann Higgins, from 'Light of the Moon', in *Philomena's Revenge*.

FURTHER READING

Anderson, Linda, 'Private Dancer' (n.d.), *Fortnight*, Supplement, No. 292, p.5.

Archer, Nuala, (ed.) Special Issue: *Irish Women's Writing* (1986), *Midland Review*, No. 3.

Archer, Nuala, *The Hour of Pan/ama* (Galway, Salmon Publishing, 1992).

Archer, Nuala, 'Sheela ˆNaˆ Gigging Around' (1994) *Poetry Ireland Review*, No. 41.

Boland, Eavan, *In Her Own Image* (Dublin, Arlen House, 1980).

Boland, Eavan, *A Kind of Scar: The Woman Poet in a National Tradition* (Dublin, Attic Press, LIP Pamphlet, 1989).

Cannon, Moya, *Oar* (Galway, Salmon Publishing, 1990).

Donoghue, Emma, *Passions Between Women: British Lesbian Culture 1668–1801* (London, Scarlet Press, 1993).

Dorcey, Mary, *Moving Into the Space Cleared by Our Mothers* (Galway, Salmon Publishing, 1991, re-issued 1994).

Frye, Marilyn, '*Lesbian "Sex"* ', in *Willful Virgin: Essays in Feminism* (Freedom, California, The Crossing Press, 1992).

Haberstroh, Patricia Boyle, 'Literary Politics: Mainstream and Margin' (1992), *Canadian Journal of Irish Studies*, Vol. 18, No. 1, pp.181–191.

Hannan Dennis J. and Means Wright, Nancy, 'Irish Women Poets: Breaking the Silence' (1991), *Canadian Journal of Women's Studies*, Vol. 16, No. 2, pp.57–65.

Hartigan, Anne Le Marquand, *Now Is a Moveable Feast* (Galway, Salmon Publishing, 1991).

Hartigan, Anne Le Marquand, *Immortal Sins* (Galway, Salmon Publishing, 1993).

Higgins, Rita Ann, *Philomena's Revenge* (Galway, Salmon Publishing, 1992).

Hooley, Ruth (ed.), *The Female Line: Northern Irish Women Writers* (Belfast, NIWRM, 1985).

Hooley, Ruth, 'Cut the Cake' (1988), in Swift, T. and Mooney, M. (eds), *Map-Makers' Colours: New Poets of Northern Ireland* (Montreal, Nu-Age Editions).

Kelly, A.A. (ed.), *Pillars of the House: An Anthology of Verse by Irish Women from 1690 to the Present* (Dublin, Wolfhound Press, 1987).

Longley, Edna, 'In Conversation with Carol Rumens' (1994), *Krino*, No. 15, pp.1–12.

McBreen, Joan, *The Wind Beyond the Wall* (Brownsville, Oregon, Storyline Press, 1991).

McBreen, Joan, *A Walled Garden in Moylough* (Galway, Salmon Press, 1995).

McCarthy, Catherine Phil, *This Hour of the Tide* (Galway, Salmon Publishing, 1994).

McCurry, Jacqueline, ' "Our Lady Dispossessed": Female Ulster Poets and Sexual Politics' (1991), *Colby Quarterly*, Vol. XXVII, No.1, pp.4–8.

Meaney, Gerardine, *Sex and Nation: Women in Irish Culture and Politics* (Dublin, Attic Press, LIP Pamphlet, 1991).

Medbh, Maighread, *The Making of A Pagan* (Belfast, The Blackstaff Press, 1990).

Meehan, Paula, *The Man Who Was Marked by Winter* (Oldcastle, Gallery Press, 1991).

Mills, Lia, ' "I won't go back to it": Irish Women Poets and the Iconic Feminine' (1995), *Feminist Review*, No. 50, pp.69–88.

Ní Dhomhnaill, Nuala, *Selected Poems*, trans. Michael Hartnett (Dublin, Raven Arts Press, 1986).

O'Connor, Mary, 'The Thieves of Language in Gaol?' (1994), *Krino*, No.15, pp.30–42.

O'Malley, Mary, *A Consideration of Silk* (Galway, Salmon Publishing, 1990).

Ostriker, Alicia, *Stealing the Language: The Emergence of Women's Poetry in America* (London, The Women's Press, 1987).

Poetry Ireland Review (1994), Special Issue: '*Sexuality*' (ed. Pat Boran), No.41.

Quinn, John (ed.) *A Portrait of the Artist as a Young Girl* (London, Methuen, 1986).

Scanlan, Patricia, *Three Dimensional Sin* (Cork, Ink Sculptors, 1988).

Senecca Review (1993), *Special Issue: 'New Voices in Irish Women's Poetry'*, Vol. 23 Nos. 1,2.

Smyth, Ailbhe (ed.), *Wildish Things: An Anthology of New Irish Women's Writing* (Dublin, Attic Press, 1989).

Smyth, Ailbhe (ed.) 'States of Change: Reflections on Ireland in Several Uncertain Parts' (1995a), *Feminist Review*, No. 50, pp.24–43.

Smyth, Ailbhe (ed.) *Writing Women* (1995b), Vol.11, No.3. Special Issue: *Irish Women's Writing*.

Smyth, Ailbhe, 'Outings, Guilt Trips and Other Kinds of Excursions' (forthcoming),

Smyth, Cherry, 'Coming Home' (1995), *Feminist Review*, No. 50.

Somerville-Arjat, Gillian and Wilson, Rebecca (eds) *Sleeping With Monsters: Conversations with Scottish and Irish Women Poets* (Dublin, Wolfhound Press, 1990; Edinburg Polygon, 1990).

Strong, Eithne, *Flesh The Greatest Sin* (Runna Press, 1980, Dublin, Attic Press, 1993).

Wills, Clair, *Improprieties: Politics and Sexuality in Northern Irish Poetry* (Oxford, Clarendon Press, 1993).

Woods, Mairide, 'Covering the Traces – A Convent Education' (1986), in *Midland Review*, No.3.

Yorke, Liz, *Impertinent Voices: Subversive Strategies in Contemporary Women's Poetry* (London, Routledge, 1991).

5

'From Room To Homesick Room':
Women and Poetry In Northern Ireland

Declan Long

Perhaps the most widely-held view about women's poetry in Northern Ireland is that it is virtually non-existent, with the solitary exception of Medbh McGuckian proving slightly too complicated a taste for the average palate. Often this opinion is difficult to contradict simply because few can name a single Ulster woman, apart from McGuckian, who has published a collection of poems with a so-called 'major' publisher in the past twenty-five years. In addition the very subject seems almost taboo: for all Ireland's political, cultural and critical controversies (even in relation to feminism) there is an apparent lack of Northern women's voices within this poetic Babel which is at the very least curious, if not downright eerie.

Yet, curiouser and curiouser, there is a substantial number of women-only writers' workshops attempting to 'make things happen' in the province. Ruth Hooley, co-editor of the poetry journal *The Honest Ulsterman* and herself an accomplished poet (though without a published book) has, for instance, commented that in her own all-woman writing group 'all the women have published, the age range is from 25–60, but none has a book yet! Eight or so women all writing poetry of quality . . . Something seems to stop them going for it.'[1] This example may well be remarkably typical despite the familiar phenomenon of the area's poetic prominence in relation to international literary developments. Should worldwide fascination with Northern Ireland's poetry Renaissance of the 1960s not have helped to discover and nurture female talents equal to or beyond those of Seamus Heaney, Paul Muldoon, Michael Longley and Derek Mahon? Can Medbh McGuckian alone have attempted to make poetry bear the weight of woman's experience throughout the past decades of conflict?

The purpose of this chapter is to examine some of the pressures which create that 'something' which Ruth Hooley perceives to be so artistically dominant and creatively restricting. In addition I will try to ask some questions about some of the poetry by women in Northern Ireland which has managed to reach publication. This chapter, though, is neither a comprehensive survey nor an 'argument'; rather, I am testing the water, tentatively exploring some aspects of an issue which has wide-ranging significance and merits more discussion within the world of Irish Studies. My title for all this, 'From Room to Homesick Room', is a line from Medbh McGuckian's poem 'On Ballycastle Beach'. It is used here as an image of displacement which has vital relevance to the way in which McGuckian's writing is itself 'Out of Place' in that it works to subvert what Thomas Docherty has called 'the "place logic" which is central to the formulation of a national culture, tradition or lineage.'[2] McGuckian's poetry will not be looked at here, since much skilled writing (such as that by Clair Wills[3]) on the subject is already available; but this chapter takes its starting point from the way in which McGuckian's work shows us no secure home or surety of place in a way that might be broadly analogous to the wider search for a woman's place in the world of Northern Irish poetry.

With regard to this notion of place, though, it is important to suggest at the outset some reasons why this chapter seeks to make its focus poetic and cultural paradigms which might be specific to contemporary *Northern* Ireland. Firstly, the purpose is not in any way an attempt to legitimise *or* condemn the present political divide within the island of Ireland. That the north-eastern corner of this small piece of land off Western Europe currently forms a state under the control of the British government is, of course, relevant but as the Dublin-born, Belfast-based literary and cultural critic Edna Longley has suggested, 'one need not endorse existing borders to feel that regional distinctiveness might be underlined here and there'.[4] And, as should be patently obvious, Northern Ireland has had a desperate and devastatingly unique 'distinctiveness'. The great danger (so frequently ignored in accounts of Irish writing which span North and South) is the affirmation of a politics of homogenous Irish national identity, the extreme consequences of such an ideological direction being terribly evident within contemporary Ireland's culture of 'rival propagandas'.[5] The novelist Colm Toíbín relates this difficulty to the representatives of an unreconstructed Nationalism who, he claims, 'have always had real difficulty with the twenty-six counties' of the Republic.

> The twenty-six counties are in Limbo, they believe, waiting for the day when our island will be united and the British will leave. This leaves out any idea that Southern Ireland has been forming its own habits and going its own way.[6]

More obviously, Northern Ireland has formed habits and habitats which are utterly distinctive. Toíbín's target here is the projects of the Derry-based *Field-Day Theatre Company* and specifically its controversial anthology of Irish Writing; of which, more later. At this point a central reason for the regional emphasis becomes clear: that of the changing relationship between the social and political circumstances of women in the North and those of their Southern counterparts. While the political interests of the island have tended in general towards the addressing of questions of national allegiance and aspiration, the politics of the South have in recent years moved (slightly) in the direction of what has been termed the 'Liberal Agenda' of divorce, gay rights, contraception and abortion reform; this shift in public policy campaigning arising partly as a consequence of (and co-incident with) the election of Mary Robinson as President and culminating in the 1995 divorce referendum. Such issues of immediate relevance to the struggles for female autonomy and the broadening of legal definitions of sexuality may paradoxically have their few Northern public equivalents in the 'Save Ulster From Sodomy' campaign from some years back and furores such as that over the opening of a Brook Advisory Clinic in Belfast. Nevertheless the pressures of the Catholic Church remain powerful in the South as the controversy surrounding the 'X' case might suggest.[7] The point here is that while on both sides of the border women could be seen to be held back by religious, legal and political restraints there are certain differences in emphases.

Yet it should not be forgotten that Northern Irish women cannot be viewed as living within a sociocultural setting which is fully equivalent to that in Britain either. Direct rule from Westminster (as opposed to the failed Northern Ireland government) may have enabled the Catholic/Nationalist community to be partly freed from religious discrimination, but changes in British social policy have regularly been resisted in Northern Ireland when they have involved issues of gender or sexuality, so maintaining a further set of discriminations which are particular to the area. Northern Ireland in the past has been excluded from legislative changes in Britain relating to battered women and rape; it has been the only region of the United Kingdom without a single state day nursery and, extraordinarily, the illegality of abortion is perhaps the fullest source of cross-community agreement in the Province. Nevertheless these legal and ethical peculiarities have their antagonists in the North's considerably active range of women's groups which, while emerging later than those in the rest of the UK and the Republic of Ireland, have played an indispensable role in political campaigning and consciousness raising. That I say there is a 'range' of women's groups is, though, an indication of a further element of regional specificity. For the euphemistically labelled 'Troubles' have not only strengthened the resolve of the most reactionary moral forces on both sides but have also created a barrier between women in Ulster who feel (perhaps rightly) that feminism cannot be disassociated from debates surrounding questions of nationality and cultural identity. 'Unity' of women has been halted by the sectarian problematic to such an extent that many women's groups have vowed publicly to avoid consideration of the 'Troubles' in order to construct a short-term campaign of social pragmatism.[8] Feminism in Northern Ireland, it seems, has been fissured at its base by national conflict, and the consequent apparent sacrifice of diversity and difference for the cause of constructing 'sisterhood' can be shown to have direct relevance to poetry written by women since the dawn of these present 'Troubles'. Following on from these suggestions of regional idiosyncrasy the next step is to direct attention towards the literary contexts within which Northern Irish women are placed – what Ulster writing, for instance, is viewed as being somehow valuable? If poetry can be seen as having 'representative' potential for a given historical moment or epoch, what 'history' of Northern Ireland is underwriting the various anthologising and publishing projects which have gained prominence within both the British and Irish literary 'communities'? Among the many putatively 'important' and supposedly non-gendered anthologies which might be relevant I want to mention three: Frank Ormsby's *A Rage For Order: Poetry of the Northern Ireland Troubles*, the Bloodaxe collection *The New Poetry* and (perhaps predictably) the astonishingly ambitious *Field Day Anthology of Irish Writing*. From these I wish then to move on to a consideration of how certain all-women anthologies have been fascinatingly disruptive of nationalist metanarratives while simultaneously raising difficult questions with regard to the relationship between women and poetry.

Frank Ormsby's *A Rage For Order* is at first glance an impressive and intriguing volume; its cover image of a skeleton riding a white horse among gantries and tower blocks (a direct reference to Loyalist iconography of King William of Orange) suggesting the state of decay in the Northern body politic. The painter of this image, Rita Duffy, is renowned for her uncompromising satirical eye for the Ulster grotesque, her work frequently focusing on the roles and representations of women within the 'Troubles'. However this anthology of 'Troubles' poetry is certainly not a book to be judged by its cover artist. For despite the claims of the volume's cover blurb that the poetry: 'faces up to the passionate intensities of the North, making this collection compulsory reading for anyone with a serious interest in modern Ireland'[9] it is difficult not to feel that a particular set of 'intensities' has been ignored. The lack of local female voices in *A Rage For Order* is at once astounding and wholly predictable, the diversity of women's experiences of the violence and its economic, social and domestic ramifications being almost entirely written out of the literary history of the province. There are nevertheless women poets in the book – most of whom are particularly well-known: Fleur Adcock for instance, or Eavan Boland, Rita Ann Higgins and Carol Rumens. Of course, none of these writers is a native of Northern Ireland and only Carol Rumens is a resident. This, though, is not the main source of my complaint. As the blurb states, the collection does seek (validly) to include the voices of poets who have 'responded to the violence from . . . more distant perspectives'. What seems to be problematic about Frank Ormsby's editorial policy, though, is the virtually blinkered approach to politics and poetical 'speech' — the anthology becomes an old-fashioned debate on the relationship between 'men of action' and 'men of words', with complex, ambiguous poetry such as that of Paul Muldoon being included on the basis of (albeit oblique) attempts to 'refer' to the violence and not because of the more adventurous formal interrogations which (as Muldoon's work implies) are imperative within the context of the conflict. So while Ormsby can propose in his desire to define a 'Troubles' poem that 'it is arguable that any poem by a Northern Irish poet since 1968, on whatever subject, could be termed a Troubles poem', he refrains from pursuing this notion by claiming that 'the unconscious element can only be a matter for speculation' (*ARFO*, p.xviii). It is through the implementation of this definition of 'Troubles' poetry and his anthologising policy, in fact, that Ormsby excuses himself from including any of the work of Medbh McGuckian, the major female poet to have emerged from Northern Ireland since the 1960s. McGuckian's poetry is remarkably complex, baffling even, but the hermeneutic difficulties presented to the reader by the work reveal a 'critical' political strategy which, rather than ignoring the poet's devastated social surroundings, challenges our understanding of them at the deepest level.

A further obvious reason for the lack of native women writers in the anthology is, naturally, that the editor has followed some form of aesthetic criteria; though what this may be is far from clear as there are included several poems written by young teenagers — highly developed, acclaimed or supposedly 'mature' writing cannot then be what is constantly required. Neither, it must be assumed, must previous publication have been a condition of entrance. Is the problem simply that women, published or not, do not directly address problems involving political violence? Even indirectness is not seen to be a crime among the male poets, so do women reject association with the 'Troubles' entirely when writing poetry (as some have done when forming women's groups)? This, of course, is a possibility; but, if it is the case, what exactly do women write about and why are so very few publishers interested?

In attempting (perhaps only partially) to answer these questions I should try to set Northern Ireland within a wider Britain/Ireland publishing context. Asking what publishers are interested in may well invite the facetious reply, 'Sales'; but in this instance it is worth noting the attitude of the editors of the oft-challenged anthology from Bloodaxe, *The New Poetry*. The compilers here (Michael Hulse, David Kennedy and David Morley) have sought to collect work from Britain and Ireland which is, in their words, 'at last responding to the imperatives of the times'[10]. They claim that this 'new poetry highlights the beginning of the

end of British poetry's tribal divisions and isolation, and a new cohesiveness –
its constituent parts "talk" to one another readily, eloquently and freely while
preserving their unique identities' (*TNP*, p.16). These are grand claims indeed.
But once again no-one seems to have wanted to talk 'readily, eloquently and freely'
with Northern Irish women. Of course, this silence is not necessarily the fault of
these editors as it is likely that they came across little published work in this area.
An acknowledgement of this situation may not have gone amiss, though, if the
editors are to claim in their introduction that 'the new Irish Poets ... included
here have been chosen because they confront the dilemmas of modern Ireland'
(*TNP*, p.25), while finding room for only one poet from Northern Ireland.

This problem of perspective which leads to an editorial blind-spot with regard
to women in Ulster does nevertheless have many (the majority even?) of its roots
across the Irish sea from Britain. The case of Frank Ormsby's collection has been
illustrated but that of the more theoretically ambitious *Field Day Anthology* has
proved to be even more illuminating. Published in 1991 by Faber and Faber
under the editorial control of the poet and critic Seamus Deane, *The Field Day
Anthology of Irish Writing* claimed to be the most comprehensive anthology of
Irish writing ever; its three volumes (totalling over four thousand pages) spanning
fifteen-hundred years of literary and political activity. Unlike Ormsby's *A Rage for
Order*, The Field Day project explicitly legislates against inclusion of writers on
aesthetic grounds, seeking to challenge conventional distinctions in Ireland between
art and politics: as Seamus Deane says in his introduction: 'The aesthetic ideology
which claims autonomy for a work of art is a political force which pretends not to
be so.'[11] By now this line is a theoretical commonplace but a nonetheless useful one.
The consequent cultural intervention which these volumes purport to make surely
should involve a challenge to the artificial (and silently political) processes of literary
value-judgement which have led to masculinist discriminations. After all, even the
loaded term 'literature' is consigned to the theoretical scrapheap in favour of the less
ideologically freighted 'writing'. Yet, typically, the anthology's putatively pluralistic
agenda, as Siobhan Kilfeather has said, involves 'the construction of a politics that
is almost completely dominated by issues of National government and sectarian
difference'.[12] Rightly, Kilfeather observes that there is 'no acknowledgement of
the debates over women's rights, sexuality and reproduction in which Mary
Robinson, for example, established her reputation'. Directly in relation to the
North, this means that once again despite the desire for 'comprehensiveness',
the 'voices' of women (both in poetry and politics) have been excluded, shouted
down perhaps by male appeals to opposing 'motherlands'. In one way the problem
might involve the point made by Edna Longley that 'Women's issues embarrass
Northern Nationalists because they highlight the controversy about Church and
State in the Republic',[13] but more simply the difficulties for women writers in

the North in gaining key positions within the anthologising race are based on the fact that ceaselessly (as Kilfeather says of *Field Day*) 'the Nationalist/Imperialist and Protestant/Catholic dichotomies are established at the expense of other neglected constituencies and forms of discrimination within Ireland'. *The Field Day Anthology*, like so many other Irish and British publishing enterprises, has missed opportunities for valuable re-evaluation of gender borders as well as geographical ones. Ironically the often angry debate it provoked has helped to amplify the noise of feminist debate: and, however tokenistic or tacked-on it might seem, the 'afterthought' fourth volume of women's writing is to be eagerly anticipated.

Other anthologies, though, have attempted to redress the gender imbalance within Irish studies and I wish to consider a sample of these. Bearing in mind what has been said about the above male-edited anthologies, Ruth Hooley's *The Female Line* is intriguingly different. Published in 1985 to celebrate ten years of the Northern Ireland Women's Rights Movement (and tellingly published *by* the Northern Ireland Women's Rights Movement) the collection claims to be unusual 'in two ways: it includes both published and unpublished female authors side by side, writing in a range of forms and styles' (*TFL*, p.2). Mixing prose, drama and verse Hooley states that her editorial aim derives from the need to 'highlight what is being written and to encourage more women toward publication', adding that 'as editor I have tried to select what is representative and of genuine interest' (*TFL*, p.2). Unlike the more general anthologist, then, the issues which are perceived to be of 'genuine interest' here are directly woman-centred; so that while Hooley notes how the troubles are 'never far from the door' she finds the 'predominant themes ... relate to family and personal life' (*TFL*, p.2). This 'personal' element, though, does not necessarily imply privacy, themes such as rape and physical abuse having a particular public resonance. In relation to the poetry in the volume this odd inversion of the received public/private binary tends to link with notions of lyrical and (political) 'self'-discovery, a majority of the poems concentrating on the quest for a fully developed 'identity'. Hooley, in fact, structures the book in terms of such personal and cultural growth, arranging the works in what she calls 'an informal sequence which moves through childhood, adolescence, growing awarenesses, personal relationships at various stages, marriage, motherhood, disillusionment, independence and old age'. (*TFL*, p.2).

'Growth' in various forms pervades the anthology, many of the poems using images of the land and rural cultivation as their metaphorical centres. Francine Cunningham, for instance, in 'Mandrake' makes clear this link between sexuality, growth and a form of 'rootedness':

Your wit was my cutting

You planted me
inside that hot house,
stalking in contingency,
not caring to sow
alone.

Rootless
I withered ...

Soiled,
I've twisted, but grown
hybrid.

(*TFL*, p.46)

The poem ends with a 'fear of being uprooted' and this relationship between woman and the land echoes throughout this anthology in the way that many of the speakers are concerned with either freeing themselves from a relationship or cultural 'root' or discovering identifications with others. Often such imperatives in the identity quest involve negotiations with a father figure – Maura Johnston (in the poem 'Father Figure'), for instance, 'can face him now, unafraid' (*TFL*, p.33) – but more importantly perhaps, links with mothers (and grandmothers) become crucial for many of these poets. Yet two poems in particular suggest the often tricky consequences of such identity forging. Ruth Hooley's 'My Mother's House' laments the death of the speaker's mother in terms of the changes in domestic atmosphere – rooms in the house becoming 'stagnant without/you to open doors and windows to the light' (*TFL*, p.169). The problem which the poem presents is that of losing the 'bright/attentive ways' (*TFL*, p.169) of the mother through the natural process of ageing, though this notion broadens to become a contemplation on what Hooley calls 'finding a way to house the past' (*TFL*, p.169). The result of this 'housing' is that the poet learns to 'see better': 'when you visit me/it will always be summer in a shady room' (*TFL*, p.169). What seems to be on offer here is the possibility of an eternal positive link, a constantly remembered summer, between women throughout history. But is this really a way of 'seeing better'? Does Ruth Hooley's poem and this notion of 'a female line' seek to *avoid* history? Mary Twomey's poem 'Sunday Visit' suggests a different version of 'the female line'. Again readers are offered two images of a woman – youth and age – yet a direct continuity between separate moments in history does not seem to be suggested. The opposite, in fact, may well be the case:

> There she sits
> Unchanged
> In the same
> Precise museum arrangement
> Of meal chest and butter churn . . .

(TFL, p.174)

Is it the domestic context which holds the woman down or is it the very concept of an essential female identity? Is there a real danger in substituting a patriarchally constructed female archetype for a different but equally monolithic idea of femaleness? Certainly Mary Twomey's poem does seem to raise such issues, moving itself in the direction of an idea of women living within history:

> I think
> Of the proud girl
> I've heard about
> Long brushed hair
> Thick velvet dresses
> Riding high in a pony trap
> When all around her
> Went on foot.

(TFL, p.174)

This poem's lively historical approach – considering time and context and reflecting on change rather than continuity – emphasises that women (to paraphrase Mary Twomey) are 'alive today'.

The troubles of essentialism, of course, are not particular to Northern Irish women's writing: what is crucial though is a recognition of the recurrent essentialism of the 'Troubles'. The particular problems in the province are often thought to derive from an identity politics which is ultimately beyond the realm of history – both sides constructing Irishness and Britishness as unambiguous and somehow 'pure' opposites. It is likely therefore that the poetry by women in Northern Ireland is at its best when avoiding or subverting this discursive framework; a female line may not need to be a straight one – discussion of difference and diversity may be advantageous politically and artistically. Eve Patten has suggested in an essay on women and fiction in Ireland that genuine diversity is often disguised in all-women anthologies because of the attempts to look for unity of experience. Of Ailbhe Smyth's anthology *Wildish Things*[14] (which admittedly is more relevant to discussions of southern Irish writing) Patten observes that while the book does seek to represent what Smyth calls 'women's lives diversely lived' the subject matter of the majority of the poems seems to imply that 'women have diversely lived more or less exactly the same experience'.[15] Perhaps the northern women in particular might learn from such challenges to homogenising critical or editorial drives. It is unlikely that Ailbhe Smyth's anthology (intentionally or not) suggests something as straightforward as an eternal female identity but as Eve Patten asks: 'is there any real gain in exchanging a masculinist made myth for the "struggling women" – stoical, angry, victimised – of a new iconography?'

A crucial element in this discussion, particularly in relation to the predominantly 'personal' subjects of *The Female Line*, is the tendency towards writing in an autobiographical or confessional mode; but again Patten's comments on fiction can be related to Ulster poetry – 'the historical attachment of female writers to confessional or autobiographical realism is a tradition but not a necessity'. The lyric form is 'traditionally' a vehicle for self-expression but the experiments of a poet such as Medbh McGuckian suggest a usefulness in challenging the expressive approach. *Form*, as we well know, is political.

With the problems faced by women in Ireland, North and South, the possibility is that the subject matter is too urgent to be presented in an overtly coded way. My comments on identity politics may push too far towards ditching a construct such as the fully formed individual self when women have been working for so long to create their own version. Can the expressive rewards of being an 'author' be discarded when as Eavan Boland has said, 'Irish women have finally moved from being the subjects and objects of Irish poems to being the Authors of them'?[16] Is the ability to discard or play around with the idea of 'self' a perk of being in a position of male cultural authority?

Ruth Hooley has answered some of the above questions in one way by suggesting that there is a strong element in Northern Irish women's poetry which is purely 'therapeutic' (it is notable how in the biographical notes to *The Female Line* one contributor states that she began writing to 'come to terms with things'); maintaining the division between poetry for so-called therapy and poetry as high-art is, according to Hooley, 'the last bastion of male authority'. This idea seems slightly excessive (if it is true, feminism has a lot less to overthrow than might previously have been thought), but it does convincingly hint at how poetry in Northern Ireland might not be handicapped by a lack of publication but, instead, differently abled.

NOTES

1. Ruth Hooley, introduction to *The Female Line* (Belfast, Northern Ireland Women's Rights Movement, 1985).
2. Thomas Docherty, 'Initiations, Tempers, Seductions: Postmodern McGuckian', in Neil Corcoran (ed.), *The Chosen Ground: Essays on the Contemporary Poetry of Northern Ireland* (Bridgend, Seren Books, 1992), p.192.
3. See Clair Wills, *Improprieties: Politics and Sexuality in Northern Irish Poetry* (Oxford, Oxford University Press, 1993).
4. Edna Longley.
5. Edna Longley uses this phrase as a more sceptical alternative to the common concept of 'competing discourses'. See her *Poetry in the Wars* (Newcastle-upon-Tyne, Bloodaxe Books, 1986).
6. Colm Tóibín, review of the *Field Day Anthology of Irish Writing*, Sunday Independent, Dublin, 24 November, 1991, p.8.
7. A circuitous legal wrangle took place in March 1992 over a minor's right to travel to England for an abortion after being raped. The convoluted case had immense political implications in the Republic of Ireland when the Supreme Court overturned the Attorney General's ruling. Fallout from the 'Child X' case contributed to the eventual collapse of Albert Reynolds' coalition government (*ILRM*, 1992, p.401).
8. Here I am referring to the 1990 Committee For the Liberation of Irish Women which, in order to avoid a potential split, announced a unanimous resolution not to discuss the Northern question.
9. Frank Ormsby (ed.), *A Rage For Order: Poetry of the Northern Ireland Troubles* (Belfast, Blackstaff Press, 1992).
10. Michael Hulse, David Kennedy and David Morley (eds), *The New Poetry* (Newcastle-upon-Tyne, Bloodaxe Books, 1993), p.28.
11. Seamus Deane (General Ed.), introduction to *The Field Day Anthology of Irish Writing* (London, Faber and Faber, 1991).
12. Siobhan Kilfeather, 'The Whole Bustle,' review of *The Field Day Anthology of Irish Writing*, London Review of Books, 9 January 1992, pp.20–2. Further Kilfeather references are to this review.
13. Edna Longley, 'Belfast Diary', *London Review of Books*, 9 January 1992, p.21.
14. Ailbhe Smyth, *Wildish Things: An Anthology of New Irish Women's Writing* (Dublin, Attic Press, 1989).
15. Eve Patten, 'Women and Fiction', *Krino* 8/9, 1990, pp.1–7; also published in *Krino 1986–96 Anthology of Modern Irish Writing*, ed. Gerald Dawe & Jonathan Williams (Dublin, Gill & Macmillan, 1996), pp.8–17.
16. Eavan Boland, *A Kind of Scar – The Woman Poet in a National Tradition* (Dublin, Attic Press, 1989), p.6.

FURTHER READING

As the point of the chapter has been that this topic is rarely discussed, there is little published material available. The texts listed below do, nevertheless, provide an insight into some of the related debates and give a sense of the wider picture of how women fit into the male-dominated world of Irish Studies.

Boland, Eavan, *A Kind Of Scar: The Woman Poet in A National Tradition* (Dublin, Attic Press, 1989).
Corcoran, Neil (eds), *The Chosen Ground: Essays on the Contemporary Poetry of Northern Ireland* (Bridgend, Seven Books, 1992).
Hooley, Ruth, *The Female Line: Northern Irish Women Writers* (Belfast, Northern Ireland Women's Rights Movement, 1985).
Kelly, A.A., *Pillars of The House: An Anthology of Verse By Irish Women 1690 to the Present* (Dublin: Wolfhound Press, 1987).
Longley, Edna, *The Living Stream: Literature and Revisionism in Ireland* (Newcastle-upon-Tyne, Bloodaxe Books, 1994).
Wills, Clair, *Improprieties: Politics and Sexuality in Northern Irish Poetry* (Oxford, Oxford University Press, 1993).

6

Writing Near the Fault Line: Scottish Women Poets and the Topography of Tongues

Helen Kidd

If I choose the word topos, the site, then you will know that this is mutable and movable; that it is more than geography because it is less rigid, and chooses to be less than geography because it refuses to be universal. It may be urban or rural, water or land or even air, and certainly space. The site is split – not into two – but into many. There is the Highland Fault Line that traverses Scotland diagonally. South of it lie the two principal cities, Edinburgh and Glasgow, the (once upon a time) Industrial Belt, the Border counties, Lallans speakers. North of it lie the mountains and the lochs, the main whisky distilleries, kilts, bagpipes, the islands, the Gaidhealtachd (Gaelic speaking areas). So that's clear isn't it?

No. Too simple. Remember that the Great Glen splits off the Great Caithness Bog – the wild landscape of Assynt – and the remote fertility of the Black Isle from the northern cities of Inverness and Aberdeen, the ski slopes of the Cairngorms and the major tourist areas. So that's clear isn't it?

Not yet. The Pentland Firth splits the islands of Orkney and Shetland from the mainland. Then there is the Minch, the sea that connects the Hebridean Islands, hundreds of them – most of the islands of the British Isles in fact – and the language of Gaeldom connects what the waters sunder, connects a people whose tongue differs from the Doric vernacular of the east coast.

There is the Free Kirk, the Scottish Episcopal Church, the Catholics. There are incomers: Italians, Poles, Asian and Black Scots, Gay and Lesbian Scots,[1] fishers and farmers, out-of-work miners, royalists and nationalists and devolutionists; there are rather too many absentee landowners, a few tories, and, of course, men and women. Is this still clear?

The tongues lick at the fault lines . . . differences, cultural diversity. Scotland has the blues (some kinds of political blues make the blues worse). The blues is an oral tradition. The blues give shape to desire. Desire is subversive. The blues arise from loss, dispossession, displacement; urban blues where communities have been shifted to peripheries, to the high-rises, to 'clean up' and gentrify the city centres; industrial blues where industries have been dismantled and wealth and jobs drained off to the south (England).

All around the world every New Year people sing 'Auld Lang Syne'. We know Burns wrote that. Few people know that Carolina Oliphant wrote 'Wi' a Hundred Pipers in A' and 'Will Ye No Come Back Again?',[2] or that Jean Elliot wrote 'The Flowers of the Forest'.[3] Scottish songs have been reivin' (raiding) across the border for centuries, colonising the hearts and minds of the colonisers. But where ballads and songs have been collected they have frequently been recolonised, bowdlerised and claimed by the male antiquarians who have collected them.[4] Paradoxically the act of transcribing the oral tradition has often resulted in a form of silencing.

But silencing the oral resonances of poetry is well-nigh impossible. Into the gap between writing and speech comes the gesture, the indication of speaking differences, the topographies of language that defy dominant colonising utterance. Scottish literature produces what the dominant English hegemony perceives as monsters. Magnificent monsters, not the tame tourist beasties like the one that eludes visitors to the shores of Loch Ness and appears only in tartan grockle-trap replicas, but the monsters of desire that threaten to reclaim the so-called 'cleared' landscapes of ben and glen, and to stalk the haunted wynds and closes of Edinburgh, Glasgow and St Andrews, among others.

These are not the tame ghosts and fairies that inhabit the devalued currency of popular culture in England, but the fully fledged *unheimlich* presences/absences which fly from the pages of Scottish literature that has been assimilated into the English canon: Jekyll and Hyde, Burke and Hare, the ghost of the Sad Queen, headless pipers, Glencoe wraiths, selkies and seers, martyrs and murderers; not to mention deals and parleys with the Deil. The tighter the attempt at southern control, the larger the ghostly army grows. The more barbarian and superstitious the Scottish imagination is labelled, the stronger its influence is felt; and no matter how insistently only the Scottish Gothic is stressed, the more the diversity of the International Festival and the importance of the Scottish Enlightenment must also be acknowledged. Cultural giants then, these monsters, rather than cultural barbarians.

The waters that fill the divides between regional and cultural differences north of the Border produce the play of possibilities, unsettle the 'clarities' of the colonising language and its cultural 'certainties'. What is perceived as quintessentially Scots is continuously dissolving into unsettling differences. Even the landscape cannot be totally controlled and refuses the image of a country as a woman, to be tamed, domesticated, entered, used. So there are fault lines; there are also granite stacks, erect old men, constantly whittled by the sea at their base, and there is also the negotiable, and less challenging droop of Kintyre. Caledonia may sound like a woman's name, but it has remained stubbornly '*it*', despite MacDiarmid's Gaelic muse.[5]

Yes, there is a Scottish Mac/hismo, as the poet Liz Lochhead points out,[6] but it covers a subtext of topographical bisexuality and cultural codes at odds with those of English constructions of gender. Plumage and kilts are feared battle dress and indexes of Scottishness, and are recognised world-wide. Prince Charlie was a symbol of resistance who took to the hills disguised as a woman. Mary, Queen of Scots was a Catholic who frequently flouted sexual decorum, tall as a man and sharp enough to take on the arguments of John Knox. Big Mary of the Songs, the great political campaigner for land rights, was seventeen stone, and a verbal match for anyone.[7] J.M. Barrie was a tiny man who never actually reached physical maturity, and George MacDonald wrote children's stories that place a numinous grandmother with a spinning wheel at the heart of the universe.[8]

The crossovers are significant and manifold: the strength of the fishwives and the strength of their swearing, the linguistic gymnastics of Scottish women matched only by their strength and ferocity in battle. Small wonder that to English standards and standard English Scotland looks like a cradle of monsters! And is it not the case, as Spivak points out, that colonisers create either Ariels or Calibans out of their colonised subjects?[9] Small wonder, either, that the colonised exploit this confusion.

> A little bit of language goes funny. An ordinary phrase'll suddenly strike you in a new way. It'll turn itself inside out in some way ... It's always a phrase that sings out in your brain. You hear it with its own rhythm and that gives you the clue how to build the rest.[10]

Try as we might we cannot separate sound from the written word. Of course the shape on the paper bears no relation to the sound in flight, but we read with the inner ear, pause at commas and spaces, pick out echoes and musical patterns, just as musical notation is read. The gap between speech and writing is filled with the movement between the two, the air-waves that recreate the performative utterance. Sometimes the gap foregrounds itself, as Lochhead points out. All this is a contrast to what she calls 'English-male-posh-grown-up-dead speech ... which is regarded as being the norm, voiceless, neutral, but these things are not neutral.'[11]

When Hugh MacDiarmid began writing in Scots it was, as he termed it, a synthetic Scots, ransacking recognisable Scots regionalisms, to express the whole.[12] His pissed thistle epistle[13] may be an attempt to 'aye be whaur extremes meet',[14] but *A Drunk Man Looks at the Thistle* dislodges its own syncretising claim in the final three lines when the woman's voice enters and in response to the poet's 'Oh I hae silence left,' Jean says, ' "And weel ye micht," sae Jean'll say, "eftir sic a nicht." '[15] A woman's point of view and the re-entrance of the other is signalled, given the final say, the gesture beyond extremes to the relational, the modality of the verb 'micht', which emphasises movement and possibility, rather than the inertia of nationalist debates, prostrate with its own weight of loquacity, and inebriated with its own national spirit. Thus MacDiarmid unwittingly introduces the voice of interaction and responsiveness and, by implication the inevitable interrelation between utterance and silence. The drunk man has created an illusion out of his 'silken leddy'/Jean, and now she returns as the voice of the light of dawn rather than 'munelicht'. The cold light of day produces the physical reality, rather than the wet-dream, of Jean and word-drunkenness turns to the need for a new direction and treatment of the diversity and dailyness of Scottish experiences. MacDiarmid's project is to 'circumjack',[16] or fit itself, in a grand poetic sweep, to all that is Scottish. A heroic project, messianic even, in its magnitude, but we don't need heroes any longer. What we need is co-operation and recognition of the multi-faceted nature of culture north of the Border. Jean gets to business where the drunk man leaves off his ranting.

I mention MacDiarmid here because his work is undoubtedly important, especially in the current revival of interest in Scots as a viable medium for poetic expression, so vigorously espoused by Lochhead and Sheenagh Blackhall for example, or W.N. Herbert and Robert Crawford.[17] The importance of the Scottish Renaissance, and its effect on twentieth-century Scottish literature is unavoidable in any discussion of this kind. However the impulse to stand as a definitive literary figure amongst one's peers is, I am convinced, a very phallocentric one, and this can be inferred from the epic sweep of Alasdair Gray's *Lanark*,[18] the mythopoeic approach used by George Mackay Brown in both his prose and his poetry,[19] and the weighing of such verities as Love and Grace in the work of Iain Crichton Smith.[20] Even more ludic poets of the younger generation, such as W.N. Herbert,[21] display a tendency to elaborate architectonics which suggests a more monolithic attitude to their own work than might be found among women writers. Although I want to make it clear here that I also greatly appreciate and enjoy what these male writers add to the cultural scene, often despite these characteristics. It also needs to be noted here that Edwin Morgan alone defies these categories, and for this reason I accord him particular esteem amongst male writers, as a poet who pays heed to the needs of the poetry before the position of poet, and a true egalitarian who respects cultural interaction and dialogue.[22] However, it is more noticeable among women poets that the urge to express and encompass the whole is predominantly absent. The recognition that differences are not to be elided but celebrated is what distinguishes the range of women poets in Scotland, and hence a synthesis of Scottish tongues is not on the agenda as it is simply too universalising. It is the task of the Scottish Constitutional Convention to establish a common sense of purpose, but it is hardly the point of cultural expression to reach for universals, but rather to explore and expand creative and linguistic diversity. Scotland possesses more than one tongue, and it is precisely this polyphony that emphasises the scope of creative responses and strategies, and highlights the potential within language to 'go funny', to defamiliarise the familiar. Lallans, Doric Scots, Gaelic, standard English with regional syntax and idioms: these all cause critical moments in utterances. Fault-lines gape – the tidal waters of possibilities flow into them, create surface interferences, unsettle the fixed meanings of the official tongue. There is no single essential Scottish voice. Women poets recognise this, and there is an unabashed espousal of, and fidelity to, regional differences. As Sheena Blackhall puts it,

> Abydan, thrawn.
> Yon merks wir Nor East Scots
> A tongue baith braid and braw,
> Nae a Joseph's coat, for polyglots.[23]

In this poem 'Doric', the canny careful 'death' of Doric Scots before the formal English of the schoolmaster (the dominie) is revealed. He acts as another Edward the First, the Hammer of the Scots, hammering out differences into a bland English 'norm', and in so doing he is acting as a traitor to his own linguistic origins. But Doric is merely acting strategically, playing possum, 'abydan' and stubborn. The poem rebuffs the mealie-mouthed urbanities of southern tones, as it does any implication of a synthetic tongue. Thus we might infer a challenge both to MacDiarmid's 'Joseph's coat' of Macaronic Scots, and to Edwin Muir's controversial questioning of Scots dialects and their usefulness to literature in *Scott and Scotland*[24] (where he states that intellectual activity takes place in standard English, and feelings are expressed in Scots). So Blackhall's poem simultaneously grasps the nettle of fidelity to the regional specificity of language and the linguistic textures which any synthesising project would destroy. On one level then this is an out-and-out manifesto poem, whereas on the page the poem also presents us with the falsity of a simple binary divide between spoken and written language. It reveals both the strangeness of formal literary English, reserved for so-called academic pursuits (we might say the masculinist or colonialist pursuit of rational discourses), and the irrational insistence on the superior rationality of standard English. At least, she points out, Doric has 'smeddum', integrity and gumption, whereas English merely flaunts itself as a medium of militaristic control.

Blackhall recognises the bifurcated nature of the writing process for a Scot in an interview with Rebecca Wilson: 'The Scottishness makes for individuality . . . I sometimes swither because it decreases the size of your reading public . . . I think anybody writing in Scots should be able to write in English as well.'[25] But there are further gaps which exist between the prospect of acceptance and the mapping of literary territory. Doric, as the poem suggests, is a hardy tongue, 'stinch, roch wirds, quarried frae centuries', and whilst the language of authority and the establishment might seek to eradicate it, and replace it with a 'Suddron rose,/Kittle, an coy, an smert', Doric resists, as stubborn as a nettle. It is this that the poet celebrates, simultaneously decrying the bad faith of schooling's normalisation process by the use of associations such as Judas, Cain and Edward I, all murderers or traitors. The fierce oppositional loyalty of the poem is embodied in its dialect, and the rooting of Doric in the landscape and climate, the 'thin hairsts, the blatter o reivin sizzens'. Thus the topos of the poem is imaged as the site of the resistance of poetic language to the standardising reductivity of the language of the symbolic order.[26]

Liz Lochhead specifically states that being a woman adds another layer of difference to language usage: 'I don't write in standard English. I write in Scots English and sometimes actually in Scots. . . . I think it's about what colour your English is. . . . My language is female coloured as well as Scottish-coloured.'[27] Admittedly this is a problem, in that Scots English is recognisable by certain tropes, whereas women do not have a language that is specifically female, nor a specific set of dialects which are identifiable by women from other cultural contexts. What we do have, however, is a sense of the subversive qualities of language: ironies, digressions, musicalities, as well as a sense of the dangers of certain male discourses which place the female subject in a subordinate position.

The equation between colonial discourses and patriarchal ones is readily observable, and women are easily able to see such parallels. The attempted eradication of the Gaelic tongue by English schooling, media and culture, which continued on the tail of eighteenth- and nineteenth-century crimes of land clearances, has led to a profound sense of dispossession in the Highlands. The burning of crofts and pillaging of land rights by absentee English lairds has been paralleled by the marginalisation of Gaelic culture and language, until it has totally disappeared in many areas. Similar examples can be seen in other parts of the world: Native American children strapped across the tongue for speaking in their own languages, the recitation of poetry in Irish Gaelic made punishable by death by the Statutes of Kilkenny, to name but two. Under colonial domination a subject people must be controlled through law, economic constraints and through language. The coloniser must be able to understand what the people are up to, hence cultural freedoms can be seen as potentially subversive, as they establish a basis for resistance. Within different cultural systems women's roles have been perceived differently, and whilst not necessarily being liberating, nevertheless they have still posed a threat to the forms of patriarchy enacted by dominant systems. Hence, the importance of Gaelic-speaking women in relation to Highland culture. Women have been the custodians of the oral tradition, and the songs of women working together in the wool-waulking sheds, for example, were political, bawdy and challenging. They cut across 'polite' notions of what was proper for women to discuss, and they expressed views of men and authority which were frequently honest, irreverent and sexually explicit. It is therefore highly transgressive, and destabilises the view a dominant grouping would disseminate of itself, to speak from the position of the colonised, doubly so as a woman. Hence the attempt to belittle women's cultural productions as lesser, subjective, dealing in daily trivia rather than universals and 'eternal verities'. But looked at from a woman's perspective it is precisely those relational, interactive and heterogeneous processes that form societal and cultural texture, and provide the material for transformation into art. In most cultures women have performed interactive tasks such as nurturing and nursing, hence subjectivity for women is formulated as process rather than fixity, as mutability required from sustaining a sense of identity as part of community. This adaptability of identity necessitates a sense of contact and communication which is subtle enough to be aware of the primary material of social interaction, language itself, and the way language can either trap, challenge or celebrate cultural and gendered expectations.

The Gaelic poetic heritage is predominantly an oral one, and as the Skye poet Catriona Nic Gumeraid points out: 'in Gaelic society the better poets were the women. They wrote the wonderful work songs when they waulked the tweed. There wasn't much difference then between a song and a poem.'[28] She describes herself as a 'language loyalist' and says that in her imagination she is living in a Gaelic world all the time. Once again we find that she feels her language to be more appropriate to dealing with emotions. We could challenge this and argue that, like women generally, Gaels are placed on the side of the emotional versus the rational, and also that poetry is once more being placed in the romantic camp of spontaneous self-expression. But I would argue that the patterns of Gaelic poetry are in themselves complex, specific, densely textured music, and this adds yet another formal set of variations to the art. Developing specific oral properties may well enhance the shades of feeling-tone, even in translation, which cannot in itself be a bad thing. It is the linguistic energy of Gaelic poetry which creates emotional complexity, and the schism between feeling and language is bridged. In fact this is a false divide which relates to more referential aspects of literature, those which attempt to disguise subjectivity behind flat, untextured, lifeless language.

Disparagement of Highland Scots, originally emanating from England has, however, been perpetuated by southern Scottish snobbery and prejudice of the kind meted out to other social and racial groupings, such as the Anglo-Irish to the Irish Gaels, white to Black, straight to Gay and men to women. Accompanying the sneers levelled at the 'teuchters' is the noble savage kind of fetishisation, which sentimentalises and yet still manages to ignore the political and economic realities of the Highland situation. Dilys Rose, in her poem 'A Gael in Glen Street', exposes the enforced alienation of a highlander in an urban environment, ending the poem with:

> but he creeps along
> as if on his feet
> he wears ill-fitting slippers
> and over his shoulders
> a heavy coat of pibroch.[29]

The heavy coat suggests the weight of dispossession, and yet the final word reclothes him in a language and culture of his own. The lament of the pibroch, of bagpipe music for the fallen, is also a culturally specific way of dealing with loss, of creating shape and meaning out of hostile circumstances, and a reminder of a heritage which, although weighty, is also a means of survival, just as the blues are part of a legacy of resistance.

So far I have concentrated on white Scots, but it is time to remember that Scotland contains a wider cultural and racial diversity. A few years ago I was in a shop in Tarbert on South Harris. The shop was owned by an Asian family. Together they were speaking Punjabi. To the locals they slipped into Gaelic, and for the rest of us they spoke English. Even the young children managed the transition between the three. There are telling omissions in Catherine Kerrigan's *Anthology of Scottish Women Poets*,[30] excellent though it is. It would be interesting to have a cross-cultural section. As Maud Sulter, a Black poet and artist from Edinburgh, says: 'Black people have been in Scotland for over four hundred years ... It's another disheartening thing that in a country that claims such a radical rebellious nature ... there is such a hesitation to take on board other people's voices.'[31]

It is certainly not before time that a Black Scots writer like Jackie Kay has achieved recognition, and it is lamentable and discouraging that Scots Asians are even harder to find in print, although Poles, Italians and Canadians are very much part of the cultural landscape.[32] Sulter also denies the fact that poetry is a male preoccupation, saying:

> The power of oratory, the power of memory, the power of keeping lines of communication open, is very much a role that women fulfil and have every right to do so ... My reaction ... was to dismiss it as a white Western

bourgeois idea, that a poet must inherently be male, and that to be a poet one must adopt a male voice and stance and perspective on life.[33]

She goes on to say that poetic material can and should be found in everyday life and that 'you have to take on board the contradictions of your life and experience ... There are lots of communities you can operate in.'[34]

This comment paves the way for the dialogues and interactions which her poetry addresses. The poem 'Thirteen Stanzas' in *As a Black Woman*[35] makes connections between women, both white and Black, united by common experiences of gender and class, and written in Glaswegian Scots. It is a lament for Carrie who has died of cancer. Simultaneously it is a litany of her qualities, a working-class elegy. The internal breaks and the dots between phrases slow the movement of the poem, and also are mimetic of her persistent struggle with the economic stringencies of her life, the interruptions, changes of direction, layers of activity and the connections that women make. Hence the dots can be seen as full stops, or as pauses and connecting breaths. They also create a space which emphasises loss, the absence occasioned by death, untimely and institutionally caused by inadequate medical attention: 'medikill' as the poem darkly puns. As it develops the phrases become less staccato, longer and more lyrical, and this more traditionally elegiac manner reinforces the stress on memory as an important continuum, an affirmation of 'a way of life that is its own witness' (Eavan Boland's apt expression),[36] and what that means to the life and survival of a community. Carrie is transformed in the poetic moment into an image of resistance and inspiration:

> flowers . golden white tokens . bright . light the lights in your
>   hair . here in
>
> remembrance . of yir fair self . of a friendship between
>   women . white working
> class woman . black working class girl . a cross . the divide
>   of race . we were
> women in struggle . women in struggle . women in
>   struggle . united.[37]

These connections between women across the divides of race, cultures, class, language and geography are persistently celebrated by Sulter and Jackie Kay. Kay also explores the links between the women of a family across time in a series of interlocking narratives in her sequence *The Adoption Papers*.[38] She says that being Black and Scottish is treated as an anomaly, and explores the situation of a Black adopted child within a white working-class Glasgow environment. The strategy of the subject is to shuttle between her Highland/Lowland, Black/white, public/private, internal and external voices, all of which tend to strengthen the subject and her understanding of differences. She also writes as a Lesbian and a young Black woman making connections with the experiences of other women. She never reaches simple or simplistic conclusions, and the poems enact a variety of situations, dialogues and positions which question one another, revealing gaps and inconsistencies which create surreal imagery. Here internalised experience and external fact become a complex movement between self and other which deflects any crude exegesis of the poetry and its transformation of autobiographical material. A fine example of this subtle movement is 'Sound' from *Other Lovers*:

> Inside the fast world,
>   my hands talk to themselves at night.
>   In my head the water tank babbles
> incoherent language. There is
> the small cough of a house in the dark.
>   There is the feather weight of my cover.
>   Inside my head I am full of light.[39]

This poem is followed by 'Sign', which explores the difficulty of finding a language to fit one's topos, and yet one which is recognisable as meaningful to those that receive it. Ostensibly the poem is about a mute woman, but it uses this image to explore the difficulty of speaking and writing difference. It demonstrates the gaps between cultural codes, between languages – oral and literary, thought and the way dominant language silences the nuances of difference. It is not in the interests of those in control to acknowledge these nuances, and maybe the language of the symbolic order is not even able to recognise such subtleties.[40]

> All this
>
> *distance*
>
> between one language and another, one
> culture and another; one religion
> and another. The *little languages*
> squashed, stamped upon, cleared out
> to make way
> for the big one, better tongue.[41]

By placing the '*little languages*' and '*distance*' both in italics, the gaps in comprehension between dominance and the cultural heterogeneity it seeks to suppress are visually emphasised. The poem plays with loss and silencing through the visual equivalents of spaces, and stresses diversity through changing fonts as well as imagery. Thus it adds an extra dimension to the page, a concrete on-the-page level which works alongside the oral and the three-dimensional physicality of sign language (a language quite literally written on the body).

It is not surprising, given the nondescript nature of standard English in relation to the polyphony of Scottish tongues, that a bit of language goes funny from time to time and reveals its artificial nature, its arbitrariness. Also, given the historically important role of women within Scottish communities as balladeers and bearers of the cultural continuum, no wonder there is an acute awareness of the limitations of official, and traditionally male, discourses. The songs collected by the bowdlerisers of the nineteenth century have become internationally famous certainly – 'Ca' the Yowes' by Isabel Pagan[42] and 'Oh Where Tell Me Where' by Ann Grant,[43] for example – but not the women who wrote them. Women writers are still strenuously drawing on the ballad tradition and reimbuing it with the political and sexual energy that it earlier embraced. In this respect women are thinking back through their literary mothers. Liz Lochhead explores the ironies at the core of twentieth-century machismo, exposing the creative contrasts and contradictions of Scottish tongues. She provides a dialectic which explodes the simplistic universalising impulses of 'mainstream' Scottish male writers. It is not enough to see the world 'tapselteerie', as MacDiarmid does in *A Drunk Man*.[44] Lochhead herself certainly appropriates his 'antisyzgy' as a technique, that concatenation of confused and contradictory particulars, both linguistic and referential,[45] to expose the monsters of control, gentrification, consumerism and plastic tartan tourism, as well as to celebrate the united differences and the colourful caprices of bad faith amongst Scottish women.

Her poetry and her dramatic pieces suggest the impossibility of political correctness, given the persistence of those twin colonisations, maleness and Englishness. If any fault there be it does not exist so much within the women themselves, their dogged loyalty to domineering men or their middle-class social pretensions, but within the prolonged superimposition of a particularly southern form of patriarchy which began long before the troublesomely named Act of Union of 1703. The internalisation of this kind of process finds an apt metaphor in her poem 'Dreaming Frankenstein',[46] which maps Mary Shelley's inklings of her now famous monster. 'Getting him out again/would be agony fit to quarter her/unstitching everything', the penultimate section of the poem states, and its economy creates resonances by which we know that this is not merely her monster but also her husband, and also the internalisation of patriarchy itself. Lochhead's poetry presents us with a rebellious defiance which persists in tracing the patterns that gave birth to the monstrously stitched up Act of Union, a union which reproduces Scotland as a monster, just as heterosexual power relations, though movable, still insist on reproducing women as monsters.

The English construct of the Scottish urban male is one that Scots all too readily embrace, a Rab C. Nesbit of self-destructive and uncontrollable dimensions, which serves nicely to justify English claims to hegemony and social control. Lochhead's 'Bagpipe Muzak, Glasgow 1990' points this out:

> Malkie Machismo invented a gismo for making whisky oot
>   o' girders
> He tasted it, came back for mair, and soon he was on to his
>   thirders
> Rabbie Burns turned in his grave and dunted Hugh
>   MacDiarmid,
> Said: It's oor National Thorn, John Barleycorn, but I doot
>   we'll ever learn it . . .[47]

In its final stanza, however, the poem refocuses as a rallying call, a sobering up, and therefore presents a strong contrast to the drunken prostration of MacDiarmid in *A Drunk Man*.

Like Liz Lochhead, Alison Fell has a strong sense of visual precision, which is complimented by her richly textured treatment of language. In her poem 'August 6th, 1945' in *Kisses for Mayakovsky*,[48] we have a powerful critique and presentation of the destructive forces of patriarchy, and this is contrasted with the creative links between women. The visual reconstruction has elements reminiscent of medieval descriptions of Hell, where the apparently normal is oddly distorted: bees 'drizzle', flowers are 'hot and white', people are transformed into lizards and salamanders. The view from above of Hiroshima is described in terms which are akin to soft focus pornography: 'the eye/of his belly saw Marilyn's skirts/fly over her head forever'. By contrast the girl on the ground is stripped much more horribly, 'her whole stripped skin/at her heel, stuck like an old/shoe sole or a mermaid's tail'. Unlike the voyeuristic bomber, the girl is blinded. As with 'Dreaming Frankenstein', the poetic economy conveys more than a theoretical work on sexual politics could cram into an entire chapter.

Fell's celebrations of the courage and contrariness of women extend to her moving poem 'Bourj al Barajneh',[49] which deals with young girls running the corridor of death outside Palestinian camps to bring back food and, in contrast, her poem about her grandmother, 'Border Raids'.[50] The title is a play on the raiding, 'rieving', habits of her forebears in the district around Annan, and the garden borders where she sets her last reminiscences of her grandmother. But these raids, the poem suggests, might be across any borders, including those of social convention. The link is made with the lawless and irreverent ancestors through contemporary familial links, and the implication is that under the domestic associations conjured by 'granny' and 'garden' lie older disruptive, and more vital, roots, as rebellious as 'the old bunch'. The poet is in the gleeful position of using the compression of poetry to create less decorous links with

familiar subjects. The death of an elderly female relative is depicted as a bang
not a whimper; 'When she went,/she went like the old bunch, cursing/blue
as smoke,/you could almost smell the burning'. The grandmother is pictured
in adjectives such as 'fierce' and 'angry' coupled with energetic verbs such as
'electrifying' and 'glints'. She is an old pagan who is associated with ancient gods
and broomsticks, and whose transgressive presence derives from the supernatural
activities of the border ballads. These are the roots that fertilise the soil of the
more domestic present, roots which Fell invokes as a living and bawdy tradition
which overturns less vigorous elegiac pieties:

> If I could go back,
> stealing up the cemetery hill
> to borrow back her bones,
> I'd give her to the merry gods
> of the midsummer garden
> who dance among the columbines
> who fib and fart
> and I'd tell them to trumpet her out[51]

Scottish women have never been meek or silent, and contemporary women
writers are rieving back their territory, whilst at the same time raising the standard
of post-modernism and post-colonialism, recognising the gaps, the inconsistencies,
the varieties of being which render visible the connections between sexuality,
gender, race, class and nationality. Rather than these connections being fixed
for all time, women poets explore them to reveal the strategic complexities
of the processes for contemporary Scots, processes which are open, defiant
and charged with linguistic, and therefore poetic energy. These processes
inevitably stand in contrast to fixed expectations about literary forms and
expressions, and these expectations are formulated by patriarchal and southern
codes. The lineage of creative resistance has been recruited by these women
writers, and reclaimed as part of their own contribution to the landscapes
of Scottish history, culture and languages. Like Alison Fell's outrageous
granny, women writers have recouped their pasts in order to move on:
they have explored the lie of the land, as well as the lies of the land,
and sailed the linguistic variables of Scots. Unlike the male canon, the need
to outwrite or out-universalise one another is not manifest. This women's
writing is a collective process, a co-operative venture, delighting in the gaps
as well as the seams. The gaps are where, through play and negotiation,
changes might take place, just as ambiguity in poetry hinges upon the
line and rests upon the presence of space. And, to marry topos to history,
women writers in Scotland have borrowed back their foremothers' bones and

reclothed them in order to fib and fart and trumpet them out in a defiantly transgressive fanfare.

NOTES

1. For the purposes of this chapter I have chosen to capitalise Gay, Lesbian and Black, but use lower case for white in order to reverse its significance.

2. Carolina Oliphant, Lady Nairne, wrote under the pseudonym of 'Mrs Bogan of Bogan'. Born 1766, Gask, Perthshire. Died 1845. Hence her life spanned the period of the most intense persecution of the Highlanders by the English, following the Jacobite rebellion. This was a period when the English army, including many Scots from the Lowlands, carried out wholesale ethnic cleansing, and assisted in putting the crofters off their lands to be replaced by sheep. See *Life and Songs of the Baroness Nairne*, ed. Charles Rogers (London, C. Griffith, 1869).

3. Jean Elliot of Minto, 1724–1805. No other writings survive. See *An Anthology of Scottish Women Poets*, ed. Catherine Kerrigan (Edinburgh, Edinburgh University Press, 1991), p.163. Hereafter referred to as Kerrigan.

4. Burns, Scott, Stevenson, Hogg and Greig-Duncan all attribute most of their material to women, but as Catherine Kerrigan points out in the introduction to her anthology, 'the recounting of intimate experiences is often direct and frank, but it has to be borne in mind that a number of these works have been bowdlerised. Many ballads in performance were bawdy, but when they began to be written down and published they were modified in order to make them acceptable to bourgeois tastes.' She goes on to cite Greig-Duncan as a case in point. Kerrigan, pp.3–4.

5. MacDiarmid refers to Alba (the Gaelic for Scotland) as female in the poem 'Direadh 111', and the speaker of the poem celebrates 'her' as a lover. *Hugh MacDiarmid: Selected Poems*, Alan Riach and Michael Grieve (eds), (Harmondsworth, Penguin, 1992), pp.237–8 in particular. This edition will hereafter be referred to as MacDiarmid *S.P.*

6. 'At the moment I don't like this macho Scottish culture, but I also know that I want to stay here and negotiate it.' Quoted from an interview with Colin Nicholson in Dorothy McMillan's 'The Ungentle Art of Clyping', *Liz Lochhead's Voices*, Robert Crawford and Anne Varty (eds), (Edinburgh, Edinburgh University Press, 1993), p.32.

7. Mairi Nic a Phearsain or Mairi Mhor Nan Oran, Big Mary of the Songs, 1821–98. She used her songs to campaign for the crofters' rights, especially on her native Skye, most notable of which is *Brosnachadh nan Gaidheal* 'The Incitement to the Gaels'. The English spelling of her name is Mary MacPherson.

8. George MacDonald, *The Princess and the Goblin* (1872) and *The Princess and Curdie* (1883), in *George MacDonald: The Princess and the Goblin and The Princess and Curdie*, ed. R. McGillis (Oxford and New York, Oxford University Press, 1990).

9. Gyatri Chakravorty Spivak, 'Three Women's Texts and a Critique of Imperialism', in *The Feminist Reader*, Catherine Belsey and Jane Moore (eds), (Basingstoke, Macmillan, 1989), pp.177–8.

10. Liz Lochhead in S.J. Boyd, 'The Voice of Revelation: Liz Lochhead and Monsters', Crawford and Varty *Liz Lochhead's Voices*, p.39.

11. *Sleeping with Monsters: Conversations with Scottish and Irish Women Poets*, Gillean Somerville-Arjat and Rebecca Wilson (eds), (Edinburgh, Polygon, 1990), p.11.

12. For a comprehensive comment on this see *Edwin Morgan: Nothing Not Giving Messages*, ed. Hamish Whyte (Edinburgh, Polygon, 1990), pp.30–1.

13. *A Drunk Man Looks at the Thistle*, *MacDiarmid: S.P.*, pp.24–113. Hereafter, *DM*.

14. Ibid., p.30, ll. 149–50.

15. Ibid., p.113, ll. 2683–5.

16. The word 'circumjack' is most notably used in MacDiarmid's lengthy poem *To Circumjack Cencrastus or The Curly Snake*, in which the windings of the serpent about the roots of the world are equalled by the windings of the poetic work. For a complete version see *The Complete Poems of Hugh MacDiarmid: 1920–1976*, Michael Grieve and W.R. Aitken (eds), (London, Martin Brian and O'Keeffe, 1978), pp.181–291.

17. W.N. Herbert's own version of macaronic Scots is undoubtedly inspired by his work on MacDiarmid; see W.N. Herbert *To Circumjack Cencrastus: The Poetry and Prose of Hugh MacDiarmid* (Oxford, Oxford

University Press, 1992). Robert Crawford's third collection of poetry is *Talkies* (London, Chatto & Windus, 1992).

18. Alasdair Gray, *Lanark: A Life in Four Books* (London, Paladin, 1987).

19. George Mackay Brown, *Selected Poems 1954–83* (London, John Murray, 1991). See also *Beside the Ocean of Time* (Glasgow and London, HarperCollins, 1995).

20. Iain Crichton Smith, *Selected Poems* (Manchester, Carcanet, 1985), and *Listen to the Voice: Selected Stories* (Edinburgh, Canongate, 1993).

21. For the poetry of W.N. Herbert see *Forked Tongue* (Newcastle-upon-Tyne, Bloodaxe Books, 1992) and, with Robert Crawford, *Sharawaggi* (Edinburgh, Polygon, 1990).

22. Edwin Morgan, *Collected Poems* (Manchester, Carcanet, 1992).

23. Sheena Blackhall, 'Doric', *Fite Doo Black Crow* (Aberdeen, Keith Murray Publications, 1989), pp.46–7.

24. Edwin Muir, *Scott and Scotland* (Edinburgh, Polygon, 1982), p.9.

25. Somerville-Arjat and Wilson, *Sleeping With Monsters*, p.186.

26. For a full discussion of the power and subversive characteristics of poetic language see Julia Kristeva, *Revolution in Poetic Language*, trans. Margaret Waller (New York, Columbia University Press, 1984).

27. Somerville-Arjat and Wilson, *Sleeping With Monsters*, pp.10–11.

28. Ibid., p.40.

29. Dilys Rose, *Madam Doubtfire's Dilemma* (Blackford, Chapman, 1989), p.51.

30. Catherine Kerrigan, *An Anthology of Scottish Women Poets* (Edinburgh, Edinburgh University Press, 1991). See note 3.

31. Somerville-Arjat and Wilson, *Sleeping With Monsters*, p.29.

32. Catherine Czerkawska has written poetry, prose and radio plays. See *A Book of Men and Other Poems* (Nottingham, Akros, 1976). Valerie Gillies, a poet from Canada, has lived and worked in Scotland for many years. See *Each Bright Eye* (Edinburgh, Canongate, 1977). Richard Demarco is probably Scotland's best-known Italian in the world of the Arts: a gallery owner who has long had a marked influence on the Edinburgh International Festival.

33. Somerville-Arjat and Wilson, *Sleeping With Monsters*, p.29.

34. Ibid., p.30.

35. Maud Sulter, *As A Black Woman* (Hebden Bridge, Urban Fox Press, 1985), pp.13–15.

36. Eavan Boland, 'Domestic Interior', *Selected Poems* (Manchester, Carcanet, 1989), p.57.

37. Sulter, *As a Black Woman*, p.15.

38. Jackie Kay, *The Adoption Papers* (Newcastle-upon-Tyne, Bloodaxe Books, 1991).

39. Jackie Kay, *Other Lovers* (Newcastle-upon-Tyne, Bloodaxe Books, 1993), p.19.

40. See Kristeva, *Revolution in Poetic Language* for a full account of the symbolic order and how poetic language exists outside this, representing a return of the repressed, which the symbolic order cannot assimilate.

41. Kay, *Other Lovers*, pp.20–1.

42. Isabel Pagan (1741–1821), *A Collection of Songs and Poems* (London, The Theosophical Publishing Society, n.d.).

43. Anne Grant (1755–1838), *Poems on Various Subjects*, (London, Longman, Hurst, Rees and Orme, 1803), *The Highlanders and Other Poems* (London, Longman, Hurst, Rees and Orme, 1808), *Eighteen Hundred and Thirteen: a poem in two parts* (London, Longman, Hurst, Rees and Orme, 1814).

44. Hugh MacDiarmid, *DM*, p.89. l. 1927.

45. The poem 'The Caledonian Antisyzygy' best demonstrates the contradictory, contrastive and conflicting voices and styles that MacDiarmid employs, whilst commenting on the process at the same time. There is a continual dialectic in his approach to Scotland, both drawn and repelled at the same time. See Mac Diarmid *S.P.*, p.262.

46. Liz Lochhead, *Dreaming Frankenstein and Collected Poems* (Edinburgh, Polygon, 1984), pp.11–12.

47. Liz Lochhead, *Bagpipe Muzak* (Harmondsworth, Penguin, 1991), pp.24–6.

48. Alison Fell, *Kisses for Mayakovsky* (London, Virago, 1984), p.56.

49. Alison Fell, *The Crystal Owl* (London, Methuen, 1988), pp.27–8.

50. Fell, *Kisses*, pp.34–5.

51. Ibid., p.35.

FURTHER READING

Boland, Eavan, *Selected Poems* (Manchester, Carcanet, 1989).

The Complete Poems of Hugh MacDiarmid, 1920–1976, Michael Grieve and W.R. Aitken (eds), (London, Martin Brian and O'Keefe, 1978).

Crawford, Robert, *Devolving English Literature* (Oxford, Oxford University Press, 1992).

Crawford, Robert, *Talkies* (London, Chatto and Windus, 1992).

Crawford, Robert and Herbert W.N., *Sharawaggi* (Edinburgh, Polygon, 1990)

Crichton Smith, Iain, *Listen to the Voice: Selected Stories* (Edinburgh, Canongate, 1993).

Crichton Smith, Iain, *Selected Poems* (Manchester, Carcanet, 1985).

Czerkewska, Catherine, *A Book of Men and Other Poems* (Nottingham, Akros, 1976).

Fresh Oceans: An Anthology of Poetry by Scottish Women, Stramullion (eds) (Edinburgh, Stramullion, 1989).

Gillies, Valerie, *Each Bright Eye* (Edinburgh, Canongate, 1977).

Gillies, Valerie, *The Chanter's Tune* (Edinburgh, Canongate, 1990).

Grant, Anne, *Poems on Various Subjects* (London, Longman, Hurst, Rees and Orme, 1803).

Grant, Anne, *The Highlanders and Other Poems* (London, Longman, Hurst, Rees and Orme, 1808).

Grant, Anne, *Eighteen Hundred and Thirteen, a poem in two parts* (London, Longman, Hurst, Rees and Orme, 1814).

Gray, Alasdair, *Lanark: A Life in Four Books* (London, Paladin, 1987).

Herbert, W.N., *To Circumjack MacDiarmid* (Oxford, Oxford University Press, 1992).

Herbert, W.N., *The Testament of the Reverend Thomas Dick* (Todmorden, Arc, 1994).

Hugh MacDiarmid: Selected Poems, Alan Riach and Michael Grieve (eds), (Harmondsworth, Penguin, 1992).

The Life and Songs of the Baroness Nairne, ed. Charles Rogers (London, Griffith, 1869).

Lochhead, Liz, *True Confessions and New Clichés* (Edinburgh, Polygon, 1985).

MacDonald, George: *The Princess and the Goblin and The Princess and Curdie*, ed. R. McGillis (Oxford and New York, Oxford University Press, 1990).

Mackay Brown, George, *Beside the Ocean of Time* (London, HarperCollins, 1995).

Mackay Brown, George, *Selected Poems, 1954–1983* (London, John Murray, 1991).

Morgan, Edwin, *Collected Poems* (Manchester, Carcanet, 1992).

Pagan, Isabel, *A Collection of Songs and Poems* (London, The Theosophical Publishing Society, n.d.).

Sulter, Maud, *Zabat, Poetics of a Family Tree: Poems 1986–1989* (Hebden Bridge, Urban Fox, 1989).

Section Three: (Post) Colonial Contexts

This section explores poetry in colonial and post-colonial contexts. It probes the tensions between feminist and post-colonial perspectives, as revealed in the poetry and in terms of the way the poets themselves are represented in literary tradition.

Alison Donnell considers a little-known sonnet sequence by Una Marson. She notes that the apparent sentimentality and conventionality of the poems is embarrassing both to those who wish to celebrate Marson as a feminist foremother, and to those who seek a poetry of colonial resistance and the emergence of indigenous Caribbean literary forms. Challenging such avoidance, she argues that the sequence can be read as subversive both in terms of form and content. Willing enslavement – a familiar trope of the sonnet form – carries an obvious political import in the context of 1930s Jamaica, and contributes to a complex interrogation of the dynamics of heterosexual love. Furthermore, the sequence reworks conventions of female objectification in love poetry, by making the man into a silent Muse while its real interest lies in the exploration of female desire and creativity. Drawing on post-Structuralist theories, she argues that the sequence's 'cyclical, multi-climactic structure' deliberately undermines the sonnet form's normal progression to heterosexual union and the securing of patriarchal lineage.

Paraskevi Papaleonida offers a critique of some aspects of post-colonial theory via the poetry of Jackie Kay and Grace Nichols. She focuses on the idea of 'syncretism', held by many to be a hallmark of post-colonial writing. Papaleonida argues that in describing the meeting and fusion of different elements or identities, syncretism risks erasing their separate distinctiveness; this could, she suggests, seem to indicate 'a melting pot where distinct identities are in danger of being fused'. In its place she proposes a model of 'dialogic synthesis', wherein differences of vernacular and culture are held alongside one another, creating a mosaic of individual elements. It is this kind of plurality she finds in the poetry of Kay and Nichols. She further challenges the assumption that these differences are inevitably participating in a struggle between 'centre' and 'peripheries' by demonstrating how, in the poems, there is no such oppositional scenario. In the latter part of the chapter she applies Mikhail Bakhtin's theory of polyphony and dialogue to the poetry in order to show that, while the poems are multivocal, they are certainly not neglectful of the differential power relations that accompany different subject positions and voices. Her chapter illustrates the obliquely political impulse within all theorising, and demonstrates how the poems of Nichols and Kay enact a more complex representation of difference than post-colonial theory's version of syncretism is currently able to accommodate.

Paula Burnett explores recent experiments with the epic genre by Derek Walcott and Jean Binta Breeze. Commenting on the apparently unlikely suitability of epic for the subversion of patriarchal colonialist legacies, she shows how two contemporary Caribbean poets have employed its traditional scale and dignity to commemorate the trauma of black history. In Walcott's *Omeros* she notes the reversal of the traditional roles of active hero/passive heroine, and their replacement with a triad of powerful and independent-minded women. Turning to Breeze's more recent epic she points out its innovative quality in restoring the centrality of the oral and spiritual dimensions of epic poetry. In her 'womanist' epic, the speaking voice is 'female in a suprahuman way': its dispersed, depersonalised quality successfully deconstructs earlier associations of epic with individual heroism and nationalist discourse, gesturing towards a new ethical and political agenda no longer shaped around racial and national boundaries.

7

Sentimental Subversion: The Poetics and Politics of Devotion in the Work of Una Marson

Alison Donnell

Whatever is anachronistic is obscene ... The lover's sentiment is old-fashioned, but this antiquation cannot even be recuperated as a spectacle: love falls outside of interesting time; no historical, polemical meaning can be given to it; it is in this that it is obscene.[1]

In *A Lover's Discourse* Roland Barthes questions the 'unwarranted' and problematic status of love. His questioning is particularly pertinent to my reading of the love sonnets of Una Marson, a black woman poet writing in 1930s Jamaica. Marson's sonnets have perplexed and outraged critics who do not know what meaning can be given to them. They cannot be comfortably accommodated by the critical schools most readily evoked in a reading of women's poetry or poetry written during the colonial period, as they disturb the thresholds of feminist and post-colonial theories and bring to the fore the tensions as well as the overlaps between these two. By offering close readings of strategic moments in the ten-sonnet sequence from Marson's first volume *Tropic Reveries* (1930), I shall address the critical problems generated by these love poems.

Clearly, the gendering of literary taste and of what constitutes serious, 'great' poetry has played no little part in creating a climate of embarrassment around the reception of love poetry. As Louise Bernikow has observed,

It is interesting how the preoccupation with love, in life or literature, has been turned against women ... The heightened states of emotion out of which male poets were creating poetry were praised as revolutionary; the heightened states of female emotion were denigrated and dismissed as second-rate.[2]

Although the need to reconsider the preconceptions and value judgements concerning women's love poetry has been argued by several critics,[3] it is, nevertheless, possible that the conscious re-gendering of literary taste by certain schools of feminist criticism has also contributed to the denigration of works which write of love. In a desire to shift the reductive and persistent relation often drawn between women's writing and notions of femininity and feeling, some feminist critics have sought to highlight the political and the polemical aspects of their writing. While a reconsideration both of texts and of ways of reading which had been previously obscured has clearly been an important project, it is possible that the legacy of this critical realignment is an inability to respond to women's love poetry. As readers, feminists perhaps feel more confident and comfortable with Elizabeth Barrett Browning's *Aurora Leigh* than with her *Sonnets from the Portuguese*, with Grace Nichols' *The Fat Black Woman's Poems* than with Lorna Goodison's *Heartease*. Yet, if feminist critics stand anxious and unarmed in the face of love poetry and its potentially unsettling influence on our desired perceptions of each other and ourselves, post-colonial feminist critics are further troubled.

If these sonnets by Marson, with their concentration upon romantic love and conventional and stylised female personae, are not so appealing to a late-twentieth-century reader in terms of gender politics, then a consideration of the cultural context in which they were written may suggest why they have been further stigmatised. In the context of Jamaican colonial culture, in which acquiescence, mimicry and subordination were everyday imperatives, the presenta-tions of willing devotion and dependence which inform these poems are even more highly charged. It is perhaps not surprising that in their assumed demonstration of (emotional and literary) dependency, immaturity and excitability, Una Marson's love sonnets represent the neglected archive of an already marginalised poet. Her blues, her parodies, and her nation language poems represent the known archive of her work, and criticism to date has attempted either to suppress, dismiss or devalue the love poetry.[4] In contrast to these, the love poetry is commonly considered to be embarrassingly bourgeois and colonial (as well as a saccharine sub-genre of gendered verse) and has failed to offer either aesthetic or cultural statements helpful to post-colonial or feminist readers.

This double disavowal may not be surprising when we consider that, despite significant cultural tensions between the two, feminist and post-colonial approaches have often worked in parallel to highlight questions and moments of agency within regulating and disempowering systems which are both political and discursive. Consequently, subversion of and resistance to patriarchal and colonial ideologies and writings have been well-documented by feminists and post-colonial scholars, and there is often a consensus between the two schools on writers worthy of attention (Jean Rhys, Margaret Atwood and Alice Walker are obvious examples).

It is one of my aims in this chapter to extend this mode of scholarship to a study of Una Marson's sonnets and therefore to explore how devotional poetry, and in particular the poetic staging of extreme (elected) female servitude presents a rather difficult and disquieting textual field for a post-colonial feminist critic seeking to locate agency. However, I also wish to consider the problems of this approach which privileges resistance and to be aware of the danger inherent in an archive defined only by those texts which are suitably insubordinate and rebellious to fulfil counter-discursive agendas. It is perhaps important to be aware that the ways of reading offered by these 'new' disciplines (post-colonialism and feminism) also have their own exclusion zones, and it is equally important to address the more vexed question of what value can be given to texts which do, to a certain extent, collude with or work with the dominant ideological and discursive structures that are assumed to be oppressive. A reading of Marson's sonnets necessitates a consideration of both exclusion and collusion.

In this way, the aim of this chapter is not simply to justify these sonnets on the grounds that they are resistant, nor to offer a reading through which we can recuperate these texts by arguing that they are not after all really eurocentric or feminine. Rather, I wish to re-evaluate their resistance within the context of the choice of the sonnet form and the genre of love poetry, and to give critical attention to the possibilities for meaning engendered by the nexus of resistance and collusion which these devotional works present. In the light of both previous refusals to read and recent re-readings of (post-colonial) women's love poetry, I wish to engage in a detailed exploration of these poems tracing the subtleties and ambiguities which underlie Marson's, and many other women's, 'conventional love poems' in order to question this designation and the reasons why women's love poetry has been such a discredited genre.

It is my argument that by locating her poetry within what appears to be a 'natural' genre for a woman, Marson is able to exploit dominant expectations of love literature without endorsing them, and to carve out a space from which to explore the workings of love and the politics of romance. As Robin Dizard argues in her analysis of Christina Stead's stories,

> Sentimental love is a major Western cliché. Its icons and gestures are common property. Having the status of second nature, it is taken for granted, and as such not expected to tangle with serious pursuits like business, politics and the life of the mind. This intellectual prejudice, aided by sexual prudery, makes love an ideal subject for a woman writer. She can examine conventions, what everyone knows, as an insider.[5]

I hope to be able to show how, in the work of a female colonial subject, love poetry can function as cipher for cultural politics as well as gendered ones. Certainly,

Marson explores the sonnet sequence with both daring and decorum, following the plot of the romantic quest from the need and desire for love, into the complex web of expectation and fulfilment, and beyond the encounter with the lover – and therefore beyond the conventional consummation – into an aestheticised indulgence of love as an ideal. The first four sonnets of this sequence deal with emotions expressed towards the lover before he actually enters the romance situation. I wish to focus in some detail on the first two poems in order to explore how their adoption of a stylised language system highlights the processes and politics involved in reading a Jamaican woman's love poems.

In 'Renunciation', the opening sonnet, the poetic persona holds a wondrous mirror up to nature, only to dispel its beauty as utterly worthless in a universe where her love remains unreciprocated. The three quatrains of the sonnet personify the natural world, celebrating the vivacity and vitality with which it responds to her. The use of rhyming couplets and of unifying alliteration establish a sense of energy and harmony:

> For me the waves of ocean sigh
> Or dance with sunbeams darting by,
> For me the shades of twilight fall
> And beauty doth the earth enthral.[6]

The anaphora is used here to stress that this natural performance is personally directed, with nature animated – indeed transformed – by the force of her love. However, while the emotions which she projects onto the natural world return to her with equal power, the final couplet denies this ethic of mutuality as the relationship to nature is revealed as a conceit for her desired relationship to the lover:

> But not for me what most I crave, –
> To call thee mine, – to be thy slave.

The desire which the poem finally articulates is both solution and paradox, for the balance of mutual possession is tipped by the ultimate power divisions of slavery. In the scenario of renunciation and the reference to enslavement this first sonnet both draws on and draws our attention to significant cultural myths.

'In Vain', the second sonnet, begins from the final image of 'Renunciation' in order more powerfully to reiterate the absence of female fulfilment through the imperialism of romance.

> In vain I build me stately mansions fair,
> And set thee as my king upon the throne,
> And place a lowly stool beside thee there,
> Thus, as thy slave to come into my own.

> In vain I deck the halls with roses sweet
> And strew the paths with petals rich and rare,
> And list with throbbing heart sounds of thy feet,
> The welcome voice that tells me thou art near.
>
> In vain I watch the dawn break in the sky
> And hope that thou wilt come with coming day:
> Alas, Diana calmly sails on high,
> But thou, king of my heart, art far away.
>
> In vain one boon from life's great store I crave,
> No more the king comes to his waiting slave.[7]

The mirrored rhymes of the final couplets of 'In Vain' and 'Renunciation', which link the desire to be loved with the impulse towards self-sacrifice in the 'slave/crave' association, clearly call for further analysis in a reading focused on gender and cultural politics. The fact that slavery appears as a field of signification within a 'love' poem written by a black Jamaican woman is troubling and demands reference to several literary and cultural contexts.

The language and imagery of imperialism could evidently be traced to the Elizabethan sonneteers. Living in a time contemporary to the continuing 'discovery' of the 'New World' and the strict hierarchy of courtly love, for these poets the image of the slave was possibly an expedient and effective emblem of submission to 'love'. But nevertheless there is a crucial difference between images of willing slavery which are mainly to love in the abstract within the poetry of 'free' white men, and images of desired bondage which are to the lover in particular within the poetry of a black female colonial subject. The overlapping of romance and mastery, and of cultural and gendered subordination here creates a matrix of signs from which meaning is not easily resolved.

The cultural discensus which separates the literary context of a poetic code of Elizabethan romance and a social context of colonial Jamaica where slavery had been practised as a brutal and inhumane reality has an implicit effect on the availability of meanings within the poems. While the formal framework of the sonnet, the thematic significance of romance and the ideological workings of the slave trade all offer some kind of boundary to the meaning of these poems, the very plurality of these boundaries points to the plurality of texts and thus to the different possible meanings which the works offer. Although we may pursue these individually within the poems in order to stabilise their meaning, the competing and colliding frameworks cannot be disentangled without reducing the innate complexity of the text or compromising the range of intertextual and contextual connections. 'In Vain' is evidently an interesting text through which to address the power politics of eroticism and of heterosexual relationships within patriarchal colonial societies. However, to concentrate on the poem as a clear critique of the eroticisation of the female slave without mention of the engagement with high literary forms and language codes would be as misleading as to construct a reading of the devotional poem which does not discuss the startling imagery of slavery. It is precisely the co-existence of the highly conventional aesthetic rendition of the lover's plight and the highly politicized references to slavery within 'In Vain' which forces us to perceive the limits which certain ways of reading (post-colonial and feminist criticism included) may seek to exert upon meaning. The obscenity of love within these opening sonnets then is revealed not in the anachronistic European and patriarchal legacy but in the conflation of desire and dependency and of aesthetic and cultural politics. In Marson's poem, it is the relation between the text and context – the slave sonnet and the colonial (ex-slave) culture of 1930s Jamaica – which makes the 'slave image' such a disturbing, difficult and fascinating one. Both sonnets strikingly call the gender and cultural orientations of romance and of certain poetic genres into question, challenging the universal currency of love and poetic conceit.

However, although the utilisation of classical language and imagery (particularly of imperialism) is probably the most striking feature of 'In Vain', I wish to offer a reading of this sonnet which takes us beyond the intertextual and contextual complexity in order to argue that its textual workings actually disrupt its ostensible dependence upon a eurocentric and masculinist culture. The poem may ring many of the lexical bells of Elizabethan love poetry, of Biblical rhetoric (the powerless as the powerful) and of the discourse of slavery, but its meaning is not equivalent to any of these.

While 'In Vain' does offer the same classical framework of courtly love poetry to be found in Edmund Spenser's *Amoretti* and Sir Philip Sidney's *Astrophil and Stella*, in which the lover is apotheosised with the characteristic blurring of religious and amatory imagery, Marson writes in a gender inversion. In this sonnet, it is the man who is unattainable, on a monarchical throne rather than an aesthetic pedestal, and the woman who devotes herself to him, somewhat unsurprisingly 'in vain'. Although the female role in this poem could be read as mere convention, it is interesting to consider the significance of this re-gendering of the courtly love scenario in the light of Hélène Cixous' discussion of the ambivalent positioning of woman within this paradigm:

> Courtly love is two-faced: adored, deified, assimilated to the idol that accepts homage, she has the rank and honours of the Virgin. Conversely, and the same position, in her powerlessness, she is at the disposition of the other's desire, the object, the prostitute. Under these conditions, what is a woman's desire?[8]

In the act of inversion Marson may be seen to liberate the woman from the virgin/whore dichotomy so endemic to a patriarchally-ordered culture, and it is certainly interesting to consider to what extent she repositions the male lover in relation to this ambivalent status. Yet, what is also interesting is that even in the 'masculine' role of devoted suitor, the woman is still commonly read as the oppressed figure of the sonnets, a reading which is perhaps more suggestive of intransigent notions of gendered subjectivities than of the textual intimations at work in this sonnet.[9] Moreover, Cixous' suggestion that woman's desire is written out of this scenario is an interesting one to pursue, as it is by appropriating this paradigm from a woman's perspective that Marson is able to centre poems on the question of woman's desire.

The very fact that willing devotion and a desired enslavement allow the poetic persona 'to come into my own' in the first stanza of 'In Vain' fundamentally disturbs the assumption that sacrifice is about the effacement of subjectivity in the face of another, and also the attendant assumptions that this form of masochism is both gendered and cultural in its association with powerlessness. By reclaiming subjectivity at the moment of sacrifice and devotion, Marson's poem allows the 'slave' to be an agent and thus reveals how collusion can be an act of self-definition and of choice. The 'slave' in this sonnet therefore serves to question the preordained cultural significance of the slave as both the sign of possession of another's self within the context of a society built upon slavery, and as the surrender of the self within the context of European love sonnets. Marson's use of this image highlights the semantic instability and polysemy of 'slave' within a colonial, patriarchal language system, making the possible meanings of these love poems both more difficult to apprehend and perhaps more urgent to consider.

By staging a scene of extreme devotion by consent, this poem is able to open up a space in which the poetic subject can position herself within slavery – a system of oppression which is most clearly defined by its denial of personal agency. Reinscribing the surrender of self – which might be seen as the approved, perhaps 'natural', destiny of the feminine and colonial subject – as a moment of self-empowerment, this sonnet seeks to question rather than to affirm that the meaning of this submissive act resides in the dependency on the man/master.

We might wish to extend this principle to a consideration of Marson's poetics here and suggest that by consciously crafting a poem in which subordination as powerlessness is undermined, any relationship of 'In Vain' to the European sonnet tradition is similarly subverted. By drawing on the established signifying material of Elizabethan love sonnets, Marson creates a signifying system which by the very nature of its transposition operates on several levels, thereby challenging the seeming conformity and conventionality signalled by her 'imitation', and allowing collusion with this tradition to function as poetic choice rather than ideological oppression. In this way the achievement of self-definition through the act of giving the self disrupts both eurocentric (colonial) ideological security in its refusal of self-denial in the act of feminine and colonial devotion, and also eurocentric (colonial) discursive confidence in its appropriation rather than replication of a received poetic and cultural form.

From such an arresting image of desire, the sequence continues with 'I am Content' in which the level of emotional dependence becomes more pronounced as the female subject assumes a position of utter passivity and devotion:

> I am content to love you to the end,
> To have you fill my thoughts both night and day,
>
> . . .
>
> I am content to listen for your call,
> To hasten or delay at your behest[10]

Although the sense of disproportionate devotion and selfless love remains, the desire for self-sacrifice as a means to romantic fulfilment is replaced by an acceptance of love as unfulfilled. The emotional momentum of her love exists without reaction, creating a self-sufficient female romance plot in which the presence of the lover is dispensable. The sacrifice to the lover becomes more of a surrender to an ideal which embraces an acceptance of unrequited emotions, as 'love' achieves an abstract rather than a personalised quality.

Indeed, it is interesting to note the shift in tone and bearing in the fourth sonnet 'Love's Lament', as the 'subject' of these poems gradually emerges. The actual relationship to the lover emerges as a painful and trifling affair burdened by the insignificant details of real life: 'I cannot let you hold me in your arms/And listen while you talk of trivial things'.[11] The whole structure of the devotional poem is overturned at this point, with the pain previously associated with the lover's absence now caused by his presence which 'brings me bitter pain'. The tension between the poetic persona's longings for a 'true love' and her awareness of the lover's inadequacy places her in an emotional limbo incapable of either ending or preserving the relationship: 'I cannot bid you stay,/Though as you go you take my life away'. The context of a real romance marks a loss of innocence on her part: 'daily from my heart your image slips', signalling the 'fall' of her archetypal ideal and her slippage from the prescribed boundaries of the feminine lover which this precipitates. Moreover, this poem which articulates the inability to be fulfilled by the lover is the clearest disclosure of the way in which the focus of the romance, and thus of the poems, is the woman's own desire rather than the male lover. Such a focus would seem to suggest a way of re-reading the extreme altruism of the female subject within these sonnets. Perhaps this 'emotional impulse' needs to be reconsidered as a conscious device which serves to conform to the masculinist icon of womanhood only in order to find an acceptable mode through which female emotional autonomy can be achieved.

In 'Love's Farewell', a valediction, the rehearsal of the acceptable 'tears' may be read as a strategy in which femininity is masqueraded in order to achieve the unacceptable status of female control within romance:

> Tis best that we should say farewell for aye,
> And never meet again in fond embrace;
> Away I go, some thousand miles away,
> And I may nevermore behold your face.
>
> Oh love, I know you would not have me go,
> But be content, the Fates have willed it so.[12]

Significantly, the repetition of 'Tis best' and the turn of destiny manoeuvred by the Fates neutralises the situation, abnegating her of any responsibility for this parting. Moreover, while the poem ostensibly seeks to reassure the lover of her pain and therefore his significance, the distance which will intervene between them is not one which elicits the pain of absence or of solitude, but rather one which solicits the space for imaginings and the romance of poetry and of emotional life. Although the exercise of control and emotional authority is carefully disguised, I would argue that a gendered inversion of Cixous' model, with the male lover: 'at the disposition of the other's desire', is being suggested here.

The final poem in the sequence of ten, 'Absence', delivers us back to the opening frame, with desire for the lover being so great that it obscures any sense of her own existence. This poem paradoxically meditates on the abyss of each lonely day fulsomely and self-indulgently. Inverting a masculinist model of romance poetry, Marson overturns the *carpe diem* in order to convey the way in which time lengthens as it is stretched over the distance of separation and thoughts of the day that can never be seized: 'What shall I do to bribe the hours of day/And long, long hours of night to hasten on'.[13] Although the sonnet is a lament for the loss of the lover, it is the sense of lament rather than of the lover which pervades the poem, making the discourse of love rather than the lover himself the *raison d'être* of the work. The statement of dependence at the very end of poem appears to be conjured by her need for an absent, fictive lover who can sustain her emotional life: 'And never, night or day, will be at rest/Until once more I hold thee to my breast'. In this way, the sonnet sequence could be read as ending, not with union, reunion or consummation, but rather with a projection of love beyond the restrictive dimensions of corporeal being into the imagination where desire can remain 'free' (although not beyond an orthodox heterosexual model).

With this final portrait of 'Absence', it is interesting to return to Barthes who comments that:

> Historically, the discourse of absence is carried on by the Woman ... It is the Woman who gives shape to absence, elaborates its fiction, for she has time to do so; she weaves and she sings; the Spinning Songs express both immobility and absence.[14]

While this gendering of the absent song may appear to stress female stasis, it also establishes a relationship between absence and creativity, between a bodily stasis and imaginative motion. Released from the actual lover, the woman begins her search for a perfect love, once more suggesting an unusual gendering as the poem functions as an emotional and intellectual utopia for women.

While Marson's sonnet sequence does explore the conventional placing of woman within the romance sphere of devotion and dependence, the cycle as a whole inverts convention in order to establish and explore a woman's experience of love and thereby create an aesthetic icon of the male lover. From the indifferent and insubstantial figure of reality, swiftly and indifferently dismissed, the male lover is metamorphosed into a Muse, a 'model' man. Thus, the romantic quest becomes a poetic and intellectual adventure through which the female persona finds not her 'master lover' but the traces of her own desire and her poetic inspiration. In this sense, Marson's sonnet sequence illustrates Adrienne Rich's belief that: 'The most revealing and life-sustaining love poetry is not actually about the lover but about the poet's attempt to live with her experience of love, to fathom how she can order its chaos and ride out its storms'.[15]

I have already argued that this sequence operates within masculine expectations of female destiny without necessarily promoting these, and I would further suggest that it also works within expectations of a (sonnet) sequence without endorsing this structure in any conventional sense. I am interested in the ways in which Marson's ten sonnets disrupt the notion of sequence as logical progression, working against a teleology of heterosexual romance which in its fulfilment in marriage or union secures masculine fulfilment and lineage. Perhaps even more fundamentally than this, Marson's cyclical and multi-climactic structure, which defies any direct linearity, may represent a distinctly female engagement with the master narrative of love leading to social integration and hence a stabilisation of female sexuality and emotion. Most crucially then, this sequence which presents the voice of extreme female devotion, even martyrdom, within the framework of conventional poetic form, might be read as a strategic positioning of female subjectivity at a seemingly safe point from which to explore the possibilities for female desire and aesthetic re-invention.

In this sense, Marson seems to approach a strategy within this sequence which both addresses and begins to answer the 'urgent' question which Julia Kristeva believes women face:

> If the social contract, far from being that of equal men, is based on an essentially sacrificial relationship of separation and articulation of differences which in this way produces communicable meaning, what is our place in this order of sacrifice and/or of language? No longer wishing to be excluded or no longer content with the function which has always been demanded of us ... how can we reveal our place, first as it is bequeathed to us by tradition, and then as we want to transform it?[16]

As both Kristeva and Marson remind us, there is a relationship between the sacrifice to men and to language, a relationship (to patriarchy) which secures women's (subordinate) place in the symbolic order manifest in both social and discursive forms. I would argue that these sonnets powerfully reveal the politics of the place bequeathed to women within linguistic and social structures while simultaneously transforming this place by taking creative control. Both in subject and in form Marson's sonnets work within and yet against an aesthetic and ethic of 'feminine feeling' that was designed to be a clear statement of patriarchal interest and a eurocentric form and language which declares its colonial affinities.

Nevertheless, I do not wish only to demonstrate how these poems employ the conventions of love sonnets and of 'feminine feeling' as an expedient discursive camouflage from under which subversive and politicised meanings can be ventured. Indeed, to do so would be to run the risk of further endorsing resistance as the only interesting or worthwhile articulation of a woman or (post)colonial poet. As I have argued, the 'resistance' of this sequence is given subtle voicing through a re-gendering of accepted roles and the claims for agency. Read thus, this sequence bids for acknowledgement against a previously dismissive reception which read only submission and imitation. However, Marson's decision to write love poetry and to harness the emotional valency of these works also needs to be recognised as an attempt to reclaim love poetry as a form capable of expressing the complex configurations of desire and to return an epistemic value to 'feeling'.

In conclusion, I shall return to Barthes' proposition with which I began. It would seem to me that Marson does recuperate the spectacle of love through a text (in Barthes' sense of the word) in which historical and polemical meanings cannot be denied. Her engagement with romance and love poetry, and her insistence upon devotion, place demands upon the reassuring narratives and orthodoxies through which we seek to make meanings. Yet this same focus simultaneously instructs us of the value of poetry which is willing to be a spectacle and which reminds us of the need both to voice and valorise the complex and perplexing matrix of desire, culture and language from which our emotional lives takes form.

NOTES

1. Roland Barthes, *A Lover's Discourse* (New York, Hill and Wang, 1978), p.178.
2. Introduction to *The World Split Open: Women Poets 1552–1950*, edited and introduced by Louise Bernikow (London, The Women's Press, 1974), p.5.
3. For examples of works which re-evaluate women's love literature see Angela Leighton, *Victorian Women Poets: Writing Against the Heart* (Hemel Hempstead, Harvester Wheatsheaf, 1992) and Suzanne Clark, *Women Writers and the Revolution of the Word* (Bloomington, Indiana University Press, 1991).
4. See for example Lloyd Brown, *West Indian Poetry* (London, Heinemann Educational Books Ltd, 1984), p.34 and John Figueroa 'Review', *Caribbean Quarterly*, Vol. 32, Nos 1 and 2.
5. 'Love Stories', in *From Commonwealth to Post-Colonial* (Coventry, Dangaroo Press, 1992), p.399.
6. 'Renunciation', in *Tropic Reveries* (Kingston, Jamaica, Gleaner, 1930), p.20.
7. 'In Vain', ibid., p.27.
8. 'Sorties' in Hélène Cixous and Catherine Clément, *The Newly Born Woman*, trans. Betsy Wing (Manchester, Manchester University Press, 1986), pp.63–132, p.117.
9. See Erika Smilowitz, 'Weary of Life and All My Heart's Dull Pain': The Poetry of Una Marson', in *Critical Issues In West Indian Literature*, Erika Smilowitz and Roberta Knowles (eds) (Iowa, Caribbean Books, 1984), pp.19–32.
10. 'I Am Content', in *Tropic Reveries*, p.29.
11. 'Love's Lament', ibid., p.32.
12. 'Love's Farewell', ibid., p.33.
13. 'Absence', ibid., p.35.
14. Barthes, *A Lover's Discourse*, p.14.
15. Adrienne Rich, *On Lies, Secrets and Silences* (London, Virago, 1980), p.251.
16. 'Women's Time' in *The Kristeva Reader*, trans. Margaret Waller, ed. Toril Moi (Oxford, Blackwell, 1986), pp.187–213, 199.

FURTHER READING

Ashcroft, Bill, Griffiths, Gareth and Tiffin, Helen (eds), *The Empire Writes Back* (London, Routledge, 1989).

Barthes, Roland, *A Lover's Discourse* (New York, Hill and Wang, 1978).

Bernikow, Louise (ed), *The World Split Open: Women Poets 1552–1950* (London, The Women's Press, 1974).

Brown, Lloyd, *West Indian Poetry* (London, Heinemann Educational Books Ltd, 1984).

Cixous, Hélène, 'Sorties', in Hélène Cixous and Catherine Clément, *The Newly Born Woman*, trans. Betsy Wing (Manchester, Manchester University Press, 1986), pp.63–132.

Clark, Suzanne, *Women Writers and the Revolution of the Word* (Bloomington, Indiana University Press, 1991).

Dizard, Robin, 'Love Stories', in Anna Rutherford (ed), *From Commonwealth to Post-Colonial* (Coventry, Dangaroo Press, 1992), pp.399–406.

Duncan-Jones, Katherine (ed), *Sir Philip Sidney: Selected Poems* (Oxford, Oxford University Press, 1973).

Figueroa, John, 'Review', *Caribbean Quarterly*, Vol. 32, Nos 1 and 2 (1986).

Kristeva, Julia, 'Women's Time', in *The Kristeva Reader*, trans. Margaret Waller, ed. Toril Moi (Oxford, Blackwell, 1986), pp.187–213.

Leighton, Angela, *Victorian Women Poets: Writing Against the Heart* (Hemel Hempstead, Harvester Wheatsheaf, 1992).

Marson, Una, *Tropic Reveries* (Kingston, Jamaica, Gleaner, 1930).

Rich, Adrienne, *On Lies, Secrets and Silences* (London, Virago, 1980).

Slemon, Stephen and Tiffin, Helen (eds), *After Europe* (Coventry, Dangaroo Press, 1989).

Smilowitz, Erika, ' "Weary of Life and All My Heart's Dull Pain". The Poetry of Una Marson', in *Critical Issues In West Indian Literature*, Erika Smilowitz and Roberta Knowles (eds), (Iowa, Caribbean Books, 1984), pp.19–32.

Smith, J.C. and De Selincourt, E. (eds), *The Poetical Works of Edmund Spenser* (Oxford, Oxford University Press, 1912).

Williams, Patrick and Chrisman, Laura (eds), *Colonial Discourse and Post-Colonial Theory: A Reader* (London, Harvester Wheatsheaf, 1993).

8

'holding my beads in my hand':
Dialogue, Synthesis and Power in the
Poetry of Jackie Kay and Grace Nichols

Paraskevi Papaleonida

> Colours reds and yellows
> bites of pink and orange,
> the sun going down casting shadows
> as the old Indian sits curled up,
> playing a Scottish bag-pipe at
> the snake charmer's ball.[1]

In this poem we have a vivid dance of colours, shadows casting a bewitching atmosphere and an Indian to make magic by playing, of all things, a Scottish pipe. This image, like post-colonial women's poetry, is something to be represented in the plural, by 'colours reds and yellows'. When it comes to theorising post-colonial writing it is recognised that:

> today there is a multitude of Gods and Goddesses from cultures throughout the world, a vitalising exchange of philosophies and ethics, a flood of unfamiliar rhythms, images and visions in the poetry being written in many languages that take their roots from the same form of 'English'. The old tools of critical exegesis are hopelessly inadequate.[2]

Post-colonial critical theory, which has partly been formulated in an attempt to account for this multiplicity, has shown that the available analytical tools are not good enough for analysing post-colonial literature. If we add to this the 'double colonisation' women are subjected to, the need for 'adequate' critical exegesis becomes even more pressing. Testing out a central part of post-colonial theory, syncretism, and a particular kind of post-colonial poetry on each other reveals some interesting things about the formation of boundaries in literary theory. The post-colonial poetry I am dealing with is poetry by two contemporary 'post-colonial' black women poets. Grace Nichols was born and brought up in Guyana and moved to Britain as a young woman. Jackie Kay, an Afro-Scot of Nigerian descent, was adopted by a Scottish family and was brought up in Glasgow. Both poets live and work in Britain. My understanding is that in their poetry the voices (languages) of present and past, of colonised and coloniser, are dialogically synthesised; they interact and make up a new creation while retaining their distinct identity. At the same time, putting these voices side by side does not make them 'equal in difference' because certain voices are more powerful than others and are therefore capable of exerting control.

My discussion of post-colonial literary theory takes as its focal point *The Empire Writes Back: Theory and Practice in Post-colonial Literatures.*[3] *The Empire Writes Back* emphasises that 'the strength of postcolonial theory may well lie in its inherently comparative methodology and the hybridised and syncretic view of the modern world which this implies'.[4] Syncretism, which is the model I want to isolate and discuss, is not just a term but is identified as a whole new viewpoint and is approved by the authors of the book who treat it as a constitutive element of all post-colonial literature; indeed, they find, 'post-colonialism privileges syncretism'.[5] The way syncretism is used in the book can be summarised by the following definition: '[s]yncretism is the process by which previously distinct linguistic categories, and, by extension, cultural formations, merge into a new single form'.[6] There are two things worth noting here, two main characteristics of syncretism: first, that linguistic categories are thought of as 'previously distinct', and second, that they 'merge into a single new form'.

Syncretism, as defined by the *Oxford English Dictionary*, is aiming at a 'union or reconciliation of diverse or opposite tenets', beliefs, systems or practices. The word connotes a merging; it is a fusion of elements from diverse cultural sources that are combined as harmoniously as possible. In psychology, for instance, a syncretic state is characterised by fusion of concepts or sensations that are not discreet any more, and in theology the term stands for a seventeenth-century school which aimed at harmonising different Christian sects. What is important from my point of view is that the end result is a fusion, a chemical merging where diverse beliefs lose their distinction and specificity and any contradictions or oppositions are collapsed. To come back to the poetry under consideration, applying a syncretic reading to it would subtly suppress its heterogeneity, since 'syncretism' could potentially be perceived as connoting a melting pot where distinct identities are in danger of being fused. In its place I argue that the notion of 'synthesis' would be more useful in an analysis of this poetry in which, as we will see, it is clear that rather than a chemical merging we have a choric synthesis of voices. The difference between synthesis and syncretism might not seem striking but it is, as I see it, a basic one. In synthesis, like syncretism, combining and unifying are also emphasised. Again as the *OED* reports, synthesis in its wider, philosophical use denotes the putting together of parts or elements so as to make up a complete whole. Unification, as a goal, might be present in both conditions; there is, nevertheless, a difference in the status of the elements within the resulting 'product'. Synthesis is a 'putting together' rather than a chemical merging; it creates the idea of a mosaic, in which each 'bead' can keep its concrete and separate individual identity. A mosaic, according to the *OED*, is produced by the joining together, 'cementing together' of minute pieces of glass, stone, or other hard substances of different colours. It is these different colours that a 'synthesis' – as achieved in and exemplified in this poetry – will not sacrifice, whereas in a syncretic model relationships between different elements can only be represented as dichotomies, for instance centre-margin and present-past, which consequently 'merge into one single form'.[7]

Vicki Bertram writes that '[Nichols'] poetry transcends national, linguistic and cultural conventions to effect a rich and original synthesis'.[8] To qualify the nature of this 'transcendence' we can consider her treatment of the issue of language. In *i is a long memoried woman*[9] Nichols uses dialect ('dih' instead of 'the'), and incorporates different voices, like those of the Caribbean woman or the English migrant. The image of the bead, as something that is scattered and then gathered together, is common: in 'Sacred Flame' for instance, alluding to multi-cultural cross-influences among indigenous, African, Asian, and European peoples in the Caribbean. As Nichols points out, she likes 'to create or chisel out a new language': 'I like working in standard English and Creole', she says; 'I tend to want to fuse the two tongues'.[10] At first glance the process that results in a new language might seem like a syncretic fusion: the final conclusion that she draws, in 'Epilogue', the poem which comprises her position regarding the coloniser/colonised language debate, is that a new language can spring from 'the root of the old one'. She acknowledges that she has lost her tongue, but this does not stop this procedure of growth/rebirth from taking place. Yet, if we take a closer look, the emphasis put on 'one', which enjoys the status of a line all by itself, makes us wonder. Will she speak just one language or does she only want to give the old one its due attention?

> I have crossed an ocean
> I have lost my tongue
> from the root of the old
> one
> a new one has sprung[11]

What characterises this 'fusion of the two tongues' is creolisation, the creation of something new out of an adaptation process within a split racial context. Yet in Nichols' case it is not a syncretic creolisation. Rather, it operates as a manifold-visioned poetic discourse. For her, '[p]oetry, thankfully, is a radical synthesising force. The erotic isn't separated from the political or spiritual, and a lot gets said.'[12] We are implicitly reminded that the old, colonised tongue was violently torn from its root. And the new tongue did not just take its place, it was chiselled out, it 'has sprung'; it is, after all, a tongue (as in 'mother-tongue') and not a language, the coloniser's language.[13] Furthermore, Nichols creatively moves on: '[d]ifference, diversity and unpredictability make me tick,' she writes.[14] Her poetry is aware of both the painful circumstances of its creation as well as the endless possibilities it can create for itself. In the following poem, 'In My Name', a black woman is giving birth to the child of the overseer in the plantation:

> Heavy with child
> . . .
> I squat over
> dry plantain leaves
>
> and command the earth
> to receive you
>
> in my name
> in my blood
> . . .
> my tainted
> perfect child
>
>> my bastard fruit
>> my seedling
>> my sea grape
>> my strange mulatto
>> my little bloodling
>
> . . .
> Let the evil one [snake] strangle on his own tongue
> even as he sets his eyes upon you
>
> For . . . with my tears
> I've pooled the river Niger
>
> now my sweet one it is for you to swim[15]

The poem talks of giving birth and makes giving birth a metaphor about itself: I think we can fruitfully read it as a parable for the new post-colonial mulatto women's poetry, a comment on the multidimensional character of this poetry. The woman is not drowning this 'strange mulatto', that carries in its own being its white father. Rather, the baby will 'swim'. Likewise, on a different level, the 'painfulness' of such a creation of post-colonial women's poetry could well lie in its attempt to escape the existing theoretical frameworks, which are dualistic and oppositional rather than pluralist and synthetic.

An important way through which syncretism, as described in *The Empire*, is thought to be achieved is by a process of abrogating and appropriating the language of the colonial centre. So, in connection to syncretism the (problematic) relation of centre to margin, and vice versa, becomes so important as to be definitive of post-colonial literature. *The Empire* explicitly states that the defining common characteristic of post-colonial literatures is that they 'asserted themselves by foregrounding the tension with the imperial power and by emphasising their differences from the assumptions of the imperial centre. It is this which makes them distinctly post-colonial.'[16] This preoccupation with the tension between centre and margin is part of the syncretic boundary post-colonial theory has set and questioning it should be part of the post-colonial critique itself. It is recognised that there is a 'dynamic interaction between European hegemony and "peripheral" subversions'[17], yet *The Empire* insists that such an interaction functions as some kind of battle between two, whereas in Nichols' and Kay's poetry cross-cultural elements are stressed and we can identify multiple influences.[18]

In Kay, for instance, we do not find friction between margin and centre. In 'Kail and Calloloo'[19] she writes in a mixture of English and Scottish, about the different heritages that an Afro-Scot carries, and about society's obsession with labelling. In the same way as passport forms and application forms do not contain the category 'Celtic-Afro-Caribbean', her poetry cannot be labelled and categories are rendered inapplicable:

> you know the passport forms
> or even some job applications noo-a-days?
> well, there's nowhere to write
> Celtic-Afro-Caribbean
> in answer to the 'origin' question;
> they think that's a contradiction
>
> how kin ye be both?[20]

She is using the Scottish accent, as in 'how kin ye be both', to point out that you *can* be both. She then goes on to describe Afro-Scots, and what their possible attributes would be. She finishes with 'Aye Actually. I'd love to go to Lagos someday/ and I'll aye be back again.' This synthetic treatment of ingredients becomes clearer in *Lazy*

Thoughts of a Lazy Woman, Nichols' third collection of poetry. 'Tapestry' is the
last poem of the collection:

> The long line of blood
> and family ties
>
> An African countenance here
> A European countenance there
> An Amerindian cast of cheek
> An Asianic turn of eye
> And the tongue's salty accommodation
> The tapestry is mine
> All the bloodstained prints
> The scatterlinks
> The grafting strand of crinkled hair
> The black persistent blooming.[21]

Fullstop. This 'tapestry' belongs to her and she acknowledges it; it is a mosaic and it
is going to be 'blooming', while at the same time she does accept the upsetting parts
of the heritage, the 'bloodstained' bits. Nichols astutely refuses categories, as Kay
does; she declares that 'there ain't no/easy-belly category/for a black woman/or
a white woman/or a green woman'. Her black women are full of self-awareness
and are depicted as '[c]rushing out/ with each dancing step'.[22] This awareness is
almost celebrated when she combines the (stereo)typically English 'cup of tea'
drinking with its Caribbean dialect equivalent of 'a lickle cup of tea':

> *But a have me lickle flat*
> *An a have me lickle key.*
> *You want to come in*
> *For a lickle cup-o-tea?*[23]

The poem is written in non-standard English and is italicised, acting out a different,
mixed, language. In 'Configurations', the private–public, or Empire–Colony are not
set up as oppositions; instead, we witness a genuine 'giving' in the private space of
two lovers as well as some first-class post-colonial irony: 'but this time her wide
legs close in/slowly/Making a golden stool of the empire/of his head', while 'he
does a Columbus'. In 'Out of Africa' Nichols transcribes her colonial/post-colonial
'memories', and even though the title of the poem together with certain repetitions
in it seem to indicate a preoccupation with the 'passage' to slavery, actually equal
status is given to the three points of her personal/cultural history: Africa is 'the
first mother', the Caribbean has contributed the 'happy creole so-called mentality'
and in England people are kind, even though, she finds, sometimes too obsessed with
politeness. Most importantly, there is no obvious uneasiness or struggle that would

potentially have been detrimental to the co-existence of the three 'experiences'; on the contrary Nichols retains the positive bits of each. She doesn't have to appropriate one of the three as truly her own and make it definitive of her identity. Instead a humorous turn is given to this dramatic and important question of belonging with the poem 'Wherever I Hang': 'I don't know really where I belaang/Divided to de ocean/Divided to de bone/Wherever I hang me knickers – that's my home.' In another instance of Nichols' multiple vision, the heroine in 'In Spite of Me' is graceful, indiscreet, obsessional, dissatisfied, focused and reassuring, all at the same time and all her magic attributes are vividly personified:

> In spite of me
> the women in me
> slip free
> of the charmed circle
> of my moulding

Vicki Bertram writes in her perceptive study, *Muscling In: A Study of Contemporary Women Poets and English Poetic Tradition*, that Nichols' work is a 'multivocal testimony of remembrance, recognition and celebration'.[24] Anticipating this 'multivocality', my next step is to show that a critical method focusing on synthesis can be enhanced by Mikhail Bakhtin's idea of polyphony and dialogue, in two important ways: first, in drawing attention to the possibility of the elements synthesised being distinct but not necessarily oppositional and, second, in making visible the power play involved in any synthetic enterprise. Polyphonic dialogue is characterised by lack of finalisation. The different pre-colonial, colonial and post-colonial experiences and traditions (literary or not) take part in such a dialogue in post-colonial literature. Applied to post-colonial literature, a Bakhtinean understanding avoids polarisation – the languages of coloniser, colonised and post-colonial would be inscribed within each other, each contributing to the dialogue. The sensitive pluralism the poetry points to can be found in Bakhtin's formulation of the dialogic encounter of two cultures. For Bakhtin dialogic relations are 'possible only between complete utterances of various speaking subjects'.[25] The members of a dialogic relation are kept complete, distinct, and so Bakhtin writes that 'a dialogic encounter of two cultures does not result in merging or mixing. Each retains its own unity and *open* totality, but they are mutually enriched'.[26] This first point is displayed in Jackie Kay's amazingly multi-levelled synthesis of voices. Hers is a poetry-narrative, a poetry with a narrative style, in which the personal is emphasised over the objective. In *The Adoption Papers*, her adoption narrative, we listen to different voices: the daughter's, the natural mother's and the adoptive mother's, which are distinguished by different fonts. As Ama Ata Aidoo, a performance poet like Kay herself, says:

'[w]e don't always have to write for readers, we can write for listeners . . . All the art of the speaking voice could be brought back so easily'.[27]

Kay breaks the tradition of lyric poetry with this narrative multi-voiced poetry and she seems to create and draw on an oral tradition. In 'The Seed' she uses a technique of mixing two of the voices in a 'democratic' way, allocating them the same space, while the device of narrating the story in chapters has the same effect. All the time we are aware that 'facts' are given through her own perception, the child's; she intervenes by using her typeface to introduce what happened. For instance she starts with 'On the first night', goes on with the events, then writes 'On the second night', and then lets the other voices speak. In 'The Telling Part,' there is an interweaving choric schema:

> *Ma mammy says she's no really ma mammy*
> *(just kid on)*
> It's a bit like a part you've rehearsed so well
> you can't play it on the opening night
> *She says my real mammy is away far away*
> Mammy why aren't you and me the same colour
> *But I love ma mammy whether she's real or no*[28]

The pattern is like an embroidery where she juxtaposes what each voice – each point of view – is supposed to be actually saying. Furthermore, two additional 'voices' can be said to join the choir. First, in 'The Meeting Dream' we are made aware of the fictitious character of the construction when the original (the daughter's) speaking voice admits that 'if I picture it like this it hurts less'. Second, we are made aware of our (reader's) active role in constructing the text's meaning since the narrative is left open-ended and so the ending can be 'pictured' in many different ways.[29] Having established the existence of different voices in dialogue with each other, Kay goes on, in the second part of *The Adoption Papers*, to talk about London life, the NHS, banking, the Poll Tax, healthy eating, transvestism, while at the same time the mask-taking, point-of-view-voicing process involved in her poetry is explicitly dramatised in the form of a powerful dramatic monologue, 'The Underground Baby Case', where a baby's kidnapper claims that

> his mother
> gave him to me really, she must have wanted
> me to have him – perhaps she planned it
> for weeks, following me about,
> picked me like you pick a disciple.[30]

'The Underground Baby Case' reminds us that not all of the depicted points of view have the same strength, which relates to my second point about the power play in the relationship of 'voices' after they have been synthesised. Indeed I find that the most valuable contribution dialogism can make to synthesis as a critical tool is a sensitivity to such a play, which will also expose the way in which syncretism operates by covering up the power interests involved.[31] A synthesis of consciousnesses and languages implies that these co-exist, are put side by side. Yet, as David Shepherd notes, Bakhtin teaches that some voices are louder than others. 'Bakhtin's work demonstrates an acute understanding of just how naively idealistic it would be to assume that in any dialogue, literary-critical or otherwise all contributors carry equal weight.'[32] Bakhtin reminds us that we should be aware of the constraints at work in the cultural and social life. As Shepherd puts it, since Bakhtin's dialogic production of meaning functions within a socially stratified and historically developing language, there are always forces of centralisation in operation. In the poetry under consideration some of the elements synthesised are felt to be stronger than others. This is an important element in the poetry, important enough to qualify my understanding of it being involved in a 'dialogic synthesis': the dialogic part of this formulation shows an awareness that some voices are (have been) dominant, sometimes to the point of controlling or repressing others: for instance colonial, post-colonial or neo-colonial oppression represents such a loud voice. For *The Empire* a syncretic view 'provides a framework of 'difference on equal terms' within which multi-cultural theories, both within and between societies, may continue to be fruitfully explored.'[33] Rather than a syncretic 'difference on equal terms', synthesis, to me, can represent 'identity in difference', or even better, dialogic synthesis renders 'loudness within difference'. The politics of dialogic synthesis would be an awareness of difference as well as an acknowledgement of the existence of loud voices in any one dialogue. It would allow for an analysis of the operations of power by recognising that cultural, sexual and racial difference has not been on equal terms.

In Kay's second collection, *Other Lovers*,[34] we have a fine dialogic synthesis, with its recognition of the loudness of certain voices over others. She still feels the need to make clear her Scottish identity: ' " *Where do you come from?/* "Here," I said, "Here. These parts." '[35] But she highlights, more explicitly and even bitterly this time, the presence of her black roots; a stronger link with her racial past is established in a mixed memory of two traumatic moments of the past, that of slavery and of the American experience of racism. In 'Even the Trees', the opening poem of the collection, she asks 'for forgiveness/to come in a storm', warning that '[e]verything that's happened once could happen again'.[36] Synthesised we find the American Blues, the noise of the bass, the whip, a scream of warning, and the wind, the life in the plantations and the operations of the Ku Klux Klan. The figure of blues singer Bessie Smith is prevalent and forms an important motif in a Bessie Smith-cycle that consists of more than half a dozen poems. Kay uses the

Blues tour, the wandering Pullman as a memory of her own, and at the same time
a kind of collective memory of which she partakes. In 'The Right Season' the Blues
singer, 'the Empress, the Voodoo Queen' with the 'cast-iron voice', is the female
figure she will identify with and the figure that will offer the link with the past.
Kay manages to synthesise these memories with her present reality. In 'Watching
People Sing', two voices are included (one italicised). She thinks of herself mainly
as the audience, listening to the blues; yet, since we normally expect the audience
to be an active participant in the blues, her own voice is present as well. She may
be saying 'I can't sing. All I can do is watch/and clap, and clap, and clap',[37] but
obviously this is not true since the poem exists. Transported to the present '[t]he
noises of the past' are made meaningful in 'Sound', representing both a historical,
racial past and the past of her childhood. She seems to be following a different
direction from Nichols, writing the story of slavery after she has dealt with the
things close to home:

> Why do I remember the blues?
> . . .
> Why do I remember her voice and not my own mother's?
> Why do I remember the blues?

she asks in 'The Red Graveyard', only to go on to say that her parents played the
blues all the time and that she does remember her mother's voice, which was like
a 'peach', or 'old rock', 'Long long grass. Asphalt. Wind. Hail./Cotton. Linen.
Salt. Treacle.'[38] Who is this mother? It is both her 'own' mother and at the
same time Bessie Smith herself: the speaker is in her father's house, we find,
her 'real' father's house, listening to Bessie's records. So Kay is succeeding both
in being close to the roots of the past and in maintaining her current identity,
in the present time and place. In 'Watching People Sing' she is helping with
the entertaining while friends, including her father, in her mother's absence,
dance and sing 'in a semi-/American accent learnt in the Glasgow Odeon'.
The voices of the past speak in an incoherent language in her head, which is
full of light, in 'Sound', but singing and dancing have been established right
before as a very precise and coherent language. In 'Sign' she speaks of the need
for one's 'little' language to be heard, and not let an imposed 'big one, better
tongue' prevail:

> The day they forced her to speak
> their tongue, she lost
> the black-eyed susan.
> She went back in
> time

> They say her voice is very strange.
> They tie her hands behind her back.
> They say repeat after me until
> she has *no language at all.*[39]

Kay talks about how they forced her out of her linguistic space into a white, male, hegemonic language. What was demonstrated in her first collection is here conceptualised, 'my mother's voice split open'.[40] Still we have the same concreteness; she uses all her senses to let '[t]he noises of the past/float into my room at night.'[41] These voices, together with the imposed muteness of her present post-colonial situation, are juxtaposed with the love poems of the second section of the book. The forgiveness which she is imploring in the beginning of the book will come in the guise of love. Love is depicted as being capable of transcending boundaries and giving a bitter-sweet taste, looking afresh at the way we live. Different personae, in a variety of situations and from different points of view, are entangled within love relationships – daughters, sons, mothers, fathers, lovers in different configurations, adults 'visiting' their childhood. These are 'Other Lovers' (the poem which gives the collection its title as well), other than the ones of the past, 'when the young danced to an old song,/the moon split in two, the stars smashed':

> One day you find you are your other lover.
> . . .
> You have actually done it.
> You would never have believed it.
> You have a whole new life.[42]

Still, this optimistic feeling of synthesis of past and present is denied in the final poem of the book. The sequence ends with 'Finger' – pointing perhaps to the 'loudness' of certain voices – an accusing finger, not forgetting about '[b]reeding in the dead heat of a tiny room for the master./Or him groping you as your man stands by.' The tone is demanding: 'Answer me . . ./This is another century. Take my fingerprint.'[43] It is an ambiguous ending, making sure nothing is erased from cultural memory.

The operations of dialogic synthesis, as I understand them, are also crystallised in *i is a long memoried woman*, where Nichols transcends boundaries of space and time, moving backwards and forwards from the Caribbean and the past to Britain and the present and uses both female and male consciousnesses to convey her own complex vision of the future. She, in the poem with the same title, is 'holding her beads':

> Unforgiving as the course of justice
> Inerasable as my scars and fate
> I am here
> a woman . . . with all my lives

strung out like beads
> before me

It isn't privilege or pity
that I seek
It isn't reverence or safety
quick happiness or purity
> but

the power to be what I am/ a woman
charting my own futures/ a woman
holding my beads in my hand

It is a synthesis of control, the beads of her life – and her poetry – different, shining, ever-present are held in her hand; she is in control of her many 'lives'.

Finally, it is the 'post-coloniality' of both poetry and theory that should enhance our understanding of the following: since not all readings (and especially not one reading) are good for all texts, particular texts need particular readings and no one reading is to be used for 'post-colonial literature' as a whole. In this direction I find Laura Donaldson's *Decolonizing Feminisms* useful. Her ideas of what constitutes a post-colonial reading are a reminder that since there is no single hermeneutic truth, our critical story of post-colonialism should not privilege any one plot. Donaldson coins the term 'Miranda complex' for the kind of analysis that suppresses heterogeneity. Miranda, Prospero's daughter in Shakespeare's *The Tempest*, although a victim of sexual oppression herself, cannot see the racial oppression Caliban is subjected to. And vice versa. Realising that both are victims and victimisers at the same time would prevent us from identifying Caliban as the colonised other and Miranda as the coloniser. Donaldson uses the complex as a 'parable about the dangers of monotheistic reading'.[44] In her own readings she 'perceives meaning as contradictory and dialectical and society as the product of a divisive and dialogical process'.[45] The need, then, has been realised (as exemplified by the work of Donaldson and Mishra and Hodge among others)[46] for no single post-colonial theory but many. Contributing to this particular part of the post-colonial debate, dialogic synthesis might prove useful in our thinking of post-colonial women's poetry if it can serve both as a frame that will not misshape the texts in a Procrustean way as well as an approach that will allow post-colonial theories to extend, cross or overcome their boundaries. This is not a generalisation either on post-colonial women's poetry or on post-colonial literary theory. It is based on a discussion of how two very specific pieces of each interact with each other. The theoretical boundaries that are crossed by the 'synthesis' achieved in this poetry are newly-moulded ones. It is interesting that boundaries are formed the moment some new kind of theorising takes place. The implications of a critical boundary formed, or of the application of a formed boundary are 'political' ones. As post-colonial critic Ihab Hassan puts it, '[p]olitics structures our theoretical consents, literary evasions, critical recusancies'.[47] In Kay's 'Kail and Calloloo' we saw how categories can be inapplicable. More importantly, when inadequately applied, categories can be harmful. Indeed, Vicki Bertram finds that the blindness of the theory which, due to its oppositional categories, is unable to fit the poetry, and therefore ignores it, is to blame for the relative critical silence about Nichols. This makes the implications of a transgressed boundary far-reaching. 'Go to your wide futures', says the mother to her children in Nichols' 'Praise Song For My Mother'.[48] Likewise, by not being concerned with its canon-based 'marginality', by creating its own terms and thus escaping any imprisoning critical frameworking involved, this poetry can go to its wide futures.

NOTES

1. Evelin Marius, 'The Snake Charmer's Ball', in *Charting the Journey: Writings by Black and Third World Women*, eds Shabnam Grewal et al., (London, Sheba Feminist Publishers, 1988), p.70.
2. Vicki Bertram, 'Muscling In: A Study of Contemporary Women Poets and English Poetic Tradition' (University of York, D Phil. Dissertation, 1992), p.55.
3. *The Empire Writes Back*, Bill Ashcroft, Gareth Griffiths and Helen Tiffin (eds), (London, Routledge, 1989). This is one of the first coherent and influential attempts to formulate post-colonial literary theory. It is a well-known volume that has been described in the first post-colonial Reader as 'a good, teachable text' that was launched to help post-colonialism get a place in the curriculum, 'a lucid, judicious and representative text which is destined to play a decisive role in this emerging field' [*Colonial Discourse and Post-colonial Theory: A Reader*, Patrick Williams and Laura Chrisman (eds), (New York, Harvester Wheatsheaf, 1993), p.276]. I find these good enough reasons to justify scrutinising this book and identifying in it hegemonic post-colonial critical ideologies.
4. *The Empire Writes Back*, p.37.
5. Ibid., p.169.
6. Ibid., p.15.
7. As far as I know, synthesis does not exist as a term in literary theory. It does exist as a philosophical term, used in Hegelian dialectics and also in connection to the political philosophy of Marx. I am not using it in either sense but it is interesting that the most prevalent point in both seems to be the individuality of the participants. The two definitions quoted in the *OED* are 'in dialectical synthesis thesis and antithesis are resolved in such a way that ... aspects of each are retained or *conserved* in every new whole or situation and are reinterpreted' (S. Hook, *From Hegel to Marx*); and 'synthesis is the moment of "identity in difference" in the dialectical advance. Synthesis will abolish the existing opposition together with both its terms' (F.J. Copleston, *History of Philosophy VII*). 'Identity in difference' would brilliantly capture the operations of dialogical syntheses which Kay's and Nichols' poetry partake in.
8. Bertram, 'Muscling In', p.328.
9. Grace Nichols, *i is a long memoried woman* (London, Karnak House, 1983).
10. In *Let It Be Told: Black Women Writers in Britain*, ed. Lauretta Ngobo (London, Virago, 1988), p.97.
11. Nichols, *i is a long memoried woman*, p.87.
12. *Let It Be Told*, p.103.
13. Post-colonial theorist Bharati Mukherjee uses the very interesting notion of a 'step-mother tongue' to account for the relationship the post-colonial subject has with the colonial language within the responsibility, affection, accident, loss, and secretive rootsquest in adoptive-family situations (quoted in Linda Hutcheon, ' "Circling The Downspout of Empire": Post-Colonialism and Postmodernism', *Ariel* 20.4 (1989), pp.149–76, p.163).
14. *Let It Be Told*, p.98.
15. Nichols, *i is a long memoried woman*, pp.55–6.

16. *The Empire Writes Back*, p.2.
17. Ibid., p.152.
18. The main problem with syncretism as a general cultural theory is that it melts this tension away in its final stage. I should point to a view, voiced by Benita Parry in her article 'Problems in Current Theories of Colonial Discourse' (1987), and discussed in *The Empire Writes Back*, that rejects syncretism as a 'cultural esperanto' and dismisses it as merely a 'subtle device for the reintroduction and reincorporation of native "difference" into a new hegemonic totality' (quoted in *The Empire Writes Back*, p.179). Also, Mishra and Hodge in their extensive critique of *The Empire Writes Back* find that, by privileging syncretism, the book is homogenising the geographical, historical and cultural specificities of post-colonialism and applying the same model to white settler and non-settler literature alike. 'The homogenising drive of *The Empire Writes Back* leads it to seek to establish a dominant field and not a set of heterogeneous "moments" arising from very different historical processes' (*Colonial Discourse and Postcolonial Theory*, p.285). They find that the dominant tone of the book is 'the tolerant pluralism of liberal humanism' (Ibid., p.278) and that syncretism as a model copied liberal multi-culturalism (as it is found in Australia for instance). I should make clear where I stand in relation to these substantial questionings of syncretism. Syncretism as understood in *The Empire Writes Back* starts off with antagonistic elements that merge into one form. Both Parry and Mishra and Hodge attack this merging and collapse of distinctions, and I agree with them. Yet, the emphasis on opposition which makes the encounter of different elements dualistic does not seem to bother them. My reading of this poetry, on the other hand, sees different but not necessarily or problematically dichotomised elements that are put together and retain their distinct identity in difference. Distinctions still remain, and the loudness of certain voices, such that can involve silencing and oppression, is recognised in my subsequent qualification of synthesis as dialogic. I should also mention that, like synthesis, when I use the word 'pluralism' I understand pluralist approaches not as tolerant and homogenising but as respectful of difference.
19. In *Charting the Journey*, pp.195–7.
20. Ibid., p.195.
21. Grace Nichols, *Lazy Thoughts of a Lazy Woman* (London, Virago, 1989), p.57.
22. 'Of Course When They Ask for Poems About the "Realities" of Black Women', *Lazy Thoughts of a Lazy Woman*, p.52.
23. Ibid., 'Beverley's Saga', p.35. The following references are all to poems in this same collection.
24. Bertram, 'Muscling In', p.298.
25. Mikhail Bakhtin, *Speech Genres & Other Late Essays*, Caryl Emerson and Michael Holquist (eds), (Austin, University of Texas Press, 1986), p.171.
26. Ibid., p.7.
27. Quoted in Ketu H. Katrak, 'Decolonising Culture: Towards a Theory for Postcolonial Women's Texts', *Modern Fiction Studies*, 35, 1 (1989), pp.157–79, p.174.
28. Jackie Kay, *The Adoption Papers* (Newcastle-upon-Tyne, Bloodaxe Books, 1991), p.21.
29. There are actually another couple of voices echoing. To start with, it is very tempting, and is presented as tempting in the text as well, to look for realistic details since the whole thing is set up as a true story: we immediately learn, from the back flap of the book, that Kay was adopted, that we are about to witness the true story of an adoption (as opposed to the way it is given in the newspapers, for instance). So, there is another autobiography-narrative running parallel to the text itself, according to which, for instance, any reference to the real father is supposed to be 'truly' fictitious because Kay never knew anything about him. At the same time the juxtaposition of narratives resists this luring process and eventually 'encourages' an awareness of the fictitious character of the text as a whole.
30. Kay, *Adoption Papers*, p.63.
31. In my dealing with Nichols' and Kay's poetry I, contrary to Mishra and Hodge, find Bakhtin's dialogism particularly useful in exposing rather than supporting syncretism. Mishra and Hodge find that the principle of universality that creeps underneath syncretism developed from the contact of post-colonial theories to European theories. 'The post-colonial has adopted a number of propositions which are absolutely central to the rise of the bourgeois novel in Europe' (*Colonial Discourse and Postcolonial Theory*, p.287), they write. 'Beneath the strategies of *The Empire Writes Back* is the dialogism of Bakhtin; and beneath post-colonial literature lies the might of the novel form. Absence of cultural specificity leads to cultural collapse, and cultural collapse takes us to the modern genre *par excellence*, the novel' (ibid., p.280). Yet, firstly, the polyphonic novel that is central to his dialogism is actually the name Bakhtin uses to describe the entry of destabilising ideological forces (carnival) into the form of writing at any one time in history (*Bakhtin and Cultural Theory*, Ken Hirschkop and David Shepherd, eds, Manchester and New York,

Manchester University Press, 1989), p.43. Dialogism (and monologism) are not inherent characteristics of particular types of (literary) discourse or of a certain generically defined type of text (novel) (ibid., p.94). And, secondly, in an important way, since the poetry considered in this paper can aid in a process of decentralising views on literary theory – syncretism as a critical tool having become 'central' – it can be seen as polyphonic because a Bakhtinean framework enhances our awareness of such centralisation. In this sense syncretism is not sustained by dialogism. On the contrary, the project of crossing the boundaries of syncretism, i.e. of not having to overlook surviving contradictions and oppositions, which is what Mishra and Hodge support, can be accommodated within a dialogic context.

32. *Bakhtin and Cultural Theory*, p.100.
33. *The Empire Writes Back*, pp.36–7.
34. Jackie Kay, *Other Lovers* (Newcastle, Bloodaxe, 1993).
35. 'In my Country', in *Other Lovers*, p.24.
36. Ibid, p.9.
37. Ibid, p.16.
38. Ibid., p.13.
39. Ibid., pp.20–1.
40. In 'Compound Fracture', ibid, p.25.
41. In 'Sound', ibid., p.19.
42. Ibid, p.41.
43. Ibid, p.62.
44. Laura E. Donaldson, *Decolonizing Feminisms: Race, Gender and Empire-Building* (London, Routledge, 1992), p.17.
45. Ibid., p.3.
46. An example is that of Mae Gwendolyn Henderson's use of the constructive approach of what she calls 'discursive diversity' to avoid privileging race over gender, or the other way round, as analytic categories in critical readings: an approach that aims at challenging discourse categories and boundaries. Focusing on Black women writers' dialogue with otherness and difference, Henderson examines the way they speak within a hegemonic discursive order and identifies the plurality of voices, the multiplicity of discourses Black women must speak in. ('Speaking in Tongues; Dialectics, Dialogics and Black Women's Tradition', in *Colonial Discourse and Postcolonial Theory*, pp.257–67.)
47. Ihab Hassan, 'Pluralism in Postmodern Perspective', *Critical Inquiry*, 12 (1985–6), pp.503–20, p.513.
48. Nichols, *The Fat Black Woman's Poems* (London, Virago, 1984), p.44.

FURTHER READING

Breckenridge, Carol and Van der Veer, Peter (eds), *Orientalism and the Post-Colonial Predicament* (Philadelphia, University of Pennsylvania, Press 1993).

Chew, Shirley and Rutherford, Anna, (eds), *Unbecoming Daughters of Empire* (Hedben Bridge, Dangaroo Press, 1993).

Donaldson, Laura, *Decolonizing Feminisms: Race, Gender, and Empire-Building* (London, Routledge, 1992).

Grewal, Shabnam, et al. (eds), *Charting the Journey: Writings by Black and Third World Women* (London, Sheba, 1988).

Holst-Petersen, K. and Rutherford, A. (eds). *A Double Colonization: Colonial and post-colonial women's writing* (Aarhus, Dangaroo Press, 1985).

Katrak, Ketu, 'Decolonising Culture: Towards a Theory for Postcolonial Women's Texts', *Modern Fiction Studies*, 35, 1 (1989) pp.157–79.

King, D. Anthony (ed), *Culture, Globalization and the World-System* (London, Macmillan, 1991).

Somerville-Arjat, Gillean and Wilson, Rebecca E. (eds), *Sleeping with Monsters: Conversations with Scottish and Irish Women Poets* (Edinburgh, Polygon, 1990).

Williams, Patrick and Christman, Laura (eds), *Colonial Discourse and Post-Colonial Theory: a Reader* (New York, Harvester Wheatsheaf, 1993).

9

Epic, a Woman's Place:
A Study of Derek Walcott's Omeros and Jean Binta Breeze's 'A River Called Wise'

Paula Burnett

Genre is itself a signifier. In the Western tradition, literary epic as genre has acquired a very special role as a site for the inscription and dissemination of nationalism, patriarchy and imperialism. From Homer on, it has been essentially phallocentric. But it is not only the choice of genre which is significant; so also is its use – the way it is made to repeat or transgress its givens. Recent Caribbean poems demonstrate that literary epic is open to feminist expression, as to black expression, and that its co-option to patriarchy is extrinsic. The works of Derek Walcott, particularly his most recent epic *Omeros* (1990) and the epic poem by Jean Binta Breeze, 'A River Called Wise' (first performed in 1993), demonstrate radically new ways of inhabiting the genre with the result that they remake it, its recreation being a metaphor for the regeneration of society which both poets desire and prefigure.

Epic's traditional function is defined at the peak of European imperialism (fuelled by classical epic's cultural influence) in 1912 by Macneile Dixon, who defines its interest as 'rather national than individual': epic, he says, is 'the natural home of ideals – there lies open to it a region forbidden to tragedy'. It deals 'with great actions and great characters, in a style commensurate with the lordliness of its theme'.[1] However, long before Dixon's Edwardian utopianism Voltaire understood the Aristotelian epic convention of 'greatness' to be extrinsic – 'Use alone has prefixed the name of epic particularly to those poems which relate some great action' – and deconstructed its centrism, envisaging an epic set, for example, 'in the West Indies'.[2] But although Voltaire may have anticipated modern moves to democratise and decentre the epic, one thing he and Dixon both took for granted is the male gender of the hero or heroes.

From *Gilgamesh* down through the ages, epic has been a particularly effective valoriser of patriarchy. It has modelled men as heroes, as doers, in contrast to its women, admired for passivity, and it has tended to glorify patriarchal values of militarism, conquest and mission. Its mythologising has been indisputably phallocentric, which may be one reason why, in a time of growing awareness of patriarchal dominance, western literary epic as genre for new writing has almost disappeared. Early modernist revisions apart, the term 'epic' acquired a loosely defined popular meaning in the twentieth century in relation to two forms central to popular culture, the novel and film, but from mid-century onwards the epic poem began to seem a thing of the past.[3]

Given the empowering effect of the Homeric tradition on European imperialism, epic might seem a strange choice for late twentieth-century Caribbean poets seeking counter-discourses. Yet out of a tiny anglophone community of some four million people, two major epic poets have emerged, Kamau Brathwaite and Derek Walcott. Their use of epic was unusual from the early days of post-colonial experiment when a majority of writers took up the novel, and now Jean Binta Breeze joins them.[4] Epic is, of course, not reserved to the Western tradition; the post-Homeric Western literary epic is just one small branch of a heterogeneous, worldwide phenomenon. Epics have been produced at many epochs and in many parts of the world in the form of extensive, spoken or sung narratives with a particular role in the cultural construction of the collective subject.[5] Unlike the novel, then, epic is not uniquely associated with Western élite culture – far from it – and is therefore perhaps, after all, a particularly appropriate choice for the post-colonial writer inheriting both literary and oral traditions. It is worth remembering that the Homeric texts which have inspired such a lineage of literature were originally transmitted orally.

If, however, this plural epic tradition is examined for its representation of women, the picture is bleak. Epic may be indigenous to diverse cultures but as both orature and literature it has traditionally been uniformly sexist. It seems that societies all around the world have developed their epics in a patriarchal idiom, with male heroes as role models, typically remarkable for their physical power and dominance. Parallel motifs recur in widely different cultural contexts: for instance, the feat of the stringing of the great bow of Shiva in the Indian epic the *Ramayana*, by which Rama wins Sita, is reminiscent of the stringing of the bow of Odysseus which precipitates the climax of *The Odyssey*. Sita, regarded as the ideal of Indian womanhood, is passive and helpless, though admired for her stoical virtues – not so different from Penelope who waits all those years in chastity for the return of the hero husband, Odysseus. But it is above all in the

Homeric representation of Helen that patriarchy's method is exposed: the woman as object of desire is fought over by men, abducted as a chattel (so far like Sita), but then blamed for the ensuing intra-masculine conflict.[6] The question, then, has to be whether epic can be made to signify differently in gender terms: whether it can be – regardless of the author's gender – in the terms of Cixous' *écriture féminine*,[7] a woman's place.

Walcott, as Caribbean male,[8] tackles the challenge head on: his focus on Helen in *Omeros* is both revolutionary and apt, since his beautiful island, St Lucia, was fought over for so long in the imperial wars between France and England that it was dubbed the 'Helen of the West Indies'. It is radical in the way that Milton might have been if he had centred *Paradise Lost* on Eve. Walcott has been attacked by some as a sexist writer[9] but this charge is difficult to sustain in the light of his more recent work. On the contrary *Omeros* can be described in terms of *écriture féminine* in that its construction of gender contests patriarchal stereotypes, and this is as much to do with the representation of men as of women. Epic's gender convention of the active hero and passive heroine is inverted, its sexual politics revolutionised.

By using the wound as symbol of the masculine condition in *Omeros*, Walcott is drawing attention to the specific trauma suffered by the colonial male psyche under imperialism and its continuing analogues. In shifting the focus from the male as aggressor to the male as wounded, he subverts the militarist ethos of epic to investigate alternative, post-colonial ways of being. He shows the healed Philoctete dancing with Achille in a new emblem of androgyny. Like the festive dancers of West Africa they dress as women for their art – a dance which is a communal mythic rite of affirmation. This is not the androgyny of masculine dread, symbolising castration, but an androgyny which shows potent male sexuality separating itself from the oppressive roles prescribed under patriarchy by harnessing its energies to art. The bisexuality is like that described by Cixous which refuses all binary conceptualisation, residing in the 'non-exclusion either of the difference or of one sex'.[10]

The representation of women in *Omeros* is also remarkably radical. Walcott revolutionises the patriarchal Western epic with its militarist ethic and heroic action-men, to place at the centre the strong woman: principled, generous, courageous, and tough. His Helen is an independent-minded woman who walks out rather than be exploited by sexist tourists and a management which refuses to make a stand, and who leaves the partner who treats her badly. He adapts Robert Graves' interpretation of the mythic lunar triad as representing the three ages of woman[11] to a collective colonial history: the elderly white woman Maud, whose era has ended, is superseded by black Helen, the sexually potent woman, while the nymph – Christine, a teenager – is just coming into view towards the end of the poem as the new helper in the No Pain Café of Ma Kilman, the black mother goddess, the healer, of whom the three may be seen as avatars. The patriarchal classical pantheon with its rivalries is thus replaced by feminine powers.

With fine irony, in the centre of his poem Walcott has his aging white woman, Maud, ask of her former servant, Helen, 'So, how are you, Helen?', to which Helen replies, 'I dere, Madam.' In case we miss the pun, Walcott continues in Maud's interior narration, 'At last. You dere. Of course you dare.' [XXIII.iii] Ostensibly Helen answers, in her St Lucian English, 'I dere' – 'I'm there' or 'I'm still here, at least, still alive'. But there is a double meaning, as the sounds in standard English signify differently: a simple, vernacular statement of her existence reads to the self-styled 'mistress' as a statement of insubordination. As so often, Walcott encapsulates in a prism of language – specifically oral language – far-reaching meanings: in this tiny linguistic moment the history of empire is narrated and brought to closure, in the gap between the two constructions of the phrase. 'I dere' as the colonial subject's 'I exist' is construed by the dominant as subversive; from the subaltern's point of view, her resisting presence is unshakable: 'If you read my assertion of my existence as revolutionary, so be it, I dare, I have courage enough.' In the psychology of empire, the overdetermination by the coloniser of the colonised's behaviour functions to enlarge difference, as Memmi has shown. Once identified,

> this gap must be kept from being filled. The colonialist removes the factor from history, time, and therefore possible evolution. What is actually a sociological point becomes labeled as being biological or, preferably, metaphysical. It is attached to the colonized's basic nature.[12]

Maud's 'Of course' is an indicator of the imperialist's myth of generalised moral hierarchy in action: Helen is seen not as an individual, but as a member of the subaltern group, whose qualities are predetermined. As Memmi has it, 'Since the colonized is presumed a thief, he must in fact be guarded against'.[13] Maud's assumption that Helen's 'daring' is revolutionary helps deliver the revolution. Typically, it is in the interstices of language difference that Walcott sets up his most profound significance: although the dominant language of the poem is standard English, its meaning can only be understood from the standpoint of the other languages it incorporates – St Lucian English (as here) and St Lucian French. The poem enacts the revolution, the handover from white power to black power, but specifically in terms resisting patriarchy: the white woman whose day is done is superseded by the black woman, who 'dares' simply by virtue of having survived her traumatic past to come into her own like Cinderella, wearing Maud's yellow butterfly dress which has 'an empire's tag' [XI.i].

Nor is the figure of the heroic woman something new for Walcott. There is a recurrent icon in his work which goes right back to a childhood memory of the unloading of coal from the ships. With its large harbour, Castries was chosen as the coaling station of the region by the British, the fuel being offloaded onto the wharf until transshipped. The St Lucian contribution was badly paid hard labour, something that the people of a poverty-stricken community had no choice but to accept. Photographs show both men and women loading the coal, but in Walcott's work over three decades the icon is of women, carrying hundred-weight baskets on their heads up the steep gangplanks.[14] In *Omeros* his Hades is the coal-wharf of colonial Castries, with his father's ghost as guide, as Virgil guided Dante through the Christian Hell:

> From here, in his boyhood, he had seen women climb
> like ants up a white flower-pot, baskets of coal
> balanced on their torchoned heads, without touching them,
>
> up the black pyramids, each spine straight as a pole,
> and with a strength that never altered its rhythm.
> He spoke for those Helens from an earlier time:
>
> 'Hell was built on those hills. In that country of coal
> without fire, that inferno the same colour
> as their skins and shadows, every labouring soul
>
> climbed with her hundredweight basket, every load for
> one copper penny, balanced erect on their necks
> that were tight as the liner's hawsers from the weight.'

[XIII.ii]

Walcott's interrogation of the Western epic tradition and the patriarchy it valorises is symbolised in his choice of this image on which to build his poem. A new notion of woman emerges:

> The carriers were women, not the fair, gentler sex.
> Instead they were darker and stronger, and their gait
> Was made beautiful by balance . . .

[XIII.ii]

The voice of the father tells the poet it is his task to give them a heroic 'voice' to match their heroic but unhonoured 'feet':

> They walk, you write;
> . . . Look, they climb, and no one knows them;
> they take their copper pittances, and your duty

from the time you watched them from your grandmother's house
as a child wounded by their power and beauty
is the chance you now have, to give those feet a voice.

[XIII.iii]

Ma Kilman's finding of the healing herb is narrated in terms of the collective history:

See her there, my mother, my grandmother, my great-great-
grandmother. See the black ants of their sons,
their coal-carrying mothers. Feel the shame, the self-hate

draining from all our bodies

[XLVIII.iii]

This initial stage of healing, signalling its ultimate enactment, is placed in the context of the centuries of pain, looking back to an ancestral past but forward to a relieved future for the race (the first person singular migrating significantly to a plural). The central meaning of the poem is that even the worst trauma, that of black history, can be healed.

Simply by asserting that such historically invisible people are heroic, Walcott is making a political statement.[15] By centring an epic poem of some three hundred pages on the tiny island of St Lucia, and on a group of ordinary people – the antithesis of the classical epic heroes – he is engaging with a world of texts which have until now taken no cognisance of the fact that such a place and such people exist. The American search for democratic epic is given a triumphant resolution. Hence the importance of the Homer analogy: he examines the centrism of the Homeric in the Western tradition, asserting the parallel importance of his own people's story, and its difference – its value as model of un-patriarchal, non-violent, plebeian heroism. He centres the Homeric idea of Odysseus' survival by his wits – the little man as hero, who outmanoeuvres the destructive force of the Cyclops by naming himself as Nobody, thereby living on as a heroic Somebody – and interweaves this with Christian myth, showing the heroism of suffering, and delivering the magic of healing. His text enacts the handover of white power to black, and ends with the black family as its closing triangle: unlike Odysseus and Penelope, a couple with far from equal weight, shaped by a patriarchal dynastic tradition, Walcott makes Helen at least the equal of her lover, Achille, as she grows the child whose biological fathering is unimportant.

Jean Binta Breeze calls her new poem an epic, although it is unlike traditional epic of either oral or literary kinds – much more different than Walcott's is, for example. It met its first audience at the Commonwealth Institute in London in the spring of 1993; at the South Bank in London in November of the same year a shortened version was performed.[16] The full text takes about three-quarters of an hour to deliver. Its fundamental difference is immediately evident: it is a poem by a woman, and composed to be voiced in a woman's voice, live in the ear, as a shared experience. It therefore recalls the oral epic as social practice in which the shared performance consolidates a sense of community. Jean Binta Breeze is Jamaican, a talented performer who trained at the Jamaica School of Drama, and a performance poet for whose audiences the words on the page are no more than a reminder of the words in performance, so when she takes on the genre of epic, she does so in her Caribbean voice from a culture in which orality is strong.

As with Walcott's, hers is post-colonial epic, but unlike Walcott who writes within certain conventional literary expectations, Breeze shifts the emphasis away from the written form and towards the oral style: it connects with ancient practice, but also with the present orality-dominated cultures of the Third World and with the new orature of the technological age (it would be a mistake to characterise its orality as in any way primitive or nostalgic). It draws on the particularity of autobiographical experience, as does Walcott's poem – the River Wise runs through the part of rural Jamaica where she grew up – but where Walcott's style emulates in order to transform the heroic idiom, Breeze's proceeds by different bearings from the outset. Hers is an impressionistic quest narrative moving fluidly through place and time as befits its only persona, the River Wise. In place of Walcott's hexameters which provide the vehicle for a verse which captures an orality of tone almost despite its literariness, Breeze uses a light, mainly two-stress line, erratically but emphatically rhymed, which is firmly in the oral idiom, although remote from some traditional oral epic metres and from the mechanistic metrical effects of some verse in the black popular tradition. The language she chooses here is almost entirely standard English, although the Jamaican intonation is very much a part of its meaning for those who have heard her perform it.

What is radically new in her deployment of the epic is its gender significance. If Walcott's is *écriture féminine*, Breeze's is what Alice Walker would call a 'womanist' text.[17] First, it comes as something of a shock to think of a woman as author of an epic poem at all, which is in itself indicative of how deeply entrenched is the perception of epic as phallocentric. Then there is the implication of this for the content and its gender significance. Where Walcott re-maps gender in his revolutionary epic, placing the black woman

at the heart of his narrative, Breeze decentres the reading of gender as trope
of humanity in her poem, and then redeploys it as abstract symbol. It is an
eponymous poem; its protagonist *is* the river called Wise, of which the female
pronoun is used. There is thus a strongly female consciousness at the heart of
the poem.

As Breeze has said,[18] she chose water because it offered a way of showing
the connectedness of the world: the same water washes the shores of the world,
and falls from the sky to replenish the rivers and return to the oceans. But this
river is called Wise: the ubiquitous mythic association of woman with water is
doubled with a sign – a name (and naming is nearly always a symbolic act
in post-colonial writing) – which unites the notion of intellectualism with the
notion of morality. To be wise is different from being clever. Thus the idea in
'the River Wise' unites Gaia with Athena – the spirituality of nature with the
spirituality of creative thought. The third-person narration constructs the river
as a persona which is gradually established as heroic. The river on its moral
quest is moved by the suffering it sees in a world characterised by exploitation,
of human beings and natural resources. Wise is herself a variant of a traditional
'Mother Nature' figure, the embodiment of nurture and care, the life-giving force
– which is not inexhaustible.[19] The female element of water is threatened with
drought: her sexuality of wetness dreads the sterility of dryness. This quasi-divine
persona can be a fury as well as benign. In indignation the river can rage – 'and
the river roared red/tore down everything/dug holes/moved mountains' (p.9) –
yet, as the poem goes on, 'some of us know/the river's true voice/was soft like
a mother/telling children to rest' (p.10).

By constructing a Protean persona as the presiding consciousness of the poem,
Breeze decentres gender; although the River Wise is female, she is female in a
supra-human way, so that while women may wish to identify with her, they can
only do so by acknowledging first her difference, her mythic transcendence. Thus
women – and men – are returned to the worldliness of their gender positions, and
to a questioning of their ethical condition. The poem offers no human heroes, either
male or female, élite or ordinary, black or white. Unlike Walcott's poem, Breeze's
has no named location, and no implicit role in nationalist discourse. The world
that Wise visits in her Odyssean quest is marked out in symbolic divisions, its cast
playing generic rather than individual roles. It is divided between the 'have-nots'
and the 'haves', who, as the poem observes with bitter irony, bid 'always be
frightened of the/poor/for there is no such thing as the/have-nots/just the
want everything you have/more' (pp.21–2). Yet even there the division is
unworkable, the attempt to construct an Other who can be held at arm's length
eroded by eros:

and still they kept arriving
in the wrong part of town
and of the millions submitted
still one with a wilder roar
who kept on turning up
at their safe front door
they found them stretched out on their garden chairs
lying with their women
now what shall we do with the crossbreeds
you know what happens when you crossthread
the top just won't stay on

(p.6)

Racial difference is a topic in the river's story, the distinguishing mark by which racist injustice discriminates, but it is not seen as important in itself. The things that matter are the ethical questions: 'thinking black and white/could lose you your health/for Wise is a river flows clear/or flows red/and acres of poppies/does nothing for her head' (p.11). The distinctions that remain are between the exploiters and the exploited, war and capitalism as they affect the environment and people's lives, with the children as the ultimate symbol of innocent suffering. The political project, though the product of institutionalised racism in the past, is no longer confinable to categorised racial difference; as Paul Gilroy notes, there is a need to contribute to 'the politics of a new century in which the central axis of conflict will no longer be the colour line but the challenge of just, sustainable development and the frontiers which will separate the overdeveloped parts of the world (at home and abroad) from the intractable poverty that already surrounds them'.[20]

Gender rather than race becomes the predominant site of symbolic expression in Breeze's poem. The colour of blood recurs, and the grand metaphor is one of rape; the abused natural world cries out with the mermaids,

man shall not enter again
his penetration has caused great pain
all for his living in vain
. forgetting the balance he found when he came
forgetting that creation was god itself
confirming himself as the head
giving over the land to the dead
striking off starwars instead

(p.18)

Patriarchy stands accused of the ills of the world, in opposition to the poem's presiding female consciousness. Like Walcott's ubiquitous and Protean persona Omeros, Wise travels from third world to first and back again, from country to town, from outside to interior, from river to sea, vaporising to sky, falling again as rain, flowing as electricity, being piped and pumped and pressured, and sinking underground: 'that's why there are some days/when truth cannot be found'.

For Wise may be seen as truth: the embodiment of the raised consciousness which has demystified the systems that institute the macro-rape of exploitation, and has uncovered the myths by which the rape is represented as benign. The world of hegemonic power is shown, in an inset monologue of 'us' and 'them', deciding to track down and destroy Wise, who is stirring unrest:

> with all our resources
> we still can't find source
> it must be an image
> or maybe a pun
> they've got many poets
> they're just poking fun
> the educated ones have learned our sarcasm
> and our poorer trash are getting out of order
> electing a playwright for president
> it's a lucky thing their governments
> find artists so dissident

> (p.7)

But the target is not only the rich world; the patriarchy of the two-thirds world also comes under attack, with its barefoot revolutionary who delivers only death, and the treacherous lover who abandons, particularly the one who abandons the black woman for the white:

> she'd been talking
> of race
> she'd been talking
> of class
> now gender got heavy
> as lead

> (p.25)

But after a passage in which Wise is transformed into a figure of nemesis, she regains her nurturing persona 'for the children's love had to be saved' (p.25), and the poem ends in an upbeat lyrical evocation of the dawning of a new day. 'A River Called Wise' is an attack on all the abuses of power which characterise the modern world, but it is also a celebration of the miraculous nature of life and the possibility of improvement. It is epic in its scope, and in that fine balance between the honest representation of the tragic and the assertion of the open-endedness of possibilities.

Both Walcott and Breeze subvert the epic tradition with its politics of dominance, using gender as the site of radical transformation through which to model the possibility of benign societies. They affirm, from their different textual mythologising, the potential of Dantean redemptive comedy in life as well as fiction, and specifically address the trauma of black history. But in Breeze's poem, because it is a woman's voice which is speaking, as well as a non-human female persona which pervades the poem, the womanist narration encompasses and embraces the suffering world, as if to show in a textual dynamic that compassion is greater than tyranny – as if Breeze's voice were that of Ma Kilman. The hope is that the sociopolitical world might operate under a similar dynamic; if the meaning of a genre can be remodelled, it would seem, other apparently intractable cultural and social practices might also be reformed.

NOTES

1. W. Macneile Dixon, *English Epic and Heroic Poetry* (London, Macmillan, 1912), cited in *The Epic: Developments in Criticism*, ed. R.P. Draper (Basingstoke, Macmillan, 1990), pp.104–5, p.102.
2. Cited by Dixon, see Draper, *The Epic*, pp.92–3.
3. Jameson relates the standard critical position: 'In literature ... the disappearance of genres as such, along with their conventions and the distinct reading rules they project, is a familiar story.' (Fredric Jameson, *Postmodernism*, London, Verso, 1991, p.371.) His analysis of the postmodern situation in relation to genres sees them migrating 'like viruses' which have 'colonized reality itself', but does not investigate the possibility of their transformation from within.
4. Other Caribbean writers have experimented with versions of epic, among them Andrew Salkey with his poem *Jamaica* (London, Hutchinson, 1973); there is also a nineteenth-century literary epic *Hiroona* by Horatio Nelson Huggins (see Paula Burnett (ed.), *Caribbean Verse in English*, London, Penguin, 1986), but Breeze is the first to work within a specifically oral style (although it does not display the formulaic signs typical of traditional oral epic), and the first woman to use epic.
5. For accounts of oral epic and the relationship between orality and literacy, see Ruth Finnegan, *Oral Poetry: Its Nature, Significance, and Social Context* (Cambridge, Cambridge University Press, 1977); Walter Ong, *Orality and Literacy: The Technologizing Of The Word* (London, Routledge, 1982); Milman Parry, *The Making of Homeric Verse*, ed. Adam Parry (Oxford, Clarendon Press, 1971).
6. In the Christian tradition such scapegoating is reinforced by representations of the *Genesis* story, both in the Bible and elsewhere, in which Eve is singled out as to blame for the Fall.
7. For Cixous' qualification of her term *écriture féminine* specifically in relation to the male author, see 'Le Sexe ou la Tête?', *Les Cahiers du GRIF*, 13, 1976, trans. Annette Kuhn; 'Castration or Decapitation?', *Signs*, 7.1, p.52, cited in Toril Moi, *Sexual/Texual Politics: Feminist Literary Theory* (London and New York, Routledge, 1985), p.108.
8. The place of the black male writer in a world of binary oppositions is ambivalent; unlike the black woman who can claim to be at the opposite, 'innocent' pole from white patriarchy, he is racially on one side of a great divide, but genderwise on another. Alice Walker pinpoints the central difficulty: 'It

is possible that white male writers are more conscious of their own evil (which, after all, has been documented for several centuries – in words and in the ruin of the land, the earth) than black male writers, who, along with black and white women, have seen themselves as the recipients of that evil and therefore on the side of Christ, of the oppressed, of the innocent.' ('From An Interview', in *In Search Of Our Mother's Gardens*, New York, 1983, London, The Women's Press, 1984, p.251) Her implicit criticism is that others, particularly black women, may not see them entirely as they see themselves.

9. An example is Elaine Savory Fido, 'Macho Attitudes and Derek Walcott', *Journal of Commonwealth Literature*, 21.1 (1986), p.109, reprinted in Dennis Walder (ed.), *Literature in the Modern World* (London, Oxford University Press and The Open University, 1990), p.288.

10. Hélène Cixous, quoted in Moi, *Sexual/Textual Politics*, p.109.

11. Robert Graves, *The White Goddess* (revised edn, London, Faber, 1961) and *The Greek Myths* (revised edn, London, Penguin, 1960) passim.

12. Albert Memmi, *The Colonizer and the Colonized*, 1957, trans. Howard Greenfield (London, Earthscan Publications, 1990), p.137.

13. Memmi, *The Colonizer*, p.156.

14. Local postcards from the turn of the century to the interwar period feature the loading of the coal as a local 'sight' (I am indebted to Robin Hanford for his assistance in securing copies of examples from the St Lucia Library Service collection). Walcott mentions the scene in 'Leaving School' (*London Magazine*, Vol.5, No.6, 1965, p.8), in 'The Glory Trumpeter' (*The Castaway*, London, Cape, 1965), and in *Another Life* (London, Cape, 1973), as well as in *Omeros* (New York, Farrar, Straus and Giroux; London, Faber and Faber, 1990).

15. The most perceptive analysis to date of the cultural politics of Walcott's use of intertextuality in *Omeros* is David Hoegberg's 'The Anarchist's Mirror: Walcott's *Omeros* and the Epic Tradition' (*Commonwealth*, 17.2, 1995, p.67). Hoegberg does not, however, focus specifically on gender.

16. The first performance was at the Commonwealth Institute, London, on 3 April 1993; the second was on 14 November 1993 in the Purcell Room, the South Bank, London, as part of the 'Out of the Margins' festival (11–14 November) to celebrate African, South Asian and Caribbean writers in Britain. References are to the page numbers of the typescript of the poem supplied by the author.

17. See Alice Walker, *In Search Of Our Mothers' Gardens* (New York, Harcourt Brace Jovanovich 1983; London, The Women's Press, 1984), p.xi.

18. Jean Binta Breeze in conversation with Paula Burnett.

19. The River Wise persona is probably also informed by a figure from West African myth, known in Nigeria as Mamee Water, a benign female divinity associated with water, to whom Breeze alludes elsewhere in her poetry.

20. Paul Gilroy, *The Black Atlantic* (London, Verso, 1993), p.223.

FURTHER READING

Bakhtin, M.M., 'Epic and Novel', in *The Dialogic Imagination*, ed. Michael Holquist, trans. Caryl Emerson and Michael Holquist (Austin, University of Texas Press, 1981).

Brathwaite, Edward Kamau, *The History of the Voice: The Development of Nation Language in Anglophone Caribbean Poetry* (London, Port of Spain, New Beacon Books, 1984).

Brathwaite, [Edward] Kamau, 'A Post-Cautionary Tale of the Helen of our Wars', *Wasafiri* 22 (1995), pp.69–78.

Breeze, Jean Binta, *Riddym Ravings and Other Poems* (London, Race Today Publications, 1988).

Breeze, Jean Binta, *Spring Cleaning* (London, Virago, 1992).

Brown, Lloyd, *Caribbean Poetry* (London, Heinemann, 1978, 2nd edn, 1984).

Brown, Stewart (ed.), *The Art of Derek Walcott* (Bridgend, Mid-Glamorgan, Seren Books; Chester Springs, Pennsylvania, Dufour Editions, 1991).

Brown, Stewart (ed.), *The Art of Kamau Brathwaite* (Bridgend, Mid-Glamorgan, Seren Books; Chester Springs, Pennsylvania, Dufour Editions, 1995).

Burnett, Paula (ed.), *Caribbean Verse in English* (London, Penguin, 1986).

Chamberlin, J. Edward, *Come Back To Me My Language: Poetry and the West Indies* (Toronto, McClelland and Stewart, 1993).

Cooper, Carolyn, 'Words unbroken by the beat: the performance poetry of Jean Binta Breeze and Mikey Smith', *Wasafiri* 11 (1989), 7–13 (reprinted in Cooper, below).

Cooper, Carolyn, *Noises in the Blood: Orality, Gender and the 'Vulgar' Body of Jamaican Popular Culture* (London, Macmillan, 1994).

Cudjoe, Selwyn (ed.), *Caribbean Women Writers* (Wellesley, Massachussetts, Calaloux Publications, 1990).

Draper, R.P. (ed.), *The Epic: Developments in Criticism* (Basingstoke, Macmillan, 1990).

Finnegan, Ruth, *Oral Poetry: Its Nature, Significance and Social Context* (Cambridge, Cambridge University Press, 1977).

Gilroy, Paul, *The Black Atlantic* (London, Verso, 1993).

Glaser, Marlies, and Marion Pausch (eds), *Caribbean Writers: Between Orality and Writing*, Matatu 12 (Amsterdam and Atlanta, Georgia, Rodopi, 1994).

Habekost, Christian, *Verbal Riddim: The Politics and Aesthetics of African-Caribbean Dub Poetry* (Amsterdam and Atlanta, Georgia, Rodopi, 1993).

Hamner, Robert, *Derek Walcott* (Boston, Twayne, 1981; rev. edn 1994).

Hoegberg, David, 'The Anarchist's Mirror: Walcott's *Omeros* and the Epic Tradition', *Commonwealth*, 17.2 (1995), pp.67–81.

Jameson, Fredric, *Postmodernism* (London, Verso, 1991).

Memmi, Albert, *The Colonizer and the Colonized* (1957), trans. Howard Greenfield (London, Earthscan Publications, 1990).

Moi, Toril, *Sexual/Texual Politics: Feminist Literary Theory* (London and New York, Routledge, 1985).

Mordecai, Pamela, and Wilson, Betty (eds), *Her True-True Name: an Anthology of Women's Writing from the Caribbean* (Oxford, Heinemann, 1989).

Narain, Denise deCaires, and O'Callaghan, Evelyn, 'Anglophone Caribbean Women Writers', in *Post-Colonial Women's Writing*,' Shirley Chew and Anna Rutherford (eds) (Mundelstrup, Denmark and Hebden Bridge, Dangaroo, 1994).

O'Callaghan, Evelyn, *Woman Version: Theoretical Approaches to West Indian Fiction by Women* (London, Macmillan, 1993).

Ong, Walter, *Orality and Literacy: The Technologizing Of The Word* (London, Routledge, 1982).

Parry, Milman, *The Making of Homeric Verse*, ed. Adam Parry (Oxford, Clarendon, 1971).

Rohlehr, Gordon, 'The Shape of that Hurt', Introduction to *Voiceprint: An Anthology of Oral and Related Poetry from the Caribbean*, Stewart Brown, Mervyn Morris, Gordon Rohlehr (eds), (Harlow, Longman, 1989).

Salkey, Andrew, *Jamaica* (London, Hutchinson, 1973).

Terada, Rei, *Derek Walcott's Poetry: American Mimicry* (Boston, Northeastern University Press, 1992).

Walcott, Derek, 'Leaving School', *London Magazine*, Vol. 5, No. 6 (1965), p.8.

Walcott, Derek, *Collected Poems 1948–1984* (New York, Farrar, Straus and Giroux; and London, Faber and Faber, 1986).

Walcott, Derek, *Omeros* (New York, Farrar, Straus and Giroux; and London, Faber and Faber, 1990).

Walcott, Derek, *The Antilles: Fragments of Epic Memory* (London, Faber and Faber, 1992; reprinted *World Literature Today*, 67.2, 1993, 261–71).

Walker, Alice, *In Search of Our Mothers' Gardens* (New York, Harcourt Braus Jovanovich, 1983; London, The Women's Press, 1984).

Section Four: The Body

These three chapters focus on female bodies and the challenges presented by their textual representation in poetry. They explore the subversive potential of representations of body forms: both as a challenge to right-wing ideas of 'normality' and as the eruption of the unsettlingly physical into cerebral debate.

Cath Stowers explores Sylvia Plath's representations of the female body. She acknowledges the anxiety, disgust and shame that often accompany these depictions, but argues it is time to move away from the dominant critical perception of 'Plath as victim'. Instead, reading from a post-Structuralist perspective, she identifies a continual oscillation between such anxiety and a more confident, knowing embrace of the possibilities of the body's representation. Drawing on the theories of Hélène Cixous and Luce Irigaray, and following their political project to reinscribe the female body, she interprets Plath's diverse female forms as a deliberate and strategic tease. Their theatrical presentation signals the poet's perception of femininity as performance, and parodies the idea of the self as a stable entity. Stowers reads Plath as a precursor of what she calls contemporary women writers' 'emancipatory strategies' that reclaim the power of female bodies and at the same time undercut essentialist arguments about the body's innate 'meaning'.

Gabriele Griffin focuses on Jackie Kay's volume of poetry, *The Adoption Papers*. She argues that 'the question of visibility – what you see – and semantics – what it means' are crucial to a full understanding of the collection. She explores this theme as it is articulated in the poems and also in terms of the circumstances of their reception, arguing that the way in which they are read is to some extent influenced by where they are published. Kay's poems explore the lives and desires of those labelled as 'deviant': lesbians, gay men, people infected with the HIV virus. She examines what society accepts as 'normal' and healthy from this outsider's perspective, in order to reveal the violence and hypocrisy of this apparently desirable norm. Griffin argues that Kay is not seeking incorporation into the mainstream; it is precisely by remaining on the outside that these poems can challenge so-called 'normality' and reveal its oppressions most effectively.

Karin Voth Harman considers questions raised by recent anthologies of birth poetry. She asks how critics can respond to such confessional, personal and physical material – hardly beloved of traditional literary criticism, nor indeed of feminist readers. Rather than reacting with suspicion, she believes we should welcome this poetry since it offers an alternative perspective to that of the medical profession, whose versions of the female body have drowned out women's experience for too long. Voth Harman examines the language women poets are using to explore these powerful physical experiences. She argues that the use of metaphor in birth poetry is less effective than in theoretical writing, since it tends to 'lose sight of the flesh' once more. Instead she examines the effect of the poets' use of more literal, metonymic imagery, suggesting that this focus on the literal body is a way of combatting the colonisation of birth and motherhood. In the poems she finds evidence of the mother's fierce struggle to preserve a sense of self and subjectivity in the face of the tremendous physical assault of birth: evidence, at last, of the mother who writes.

10

Sylvia Plath's Revolutionary Wieldings
of the Female Body

Cath Stowers

> Until dream takes her body
> From bed to strict tryouts
> In tightrope acrobatics[1]

This chapter came out of an attempt to rethink what has been a long and close relationship with the work of Sylvia Plath. Becoming aware of how, in the past, I had concentrated on Plath's expression of that female 'anxiety of authorship' documented by Sandra Gilbert and Susan Gubar,[2] I found it increasingly difficult to reconcile such arguments with my work on contemporary women's writing. On the one hand I was highlighting Plath as a particularly powerful illustration of the suppression of the woman writer. On the other I was now claiming that it was precisely this focusing on repression which feminist literary criticism needed to move on from. I was arguing that the negative connotations which had gripped feminist literary criticism for so long were now, in the work of contemporary women writers, outweighed by aspects of freedom and escape; of re-writing and re-inventing; of re-figuring identity: but how did such claims relate to Plath's work? Was it simply a case of straightforward historical progression, with Plath the epitome of the suppressed woman writer, the mad woman in the attic, who had now evolved into the new figure of the emancipated, playful, radical woman writing today?

For me, the simplicity of such a 'before and after' formula and the suggestion that Plath should be left behind in some linear history of women's writing beggared belief. As I worked through this discomfort, so I found myself moving to an increasing emphasis on Plath's positive and deliberate strategies of subversion and escape from the earlier documented 'anxiety of authorship'. I hope here to trace this trajectory, to follow Plath's flight as a woman writer, to highlight her parody and playacting, her portrayals, through descriptions of the body, of a playfully plural self. Consequently, this chapter will move from an examination of the fear, shame and disgust at woman's body expressed in Plath's work to a consideration of the increasingly varying applications of the female form. Above all, I hope to suggest not so much a resolution or linear solution as a tension and dialectic. For, no matter how strong my resistance to criticism which erases any distinction between Plath and her autobiography, the question remains: if she found a permanent solution, why did she finish as she did? I hope to show how the range, the multiplicity of Plath's portrayals of the female body, represent an aesthetic of eternal movement, a tug of war between two poles which never really escaped its contradictions.

I shall be utilising, firstly, theories on women's autobiographical writings. To my mind, Plath's work has especially suffered from a scavenging for glimpses of some supposedly 'genuine self', with readers spellbound by the knowledge of her suicide and critics often dismissing her work as simply the transcription of a damaged personality.[3] Consequently, I am by no means suggesting that her work be reduced to nothing more than her 'autobiography'. Rather, I aim to follow Celeste Schenck's arguments that women's poetry and autobiography often share a similar concern with 'subject formation'.[4] Poetry as autobiography, Schenck continues, 'constitutes a potential space' where the woman writer may be 'repeatedly and repeatably present to herself during the act of utterance'.[5] This paper aims in particular to illustrate the ways in which the female body becomes used by Plath in images of 'hyper-self-assertion' which refuse and deflate any essential, unitary selfhood.[6]

I will also be calling on the work of French feminist writers, especially Hélène Cixous and Luce Irigaray. Arguments about the pros and cons of theories of *l'écriture feminine* are too lengthy to cover here. I hope it will suffice to say that, given that this essay concerns itself with Plath's re-presentations of the female body, I will be utilising work on *l'écriture feminine* as a major source of inquiry into the question of how woman's body and female sexuality have been represented and they should or could be re-written. It is not my intention to impose any single monolithic framework and it is, of course, vital to acknowledge the greatly differing critical, historical and political orientations of Plath and these theorists.[7] Nonetheless, I believe plausible links can be traced between the arguments of writers such as Cixous and Irigaray and Plath's re-workings of the female body. As such, I am simply using the theories as useful conceptual paradigms.

Cixous has argued, for example, that writing can enable women to re-appropriate their bodies, usurped for so long by male portrayals and male gazes; a woman can 'write to give the body its Books of the Future'.[8] At times Plath produces images of the female form that do indeed shatter the fixity of what is, for her, a threatening phallic order. It is not, then, a question of Plath simply not figuring solutions; more a question of a rise and plunge between the negative bodily images I will first be considering, and the more positive shape shiftings I will move on to discuss. However, I am not suggesting that she simply moved from one to the other, leaving the pole of negativity behind. I hope to suggest three movements in Plath's writings: one of negativity; one more positive; and one of the tension between the two. Wanting to highlight the flux of Plath's poetics, this movement between two positions which never finally settles, I will conclude with a suggestion that woman's body – and indeed subjectivity itself – becomes refigured as a fluid, quicksilver paradigm.

Virginia Woolf made clear the contradictions between female corporeality and poetic creation, wondering 'who shall measure the heat and violence of the poet's heart when caught and tangled in a woman's body?'.[9] More recently, Sidonie Smith has argued that any woman who follows the male traditions and demands of male autobiographical writings will have to assure the reader that she has successfully escaped the burden of the body and the polluting, infecting effects of female sexuality.[10] The consequent uneasiness which Smith claims the female autobiographer will feel towards her own body is indeed clearly articulated in Plath's work. Woman's body is frequently presented as an object of abhorrence and disgust, a rawness which in 'Street Song' must be hidden, so that:

> Nobody blinks a lid, gapes,
> Or cries that this raw flesh
> Reeks of the butcher's cleaver.

> (*CP*, pp.35–6)

In 'The Bee Meeting', the female form is exposed and vulnerable in a 'sleeveless summery dress' that offers 'no protection', whilst in 'Poem For A Birthday' that body so incompatible with poetic creation is secreted away, disguised, with Plath inhabiting a 'wax image of myself, a doll's body' (*CP*, p.135). Elsewhere, the body becomes something to be cleansed, purified by a hot bath in *The Bell Jar*, or erased as sign of femaleness in 'Tulips': 'And I have no face, I have wanted to efface myself' (*CP*, p.161). Abandoning and disowning her woman's body, Plath writes of how she has 'given . . ./my body to surgeons'. In *The Bell Jar* Esther desperately tries to escape her corporeality in her suicide attempts but: '. . . saw that my body had all sorts of little tricks . . . I would simply have to ambush it with whatever sense I had left, or it would trap me in its stupid cage . . .'.[11]

If the female body does become locus of creativity, source of human life or literary creation, it can often only threaten loss or leakage as in 'Three Women' – 'And what if two lives leaked between my thighs?' (*CP*, p.180) – or birth the stunted, malformed poems of 'Stillborn' which 'do not live' (*CP*, p.142). In poems such as these, woman's body becomes reduced to 'a wound walking out of hospital' (*CP*, p.184); that 'Fat and red' 'placenta' symbolising her mother in 'Medusa' (*CP*, p.225); or the 'red meat' of 'Death and Co.' which in *The Bell Jar* 'hung the raw, red screen' of eyelids and 'their tiny vessels in front of me like a wound' (*BJ*, p.130). Plath repeatedly renders woman's body in terms of blood, whether the sign of sterility of 'Childless Woman', 'uttering nothing but blood'; the signifier of suffering as in Esther's haemorrhaging in *The Bell Jar* where 'every beat' of her heart 'pushed forth another gush of blood' (*BJ*, p.244); or the mark of failure to escape the body in 'Suicide Off Egg Rock', where blood is 'beating the old tattoo/I am, I am, I am'. As object of torture, suffering is frequently inflicted on this all-too-female body where in 'Tulips' the 'smiles' of 'husband and child' only 'catch onto my skin, little smiling hooks' (*CP*, p.254). Held captive and confined by nature, a male figure, disease and death, the female form is gagged by wind and mist, racked and screwed, wrapped like a mummy, shocked and sizzled by electricity, its tongue stuck in a barbed wire snare.

There is, I believe, considerable continuity here with Cixous' claim that women 'haven't dared enjoy' their 'colonized' bodies, have perhaps 'internalized' the male fear of that 'dark continent' of woman's body and sexuality.[12] This horror felt at the female form becomes transposed to Plath's blood-soaked malignant universe, itself often imaged in particularly corporeal terms where 'trees stiffen into place like burnt nerves' (*CP*, p.151) and the 'redness' of tulips 'talks to my wound, it corresponds' (*CP*, p.161). I aim now, however, to show how this hatred of woman's body, this fear of the incompatibility of woman's body and woman's literary creation, becomes transformed at other times into a celebration of the female form as a source of writing. Realising that disguise can wither, that the 'mummy-case' of 'In Plaster' could 'cover my mouth and eyes, cover me entirely' (*CP*, p.159), Plath fulfils Cixous' demand that woman must 'kill the false woman who is preventing the live one from breathing. Inscribe the breath of the whole woman.'[13] Abandoning the 'cool calm' voice which in *The Bell Jar* concealed 'the zombie' which 'rose up in my throat' (*BJ*, p.133), Plath regurgitates false masks. An illustration of Cixous' feminine text which is 'an outpouring' like 'vomiting', 'disgorging', the body becomes a source of expulsion – expulsion, often, of writing.[14] It is not my aim to collapse Plath's texts into some autobiographical whole (so much has been made of Plath as autobiography), yet strikingly *Letters Home* here almost exactly replicates *The Bell Jar* and Cixous, as Plath writes of how she tries to 'spew out those thoughts which are like the blocked putridity in my head', of how she is 'overflowing with ideas and inspirations, as if I've been bottling up a geyser for a year. Once I start writing, it comes and comes . . .'.[15]

Continuing along this vein, the pulsing sub-text of blood in Plath's work can be read as representing more that just the seepage of suffering figured in the 'red plush' of 'Cut'. It is, I suggest, open to an alternative interpretation, whereby it can be viewed as a possible example of Gagnon's call for women to 'let the blood flow, from the inside'.[16] In this sense, Plath's proclamation in 'Kindness' that: 'The blood jet is poetry/There is no stopping it' (*CP*, p.270) could be said to parallel Cixous' equation of feminine writing and blood whereby 'silent words in all the veins of my life have translated themselves into mad blood, into joy-blood'.[17] Woman's body becomes the locus of subversive streaming: that writing which, for Cixous, 'circulates inside me. Like blood', as Plath seemingly anticipates Anaïs Nin's demand that 'woman's creation . . . must come out of her own blood'.[18] Poetry here comes forth from the body like Cixous' 'word of blood, which will not cease'.[19] Plath's blood-shot and bleeding texts quicken the pulse, an example of Cixous' feminine writing which demands:

> . . . the form that stops the least, that encloses the least, the body without a frame, without skin, without walls, the flesh that doesn't dry, doesn't stiffen, doesn't clot the wild blood that wants to steam through it – forever.[20]

Fulfilling Cixous' call for women to 'take infinite pleasure in your bodies',[21] Plath's poetry makes woman's body highly adaptable. Her prolific portrayals and performances now produce potency. Above all, the female form is wielded as a metamorphosing multiplicity, utilised in Plath's explorations of a variety of different speaking positions. It can become compressible and contractile, shape shifting in 'Poem For A Birthday' into 'all mouth' or 'one stone eye' (*CP*, p.131–6). Atrophic enough to 'sit in a flowerpot' (*CP*, p.131), it shrinks into inanimate objects such as a grain of rice: 'Sitting under a potlid, tiny and inert' (*CP*, p.135), or 'a root, a stone, an owl pellet' (*CP*, p.132). Yet this body also changes further from that burrowed in the marrowy tunnels at the 'bowel of the root', the 'nobody' who had 'nothing to do with explosions' (*CP*, p.160). Instead, stripping the artificial order of her earlier poems, Plath demands of their dessiccating formalism 'Give me back my shape' (*CP*, p.136) and re-appropriates her body. Throwing off the mask – the 'skin' of 'Face Lift' that 'doesn't have roots' but 'peels away easy as paper' (*CP*, p.156) – she exclaims 'Oh, I cry out against it. I am I – I/am powerful' (*CP*, p.62). Reclaimed and revealed, the female body is displayed as defiantly as Godiva's, 'stepping from this skin/Of old bandages, boredoms, old faces' (*CP*, p.249) – a 'White/Godiva, I unpeel' (*CP*, p.239). Is this revelation, then, subsequent to the trope of the body as blood, as wound and so forth, or is it felt more as a contradiction, a to and fro? I hope to stress not so much a resolution, a progression, as constant movement between opposing poles.

Frequently the nakedness revealed in Plath's poems is ugly and horrific, an attempt to break out of that prison of ideals constructed by male idolatry of woman's body. Thus in 'Lady Lazarus', instead of the usual sexual performance with stripped-away scarves, Plath displays a stark cadaver; instead of a titillating revelation of flesh, only 'skin and bone' and 'eye pits' (*CP*, p.244). Playing the role of the traditional monster woman in mocking self-parody, like Irigaray's theatrical staging of the mime, miming the miming imposed on women, Plath undoes the effects of phallocentric discourse by overdoing them.[22] As Christina Britzolakis has argued, the striptease artist becomes a parody of the performing poet, of the staging of autobiography; and the appearance of femininity is exposed as part of the masculine literary tradition to be confronted with sexual difference.[23] Just as in *The Bell Jar* Plath rejects the traditional role of femininity, refusing to keep up appearances and to anoint, decorate or worship the feminine body, so in the poems that body may instead become something to shock and horrify:

> Out of the ash
> I rise with my red hair
> And I eat men like air.

> (*CP*, p.247)

The female body in these poems seems to figure Cixous' 'gestation of self . . . in itself, atrocious. When the flesh tears, writhes, rips apart, decomposes, revives, recognizes itself as a newly born woman.'[24] Metamorphosed by rage, the female form becomes the 'lion-red body' of 'Stings', a 'red/Scar in the sky, red comet' (*CP*, p.215), the harem wife in 'Purdah' revealing herself as a Clytemnestra to her unsuspecting husband, the plaster of concealment ripped away, the body escaping from 'the wax house', the bell jar, the cellar, the 'mausoleum' (*CP*, p.215).

So, Plath's own body frequently seems to become the starting point for her imaginative autonomy, to be manipulated as a psychic and physical space or re-invented in new forms. Repossession thus becomes, as Adrienne Rich argues, an assertion of the female poet's activity and an exercise of the artist's power to reshape the nature given to her into free forms of energy and desire.[25] Hence woman's body can become a new agent of apocalypse and revelation. Plath takes over the task of resurrection and becomes her own miracle in 'Face Lift', 'Mother to myself', re-birthing that new body 'Pink and smooth as a baby' (*CP*, p.156). In 'Fever 103°' the body is purged, rising at the end in erotic, orgasmic transcendence as a lethal 'acetylene virgin', head 'a moon/Of Japanese paper' and 'gold beaten skin' too pure and too hot for any man's touch (*CP*, p.232). In 'Getting There',

Plath makes a birth out of the bloodshed, raising the dead like a Mother-God, her body a divine medium for human salvation from history. Plath does not, however, simply repossess her body from the old usurpation; in the flight to revelation in 'Ariel', she becomes the presiding genius of her own form. Proclaiming 'I/Am the arrow' (*CP*, p.239), woman's body is now, to quote Cixous, 'going out ahead': '... as an arrow quits the bow with a movement that gathers and separates the vibrations musically, in order to be more than her self.'[26] Released and reinvented, woman's body becomes an active agent of that feminine writing Cixous has further characterised as 'tearing away, dizzying flight and flinging oneself'.[27]

But if I am speaking of an increasing revelation of the body as part of a struggling self-expression, isn't there a danger of suggesting that this represents some revelation of a 'true self'? My arguments are emphatically not designed to produce a swing back to those notions of 'the self' as a biological or psychological essentialism which have been so prominent in much criticism of Plath. Rather I am suggesting an increasing utilisation of the female body as part of wider strategies of active autobiographical creation and re-creation. Plath's poetry does, I believe, produce new inscriptions of the female body which become linked with the expression of a dispersed, multiple subjectivity: the female form used to record Schenck's 'negotiation of the female self-*in-process*'.[28] It is a drastic reduction of Plath's skills, range and imagination to assume that the depiction of two or more selves is only a prelude to schizophrenia, falseness, or death. Rather, she tries on several provisional and often contradictory guises to flaunt the mutable nature of her body and consciousness, cultivating various poses and positions from which to speak, and parodying the way feminine subjectivity is produced and managed. Plath's articulations through body language of a multiple subjectivity can surely also partly be read as a parody of the fictional construct of 'the self' in autobiography. As the performing poet enacting a theatrical show, she illustrates Nancy Miller's arguments on 'the production of the female self as theatre', the woman writer performing on 'the stage of her text'.[29] Exaggerating Patricia Spacks' claim that autobiography commits one 'to performing one's changing selfhood in public', Plath remodels her body endlessly in a continuous play of appearances with performance and intoxication feeding off each other.[30] The re-workings of the body parallel the reworkings of 'the self' which autobiography's recollections of the past necessitate, giving expression to Mary McCarthy's argument that although 'it's absolutely useless' to look for the self on some autobiographical quest, 'it's possible in some sense to make it'.[31]

'I am', writes Plath in *Letters Home*, 'making a self, in great pain, often, as for a birth'.[32] Utilising her body she can become 'my studious self' with 'my brown hair' or 'the blonde one' with the 'creative flood'.[33] Such reworkings do, however, form Plath's admission that any attempted literary shaping of the self will, by definition, be unfinished and inadequate, and the shape shifting of woman's body is matched only by the flexibility of the I: 'I break up in pieces that fly about like clubs' (*CP*, p.192). The particularly self-conscious performances of poems using body language such as 'Lady Lazarus', 'Purdah' and 'Fever 103° ' thereby replace any fixed identity. Questions, theatrical acts, shape shifting and disappearances become Plath's forte, confounding any search for a precise revelation of either her 'genuine self' or of the poems' perfection of woman's image. She herself writes, after all, of how 'I sometimes wonder who is me',[34] the suggestions of the mutable self which it is impossible to define anticipating Cixous' theories of the possibilities for women's self-creation. In this respect, then, woman's body almost becomes Cixous' 'spacious singing Flesh: onto which is grafted no one knows which I'.[35]

Having little need for resolution or closure, Plath thus explores all the dramatic possibilities of the self. In her mercurial consciousness she allows no single state to predominate, describing mobility, not final choice, between the points of stasis and animation, passivity and theatrical display. As such, it is perhaps the image of the mercurial female body which best epitomises its position in her aesthetic. Irigaray has argued that woman as body/matter acts as the material from which the mirror is made enabling man to see his own reflection wherever he looks. Consequently, women are denied any mirror for becoming women, whilst simultaneously reminded of their sex at every turn in the great cultural hall of mirrors.[36] In 'All The Dead Dears', Plath writes of a mirror which seemingly only reflects femininity, a femininity which sucks her in and could reduce her to nothing:

> From the mercury-backed glass
> Mother, grandmother, greatgrandmother
> Reach hag hands to haul me in.

> (*CP*, p.70)

On the one hand, the mirror seems to be inhabited by these female figures with 'hag hands'. On the other, the mirror appears to produce the beginning of a possible solution and healing, the possibility of the innovative image of the self offered by mercury's silver globe.[37] Sidonie Smith has written of how the woman autobiographer seeks to 'shatter the portrait of herself' which hangs in 'the textual frames of patriarchy',[38] and interestingly Plath's writings frequently figure that 'disturbance in mirrors' of 'Couriers' (*CP*, p.247). This, then, is far from the creation of that unified subjectivity of Lacan's mirror phase; Plath is unconcerned with desperately protecting the reflected image against any division or disintegration. Appropriating the mirror and the mirrored body, asserting fragmentation and multiplicity, her poems perhaps practise Irigaray's claim that: 'That "elsewhere" of feminine pleasure can be found only at the price of *crossing back through the mirror that subtends all speculation*.'[39] Exploring that space beyond the mirror which defies the defined image of woman – the mirror's 'flux of silver' (*CP*, p.95), the body's orgasmic 'ripples of silver' (*CP*, p.268) – becomes a significant motive in Plath's aesthetic. Giving back distortions in *The Bell Jar* 'like the reflection in a ball of dentist's mercury' (*BJ*, p.20), allowing no stabilised image of the self, that silver at the back of the mirror which reflects only the patriarchal gaze becomes refigured as a nitrate of mimicry and masquerade. Woman's body can 'gleam like a mirror' in 'Purdah' (*CP*, p.242), but as it is reflected 'The image/Flees and aborts like dropped mercury' (*CP*, p.252). Thus in *The Bell Jar* that 'idealistic and beautiful' image of herself which Esther erected in her mind and which 'insinuates itself between me and the merciless mirror' (*BJ*, p.161) can return as 'a big, smudgy-eyed Chinese woman', 'a sick Indian' (*BJ*, p.118) or a 'stranger' who 'puts on a public grin' (*BJ*, p.24). Writing the body finally shatters the deadly specularity of the patriarchal mirror into that fluid quicksilver shape shifting of mercury's 'silver globe' which Esther so gleefully observes in *The Bell Jar*:

> If I dropped it, it would break into a million little replicas of itself, and if I pushed them near each other, they would fuse, without a crack, into one whole again.
> I smiled and smiled at the small silver ball.

(*BJ*, p.194)

From being simply an image to be consumed, the woman writer is illustrated as reclaiming her own body and becoming both producer and consumer of images. From being the object of male gazes, representations and fears, woman's body is re-appropriated as subject, rediscovered in its female specificity as source or feature of discursive practice in a reversal of that traditional mind/body dichotomy. Too much criticism – and, interestingly, Susan Brownmiller's work on women and rape[40] – has placed her in a tradition of female victimhood. I hope I have shown how she can be firmly situated in an alternative tradition, a tradition of women's writing which relishes emancipatory movements and displays of the female form. This tradition today includes writers such as Angela Carter, Michèle Roberts, Jeanette Winterson and, like them, Plath wields the body as a tool of narrative disclosure. Although she clearly cannot be placed with such contemporary post-modern writers without qualification, she can, I believe, be viewed as an early precursor similarly suggesting an articulation of subjectivity and representations opposed to phallocentric discourses. Disrupting the figure of (male) unitary selfhood, interrupting gendered logic, Plath ultimately portrays woman's body in and for herself, in assertions of independent creative powers. Expressing Annie Leclerc's 'multiple celebrations' of the body,[41] women's poetry is here established as a site of difference where phallocentric concepts which censure or erase woman's otherness can be challenged and deconstructed. As Arleen B. Dallery has argued, writing of the body is 'both constative and performative':

> It signifies those bodily territories that have been kept under seal; it figures the body. But, writing the body is also a performative utterance; the feminine libidinal economy inscribes itself in language.[42]

Plath is, I believe, one such writer whose re-presentations of the body overcome traditional received notions of femininity, flesh out freer texts, and give body to a new body of women's writing. In this way, Irigaray's multiplicity of libidinal energies can indeed become part of women's poetry's project, and Woolf's prophesy is fulfilled: 'the dead poet who was Shakespeare's sister will put on the body which she has so often laid down'.[43]

'Reading is no longer just an attempt to decipher; it is simultaneously a gesture of self-inscription.'[44] As the feminist critic receives the creative text actively, she is, in turn, a writer, with the poet thereby engendering new poetry. The critical act is re-creation, extending life to the original text, breaking down the boundaries between creative writing and criticism.

> *Bound*
> *By a muscle of love*
> *Tight*
> *As the band of gold*
> *Wound round my mother's finger,*
> *I've been tugged*
> *Back and forth*
> *Across the globe*
> *To keep up with the sweep of your stride.*
>
> *But being fractured female*
> *My footfalls falter,*
> *Marked by the crack*
> *Which cleaves*
> *Me*
> *From you father,*
> *The singing rib of pain*
> *Nagging in your side,*
> *Persistent, perpetual stitch.*

My body has always been one of breakages.
Of leakage and of loss.
I marked your house
Veining it bloodshot
With my trail
Now blotted to stale faded traces,
Skeleton clues still telling tales
Whispered in undisclosed spaces.

Once I dreamt
My belly was beautiful,
A true womb with a view
Crafted crystal glass.
But with sudden sickening smash
I shattered to a thousand splintered shards,
The after-birth of dream lost
Bleeding to miscarriage's pre-birth.

In the hospital bed next to me,
Wretching lungs in labour
Birth only green bile
Of cancer and of death.
Though far from the sea
Where seagulls sound my heart
My body is still rendered fluid.
Running from nostrils
Flooding in lungs —
As the marrow in my bones leaks away
I seep to pools
On my cheeks
Deep enough for ducks to wallow in.

Your bloodhound snout can still sniff me out father,
Tracking each aching clench of red —
But beware my blood pressure rising.
Remember those who feared the bleeding woman's glance
As they feared the glare of the Gorgon.
I do blood counts of books
Which add their own blood to mine
And so her wise blood circulates,

Fleshes out my skeleton texts.
Claret I blood-thirsty sup on.

The flesh of my fingers
May be furrowed with lightning forks,
Skin etched with scars
Which zipper with stitches like teeth.
But now my veins strain –
My marrow saps quicksilver –
The plastic in my fingers melts to mercury
And sparks fly when I write.

The scoop of my shoulderblades
Silently whispers wings,
And I swoop and soar through starry skies
With wings broader in spread
Than your mind.

'With one hand, suffering, living, putting your finger on pain, loss. But there is the other hand: the one that writes.'[45]

NOTES

1. Plath, Sylvia, *The Collected Poems*, ed. Ted Hughes, (London, Faber and Faber, 1981), p.331, hereafter referred to as *CP* followed by page number.
2. Gilbert, Sandra and Gubar, Susan, *The Madwoman in the Attic: The Woman Writer and the Nineteenth-Century Literary Imagination* (New Haven; Yale University Press, 1979).
3. See, for example, Butscher, Edward, *Sylvia Plath: Method and Madness* (New York, Seabury Press, 1976); Spender, Stephen, 'Warnings from the Grave' and Furbank, P.N., 'New Poetry', both in *Sylvia Path: The Critical Heritage*, ed. Linda W. Wagner (London, Routledge, 1988).
4. Schenck, Celeste, 'All of a Piece': Women's Poetry and Autobiography', in *Life/Lines*, Brodzki, Bella and Schenck, Celeste (eds), (Ithaca, Cornell University Press, 1988), p.286.
5. Ibid., p.292.
6. Ibid., p.294.
7. Although pre-dating writers such as Cixous and Irigaray, Plath's poetry presents, I suggest, an illustration of the way creative writing often seems to anticipate the arguments of theory.
8. Cixous, Hélène, *Coming to Writing and Other Essays* (Massachusetts, Harvard University Press, 1991), p.42.
9. Woolf, Virginia, *A Room of One's Own* (London, Panther Books, 1977), p.47.
10. Smith, Sidonie, *A Poetics of Women's Autobiography* (Bloomington, Indiana University Press, 1987).
11. Plath, Sylvia, *The Bell Jar*, (London, Faber and Faber, 1966), p.168, hereafter referred to as *BJ* followed by page number. I acknowledge here the need to qualify Plath's texts. My aim is not to run them all together into one seemingly continuous whole; rather I will be considering the *Collected Poems*, *The Bell Jar* and *Letters Home* as particular examples of Plath's concern with subject formation.
12. Cixous, Hélène, and Clement, Catherine, *The Newly Born Woman* (Manchester, Manchester University Press, 1986), p.68.
13. Cixous, Hélène: 'The Laugh of the Medusa', in Marks, Elaine and de Courtivron, Isabelle (eds), *New French Feminisms* (Hemel Hempstead, Harvester, 1981), p.250.

14. Cixous, Hélène, 'Castration or Decapitation', in *Signs: Journal of Women in Culture and Society*, Vol. 7, No. 1, (Autumn 1981), p.54.

15. Plath, Sylvia, *Letters Home: Correspondence 1950–1963*, selected and edited by Aurelia S. Plath (London, Faber and Faber, 1975), p.336.

16. Gagnon, Madeleine, 'Body I', in Marks and de Courtivron (eds), *New French Feminisms*, p.180.

17. Cixous, *Coming to Writing*, p.10.

18. Cixous, *Coming to Writing*, p.4; Nin, Anaïs, quoted in Stanford Friedman, Susan, 'Creativity and the Childbirth Metaphor', in *Feminisms: An Anthology of Literary Theory and Criticism*, Warhol, Robyn R. and Price Herndl, Diane (eds) (New Brunswick, Rutgers University Press, 1991), p.387.

19. Cixous, *Coming to Writing*, p.5.

20. Ibid., p.10.

21. Ibid., p.7.

22. See, for example, Irigaray, Luce, 'The Power of Discourse and the Subordination of the Feminine', in *This Sex Which Is Not One* (Ithaca, Cornell University Press, 1985), p.76.

23. Britzolakis, Christina, 'Sylvia Plath and the Spectacle of Femininity', Staff/Graduate Seminar, University of York, Spring 1993.

24. Cixous, *Coming to Writing*, p.36.

25. Rich, Adrienne, *On Lies, Secrets and Silence: Selected Prose 1966–1978* (New York, W.W. Norton and Co, 1979).

26. Cixous, Hélène, The Laugh of the Medusa', in Marks and de Courtivron, *New French Feminisms*, p.248.

27. Cixous and Clément, *The Newly Born Woman*, p.92.

28. Schenck, 'All of a Piece', p.287.

29. Miller, Nancy, 'Women's Autobiography in France: For a Dialectics of Identification', in *Women and Language in Literature and Society* McConell-Ginet, Sally, Borker, Ruth, and Furman, Nelly (eds) (New York, Praeger, 1980), p.260. I am also indebted to Christina Britzolakis' work on Sylvia Plath here: 'Sylvia Plath and the Spectacle of Femininity'.

30. Meyer Spacks, Patricia, 'Stages of Self: Notes on Autobiography and the Life Cycle', in *The American Autobiography: A Collection of Critical Essays*, ed. Albert E. Stone (New Jersey, Prentice-Hall, 1981), p.56.

31. McCarthy, Mary, in Eakin, Paul John, *Fictions in Autobiography: Studies in the Art of Self-Invention* (Princeton; Princeton University Press, 1985), p.55.

32. Plath, *Letters Home*, p.233.

33. Ibid., p.146; Plath, Sylvia, *Johnny Panic and the Bible of Dreams and other Prose Writings* (London, Faber and Faber, 1977), p.205.

34. Plath, *Letters Home*, p.166.

35. Cixous, Hélène, The Laugh of the Medusa, p.260.

36. See, for example, Irigaray, 'The Power of Discourse and the Subordination of the Feminine' and 'Questions', both in *This Sex Which Is Not One* (Ithaca, Cornell University Press, 1985).

37. The God Mercury – or Hermes – was after all an ambiguous figure, though ultimately a healing and positive one: the God of magic, medicine, speed, letters and occult wisdom. The mercurial paradigm Plath explores perhaps figures the slippage between the euphoria and depression of her manic depression; interestingly, it is a figure frequently used by another woman writer who survived manic depression – Janet Frame. (Thanks to Nicole Ward Jouve for her thoughts on mercury.)

38. Smith, *A Poetics of Women's Autobiography*, p.59.

39. Irigaray, Luce, *This Sex Which Is Not One*, p.77.

40. Brownmiller, Susan, *Against Our Will: Men, Women and Rape* (Middlesex, Penguin, 1978). Positing Plath in the discussion of what she identifies as a 'conscious female fantasy of rape' (p.322), Brownmiller writes: 'Plath's victim identification remained with her throughout her life; she could not shake it' (p.327).

41. Leclerc, Annie, 'Woman's Word', in *The Feminist Critique of Language*, ed. Deborah Cameron (London: Routledge, 1990), p.76.

42. Dallery, Arleen B, 'The Politics of Writing (the) Body: Ecriture Feminine', in *Gender/Body/Knowledge: Feminist Reconstructions of Being and Knowing*, Jagger, Alison Mary and Bordo, Susan R (eds), (New Brunswick, Rutgers University Press, 1989), p.59.

43. Woolf, *A Room of One's Own*, p.108.

44. Furman, Nelly, 'Textual Feminism', in *Women and Language in Literature and Society*, p.51, pp.45–54.

45. Cixous, *Coming to Writing*, p.8.

FURTHER READING

Alexander, Paul, *Rough Magic: A Biography of Sylvia Plath* (New York, Penguin, 1992).

Axelrood, Steven Gould, *Sylvia Plath: The Wound and the Cure of Words* (Baltimore, John Hopkins University Press, 1990).

Bundtzen, Lynda, *Plath's Incarnations: Women and the Creative Process* (Michigan, University of Michigan Press, 1983).

Butscher, Edward (ed.), *Sylvia Plath: The Woman and the Work* (London, Peter Owen Ltd, 1987).

Chesler, Phyllis, *Women and Madness* (Harmondsworth, Penguin Books, 1979).

Markey, Janice, *A Journey into the Red Eye: The Poetry of Sylvia Plath – a Critique* (London, The Women's Press, 1993).

Marsack, Robyn, *Sylvia Plath* (Buckingham, Open University Press, 1992).

Montefiore, Jan, *Feminism and Poetry: Language, Experience, Identity in Women's Writing* (London, Pandora, 1987).

Newman, Charles, *The Art Of Sylvia Plath: A Symposium* (London, Faber and Faber, 1970).

Ostriker, Alicia Suskin, *Stealing the Language: The Emergence of Women's Poetry in America* (London, The Women's Press, 1987).

Rose, Jacqueline, *The Haunting of Sylvia Plath* (London, Virago, 1991).

Showalter, Elaine, *The Female Malady: Women, Madness and English Culture, 1830–1980* (London, Virago, 1987).

Smith, Sidonie, *Subjectivity, Identity and the Body: Women's Autobiographical Practices in the Twentieth Century* (Bloomington, Indiana University Press, 1993).

Stanley, Liz, *The auto/Biographical I: The Theory and Practice of Feminist Auto/biography* (Manchester, Manchester University Press, 1992).

Stevenson, Anne, *Bitter Fame: A Life of Sylvia Plath* (London, Viking, 1989).

Wagner-Martin, Linda, *Sylvia Plath: A Bibliography* (London, Chatto and Windus, 1988).

11

In/Corporation? Jackie Kay's The Adoption Papers

Gabriele Griffin

Since its first publication amidst the rise of debates about 'the Family' in 1991, Jackie Kay's *The Adoption Papers* has steadily gained in poignancy as the issues addressed in her poetry have also extensively occupied the public domain. The issues I am referring to here include: the 'Back to Basics' campaign inaugurated by the Tories at their 1993 Party Conference; the 'lone mothers' and 'home alone' debates associated with that campaign; the renewed engagement with reproductive technologies and postmenopausal motherhood; the abortion campaigns in Ireland; discussions around mixed-race adoption; the tightening of adoption regulations to reinforce the nuclear, heterosexually oriented family as the desirable repository for children; and the House of Commons debates concerning the lowering of the age of consent for homosexuals. *The Adoption Papers* is pertinent to all of these issues. It is particularly poignant because, at a time when UK citizens are confronted with the paradox of a government which promotes individualism, privatisation and deregulation at the same time as it seeks increasingly and with renewed vigour to regulate its citizens according to its specific ideological agendas, Jackie Kay's poetry speaks, among other things, of the relationship between individual and state, and investigates the dynamic of desire and constraint which informs that relationship.

The Adoption Papers is divided into two sections: the first part is also entitled 'The Adoption Papers' and thus seduces the reader to regard it as primary since it comes first and also bears the same title as the volume as a whole. As critical reviewers like to point out, it focuses 'autobiographically' on the adoption of a black baby by a white Communist Scottish couple who, for a number of reasons, are considered unsuitable as adoptive parents. They are finally offered a baby which 'wasn't even thought of as a baby'[1] – not qualifying as such because of her colour – when they say they will adopt a baby of any colour. The section explores issues around this adoption from the three viewpoints of the biological mother of the child, the adoptive mother and the adopted child herself.

The second part of the volume, entitled 'Severe Gale 8' and of about equal length to the first, brings together a whole range of poems dealing with what one might describe as 'other lovers' (the title of another of Jackie Kay's collections of poetry[2]). This part includes explorations of lesbian and gay relationships, being foreign, issues of health, parenting, ageing, housing and the social and economic decline of Britain during the 1980s.

The volume as a whole, marketed to a general poetry-reading public, has attracted some interesting critical responses. I want to detail these briefly as they raise the question of how to situate Kay's poetry and its incorporation into, or exclusion from, canons of ideological agendas and poetry. Some reviewers have tended to treat *The Adoption Papers* as containing two discrete and incompatible halves, with a decided emphasis on the first half at the expense of the second. Thus Bruce King, for example, wrote about 'Severe Gale 8': 'The second half of the volume shows Kay, sometimes less successfully, exploring ways to write about such topics as AIDS, love between women . . .'[3]. Fleur Adcock, in *The Sunday Times*, wrote about the second section: 'Individually, some work well, but their political intent looms rather too earnestly over the group as a whole.'[4] And finally, this is what Angus Calder had to say: 'Kay's voice, whether the spelling is Scots or (as is far more usual) English, is distinctive, relaxed, fresh. Yet part of 'Jackie's' appeal is her capacity to represent an astonishing compound of marginalized and problematic existences. She is black, of mixed origin, adopted, gay, an unmarried mother: these marks alone would seem hard enough for your average Englishman [sic] to accept. But on top of all that, she has never disavowed her adoptive parents' Communism.'[5] Well, there you have it – everything which is anathema to *your average Englishman* is embodied in Jackie Kay, or is it in her poetry, or in both? Angus Calder has some difficulty distinguishing between the two, and may be gesturing towards this by putting Jackie in inverted commas. This blurring, which raises issues of similarity and difference, textuality and actuality, reflects the problematic position of all those not perceived to be part of dominant culture and ideology who, in the words of Trinh T. Minh-Ha, are therefore required 'to take on the dubious role of the Real Other to speak the "truth" on otherness'.[6] This requirement allows for the incorporation into mainstream culture of the other as simultaneously other and guarantor of self. As I shall indicate below, Kay's poetry both suggests and resists that possibility.

Minh-Ha maintains that 'Participation never goes without a certain vigilance.'[7] Such vigilance may operate at the point of the construction of the text in what is traditionally described as 'authorial intent', but this does not enable complete control of how the message is received, nor of what sort of selective attention is paid and given. For, 'what is at stake is obviously not only the Master as sovereign subject of knowledge, but also the fantasized Other as authoritative subject of an other knowledge'.[8] This is the case for the author in her construction of her poems because the process raises issues of who is 'allowed' to speak and who controls the meaning of the text. It is also thematised in the poems of *The Adoption Papers* themselves. There dominant and divergent discourses and positions are frequently juxtaposed so that they expose the limitations of the dominant and thus undercut its status as 'master' while reviewing the position of the divergent as unacceptably different. The issue of the relationship between 'master' and 'other' also applies to the reader trying to engage with Kay's work. In all three instances the same questions arise: who is the 'master'? Who is the 'Other'? And: what is the status of their respective knowledges? Kay's poems are thus open to selective readings which privilege certain meanings over others; by reading the poems in particular ways, ways which, for instance, *do not offend your average Englishman*, otherness in a variety of manifestations can be both confirmed and denied. Let me explain what I mean.

I would argue that the first section of *The Adoption Papers* has been more popular, more positively received and more extendedly discussed by reviewers of this volume of poetry because that section can be read in ways which lead the reader onto familiar ground, situating him (rather than her?) in the mainstream of contemporary cultural and political preoccupations. Formally, for instance, the use of the first person to signify a variety of personas (child, biological mother, adoptive mother), which creates ambiguity, continuity, multiple and merging points of subjectivity and identification, has become a familiar device. It is frequently associated with the specificity of women's writing. (Grace Nichols' *i is a long memoried woman*,[9] for example, makes use of this device which is also discussed as a formal strategy in Trinh T. Minh-Ha's essay 'The World as Foreign Land'.)[10]

In terms of its content, the first section of *The Adoption Papers* can (which does not mean 'should') be read in terms of a politics infused with the back-to-basics ideology: here we have the presentation of an overweening desire for maternity which, by virtue of the identifications the poems invite, reinforces the notion that every woman wants to be a mother. We also have the punishment of sex outside marriage *and* with the 'wrong' partner: the biological mother, too young to take on motherhood, gives up her 'illicitly' acquired baby for adoption and suffers the life-long consequences of being deprived of her child. The adopted child faces difficulties in coming to terms with her status as adopted and experiences the powerful desire to know her origin. Conservative ideology would construe all these concerns as 'natural' and/or desirable: it is 'natural' that women want children; it is 'natural' that children should grow up in a heterosexually oriented two-persons-of-the-opposite-sex household; it is 'natural' for a child to want to know her origins; it is 'natural' that a woman who is young, unmarried and has had sex with an 'inappropriate' partner should give up her child for adoption and suffer the consequences.

It is possible to read 'The Adoption Papers' in the terms just outlined but only if one ignores the second section and reads the two as entirely separate. As Angus Calder's comment makes clear, 'The Adoption Papers' may raise problems of identification for the white, middle-class, conservative, male English reader, but 'Severe Gale 8' invites consideration of personas who push the boundaries of convention even further while insisting that they do so in the name of precisely those desires endorsed by conservative middle England, such as the wish to have children. However, in the second section the child in 'Mummy and Donor and Deirdre' is conceived by a lesbian through artificial self-insemination; in 'The Underground Baby Case' the baby is snatched.

The continuities in the portrayal of desire (such as the one for having children) from section one of the volume to section two are disrupted by the way in which that desire is satisfied, thereby exposing some of the limits of tolerance in our society. These limits are the boundaries against which the reader's perception of convention and 'normality' is tested. By refusing to acknowledge the continuities between 'The Adoption Papers' and 'Severe Gale 8' the reader can contain the level of disturbance involved in recognising the diverse impacts of the same desire on people's actions; the couple adopting the black baby may be 'marked' (to use Calder's term) by their Communism, their Scottishness and their willingness to have a black as opposed to a white baby and so they represent, for some, an otherness. *But*: they are nevertheless a heterosexual, economically secure unit. They can thus be seen, at least in some respects, as belonging to mainstream society. Indeed, in a profile of Jackie Kay, Valerie Mason-John felt able to assert that 'Kay's aim is to convey what it is like for all those involved in the adoption process – *regardless of their race*'[11] (my emphasis) even though, a few lines later, she goes on to cite Kay as saying 'I want people to think about society's homophobia, racism and sexism'. The 'difficulty' arises when the text presents a lesbian or single mother – what attitude do you take if these positions do not offer you a point of identification?

In the same year that *The Adoption Papers* was published, Tessa Boffin and Jean Fraser's *Stolen Glances: Lesbians Take Photographs*[12] appeared, containing a version of 'The Adoption Papers' under the title 'The Soil in my Blood'. Unlike *The Adoption Papers*, *Stolen Glances* is a book by lesbians marketed to lesbians; *Stolen Glances* raises the question of family relations from an explicitly lesbian perspective which therefore de-naturalises the idea that 'family' equals father, mother, child(ren) in the nuclear, heterosexual formation portrayed as the norm in Western right-wing ideology. Significantly, the idea for *Stolen Glances* was conceived in the summer of 1988[13] in the wake of lesbians' and gay men's struggle against Section 28 of the Local Government Act which (in)famously forbids the promotion in any maintained school 'of the acceptability of homosexuality as a pretended family relationship'.[14] From its context alone, Kay's sequence of poems in *Stolen Glances* raises questions about origins, sexual identity and desire, identification and how the self is to be understood in social and in familial relations. Since these questions, often raised self-consciously, are part of lesbian identities anyway, the effect of the poems in a volume for and by lesbians is to naturalise them in a way which would be impossible in a mainstream publication. Central to the issue of incorporations, then, are questions of context and target readership.

In her essay, 'Which One's the Pretender? Section 28 and Lesbian Representation', also published in *Stolen Glances*, Anne Marie Smith analyses the relevance of Section 28 to lesbian representation and suggests that:

> Section 28 would be irrelevant to lesbian representation if lesbian representation kept its promise. That promise, which is common to all representations, is the complete, unaltered and fully accessible presentation of an original within an enclosed space. In this case, the original would be 'the Lesbian': 'our true selves', 'our true meaning', 'our true desire', constituted prior to any encounter with outside discourses. Ideally, we would enjoy 'our own' images of this original in 'our own' separate space purified of difference; the not-lesbian would be entirely absent. Actual men, and the 'male-identified element', would be excluded.[15]

Problems with this ideal representation arise when either an external reference contaminates our space or when lesbian representations are presented to the outside.[16] Demonstrating that lesbian images cannot be 'pure', Smith maintains that 'The lesbian with a child shows the possibility of a family which is not based on patriarchal and heterosexual principles ... It is by her displacement of the married man as the head of the family that she becomes a pretender to the throne.'[17] This means that 'lesbian-ness becomes dangerous not as a sexuality but as a displacement of the traditional family'.[18] I would argue that a critical reception of *The Adoption Papers* which ignores 'Severe Gale 8' and thus the lesbian parent, arises out of a perception of that parent – but not just her – as a threat to the traditional family. It is, without doubt, easier for some, to incorporate 'The Adoption Papers' into mainstream culture than 'Severe Gale 8'.

However, a careful reading of 'The Adoption Papers' reveals it too is subversive. Kay subtly exposes and defamiliarises notions of what is 'natural' throughout the sequence. Consider the very opening lines of *The Adoption Papers*:

> I always wanted to give birth
> do that incredible natural thing
> that women do – I nearly broke down
> when I heard we couldn't

Here the idea of the norm, the natural thing of giving birth, is immediately undercut by the revelation that this couple will not be able to have 'natural' children.

There are other ways in which this couple, like those portrayed later in the volume, do not conform. They – white – choose to raise a black baby whose mother, a white woman, loved a black man. The biological mother describes her community's appalled reaction:

> when we walked out heads turned
> like horses, folk stood like trees
> their eyes fixed on us – it made me burn, that hot glare; my hand
> would sweat down to his bone.
> Finally, alone, we'd melt
> nothing, nothing would matter

These lines, through the use of similes evoking 'natural' non-human objects such as horses and trees but likening people to these, raise precisely the questions around what actually *is* natural or, if you like, 'un-natural' here: the love between the black and the white person or the people's responses to seeing a mixed couple, or both, or neither. There is passion on both sides, the heat of hate and the heat of love: both seek the eradication of the lovers and are transgressive in their excess and movement towards annihilation. The very physicality of the descriptions, the focus on bodies and physical experience, emphasise the centrality of the body and the senses in the social exchange which determines the experiences described.

The question of what is 'natural' is a constant theme in Kay's poetry, highlighted by the variety of ways in which transgression is signalled. People stare at the lovers because they are noticeable, visible through their difference which surfaces, quite literally, on their bodies. These therefore become a site of marking difference. One of the major preoccupations of Kay's poetry in this volume is this issue of the marked surface, of the appearance which establishes difference, and of how that difference is read. The marking of the black baby's face in the early part of the volume ('I was pulled out with forceps/left a gash down my left cheek') is echoed in subsequent poems, including the one entitled 'Black Bottom' in which the teacher, talking of dancing, says to the black child, 'I thought/you people had it in your blood'. The difference is that the scar on the surface of the body is visible whereas what is 'in your blood' is not visible in the same way. Kay's poetry plays on the literal and metaphorical meanings of phrases like 'x is in your blood' to establish continuities and discontinuities of perceptions.

The exploration of the marked body in Kay's poetry serves to indicate that such marking, which in *The Adoption Papers* becomes a source of suffering, is the means by which individuals acquire an (attributed) identity. This identity may not be synonymous with their own experience of themselves but it is nonetheless used to distinguish them, on the basis of surfaces or appearances, from what is considered to be the norm. In Kay's poetry, however, the effect is to challenge this norm and to show its own differences, specifically its cruelty and violence. She achieves this by constructing symmetries which simultaneously suggest and belie similarity and establish a reverse discourse where what is marked as negative is re-valued in the face of the 'normal', which thus becomes a destructive other. One of the poems which most effectively demonstrates this is 'Dressing Up'[19]. The symmetry established in this poem between the victimised mother and the son victimised both by her and by his father relies on the reader's recognition of the mother's *mis*-recognition: the juxtaposition of the lines 'You look a bloody mess you do', addressed to the dressed-up son, with the persona's comment, 'She had a black eye, a navy dress', invites the reader to consider who precisely is (in) a mess here.

The poem also raises the question of what violations are tolerable in a society, insisting that built into the dominant itself are transgressions which are ultimately more destructive than those engaged in by the ostracised outsiders. As the persona says about his transvestism: 'Nobody gets hurt, it's not for/the image even I'm just dead/childish.'[20] His mother, on the other hand, would prefer him to be a killer rather 'than that'.

Death is one of the recurring themes in *The Adoption Papers*. Where it is raised it is often, as in 'Dressing Up', with reference to the deadliness of convention and the norm/al. Thus in 'Close Shave', a phrase in itself associated with danger and near death, the persona – a miner – lives a double life as a married man preserving his nuclear family and as the long-term lover of a barber. Unable to tell his family and act on his desire, the man has only twice spent a whole night with his lover, 'once when my wife's sister died,/once when the brother-in-law committed suicide.'[21] In this instance, death has facilitated love but for the miner, having internalised homophobia, his family means symbolic death to the enactment of his desire. It flourishes, underground so to speak (one explanation for the construction of the persona as a miner), but it must not surface, else he would risk becoming a marked man.

Many of the domestic scenarios and intimate relationships Kay portrays in her poetry focus precisely on the question of visibility – what you see – and semantics – what it means. To be visible as different from the norm invites violence and violation: this is one of the conclusions of her poetry. But, as the position of the mother in 'Dressing Up' makes clear, to subscribe to 'the norm' does not necessarily protect you from violence or violation either. The mother is physically marked out as an object of violence; her choice of conventional self-presentation does not guarantee her inviolability. The persona in 'Dressing Up' chooses to present an unconventional sense of self; he faces the dilemma of how to establish this identity, not for him predicated upon 'the image' but on the enactment of an infantile self, and how others will perceive him as he encodes his desire (for difference) in a particular image. In the juxtaposition of mother and son, Kay's poem suggests that while the body and its surface may be the site on which violence is inscribed, it is not the body itself which is at issue but the way that body is read, what meaning is imposed upon it. Simultaneously, the poem denies the difference between mother and son which both cultivate and insist upon. Their respective victimisation and oppression within hierarchies which are maintained through the policing of particular differences makes mother and son similar. The crucial difference between them is their attitude towards this oppression; the son rebels while the mother colludes, denying the similarity of their position in the structure of the family.

Just as visibility as a source of disturbance is one of Kay's concerns, so is its opposite, invisibility. Fertility or infertility, for instance, are not visible; yet they cause the mothers in 'The Adoption Papers' much anguish. Similarly, being lesbian or gay, and being infected by the HIV virus may not necessarily be visible, yet both involve difference and can cause disturbance, the anguish of the invisible. This is indexed in the poem 'Dance of the Cherry Blossom' which begins with the lines: 'Both of us are getting worse/Neither knows who had it first'.[22] This opening rhyming couplet suggests a symmetry which is formally both sustained ('He thinks I gave it to him/I think he gave it to me') and disrupted '(Both of us are getting worse/I know I'm wasting precious time') throughout the rest of the poem. The sustaining of the symmetry underwrites both the continuity of the relationship and the mutual continued suspicion concerning who first contracted the disease; the disruption signals the difficulty of coming to terms with this invisible but destructive and in every sense alien body, the virus, which invades every aspect of the two men's relationship.

This, I would argue, is at the centre of *The Adoption Papers* and pertains both to the volume's content and to its reception: the issue of the alien body and how it is accommodated. It *can* be visible: the black body in an overwhelmingly white community; cross-dressing in a society in which this is not the norm; the single mother in a context where the idea of motherhood is tied to heterosexual marriage. Or it can be invisible: the HIV virus circulating in the body; the desire of two women for each other. To the extent that this body/thing/desire falls outside the back-to-basics ideology it is marked, transgressive and a source of alienation. As such it cannot be incorporated into the norm, for its very difference sustains that norm. Yet through pushing at the boundaries of the norm, it indicates difference and therefore the possibility of change.

Kay's poetry does not request incorporation into convention. It is celebratory rather than pessimistic as it maps both a transgressive and a transcending alienation: those who are marked as outside the dominant survive and get what they desire – against the odds – whether these odds be simply the weather as in 'Pounding Rain', or a racially problematic past as in 'Photo in the Locket' or infection and death from the HIV virus. Kay's poetry is affirmative: love triumphs over destruction and rejection. It articulates the dream of overcoming enforced 'normality' which enables difference to be lived.

NOTES

1. Kay, Jackie, *The Adoption Papers* (Newcastle-upon-Tyne, Bloodaxe Books, 1991), p.24.
2. Kay, Jackie, *Other Lovers* (Newcastle-upon-Tyne, Bloodaxe Books, 1993).
3. King, Bruce, 'Review: *The Adoption Papers*', in *World Literature Today*, 66/3 (1992), p.518.
4. Adcock, Fleur, 'Points of No Return', *The Sunday Times*, 5 January 1992.
5. Calder, Angus, 'Consanguine Verse: Reading Jackie Kay', in *Landfall*, 46/6 (1992), p.477.
6. Minh-Ha, Trinh T., *When the Moon Waxes Red* (London, Routledge, 1991), p.185.
7. Ibid., p.186.
8. Ibid., p.186.
9. Nichols, Grace, *i is a long memoried woman* (London, Karnak House, 1983).
10. Minh-Ha, Trinh T., 'The World as Foreign Land', in *When the Moon Waxes Red*, pp.185–200.
11. Mason-John, Valerie, 'Pride of Place', *The Guardian*, 10 October 1991, p.38.
12. Boffin, Tessa and Fraser, Jean (eds), *Stolen Glances: Lesbians Take Photographs* (London, Pandora, 1991).
13. Ibid., p.9.
14. Smith, Anne Marie, 'Which One's the Pretender? Section 28 and Lesbian Representation', in *Stolen Glances*, p.128.
15. Ibid., p.128.
16. Ibid., p.129.
17. Ibid., p.136.
18. Ibid., p.136.
19. Kay, *The Adoption Papers*, p.57.
20. Ibid.
21. Ibid., p.56.
22. Ibid., pp.50–1.

12

Delivering the Mother:
Three Anthologies of Birth Poetry

Karin Voth Harman

This chapter was conceived several years ago, when, as a new mother fighting post-partum blues, I flicked through anthologies of women's poetry looking for poems about childbirth. There wasn't much there for me.[1] As Muriel Rukeyser noted (in 1949): 'One is on the edge of the absurd the minute one tries to relate the experience of birth to the silence about it in poetry.'[2] Though well-known poets such as Sylvia Plath and Anne Sexton were writing on birth in the 1960s, only very recently have we seen a rapid change in the relationship between motherhood and writing. Within the past decade, increasing numbers of writers have been motivated to address, in a variety of genres, the subject of parenthood, and their representations are gaining a much wider audience than did, for example, the poetry of maternity published in feminist magazines during the 1970s. They are reaching a wider audience primarily because the relationship between the 'literature of maternity' and the critical establishment is slowly beginning to change: on both sides of the Atlantic writers as renowned as Toni Morrison, Anne Tyler, Alice Walker, Bobbie Ann Mason, A.S. Byatt, Margaret Atwood, Sharon Olds and Buchi Emecheta are exploring aspects of motherhood in their writing, and publishers, reviewers, and scholars are being compelled to take note.

That a cultural focus on motherhood (however overdue) is occurring *now* undoubtedly rings alarm bells for those worried about the so-called 'Eighties backlash' against feminism which has, according to cultural observers such as Susan Faludi, resulted in a rampant 'pro-natalism' in the USA, and to a lesser extent in Britain.[3] Ann Snitow, for instance, suggests that the increasing involvement with motherhood in all literary genres is symptomatic of the ways in which even feminist writers have internalised the conservative agendas of the 1980s.[4] Snitow describes an intractable divide between those within feminism who would explore and expand the subject of motherhood and those who would wish to diminish its hold on the imagination. Her own preference is for the latter though she feels that the former, in the light of the conservative backlash, currently enjoy centre stage.[5]

In response to Snitow's concerns, I wish to suggest that whilst representations of parenthood might be fashionable in popular culture, 'literary' texts about motherhood have a very long way to go before they reach anything like the centre stage of academic consideration. Moreover it is precisely the concern with ways in which mindless glorification of motherhood can damage women which should compel feminist critics to get more involved with the new representations of parenting. Certainly the recent cultural absorption with 'family values' in both Britain and the United States encourages women to write and publishers to publish literature exploring motherhood. But these texts are not simply internalising a neo-Victorian reification of motherhood, as Snitow seems to suggest. In most cases, women writing poetry, fiction, and drama are using this timely opportunity to rewrite and to complicate the 'backlash script' on motherhood. They are angry with the existing discourses of maternity. By serving as midwives to writers attempting to deliver mothers, in all their complexities, to the public gaze, critics now have the opportunity to publicise and promote different understandings of motherhood. The medium of poetic language offers a crucial alternative to the potent linguistic mix of medicine, psychology and politics which currently drowns most mothers' voices.

With that plea, then, for critics to take note, I turn to the specific literary phenomenon which has inspired this chapter: the publication, within four years of my fruitless post-partum search through poetry anthologies, of no fewer than three anthologies of birth poetry in Britain: Faber's *Cradle and All* (1989), edited by Laura Chester; The Women's Press' *In the Gold of Flesh: Poems of Birth and Motherhood* (1990), edited by Rosemary Palmeira, and *The Virago Book of Birth Poetry* (1993), edited by Charlotte Otten.[6] The three editors of these anthologies have taken the significant first steps in sorting through, evaluating and publicising birth poetry; this essay asks: what might be the next step in formulating a critical response to this very personal poetry of reproduction?

My own particular interest is in the choices poets make about the representation of bodies within their writing on birth. For birth is an undeniably body-centred event, and yet questions about whose body to focus upon (and how, indeed, to centre the splitting or emerging body) are questions which are political, as well as artistic. The contemporary 'birth poet' writes at a time when political, medical and anti-abortion discourses seem to be increasingly erasing or ignoring the bodies of mothers in favour of the bodies of the foetus/infant. Moreover the poet is likely to be aware of the fundamental opposition proposed, by various branches of psychoanalytic theory, between language and the mother's body. She writes, in fact, in the face of centuries of cultural manoeuvres which have sought to mystify and silence, and/or denigrate and silence the reproductive female form. In addition she writes against the childbearing body's own resistance to language due to the highly probable presence of mind-altering drugs and/or pain. Finally she writes about an event which, in contemporary western culture, as Tess Coslett demonstrates in her ground-breaking work, *Women Writing Childbirth*, has been heavily colonised by two dominant oppositional discourses of the body: the language of medical science and the language of the natural childbirth movement.[7]

As I turn then to these birth anthologies asking: 'where's the body'? I find, not so surprisingly, less a triumphant 'essentialist' celebration of the powerful female flesh than evidence that certain taboos 'protecting' the female body are still intact. Within each of these anthologies of birth (all of which contain poetry on infertility, conception, pregnancy, miscarriage, abortion, stillbirth and early motherhood as well) is a special section devoted entirely to the actual moment, or event of childbirth. Yet less than half of the poems in these special sections of both the Virago and the Women's Press anthologies contain more than a line or two which depicts the maternal body. Not surprisingly, reviewer Blake Morrison (although it may be surprising that *he* is the reviewer of this anthology) comes away from the Virago book still wondering what birth feels like: 'plenty after birth but not much afterbirth', he writes, commenting on the 'flat abstract lack of physicality of much of the verse'.[8] Chester's Faber anthology offers a bit more 'body' – just over half of the poems in her section 'On Being Born' attend to the body of the woman giving birth.

What are all these poems in the 'birth' sections of anthologies on birth actually doing with the woman's body if they're not writing about it? Many opt to focus on the simpler, more discrete body and consciousness of the foetus or new-born baby. Others reflect upon the other issues or personalities which attend birth, depicting the mother's interaction with the father, with her birth attendants, or with her analgesics. Frequently poets apply extended metaphors to the body which metamorphose it into something else: usually a great force of nature such as the fertile earth or the stormy sea. I wish to look briefly at this latter mode of 'body-snatching' and then to discuss other aspects of the problem of metaphor for birth poets.

A title of a poem in the Virago anthology puts it most bluntly: 'Our Mother's Body is The Earth'.[9] Nowhere can the lure of the ancient alignment between woman and nature be stronger than in this area of maternity. Although I could select many poems to illustrate the effects of such an alignment I have chosen to quote from Rosemary Palmeira's poem 'Woman', which she includes in her anthology. Since this is a poem by the editor herself it can, in some sense, be seen to speak of her philosophy as editor/critic as well as to offer her own poetic representation of maternity. The first stanza carves out a space of difference in which to situate the presumably pregnant woman who narrates:

> I have come upon a spell of stillness
> out of the mainstream current
> a little bay, a sheltered pocket
> visited by boat and sea.

Into this space of diminutive stillness, the 'sheltered pocket', the poem's second stanza lobs a succession of metaphors:

> I am already making a space
> my belly a rich loamy lining
> a warm hollow, a barrel of grain
> a grass-thick valley, a nestful of birds
> a bowl of still water, a whirling eddy
> a vat full of wine, a chalice of grail
> an eye full of tear, a bay full of sea
> a well earth-deep, a bell of bronze.

The poem concludes 'I prepare myself to bear a mystery',[10] and indeed in this poem both the bodies of the child and of the mother remain a mystery. In fact the poem's title 'Woman' implies that it is the female body in general which is too great, too profound, to be depicted in 'mainstream' patriarchal language. The poem makes huge claims for this body at the same time as the particular body is wholly effaced. (An ironic sort of 'death of the author'.)

Though many feminists find 'earth mother' imagery very empowering, French feminists, in particular, having given it a theoretical underpinning, I find these metaphors work better in *theory* than in *poetry*. In poetry they run a high risk of being 'dead' metaphors: they have lost their power to jar the imagination because they compare things which readers readily accept as having something in common.[11] After centuries of comparison between women and nature, and about fifty years of being told by natural birth experts to 'imagine your body as a flower', such imagery loses impact upon the Western imagination. Extended metaphorical treatment of birth loses sight of the flesh which is so central to this act. This is both an artistic and ideological sin of omission: draping metaphor around the body tends to flatten and to etherialise a poem at the same time as it contributes to prevailing taboos about maternal bodies. Birth poetry, which is forced to navigate the tricky terrain of the ongoing arguments within feminism between so-called 'essentialists' and 'social constructionists', needs to pay very close attention to its imagery. Metaphor, which begins to make meaning out of physical difference, is so often the culprit in shifting a laudable focus on the female body into an essentialising, universalising effacement of that particular body.

Behind this problem of choosing metaphors to describe childbirth lies the greater difficulty of writing about an event which is commonly used as a metaphor for writing, at the same time as one writes about a body which is commonly used as metaphor for silence or difference. Discussing the French feminists Hélène Cixous, Julia Kristeva and Luce Irigaray, Domna Stanton notes '[i]n this symbolic context, it becomes clear that "the Mother" is, as Cixous states, "a metaphor" (Laugh, 881)'.[12] Despite some reservations, Stanton argues for a 'metonymic' rather than a 'metaphoric' treatment of the maternal,[13] playfully concluding her essay:

> But even that idea is not ... phallago-free. For metonymic deferral, postponement or putting off ironically represents the traditional feminine posture whenever a question of inter(dis)course arises. Nevertheless ... it is the more desirable course for diverse female explorations than excessive, tumescent metaforeplay.[14]

(Stanton's (metaphorical) description of the metonymic attitude of deferral seems particularly apt for women writing very soon after childbirth!)

Margaret Homans approaches the meaning of 'the mother' in Western culture from a more psychoanalytic angle. Nevertheless, like Stanton, she locates a problem with the kind of language used to speak of the mother:

> To take something literally is to get it wrong while to have a figurative understanding of something is the correct intellectual stance. And yet, to the extent that women writers are able to have a view of this situation independent of men's, women may value both the mother and the literal differently and consequently understand their linguistic situation in a way that makes their writing unacceptable to those who privilege the figurative.[15]

Both Stanton and Homans seem to suggest that a move away from metaphor (or at least from totalising figures of speech) towards a metonymic, or a more literal discourse might constitute a 'better', more subversive move for women writing the mother. And, indeed, I think this is what we do in fact find in the most powerful poems on childbirth. These poems manage to shake off the prevalent cultural ideas that childbirth in writing is only, or primarily, a metaphor for creativity and that the mother is primarily a metaphor for female difference or silence, and to focus literally and metonymically upon the mother's body in birth.

The stylistic characteristics of such poems can be summarised as follows. First, in their attempt to follow the events of the mother's body and consciousness they will often split or multiply pronouns and voices and convey uncertainty about identity. Second, these poems use metaphor sparingly and in fragmented rather than connected or extended form. Their metaphors often focus (rather metonymically) on a specific part of a body: Sylvia Plath, for instance describing the pain of labour as being 'dragged by wild horses, the iron hooves'[16] or Alicia Suskin Ostriker depicting breast feeding as her '[h]ot breast' running to her new-born like 'a dog [running] to a younger dog it wants to make friends with'.[17] Third, these poems, although they tie themselves to the maternal body through literal description, do not, as one might expect, become mere birth reports. Rhythm and syntax prevent this even when there is no figurative language: 'Oh, hands against the wall, hang on, no, let go, go into it, don't fight it (all doubled up) don't fall into the toilet.'[18] Perhaps because birth is this experience of being 'all doubled up', literal inscriptions of the different voices within the mother's consciousness readily achieve an intratextual resonance normally granted only to figurative speech. Fourth and finally, the use of dream narratives, fragments of myth and overheard voices, all of which are particularly present in the longer poems of Chester's anthology, serves to denote, and to begin to fill in, gaps in the speaker's consciousness, moments when the sensations of the body do, in fact, eclipse a literal language. Daphne Marlatt's 'Rings, iv.', Deena Metzger's extract from 'Skin: Shadows/Silence', Toi Derricote's extract from 'Natural Birth' and Bernadette Mayer's extract from 'The Desires of Mothers to Please Others in Letters', all in *Cradle and All's* section 'On Being Born',[19] make extensive use of this layering of bodily events with extracts from the social, psychological, and linguistic dramas which also play themselves out in birth.

Ironically, many of the poems which adhere most faithfully to the mother's body end up, in fact, enacting a drama about language in which language (like the body) is stretched to the very limits of its endurance, looks likely to flicker out altogether, but then delivers. Toi Derricote's lengthy poem 'Natural Birth'[20] enacts this extraordinary alignment between body and language as it illustrates the stylistic strategies noted above. I quote from the poem's evocation of transition, the stage of labour which generally presents the greatest challenge to the birthing mother's consciousness. Note the way in which Derricote splits this consciousness into an 'i', always a vulnerable, lower-case 'i' and a 'she', who represents the force of the birthing body and its threat to annihilate language. This section of the poem depicts a battle of pronouns:

> the meat rolls up and moans on the damp table
> my body is a piece of cotton over another
> woman's body. some other woman, all muscle and nerve, is
> tearing apart and opening under me.

i move with her like skin, not able to do anything else,
i am just watching her, not able to believe what her
body can do, what it *will* do, to get this thing accomplished.

this muscle of a lady, this crazy ocean in my teacup.
she moves the pillars of the sky. i am stretched into
fragments, tissue paper thin. the light shines through
to her goatness, her blood-thick heart that thuds like
one drum in the universe emptying its stars.

she is
that heart
larger
than my life
stuffed
in
me
like sausage
black sky
bird
pecking
at the bloody
ligament

trying
to get
in, get
out
i am
. . .

when i see there is
no answer
to the screamed
word
GOD
nothing i can do,
no use,
i have to let her in,
open the door,
put down the mat
welcome her
as if she

might be the
called for death,
the final
abstraction.

she comes
like a tunnel
fast
coming into
blackness
with my headlights
off
  you can push . . .

Bravely Derricote takes on the birthing mother during transition: in doing so she
provides one of the very few portrayals, in any art, of the struggle during this
time for the mother's subjectivity. The 'i' valiantly attempts to hold out, asserting
its literalness in the scriptural refusal of metaphor: 'i am'. After a fruitless appeal to
God to validate her subjectivity, the 'i' in Derricote's poem prepares to accept the
victory of the 'she', the victory of objectification, the victory of the 'final abstraction',
death. She prepares to leave her body, situating her narrative viewpoint outside of
that body. And the crux of this poem, and perhaps the crux of this chapter, is the
idea that it is the literal events of the flesh, and those life-saving literal words 'you
can push' which save this poem, and which deliver the mother. This poem works
because it pushes the figurative construction of identity to the limit (and in doing
so, embodies the torments which literally do assail the subjectivity of a birthing
mother). At the last moment, however, it looks back at the body, and locates, in
its materiality, a position from which the mother can both listen and speak.

Two final poems illustrate the ways in which birth poets who remain committed
to the maternal body can play with and against prevailing cultural myths about the
relationship between birth and language (in much the same way as they can play
with and against contemporary attitudes towards motherhood). Linda Pastan's
'Notes from the Delivery Room'[21] begins from its title to play with the age-old
metaphoric yoking of creativity and procreativity. In a wry, reflective tone, Pastan
'notes' the discrepancies between the work of birth and the work of the creative
genius. The birth-giving woman is a 'victim in an old comic book', a 'sweating
laborer', a 'new magician' struggling to produce 'the rabbit/from my swollen hat'.
These disparate images of the birthing mother all counter romantic images of both
childbirth and writing, and the alignment of the two: 'this work, this forcing/of
one life from another/is something that I signed for/at a moment when I would
have signed anything'. After a series of disconnected images and wry observations

about the work of childbirth, Pastan deconstructs one last metaphor and concludes with a literal image focused upon a specific part of her body. I find the humility and accuracy of this final depiction of mother and child intensely poignant:

> She's crowning, someone says,
> But there is no one royal here,
> just me, quite barefoot,
> greeting my barefoot child.

In a tone diametrically opposed to Pastan's, Sharon Olds also addresses the metaphorical alliance between childbirth and writing in her swashbuckling 'The Language of the Brag'.[22] This poem begins with the narrator's desire for phallic, masculine, public power, 'some epic use' for her 'excellent body': 'I have stood by the sandlot/and watched the boys play.' The thrust of this poem is that childbirth fulfils these *masculine* desires of the body rather than traditionally feminine (or fluid, earth-motherly) desires. The language here focuses mercilessly upon the literal body:

> I have wanted courage, I have thought about fire
> and the crossing of waterfalls, I have dragged
>   around
> my belly big with cowardice and safety,
> my stool black with iron pills,
> my huge breasts oozing mucus,
> my legs swelling, my hands swelling,
> my face swelling and darkening, my hair
> falling out, my inner sex stabbed again and again
>   with terrible pain
> like a knife.
> I have lain down.
>
> I have lain down and sweated and shaken
> and passed blood and feces and water and
> slowly alone in the center of a circle I have
> passed the new person out
> and they have lifted the new person free of the
>   act
> and wiped the new person free of that
> language of blood like praise all over the body.

Olds's final stanza, in a move almost calculated to offend 'staunch privilegers of the figurative', turns to the male poets, taunting them with their inability to achieve in the literal sphere of procreativity and flaunting her ability to achieve both the birth of babies and the 'glistening verb' of birthing her body into language (the poem's title, in fact, asserting that the poem is about *language*):

> I have wanted what you wanted to do, Walt
>   Whitman,
> Allen Ginsberg, I have done this thing,
> I and the other women this exceptional
> act with the exceptional heroic body,
> this giving birth, this glistening verb,
> and I am putting my proud American boast
> right here with the others.

In her celebration of the literal, Olds exemplifies Laura Chester's claim in the introduction to her anthology that 'coming through the body we go way beyond it, making valid life experience through the context of the word'.[23] In that 'language of blood like praise all over the body', the mother is delivered.

In 1976, Adrienne Rich concluded her opus *Of Woman Born* with an impassioned cry for women, at last, to think through the body.[24] Thirteen years later Marianne Hirsch, towards the conclusion of her study of mother/daughter plots, urged feminism to get over what Nancy K. Miller calls its 'bugaboo about essentialism' and to start writing about real bodies.[25] Writing about bodies is not something feminists 'mastered' in the 1970s; it remains a crucial challenge in a world which would seek to inscribe those bodies with many silencing discourses. In childbirth, women cannot avoid the literalness of the flesh. To write poetry out of this event which is so physical, and yet is our culture's predominant metaphor for the act of writing, is an achievement which deserves appreciation and further exploration from all those interested in the movement of word upon flesh.[26]

NOTES

1. The 'barren' anthologies included *Making for the Open: Post Feminist Poetry*, ed. Carol Rumens (London, Chatto & Windus, 1987), which had no poems on childbirth; *The Faber Book of Twentieth Century Women Poets*, ed. Fleur Adcock (London, Faber and Faber, 1987), which contained only Gwendolyn Brook's poem on abortion, 'The Mother'; *The Bloodaxe Book of Contemporary Women Poets*, ed. Jeni Couzyn (Newcastle, 1985) had three poems on childbirth; and *The Longman Anthology of World Literature by Women, 1875–1975*, ed. Marian Arkin and Barbara Schollar (White Plains, New York, 1989) had three poems on birth in 1055 pages of women's writing.
2. Muriel Rukeyser, 'A Simple Theme', *Poetry* 74 (July 1949), p.237.
3. Susan Faludi, *Backlash: The Undeclared War Against American Women* (New York, Crown Publishers, 1991). See, for instance, chapters 5 and 14. Suzanna Danuta Walters's *Lives Together, Worlds Apart: Mothers and Daughters in Popular Culture* (Berkeley and Oxford, University of California Press, 1992), Chapter 7, is also very illuminating on the effect of the 'backlash' on representations of maternity.
4. Ann Snitow, 'Feminism and Motherhood: An American Reading', *Feminist Review* (Spring 1992), pp.32–51.
5. Snitow, 'Feminism and Motherhood', see particularly pp.40–1.
6. *Cradle and All: Women Writers on Pregnancy and Birth*, ed. Laura Chester (London, Faber and Faber, 1989); *In the Gold of Flesh: Poems of Birth and Motherhood*, ed. Rosemary Palmeira (London, The

Women's Press, 1990); *The Virago Book of Birth Poetry*, ed. Charlotte Otten (London, Virago, 1993). In 1983, Faber published *The Naked Astronaut: Poems on Birth and Birthdays*, edited by René Graziani, in which, remarkably, only 13 of 137 named poets are women. The difference between this anthology and Faber's *Cradle and All* gives a good indication of the increased possibilities for women writing as mothers during the 1980s.

7. This is Cosslett's argument in *Women Writing Childbirth: Modern Discourses of Motherhood* (Manchester, Manchester University Press, 1994).
8. Morrison, Blake, 'From here to maternity', *The Independent on Sunday*, 9 January 1994, p.30.
9. *Virago Book of Birth Poetry*, p.145.
10. Ibid., pp.20–1.
11. This idea is developed in Paul Ricoeur's *The Rule of Metaphor: Multidisciplinary Studies of the Creation of Meaning in Language*, translated by R. Czerny with K. McLaughlin and J. Costello (Toronto, 1977), originally published in French, 1975.
12. Domna C. Stanton, 'Difference on Trial: A Critique of the Maternal Metaphor in Cixous, Irigaray, and Kristeva', in *The Poetics of Gender*, ed. Nancy K. Miller (New York, Columbia University Press, 1986), pp.157–81, p.161.
13. Roman Jakobson's seminal discussion of metaphor and metonymy, 'The metaphoric and metonymic poles', reprinted in David Lodge's *Modern Criticism and Theory* (London, Longman, 1988), positions these linguistic strategies as two opposite ways in which the mind makes connections. 'Metaphor' works by substitution based on similarity whilst 'metonymy' works by means of contiguity. 'Metonymic' treatment of a maternal body, therefore, would have to maintain some connection with that body in space and time, whilst 'metaphoric' treatment would be free to transform that body into anything which bore some similarity to it. Jakobson notes the alliance between metaphor and poetry (and scholarship) and between metonymy and realism.
14. Stanton, 'Difference on Trial', p.177.
15. Margaret Homans, *Bearing the Word: Language and Female Experience in Nineteenth Century Writing* (Chicago and London, University of Chicago Press, 1986), p.5.
16. *In the Gold of Flesh*, p.62.
17. *Virago Book of Birth Poetry*, p.90.
18. Daphne Marlott, *Cradle and All*, p.95.
19. Ibid., pp.77–135.
20. Ibid., pp.108–16.
21. *In the Gold of Flesh*, p.71.
22. *Cradle and All*, p.134.
23. *Cradle and All*, p.4.
24. Adrienne Rich, *Of Woman Born: Motherhood as Experience and Institution*, 2nd edn (London, Virago, 1977; first published New York, Norton, 1976), p.284.
25. Marianne Hirsch, *The Mother/Daughter Plot: Narrative, Psychoanalysis, Feminism* (Bloomington, 1989), p.166. Critiquing the existing so-called essentialist and liberating discourses of the body, Hirsch writes, 'The representation of the female body in French feminism is neither essentialist or experiential . . . For Cixous and Irigaray, the body is not matter but metaphor, and their gestures of reconstruction are figural enough not to have to include the mother's literally pregnant body.'
26. See Susan Stanford Friedman's rigorous essay 'Creativity and the Childbirth Metaphor: Gender Differences in Literary Discourse', the first two sections of which chronicle the pervasiveness of the childbirth metaphor for creativity in Western writing in English. Included in *Speaking of Gender*, ed. Elaine Showalter (New York and London, Routledge, 1989), pp.73–100.

FURTHER READING

Daniels, Kate, *The Niobe Poems* (Pittsburgh, University of Pittsburgh Press, 1988).
Derricote, Toi, *Natural Birth* (California, The Crossing Press, 1983).
Kay, Jackie, *The Adoption Papers* (Newcastle-upon-Tyne, Bloodaxe Books, 1991).
Olds, Sharon, *Sign of Saturn* (London, Secker and Warburg, 1991).
Ostriker, Alicia, *The Mother/Child Papers* (Boston, Beacon Press, 1980, 1986).
Pratt, Minnie Bruce, *Crime Against Nature* (Ithaca, New York, Firebrand Books, 1990).

Section Five: Radical Poetics

'Experimental' women poets have received little attention, either from within experimental poetry circles or from feminist critics. Avant-garde experimental poetry is predominantly a male preserve – at least, in so far as it gets any public attention, the figures associated with it are almost all men – and its exponents have proved ill-equipped to recognise the significance or intention of their women colleagues' work. Feminist critics have been more preoccupied with the political import of the poems' content than with the subversive possibilities of formal experimentation. The chapters in this section examine the radical poetics employed by some of these female experimentalists and suggest that their neglected work offers valuable models and useful strategies for contemporary poets.

Harriet Tarlo examines the work of American objectivist Lorine Niedecker, whose work was published throughout the first half of the century. Faithful to the tenets of objectivism, Niedecker saw the poet's role as transmitter of facts and objects from the world around, unadulterated by the poet's ego. However, Tarlo demonstrates that this impulse was tempered by her interest in the local: the lives of members of the community, their folk traditions, and the burden of a shameful colonisers' history, imprinted on the land. Niedecker anticipated many contemporary preoccupations. In her poems she expressed a radical environmental vision, in which humankind are depicted as just another part of the natural world. Fascinated by great male thinkers, she interspersed fragments of their letters or biographical information amongst extracts from their ideas, in order to disrupt their monologic authority. Delight in language play, sound, rhythms and the music of words sits alongside objectivist fidelity to the real and particular in her work: as Tarlo comments, this produces a unique tension between Julia Kristeva's semiotic multiplicity and a more solid, 'grounded' mode of writing.

Alison Mark concentrates on the early work of the poet and academic, Veronica Forrest-Thomson – a woman whose influence on contemporary experimental poets is still barely recognised. Her interest is in Forest-Thomson's exploration of the slippery, elusive nature of identity and her tantalising, yet doomed, efforts to catch it in language. Consciousness of self and of language characterise her writing, in which form is invariably the dominant element. Forrest-Thomson advocated a poetry of what she called 'suspended naturalisation', in which the urge to make narrative sense is checked by formal disruptions. Her interest was always in the processes of writing and reading poetry, rather than its 'meaning'. The reader has to work hard to follow the cryptic puzzles she sets but Mark, true to her subject's intentions, uses post-structuralist and psychoanalytic theories to explicate her method without trying to fix the works' meanings.

Romana Huk brings a valuable transatlantic perspective to bear on the issue of experimentalism. She suggests that UK suspicion of such work stems from the strength of the empiricist tradition; this also characterises feminist thought, and helps explain scepticism towards postmodern poetic experiment. Huk argues that the idea that traditional lyric and experimental 'Language' poetry are opposites is unhelpful and outdated, as is the assumption that radical politics cannot be expressed in the former, and that a hard-won sense of self is sacrificed in the latter. Using the US experimental poet Susan Howe as an illustration, she shows that formal radicalism does not in fact avoid laying claim to transcendent authority. To demonstrate her contention that radical philosophical ideas can be explored in formally conventional poetry, she looks at some of Eavan Boland's work, and finds her grappling with the same 'postmodern' problems of authority. Huk concludes that, rather than being formally conservative, some UK poets are tackling the same difficult issues as their more experimental American counterparts, only approaching these issues via a postmodern critique of empiricism. She suggests that the work of Denise Riley successfully bridges the impasse between empiricist and theoretical modes: Riley preserves an 'I' in her poems, but is constantly testing this self in the face of her understanding of the instability of identity and the problems of transcendent authority.

13

Lorine Niedecker On and Off the Margins: A Radical Poetics out of Objectivism

Harriet Tarlo

A tough game, art,
humanity's other part.[1]

'She is unknown. She is therefore erased. Every time she is mentioned, she must be re-introduced.'[2] A quarter of a century after her death, I must again re-introduce Lorine Niedecker. She lived most of her life (1903–70) on Black Hawk Island, a marshy peninsula of Lake Koshkonong outside Fort Atkinson in Wisconsin. Coming from a working family, she worked until she was sixty in a variety of jobs, from editing to hospital cleaning. She was married twice, at the beginning and end of her adult life, living most of the intervening thirty years alone.

Niedecker is known as an objectivist, the only woman to be involved in the movement established by Louis Zukofsky in his 1931 guest-edited edition of *Poetry*. Niedecker read the magazine and wrote to Zukofsky, thus initiating a lifelong correspondence. Zukofsky has, in the past, been perceived as Niedecker's introduction to the avant-garde and to publication. However, recent criticism has emphasised that she was interested and involved in surrealist and imagist poetics before 1931.[3]

Furthermore, Niedecker's letters to Zukofsky, whilst they do reveal an obvious power imbalance in their relationship (colluded in by both parties), also suggest the reciprocal exchange of support and ideas between two poets of almost the same age. Since Niedecker did not make public statements about her work, this correspondence and the later one with the poet Cid Corman, editor of *Origin* magazine and publisher of her work, are important sources for her readers.

Niedecker's publishing history reflects a life on the margins. She had been appearing in magazines for fifteen years before her first book, *New Goose*, was published by James Decker in 1946. Another fifteen years passed before her second, *My Friend Tree* (1961) and, only in the final years of her life, were three major collections achieved.[4] Even now we do not have a reliable edition of her collected poems.[5]

During her life and since her death, Niedecker has suffered neglect on three counts: as objectivist, as woman poet and as objectivist woman poet. Objectivism is regarded as a minor movement, an obscure sideline of 1930s poetry; besides, Niedecker was the only woman involved and felt herself to be 'on the periphery just after the "movement" started'.[6] Nor has Niedecker featured in the recovery work of feminist critics. Women's poetry, as Marjorie Perloff has noted, has defined itself and been defined ideologically, being scrupulously inclusive of women of differing cultural and ideological concerns, but exclusive of writers whose predominant concerns are with poetic form.[7]

Niedecker baulked at polemical writing *per se*, and she cannot be read *only* as ideologically radical.[8] Not that Niedecker was uninterested in ideology: both poems and letters indicate her awareness of international events[9] and important new readings of her work show her concern with class and gender politics.[10] Overall however, she must be seen as a poet in whose work form and ideology were symbiotically related, but for whom formal concerns were never secondary.

Returning to Niedecker's marginality, we find it rooted in her geographically marginal position 'with the persons/on the edge' (*FTC*, p.222). In her case, 'local' has been interpreted as 'minor'. It is interesting to note that William Carlos Williams' long poem, *Paterson*, with its emphasis on the local, did not condemn him to such a fate. Here Niedecker's gender is significant, influencing critical attitudes to her as a small, 'natural' talent. The brevity of her early poems, especially when compared to Williams' 'epic', only served to confirm this view in critical minds. Another factor here, which can also be seen as gender-related, was Niedecker's refusal to self-publicise and theorise. She did not, unlike Williams, theorise about her provinciality, believing that a poet should not have to become public property to be taken seriously.

Locally, she refused readings and attempted to keep her writing secret. This was not mere self-effacement, but an effort to keep her non-working time for writing and her channels of inspiration open. Asking a friend not to tell 'folks' about her poems, she wrote: 'I have to be among 'em to hear 'em talk so I can write some more! Believin' as I do that poetry comes from the folk if it's to be vital and original.'[11] In her essay, 'LN, the Anonymous', Rachel Blau DuPlessis argues that Niedecker's 'anonymity was principled; it was, in my view, a choice'.[12] Whilst Niedecker's status as a working-class, semi-rural woman both precipitated her marginalisation and remained a position from which she chose to speak, 'anonymity' is, I feel, too strong a word. Although Niedecker sought *local* anonymity, she did seek publication and appreciation of her work. She wanted her name to be known, referring for instance to the 'glorious shock' she feels when she see the names of Zukofsky, Corman and Niedecker in print.[13]

Niedecker's staying put has contributed to other patronising critical images of her as a fragile little bird or young girl. Critics have also over-stressed or romanticised her isolation, ignoring her working and neighbourly proximity to others. Ironically, given their own over-emphasis on Niedecker's personal life, critics also conflate the 'local' with the 'personal' when dealing with her work. All this means that, when attention is actually paid to the work rather than the life, Niedecker is seen to have a more restricted, personal perspective than her fellow-objectivists. Niedecker's own references, in her letters, to her critical treatment show an ambivalent awareness of such attitudes, even from the men she regarded as her champions. She despairs to Zukofsky that even Cid Corman (who did and still does much to promote her work) should call her 'slight' ('That word *slight* again!'). Another time, in the midst of a gushing paragraph on the reviews of *My Friend Tree*, she remarks about Jonathan Williams' comments, 'And LN *personally* – when what we're talking about is poetry!'[14] There are two elements to this review that one imagines Niedecker must have been referring to. One is Williams' reference to her poetry as 'local and personal in the ultimate way' and the other is the fact that he spends most of the piece describing Niedecker herself – even when he does refer to the poetry, he does so through her person: 'She is a frail person, like the poems, but sturdy as they also are'.[15] These are common critical fallacies in approaches to women's writing, as is the tendency to draw comparisons only with other 'poetesses' (in Niedecker's case, Emily Dickinson, Denise Levertov, Marianne Moore or Elizabeth Bishop), thus creating a lesser league of women's poetry in an enclave all its own.[16]

The overall impact of these critical perceptions is such that even recent critics seem to accept Niedecker as a minor rather than major talent. Here I want to bring Niedecker off the margins while refusing to disentangle her from the marginalities out of which she chose to write. I want to make the in-itself-radical claim that she crafted a radical and independent poetry and poetics that should be seriously explored.

No one is so subtle with so few words.[17]

It is important to stress the complexity and diversity of Niedecker's poetic background. We can say she came 'out of objectivism' both because it was the fertile ground out of which her poetics grew, and because, like her fellow-objectivists, she did not remain within it. From objectivism, Niedecker took certain key poetic principles of 'sincerity and objectification,' above all the rejection of lyricism, verbosity and 'strained metaphor' in favour of the clear image, the 'bringing of the rays of an object into focus'. This concentration on 'clear and vital particulars' included 'historical and contemporary particulars' which extended to the use of facts and quotations from diverse sources.[18] I shall show these principles in action in her work below.

As objectivist poet, Niedecker also rejected the confessional or sublime 'I'. It is Charles Olson, promoting his own 'projective verse' in 1950 who perhaps best sums up this objectivist principle:

> Objectism [sic] is the getting rid of the lyrical interference of the individual as ego, of the 'subject', and his soul by which western man has interposed himself between what he is as a creature of nature ... and those other creatures of nature which we may, with no derogation, call objects. For a man himself is an object ... the more likely to recognise himself as such the greater his advantages ...[19]

I shall return to this passage later. For now, we can note that in Niedecker, the rejection of the ego as outlined by Olson has played her a double trick in terms of recognition. It has functioned not only as a challenge to the lingering Romanticism of earlier ages, but also to the tendency of feminist criticism to validate the subjective voice of personal experience, its overwhelming emphasis on female identity. For Niedecker, although her use of the word 'I' becomes more common in later poems, 'the world is fact, and the poet is its agency'[20], the transmittor rather than the egotistical centre.

Niedecker's objectivism was, like H.D.'s imagism, more faithful to objectivist principles than that of her fellows, especially, as Michael Heller points out, in exactitudes of sound and form.[21] She combined a musical sense of the power of the individual word and syllable – Olson's 'elements and minims of language' – with a sense of rhythm, of 'thinking with the things as they exist ... along a line of melody'.[22] She rejected the structure of the sentence, 'all those prepositions and connectives', which she perceived as 'lying in wait for her'.[23] This allowed her to use words in multi-functional capacities, as I shall show, and to maintain the emphasis on the individual word as a musical note functioning non-hierarchically, rather than on the grammatical unit of the sentence.

Niedecker then, like 'H.D. Imagiste', has perhaps earned her reputation for having attained the ideals of her poetic movement to perfection. However, such categorisation can be dangerous. The woman poet is seen as a natural, even naive, artist, rather than a sophisticated modernist 'craftsman', the image we associate with Ezra Pound, Zukofsky and Basil Bunting. Once established in her niche, she is expected to remain static, a small but perfect talent or talisman. Her disassociation from the movement can be a tortured process and her subsequent divergent work is often undervalued or even attacked by those who were previously her champions.

Niedecker did not make a dramatic break with objectivism and, through continued contact with Zukofsky, she remained susceptible to its strictures, which were in effect Zukofsky's censures. However, throughout her writing life, she was influenced by other ideas about poetry. Some remained repressed within objectivism and are only fully visible in writing before and after Zukofsky exercised most influence; others are present throughout her work.

Niedecker's fascination with voice, dialect, slang, song and nonsense was a poetic concern which both remained within objectivism/Zukofskyism and went beyond it. We have seen that Niedecker acknowledged her roots as 'folk', her inspiration, the words of working people. Although she drew on ancient folk forms (nursery rhyme, ballad, riddle), 'folk' was not nostalgic for Niedecker, but to do with contemporary and vernacular diction and speech rhythm. Hence, the name of her first book, with reference to 'Old Mother Goose', *New Goose*.

This folk-work, married to Niedecker's objectivist clarity and economy of words, produced poetry called aptly by Kenneth Cox 'the speech of the American people whittled clean'.[24] Often, however, this 'clean' poetry is imbued with what Niedecker described as 'some puzzlement, some sharpness, a bit of word-play, a kind of rhythm and music'.[25]

The 'rhythm and music' had various inspirations including, most famously, speech-rhythm and nursery rhyme. Nursery rhyme rhythm, in Niedecker as in the rhymes themselves, varies in regularity of beat. Some rhymes, such as this one about the sora-rail bird, surely reflect Gerard Manley Hopkins' claim that such rhymes were written in 'sprung rhythm', counting their beats in stresses rather than syllables:[26]

> Don't shoot the rail!
> Let your grandfather rest!
> Tho he sees your wild eyes
> he's falling asleep,
> his long-billed pipe
> on his red-brown vest.

(*FTC*, p.25)

But we can also find in Niedecker the sounds of Hillbilly and Blues, in particular, Talkin' Blues:[27]

> Jim Poor's his name
> and Poor Jay's mine,

> his hair's aflame
> not worth a dime
> or he'd sell it.[28]

The throw away final line here, breaking the rhythm, especially characterises the Blues 'talk'.

Yet again, rhythms derived from advertising jingles or political soundbites mingle with or, as here, take over from speech rhythm:

> I doubt I'll get silk stockings out
> of my asparagus
> that grows too fast to stop it,
> or any pair of Capital's
> miracles of profit.

> (*FTC*, p.18)

In this poem of the depression years a woman relates her attempt to eke a little luxury out of private enterprise: the anti-capitalist comment turns on the juxtaposition of the language of the vernacular and of economics, while the 'pair' forms the humorous axis between the two. Characteristically, form and ideology are symbiotically interwoven.

It is of course important to emphasise, as Jenny Penberthy does, how such 'anarchic playfulness' within language 'challenge[s] convention and language habits'.[29] Yet, it is equally important that, in our attempt to provoke 'serious' interest in Niedecker, we do not neglect the sheer joy in language for its own sake that we find in her work. Niedecker delights in words, their use and misuse, sense and nonsense, in slang or in error (even twisted by politicians or advertisers), above all, simply for play: 'O let's glee glow as we go' (*FTC*, p.6). Paul Zukofsky (Louis' son), her child-muse, provided inspiration through his childish words: 'Paul's playing "Handle" ' (*FTC*, p.46).

So words in Niedecker become objects, spinning-tops of swirling multiple meaning. Within a Kristevan schema, this poetry, with its paragrammatic language-play and emphasis on the sound, materiality and doubleness or *différance* of language, represents an influx of the semiotic into the symbolic. Yet, the basis of Niedecker's poetry in 'real' particulars, be they observations of folk, birds or politics and her awareness of language as a cultural construction check this impulse. This makes for a unique radicalism, a held tension in which language (sometimes in different poems, sometimes simultaneously) presents an objectivist specificity side by side with a semiotic multiplicity.

This nonsense-*jouissance* in Niedecker's work can be related to her interest in different levels of mental consciousness. In the 1930s she read Eugene and Maria Jolas' magazine, *transition*. Produced in Paris, *transition* published the surrealists, James Joyce, Gertrude Stein and other avant-garde writing concerned with 'revolutionary' uses of language and the unconscious levels of the mind. Niedecker remained interested in this 'vertical' (rather than 'horizontal' or everyday) plane of human experience.[30] During the 1930s, and again in the 1960s (emergent from objectivist orthodoxy), she wrote 'subliminals' exploring 'dream, mind at rest, automatic writing'.[31]

We can find this 'vertical' dimension to her work in the whole oeuvre in punning word-slips, incongruous pairings of objects, and word associations which refuse to make 'reasonable' sense. All these work on the reader below the conscious level, the same level at which Niedecker wrote: 'when I'm writing it's as if my mind is operating just below the level of consciousness'.[32] Once again, the balance is complex: words, very often cited from 'real' life, are made to work at a subconscious level, producing surrealistic sound-based (rather then reason-based) verse. Niedecker defied Zukofsky to achieve this rich if seditious mixture of objectivist and 'vertical' work. He advised her to stick to real details and curb her 'surrealist' and nonsense tendencies.[33]

Such work at the subconscious level, defying both grammar and logic, liberates readers to take their pleasure of the text's sounds, sights and significances. The reader becomes what Roland Barthes describes in his definition of the avant-garde 'writerly' (as opposed to 'readerly') text, 'no longer a consumer, but a producer of the text'.[34] Niedecker's poems vary in their position on the writerly–readerly continuum, but many are 'plural' texts: the number of 'systems of meaning' which can be applied to them 'is never closed, based as it is on the infinity of language'.[35]

A last seemingly contradictory element to weigh in the balance of Niedecker's poetic scales is her sense of the importance of silence to creativity, poetic form and even reading poetry. Here again, as Jan Clausen has noted, Niedecker presents a challenge to feminist ideology with its emphasis on breaking silences.[36] She was particularly drawn to Japanese haiku with its sense of silence and space around and within each poem. Niedecker invented her own five-line stanza-form called, in tribute to haiku, *In Exchange for Haiku*:

> Fog-thick morning –
> I see only
> where I now walk. I carry
>   my clarity
> with me.

(*FTC*, p.123)

It was the silence in Cid Corman's work which appealed to Niedecker: 'each man an empire when he enters/a silence' she quoted approvingly.[37] Yet, this letter, and others, reveal Niedecker's concern over how to balance Eastern silence with American noise: 'I'm a little worried – not really tho – about my own folk impulse lost – lost? – on the way to the ice.' While silence is ultimately ice, noise is destructive fire. 'The ages have degressed (not progressed) in proportion to increasing noise until now the bomb' she wrote.[38] Once again a radical balance of voice and music out of or within silence (which we can also read as space on the page) is required.

It is out of this counterbalancing – folk speech, song and nonsense with the vertical; the vertical with silence; silence with speech, song and nonsense – that Niedecker created her distinctive poetics. It is noticeable that, though the balance changes at different times in her life (in favour of folk or haiku for instance), we find poems representing all influences at all periods of Niedecker's life. She does not reject, but as a late letter to Kenneth Cox suggests, integrates, never relinquishing her early sources for the late:

> Well – there was an influence from *transition* and from surrealists that has always wanted to ride right along with the direct, hard, objective kind of writing. The subconscious and the presence of the folk, always there.[39]

Knowledge, humanity, energy

> You ask what kind of boats in *my* country
> on my little river.
>
> Black as those beside Troy
> but sailless tar-preserve-black fish barges
> and orange and Chinese-red rowboats
> in which the three virtues
>   Knowledge, humanity, energy
> Sometimes ride.

                                                                (*FTC*, p.43)

Here I take knowledge, humanity and energy, three virtues named by Niedecker to Paul Zukofsky, as anchors or 'poetic principles' through which we can further determine the radical nature of Niedecker's poetics.

Knowledge

> To know, to love . . . if we knew nothing,
> Baruch the blessed said, would we exist?

                                                                (*FTC*, p.50)

Niedecker-the-objectivist made an inquiring study of encyclopedic and natural science books such as Carl Linnaeus' *Species Plantarum*; Gilbert White's *Natural History of Selbourne* and books by John James Audubon, M.G.J. Crèvecoeur and Jean Henri Fabre.[40] She also exploited local historical data researched for the Federal Writers Project, especially about the Native Americans and pioneers of Wisconsin.[41] However, among the many books left at Niedecker's death and the references to books in her letters, we find evidence of a reading span extending far beyond the factual.[42] Alongside a collection of literary works ranging from ancient Latin, Greek and Chinese to books by her fellow moderns, there is an idiosyncratic collection of books of philosophical, political and scientific thought. Among the thinkers of importance to Niedecker are Marcus Aurelius, Plato, Einstein, Darwin, Thoreau, Emerson, George Santayana, Swedenborg and Henri Bergson.

How does Niedecker, the marginalised woman poet, relate to knowledge in her work and how does her fascination with ideas sit with her concern with the visual and oral texture of language, with form? First, we should note the radical nature of the ideas that attracted her. In the 1930s she was drawn to communism and she remained attached to left-wing idealists such as Crèvecoeur and Thomas Jefferson. She also developed a far-seeing environmentalism of her own.

Many of the historical figures who attracted her were those who radically challenged certainties and hierarchies of knowledge, as some poems reflect:

> Species are not
> (it is like confessing
> a murder)
> immutable

('Darwin', *FTC*, p.211)

Darwin, Einstein and Freud, all present in her work, could, between them, be said to have revolutionised nineteenth-century thought.[43] Knowledge among such thinkers is an overturning force. Nor is knowledge a singular, progressive force in Niedecker, being pluralised by her interest in non-Western, especially Native American and Oriental perspectives, and by her interest in different eras, notably ancient and eighteenth-century philosophy.

Furthermore, where Niedecker presents knowledge in her poems, its weight is almost always balanced either by details of the life of the thinker, by observations or both. Thus knowledge is radically cut down to size. These moderating factors reflect Niedecker's concern with fidelity, with original sources. The personal material is mostly drawn from letters and journals; the observations from the world-as-fact. From 'Swedenborg':

Well he saw man created according
to the motion of the elements. He located the
   soul: in the blood. Retired
at last – to a house where he paid
window-tax (for increasing the light!).
Lived simply. Gardened. Saw visions.

(*FTC*, p.156)

In re-establishing their humanity around these 'big people'[44], often concentrating on relationships with wives and daughters, Niedecker refuses to be reverent. She reveals a concern that, as in the life of Crèvecoeur, action should match philosophy. Overall, she is concerned, like many early philosophers, including Marcus Aurelius whose *Meditations* she prized, with how to live happily, ethically, moderately and wisely.

It is still necessary to refute the perception of Niedecker as a naive, purely nature-learned poet.[45] However, Niedecker remained an objectivist and, like Marcus Aurelius, she felt a tension between book and world. In several poems she berates herself for burying her head in a book.[46] The aim is always to integrate what is seen with what is read. The final lines of 'The broad-leaved Arrow-head' suggest this is possible, that a body can be both tree and library, finding a relationship with the world both far-seeing and far-knowing:

Well, up
from lying double in a book,
go long like a tree
and broad as the library

(*FTC*, p.21)

Even when knowledge breeds metaphysics in Niedecker's work, the physical world is never neglected.

Her knowledge, then, is worn lightly, in fragments. Although her selections are of course biased, the fragmentary presentation leaves the reader free to agree or not. We are not worn down, as when engaged in reading weighty volumes of learning, by rhetoric and mass.

Such fragments are released from ownership, entered into free circulation. It is here, in such poems of conversation, that Niedecker finds the equivalent to the Native American 'dancing ground' she mourns the lack of in 'Paean to Place' (*FTC*, p.220): a community for sharing wisdom and delight. The fact that Niedecker's fragments are often taken from letters, which are in themselves already acts of reciprocal exchange between people, extends the circle of the dance to a full range of literary and historical ancestors.

Fragments do not suggest fragmented meaning in Niedecker's work, but represent especially nourishing words that stand alone, 'the essences, tincture' of the matter.[47] In keeping with Pound's and Zukofsky's belief that good writing should be passed on, knowledge in Niedecker is a gift to the reader, the deeply dredged fragment given free.

Humanity

> I suppose there is nothing
> so good as human
> immediacy

(*FTC*, p.133)

The words 'human' and 'humanity' crop up continually in Niedecker's poetry and letters where 'humanity' is sometimes a yardstick against which to measure poems.[48] I have already stressed how vital the human was to Niedecker in terms of sound and rhythm, but human situations and feelings are also important in her work.

The polyphony of various voices in Niedecker's work reflects her egalitarian attitudes, equal value being placed on the words of 'big people' and of 'folk'. The experiences reflected are often ones of privation, whether it be the poverty of the 'folk', as in her war and depression poems, or the dire straits of 'Indians', pioneers or 'big people' in poems such as 'Pioneers', 'Audubon', 'Van Gogh' and 'The wild and wavy event'.

The exploitation which leads to poverty, especially among the rural poor, is exposed in Niedecker's work, and governments and law-makers mocked. In 'The government men said Don't plant wheat' the speaker reveals how absurd government policies leave the poor hungry.[49] It is partly the presence of the basic stuff of life – food, water, and clothes (or the lack of them) – in such poems that leads critics to perceive Niedecker's poems as trivial, feminine or domestic. She is in fact working within an old tradition of using nursery rhyme for radical purposes:

> The land of four O clocks is here
> the five of us together
> > looking for our supper,
> Half past endive, quarter to beets,
> seven milks, ten cents cheese
> > lost, our land, forever.

(*FTC*, p.7)

In this poem, time is measured (and lost) in the search for food and, as with 'Jim Poor', the final line carries the punch.

In a letter to Corman on meaning and song, Niedecker reflects that it is not only cadence, measure and rhythm that make song, but also 'depth of emotion condensed'.[50] Those of Niedecker's poems which focused on a woman's relationships with her mother or husband/lover carry a particularly powerful charge of feeling. In their concern with female experience, personal experience and surrealistic forms, these poems carried a triple taboo for earlier Niedecker critics. Yet, they are often especially strong work in which the disturbed, subconscious mind produces surrealistic, nightmarish visions:

> I married
>
> in the world's black night
> for warmth
>   if not repose
>   At the close –
> someone.
>
> I hid with him
> from the long range guns.
>   We lay leg
>   in the cupboard, head
> in closet.
>
> A slit of light
> at no bird dawn –
>   Untaught
>   I thought
> he drank
>
> too much.
> I say
>   I married
>   and lived unburied.
> I thought –

> (*FTC*, p.176)[51]

The marriage bed here is a coffin-like cupboard, the lack of space within marriage figured by bodies disjointed, almost (as in surreal works) dismembered, wedged awkwardly into closets. The syntax, unravelling rhymes, and awkward line breaks embody this discomfort. The spaces in the text reflect that which is unsaid,

especially the space at the end of the poem which suggests thoughts stifled within
the marriage-coffin.

Different 'layers of the mind' are also an important factor in the formation
of the 'big people' poems. In 'Thomas Jefferson' the separate sections, overlapping lines, hyphens and parentheses reflect the different levels of thought in
Jefferson's mind:

> When I set out for Monticello
> (my grandchildren
> will they know me?)
> How are my young
> chestnut trees –

> (*FTC*, p.197)

In such work Niedecker, like other modernist writers, questions the idea of the
unitary self:

> Niedecker's portrait poems subvert conventions of traditional biography and
> embody her idea of the self as fluid, multiplicitous and constantly evolving.[52]

Yet though the self be questioned in Niedecker's poems reflecting the unconscious
mind, the human as species can find its place in the cycles of the universe, as the
following section shows.

Energy

> no fact is isolate[53]

Throughout her work, Niedecker expresses doubt about all forms of ownership,
especially land-ownership. Living on Black Hawk Island, she cites 'Old Chief
Black Hawk' whose dictated autobiography was one of her 'great books':[54]

> Black Hawk held: In reason
> land cannot be sold,
> only things to be carried away,
> and I am old.

> Young Lincoln's general moved,
> pawpaw in bloom,
> and to this day, Black Hawk,
> reason has small room.

> (*FTC*, p.21)[55]

Her poems and letters reveal an underlying awareness of the violent greed inherent in the history of the land of America.[56] In this context, Niedecker struggled painfully with her father's hard-earned bequest of two houses on the island.[57]

Numerous poems dwell on the problem of property which Niedecker often links to other forms of possessive materialism, including possession in relationships. In 'That woman!' a woman's desire for property governs her distorted relationship with her lover (*FTC*, p.28). In 'I rose from marsh mud' (*FTC*, p.93) marriage is seen as another form of possession, the couple 'United for life to serve/silver' (*FTC*, p.93). In 'What's wrong with marriage?' 'those "buy! buy!" technicolour ads' aimed at women are blamed for the failure of marriage (*FTC*, p.90).

The disgust with property (and typically here with the law also) leads ultimately to the desire to destroy it altogether:

> Tell 'em to take my bare walls down
> my cement abutments
> their parties thereof
> and clause of claws
>
> Leave me the land . . .

(*FTC*, p.208)

Here is an alternative to ownership and materialism, a blurring of outside and inside, found also in poems relishing the flood that destroys domestic life on Black Hawk Island:[58]

> O my floating life
> Do not save love
>   for things
>   Throw *things*
>
> to the flood

(*FTC*, p.221)

Out of this reaction against possession and desire for engulfment develops an alternative reason (of a Black Hawk kind), a radical philosophy of reciprocity, of moving energy, extending to all elements of nature and to Niedecker's poetics. This was not a new philosophy. It grew out of Niedecker's long-term interest in the 'symbiotic relationship'[59] between different natural elements, including human beings. In the early poems 'My friend tree' and 'Along the river' tree, sun, sunflower, air and silt are all friends or relatives to the human speaker (*FTC*, p.20). We are reminded of Olson's reference, quoted earlier, to human beings being on a par, as 'objects', with all other 'creatures of nature'.[60]

In late work, these ideas develop into exemplary poems and sequences. Human beings are shown not only their kinship with nature, but also their protozoic origins. From 'Traces of Living Things', a sequence laying the foundation for the long poem, 'Wintergreen Ridge':

> Far reach
> of sand
> A man
>
> bends to inspect
> a shell
> Himself
>
> part coral
> and mud
> clam
>
> (*FTC*, p.166)

In 'Lake Superior', we find images of fluid energy common to all growing things: the sap in the plant, the minerals in human blood common to those in rock:

> In every part of every living thing
> is stuff that once was rock
>
> In blood the minerals
> of the rock
>
> (*FTC*, p.161)

Each element of nature should be respected (as in 'Don't shoot the rail!' quoted above), and is shown in its strength, not weakness. Even the most modest live green matter, the lichen, may survive weapons designed to destroy humanity:

> Unaffected
> by man
> thin to nothing lichens
> grind with their acid
> granite to sand
> These may survive
> the grand blow-up –
> the bomb . . .
>
> (*FTC*, p.187)

Niedecker rightly described these poems as metaphysical and as 'poems that carry a load of ecstasy'.[61] However, they are never transcendent. Niedecker remains the scrupulous observer and researcher through this large vision and the poems remain rooted in objectivist detail, in matter-of-fact (matter as fact). The details of the system of kinship between living things are so delicately portrayed that each keeps its individual discretion.[62]

The seeing eye still carries the structure. Sturgeon notes 'objectivist reflection' alongside the 'rapid sequential sensing of a life' in the autobiographical 'Paean to Place'.[63] In 'Wintergreen Ridge' the poem's course 'derives from the shifts of thought prompted by things seen in passing'.[64] It is almost impossible to extricate quotations from these poems, their visual and oral form being utterly entangled with their philosophy, and embodying the flow of nature.[65]

In 'Wintergreen Ridge' the structure of three lines each moving further away from the margin suggests the rhythm of sea-waves, with their tidal overlap.[66] Almost devoid of punctuation marks, the words of 'Wintergreen Ridge' function both backwards and forwards, suggesting the reciprocal flow of natural energy. For example, the word 'Unaffected' in the following lines (which take us up to the lines from the poem quoted above) can be read to refer to light and silence or to lichens:

> Nobody, nothing
>   ever gave me
>   greater thing
>
> than time
>   unless light
>   and silence
>
> which if intense
>   makes sound
>   Unaffected
>
> by man
>   thin to nothing lichens . . .

In keeping with Niedecker's avoidance of the sentence, capitals are used here (and in the 'Traces of Living Things' quote above) to stress doubly-signified words rather than to begin a sentence.

In a letter to Zukofsky, Niedecker extols Pound's 'passing between and around images, from one to another, *locus*' and links it to her desire to do this with ideas, through 'the use of lines and words that look backward and forward'.[67] Here she is successful, but this writing is only an extension of her previous non-hierarchically structured poetry in which the sense of the full *différance* of the word has always been present. Here Niedecker creates a radical poetry which fulfils her own description of what 'good' poetry should do:

> [M]odern poetry and old poetry, if it's good, proceeds not from one point to the next linearly but in a circle. The *tone* of the thing. And awareness of everything influencing everything.[68]

NOTES

1. All otherwise unattributed quotations are from *From This Condensery: The Complete Writing of Lorine Niedecker*, ed. Robert J. Bertholf (Highlands, North Carolina, The Jargon Society, 1985), hereafter referred to as *FTC*.
2. Rachel Blau DuPlessis, 'Lorine Niedecker, the Anonymous: Gender, Class, Genre and Resistances', *Kenyon Review*, 14.2 (1992), pp.96–116 (p.99).
3. See Jenny Penberthy, introduction to *Niedecker and the Correspondence with Zukofsky* (Cambridge, Cambridge University Press, 1993), hereafter referred to as LN/LZ and Glenna Breslin, 'Lorine Niedecker: Composing a Life', in *Revealing Lives: Gender in Autobiography and Biography*, Marilyn Yalom and Susan Croag Bell (eds) (New York, SUNY Press, 1990), pp.141–53. These two sources discuss the complexity and significance of the relationship between Niedecker and Zukofsky in far greater detail. Breslin tells the story that cannot but be seen as significant, that Niedecker, during a brief period living with Zukofsky in New York, became pregnant by him and had an abortion against her will (p.145).
4. *North Central* (London, Fulcrum Press, 1968); *T&G* (Highlands, North Carolina, The Jargon Society, 1969); *My Life By Water: Collected Poems 1936–1968* (London, Fulcrum Press, 1970).
5. For a list of the manifold errors in Bertholf's edition, *From This Condensery*, see Jenny Penberthy's review of the book, 'The New Niedecker', *Sagetrieb*, 5.2 (1986), pp.139–51. See Tandy Jennifer Sturgeon, *A Critical Edition of the Collected Poems of Lorine Niedecker* (dissertation, University of Wisconsin-Madison, 1990) for a more reliable presentation of the poems.
6. 28 May, 1969, in *Between Your House and Mine: The Letters of Lorine Niedecker to Cid Corman 1960–1970*, ed. Lisa Pater Faranda (Durham, North Caroline Duke University Press, 1986), p.193, hereafter cited as LN/CC.
7. Marjorie Perloff, *Poetic License: Essays on Modernist and Postmodernist Lyric* (Evanston, Illinois, Northwestern University Press, 1990), pp.35–6.
8. In a letter to Cid Corman, Niedecker explains her refusal to contribute to a book of anti-Vietnam poems: 'Of course I don't write ... in that way, if a poem happens to fit the situation OK' (15 June 1966, LN/CC, p.87).
9. See Morgan Gibson, 'Lorine Niedecker, Alive and Well', *Truck*, 16 (1975), pp.120–4 (p.122).
10. See especially DuPlessis, 'Lorine Niedecker, the Anonymous', (pp.102–3).
11. Jane Shaw Knox, *Lorine Niedecker: An Original Biography* (Fort Atkinson, Wisconsin, Dwight Foster Public Library, 1987), p.20.
12. DuPlessis, 'Lorine Niedecker, the Anonymous' p.101.
13. 21 November 1968, LN/CC, 179. It is characteristic of Niedecker's own, at times distressing, self-effacement that she names the two men first in this letter.
14. 15 September 1960, LN/LZ, p.267 and 26 September 1962, LN/LZ, p.321. See Michael Heller, *Conviction's Net of Branches: Essays on the Objectivist Poets and Poetry* (Carbondale and Edwardsville, Southern Illinois University Press, 1985), p.49, for evidence that such attitudes persist.
15. See Jonathan Williams, 'Think What's Got Away in my Life!', *Truck* 16 (1975), pp.91–3 (p.92).
16. Ibid., p.91 and also Gibson, 'Lorine Niedecker', pp.120–4 (p.120), and Alan Davies, 'A Pencil for a Wing-Bone', *Truck*, 16 (1975), pp.128–30 (p.129).
17. Basil Bunting, jacket-cover quote, Lorine Niedecker, *North Central* (London, Fulcrum Press, 1968).
18. These principles and phrases are distilled from Louis Zukofsky, 'Program: "Objectivists" 1931', *Poetry* 37.5 (1930–1), pp.268–72 and 'Sincerity and Objectification', *Poetry*, 37.5 (1930–1), pp.272–85.
19. Charles Olson, 'Projective Verse', in *The Poetics of the New American Poetry*, Donald M. Allen and Warren Tallman (eds) (New York, Grove Press, 1973), pp.147–58 (p.156).

20. See Heller, *Conviction's Net of Branches*, pp.10–11.

21. Heller, *Conviction's Net of Branches*, p.49.

22. Zukofsky, 'Program: "Objectivists" 1931', pp.268–72 (p173).

23. 18 February 1962, LN/CC, p.33.

24. Kenneth Cox, 'The Poems of Lorine Niedecker', in *The Full Note: Lorine Niedecker*, ed. Peter Dent (Devon, Peter Dent/Interim Press, 1983), pp.29–35, (p.29).

25. 15 December 1966, LN/CC, p.108.

26. *The Correspondence of Gerard Manley Hopkins and Richard Watson Dixon*, ed. C.C. Abbott (London, Oxford University Press, 1935), pp.14–15. Hopkins was a favourite poet of Niedecker's and her poem, 'Otherwise', taken from his letters, shows her familiarity with his ideas about rhythm. 'Your father to me in your eighth summer' grants a similar tribute to Zukofsky, her other musical inspiration.

27. We find evidence of Niedecker's longstanding interest in blues in her letters: see 26 February 1946, LN/LZ, p.135 (about Ellington and blues music as folk music) and 21 November 1968, LN/CC, p.180.

28. Sturgeon, *A Critical Edition of the Collected Poems of Lorine Niedecker* p.136. Poem omitted from Bertholf's edition.

29. Penberthy, introduction to *Niedecker and the Correspondence with Zukofsky*, p.36.

30. See Niedecker's letter to Corman in 1968 about her continued interest in the 'vertical' (30 January 1968, LN/CC, p.149). See Douglas McMillan, *In transition: A Paris Anthology* (London, Secker and Warburg, 1990), pp.62–6 for a discussion of verticalism in transition.

31. 15 December 1966, LN/CC, p.108.

32. Gail Roub, 'Getting to Know Lorine Niedecker', *Wisconsin Academy Review*, 32.3 (1986) pp.37–41 (p.38).

33. Penberthy, introduction to *Niedecker and the Correspondence with Zukofsky*, p.40, p.63. As Niedecker wrote to Corman: 'This is the kind of thing [writing of the subconscious] that's been pushed out, down, in me all these years, but always there, dormant ... I'd think a mixture of this kind of writing and of objectification for myself' (7 March 1969, LN/CC; p.186).

34. Roland Barthes, *S/Z.*, trans. by Richard Miller (Oxford, Blackwell, 1990), p.4.

35. Barthes, ibid., p.6.

36. Jan Clausen, 'Lorine Niedecker', *Belles Lettres*, 2.5 (1987) p.11.

37. 13 January 1963, LN/CC, p.38.

38. 17 October 1961, p.293.

39. 10 December 1966, in Lorine Niedecker, 'Extracts from Letters to Kenneth Cox', in *The Full Note* ed. Dent, pp.36–42 (p.36, hereafter cited as LN/KC).

40. See letter to Cid Corman, 10 January, 1968, LN/CC, p.146 and p.148 n.7.

41. Both lines of reading can be seen to take up and deepen William Carlos Williams' challenge to poets in *In the American Grain* (1925) (which Niedecker owned) to know their land and its history.

42. See Appendix 5 of Sturgeon, *A Critical Edition of the Collected Poems of Lorine Niedecker* for a list of Niedecker's library holdings, although this obviously does not list all her reading.

43. Freud is not a named presence in Niedecker's work, but her interest in the subconscious must ultimately be seen to derive from his thought. She would have been familiar with Freudian and Jungian ideas through *transition* and she did own Freud's letters, a sure sign of her interest in a thinker's mind.

44. 2 May 1969, LN/KC, p.37.

45. It was only in the 1970s that Thomas Meyer likened Niedecker to Socrates' 'slave-boy' solving geometrical problems without knowing geometry and asked (of the poem, 'Thomas Jefferson'), 'Where did she get this from? ... Did it come from peeling potatoes?' (Thomas Meyer, 'Chapter's Partner', *Parnassus: Poetry in Review*, 5 (1977), pp.84–91 (p.88, p.90). Unpacking his equation of woman with slave with worker (potato-peeler) and his assumption that all three categories cannot possess knowledge, we need to stress that Niedecker, though working class and provincial, was a self-taught, book-learned scholar.

46. 'A Student'; 'The broad-leaved Arrow-head'; 'Lake Superior' (*FTC*).

47. 'the essences, tincture' refers to Niedecker's long project of cutting fragments from Zukofsky's letters to her for a book which Zukofsky did not allow to be published (6 August 1965, LN/CC, p.59).

48. See 29 September 1955, LN/LZ, p.224.

49. Sturgeon, *A Critical Edition of the Collected Poems of Lorine Niedecker*. p.149. Poem omitted from Bertholf's edition.

50. 2 July 1965, LN/CC, p.64.

51. Interestingly, Niedecker acknowledged two sources to this poem: the subconscious, to which 'we shd try to be true' and 'a folk conversation' (20 July 1967, LN/CC, p.128).

52. Glenna Breslin, 'Lorine Niedecker: Composing a Life', in *Revealing Lives: Gender in Autobiography and Biography*, ed. Marilyn Yalom and Susan Croag Bell (New York, SUNY Press, 1990), p.142.

53. From an early draft of the poem, 'Swept snow, Li Po' (*FTC*, p.109).

54. A letter to Zukofsky tells of Black Hawk's defeat: 'After I read about the Black Hawk War I don't think much of white people' (18 May 1941, LN/LZ, p.128).

55. See also the later poem, 'Don't tell me property is sacred!/Things that move, yes!', showing Black Hawk's continued influence (*FTC*, p.98).

56. See 'Pioneers' and 'Lake Superior' (*FTC*).

57. 'Point is, of course, I don't want property on Blackhawk [sic] Island – what a terror just to think of it, to try to earn money by property here. But I won't at the same time, let one penny be lost of me [sic] inheritance' (14 March 1962, LN/LZ 304).

58. See Kenneth Oderman, 'Lorine Niedecker: Houses into Hoopla', *Sagetrieb* 7.2 (1988) pp.81–6.

59. 19 June 1948, LN/LZ, p.150.

60. Charles Olson, 'Projective Verse', in *The Poetics of the New American Poetry*, (eds) Donald M. Allen and Warren Tallman (New York, Grove Press, 1973), p.147–58 (p.156).

61. 10 June 1969, LN/LN, pp.358–9.

62. See Richard Caddel, 'A Poem in Its Place', *Sagetrieb*, 3.3 (1984), pp.115–22 (p.120).

63. Sturgeon, introduction, *A Critical Edition of the Collected Poems of Lorine Niedecker*, p97.

64. Kenneth Cox, 'LN's Longer Poems', *Bête Noir*, 12/13 (1991–2), pp. 396–401 (p.397).

65. See Caddel, 'A Poem in Its Place', pp.115–22 (pp.116–7) for detailed discussion of how this works in the lines from 'Lake Superior' quoted above.

66. This is perhaps the movement Niedecker reflects on in 'Paean to Place':

> I must tilt
> upon the pressure
> execute and adjust
> In us the sea-air rhythm
> 'We live by the urgent wave
> of the verse'
>
> (*FTC*, p.218)

67. March 1951, LN/LZ pp.177–8.

68. Knox, Jane Shaw, *Lorine Niedecker: An Original Biography* (Fort Atkinson, Wisconsin, Dwight Foster Public Library, 1987), p.45.

14

Reading Between the Lines: Identity in the Early Poems of Veronica Forrest-Thomson

Alison Mark

Veronica Forrest-Thomson (1947–75) was a poet, literary theorist and academic. Though her body of work is substantial and accomplished, it has been, until recently, largely unknown. Nonetheless, Forrest-Thomson's work has been a central influence upon the writing of subsequent experimental poets in both Britain and the United States, particularly the Language poets, who have taken up her poetics in their own theoretical and poetic work.

> It was, therefore, quite right
> of Chiang Hen to write down
> the text only. For if the student
> concentrates and uses his mind
> he will discover the process
> between the lines[1]

Veronica Forrest-Thomson, of course, does not always follow the textual prescription approved in this poem from her last collection, 'Pfarr-Schmerz (Village Anguish)'. In addition to the books of poems, with their explanatory notes and prefaces, she published numerous articles, for the most part on poetry and poetics, as well as her major theoretical work: *Poetic Artifice: A Theory of Twentieth-Century Poetry*.[2] However, as well as contributing to my title, the epigraph serves to focus attention appropriately on the aspect of process, for, according to Forrest-Thomson: 'The question always is: how do poems work?'[3] Always how they work, rather than what they mean.

They work by both what is said, and what is unsaid – the experience of which is made available to the reader by the choice and arrangement of the elements of poetic language. The poems work both intellectually and emotionally on at least two levels: the conscious and the unconscious; poetry itself being a form of memory, or rather a memorialisation, of experience. And memory is fundamental to identity. Here I explore the question of identity in Forrest-Thomson's early poems, concentrating for the most part on four poems in particular, the first of which was unpublished prior to Anthony Barnett's invaluable edition of the *Collected Poems*. The following two poems are from *Identi-kit*, her first collection, published in 1967. The final poem is from a later collection, *Language-Games*, published in 1971, but which first appeared together with most of the poems later published as *Language-Games* in *Twelve Academic Questions* (1970), a collection that also included one other poem: 'Variations from Sappho'.[4]

The first poem, 'Sagittarius', states the problem, which for poetry more acutely than for any other operation in language is one of articulation. And in addressing the subject of articulation I am playing – as does Forrest-Thomson – with an ambiguity of meaning in the word itself, with its dual senses of jointing or connecting different elements, and of the capacity for utterance or coherent speech. I then trace further attempts to capture the elusive subject from the stereotype of 'Identi-kit', the title poem of the collection, to the photograph concealed in 'Ducks and Rabbits', through the medium of the mirror in 'Gemini', and the camera lens in 'Identi-kit'.

Suzanne Raitt, in her perceptive review of the *Collected Poems and Translations*, remarks that Forrest-Thomson's 'search in *Identi-Kit*, and in the uncollected early poems . . . is for a reliable blueprint for the self'.[5] A blueprint is of course a photographic plan; figuratively a detailed plan of work to be done. This search will be for a blueprint of the self, of identity, and of the other – the 'wanted person' of the identikit – which of course includes the reader: for the 'I' in the text sets up a relationship with, and calls into being, this other. The search is conducted through language: for a poet the only available, always inadequate medium.

This search for identity begins with 'Sagittarius', probably the earliest poem in the *Collected Poems*, which from the date on the manuscript was apparently written on or for her nineteenth birthday, under the astrological sign of Sagittarius.[5] Paradoxically, in this poem the pleasures and pains of the dissolution of self, of identity, also feature, for 'a blueprint is no guarantee/against anonymity.'[6]

SAGITTARIUS

Something dislocates.
I find me trying, to be
without a predicate.
For once a blueprint is no guarantee
against anonymity.

The self-set questionnaire
of circumstance
can't make all square.
Aspects jar.
A day with jagged edges and
minutes sharp to breathe through
bars retreat to neat
articulation;

derides the jingling skeletons
of sounds I blame
for these complexities:
Mercury, Moon, Jupiter,
when I was born,
were placed all wrong.
Sometimes the stars' perplexities
are fun, but now, not even names,
just pain; thoughts hurt.

The mind's an aggravated boil,
needs lancing; but no tool
– unless maybe
these jigsaw shards
of useless personality.

At last I can forget
the self-made self and work
to turn the spheres and all
that matters of "I am"
into this it
that is.

'Something dislocates.' Something that dislocates was, by inference, once articulated, or joined, jointed. Now it is out of place, out of the place where it belonged, moved to another place: perhaps to Freud's *andere Schauplatz*, the 'other scene' (literally showplace) of the operations of the unconscious. In the other sense of articulate, something is dislocated from the field of speech, is no longer speakable. The sentence order suggests that it is the missing predicate of line three that has dislocated, moved out of place, the predicate without which 'I find myself trying' – and here the syntax allows, the punctuation insists, in frustration of the urge to carry on to the end of the line, on the interpretations of both irritating and attempting. The absence of the predicate - the descriptive, that which is affirmed or denied of the subject by means of the copula – that which gives an identification or identity, makes being difficult.

This tremendous compression of sense and the issue of verbal connection is also seen in this extract from a later poem, 'Antiquities', from *Language-Games*[7] which is concerned with very similar verbal and psychic issues:

> Glance is the copula
> that petrifies our several identities,
> syntactic superficies.

As in 'Sagittarius', so too in this poem the manipulation of syntax – to which added attention is drawn here by the use of the word 'syntactic' – doubles the sense of the lines. The glance petrifies: the gaze fixes and terrifies – and the suggestion is that it terrifies precisely because it fixes – that which it looks upon. The child's first perception of identity at the Mirror Stage – an issue to which I will return in discussing 'Gemini' – essentially devolves upon the gaze, either that of the self as viewed in a mirror, or as constituted in the gaze of the mother, depending on one's theoretical preference. This conceit creates a Gorgon whose power can frighten and freeze – petrify – whose gaze can be the 'copula' that connects as it turns to stone our multiple and separate (another doubling), our 'several identities'; those identities which are, like part of the art which informs these lines, 'syntactic superficies': clever arrangements of surfaces. Through the manipulation of the formal elements of language, voice is given to that which cannot be spoken directly for the want of a form of articulation that can capture the duplicities, or multiplicities, of identity; the paradoxes of being.

The abrupt and awkward punctuation of the first stanza of 'Sagittarius' mimics and displays just this sense of hiatus, blockage, and disruption: 'retreat to neat/articulation' is barred; the 'jingling' – articulated – 'skeletons/of sounds' may be blamed, but not outmanoeuvred, for language is itself constitutive of identity. Indeed Forrest-Thomson used the restrictions placed on her by the constrictions of the conventions of language to create special effects, to 'challenge the strait-jacket of meaning', as Raitt puts it.[8] For she believed that the future of poetry lay in a new formalism, and what she called in *Poetic Artifice* 'suspended naturalisation' rather than in premature, 'bad naturalisation' or the rush to join words to world.[9]

Suspended naturalisation allows the constraints imposed by the formal patterning of the poem to govern the range of interpretation applicable, resisting the tendency to a premature narrative assimilation of the poem, particularly where that involves material imported from outside the text. It simultaneously relies on the connective powers of readers and on their patience in their exercise; willingness to wait in a cerebral negative capability.

'Anonymity' suggests a namelessness which hints at non-existence, at the least the lack of an individual identity; and, perhaps, the fear of failing to establish originality through the painful, continuous process of constructing 'the self-made self'. Even a blueprint – and the technical language is itself distancing – offers only a plan, no elevation: it is two-dimensional, just the outline, a stereotypical image, like the astrological chart from which Forrest-Thomson quotes:

> Mercury, Moon, Jupiter,
> when I was born,
> were placed all wrong.

These scraps of lines – blueprint, astrological chart, poem – offer no defence 'against anonymity'; no passport to identity and significance, let alone immortality, the desire for which, the immortality of the text, is such a traditional and powerful theme of poetry.

> At last I can forget
> the self-made self and work
> to turn the spheres and all
> that matters of "I am"
> into this it
> that is.

Desire also encompasses death, desire's end, of which oblivion or forgetting is the precursor. The 'self-made self' gets no further description than the deep relief of forgetting it, turning to the narrowing compass of the last three lines, where the emphasis falls successively on ' "I am" ', 'it' and 'is'. This images the dissolution of 'the self-made self' that can say, by virtue of the effort that went into making it, 'I am' (first person singular) into the neutrality and impersonality of the third person 'it is'. Turning everything of being, of subjectivity, back into the simplest of objective descriptions, 'it is.'

There are few categories more contested at the latter end of the twentieth century than that of the subject: of the construction of identity, of subjectivity, and its relationship to language. Under the rubric of what has become known as the post-structuralist concept of the decentred subject, and its consequent accompaniment the destabilisation of meaning, the theoretical initiatives of the

1960s and 1970s effectively foreclosed the possibility of any certainty about the nature of the self and its observations of the world. As Jonathan Culler succinctly explains, a concomitant of what he calls 'the pursuit of signs',[10] is that:

> the subject is deprived of his role as a source of meaning. I know a language, certainly, but since I need a linguist to tell me what it is that I know, the status and nature of the 'I' which knows is called into question.[11]

Some of these ideas, and their intellectual pedigree, were registered by Forrest-Thomson even before she became – as she rapidly did – familiar with the work of the structuralist and post-structuralist theorists responsible, and forms part of the argument of my thesis on Forrest-Thomson.[12]

Identi-kit was published in 1967 under her original name of Veronica Forrest, without the hyphenation (an issue of naming to which I will return). It is worth noting here that in the original edition the title was printed with the k of 'kit' in lower case, rather than upper case, as it appears in the *Collected Poems*. I maintain this usage (presumably the author's preferred format) which indicates a hierarchy of value of the two terms of the title divided and united by the hyphen, the hyphen whose use she was to celebrate in a poem of that title in *Language-Games*. The self and language-consciousness of her work is established from the beginning by just such details.

As the title suggests, the poems in this collection embody the theme of the search for identity, with poetic language providing a kit of tools for its investigation. Here, in a group of poems written prior to the influence of Wittgenstein's theories of language on her work, the beginnings of Forrest-Thomson's formal experimentation show already the importance of language play, quotation, imitation and innovation to her poetic project.

The title 'Identi-kit' is a play on the name of the police method of developing a composite picture of the wanted person – a wanted person who could here be either self or other. It was the quest for the other which explicitly underlay her final, posthumous, collection of poems, *On the Periphery*,[13] as her preface to that volume reveals:

> [T]his book is the chart of three quests. The quest for a style already discussed, the quest for a subject other than the difficulty of writing, and the quest for another human being.[14]

It is conspicuously hyphenated, against the common usage, on the pattern of her chosen use of the hyphen in her own name. This simultaneously draws attention to the split she has created and attempts to bridge it, as she describes in 'The Hyphen':

> i hyphen (Gk. together, in one)
> a short dash or line used to connect

two words together as a compound [. . .]
But also: to divide
for etymological or other purpose.

(*C* 35)

Typically, as in 'Sagittarius', the line breaks underline her theme: 'connect/two words', and 'divide/for etymological or other purpose.' As to purpose: in the case of 'Identi-kit' it is an effective device to call attention to the elements of the word, at once discrete and united. It serves, introducing her first published collection, to emphasise the theme of identity, and also indicates the possibility of discovering or creating a kit of tools for its investigation. It is a technique she continued to use in the collection *Language-Games*, where it also repeats Wittgenstein's use of the hyphenated concept of the language-game. The title of the collection is also the title of one of the poems from this collection on which I focus here:

IDENTI-KIT
Love is the oldest camera.
Snap me with your eyes.
Wearied with myself I want
a picture that simplifies.

Likeness is not important
provided the traits cohere.
Dissolve doubts and contradictions
to leave the exposure clear.

Erase shadows and negative
that confuse the tired sight.
Develop as conclusive definition
a pattern of black and white.

For I wish to see me reassembled
in that dark-room of your mind.

(*C* 208)

An identikit picture invites a form of identification that is not equivalent to a portrait. It invites partial rather than full recognition, and is more like the sketch of an idea of the person, a stereotypical image created as an improvisation on the possibly slender evidence of the memory of one person by another, who has no material knowledge of the subject:

> The system known as 'Identikit' is . . . a pure form of stereotype in that its incomplete and tentative images know only a generalised outline of the face; they are built up in a state of ignorance, a state of separation from material knowledge which they constantly strive to overcome; at the end of the successful process the provisional hypotheses of Identikit can be replaced by the use of the real thing – the photograph.[15]

Norman Bryson's discussion of the visual stereotype clearly delineates this process, the end of which is implicitly the discovery of the 'true' identity of the subject, tentatively recorded in their absence. The narrative withheld from the observer in the composite picture built up of lines is filled out in the photographic representation. Forrest-Thomson's interest in this development from the graphic to the photographic image, its metaphorical progression, is recorded in the title poem of this collection, and further developed in 'Ducks & Rabbits' (which I discuss later) where the photograph remains implied, withheld, still not overt. The importance of metaphors of visual imagery in the early poems demonstrates Forrest-Thomson's concern with perception. Of course the camera employs monocular vision: 'Love is the oldest camera./Snap me with your eyes.' Monocular vision erases depth, records everything in the same plane, flattens out the subject to give: 'a picture that simplifies'.

Bryson also compares the stereotype, as exemplified by the identikit picture, to the pre-recorded message, most familiar to us through the telephone answering machine, and which bears comparison with the text of the poem:

> The stereotype resembles, one might say, the pre-recorded message, in that besides its content it also indicates, fairly safely, that the speaker is elsewhere: it is an alibi that always works . . . the authority which so masterfully addresses the viewer is sure to be somewhere else . . .[16]

The text on the page also indicates an absence: that of a clearly identifiable speaking subject, for who is the 'I' set up by the poems?

The original printing of *Identi-kit* with the k of 'kit' in lower case indicates the relative importance of the two sections of this idiosyncratically hyphenated word, suggesting a focus here on the Identi(ty), rather than on the 'kit' for discovering it. This represents a foregrounding of theme over form that she was to reverse in her later poetry, for here language is the toolkit with which simultaneously to explore and to construct both identity and experience, whereas later it is language, always language that is foregrounded, as she confirmed in *Poetic Artifice*:

> The basis of continuity between poetry and the rest of one's experience is the essentially verbal nature of that experience: the fact that it takes shape through language. What we can know of experience always lies within language.[17]

As Suzanne Raitt observes: 'for Forrest-Thomson, theories of poetry are also beliefs about identity',[18] and Forrest-Thomson expressed her belief about the relationship between poetry and identity in an explanatory note following the poetry text of *Language-Games*:

> The construction of poems becomes the record of a series of individual thresholds of the experience of being conscious; they form the definitions, or affirmation, in time and language of human identity.[19]

Here the use of the word 'thresholds' evokes that periphery of conscious awareness, implicitly also the periphery of the unconscious, to which the title of her last collection, *On the Periphery*, alludes. She explicitly connects the practice of poetry with an attempt to define and simultaneously to affirm, or attest to, the experience of consciousness and identity through the mediating power of language. It is language which is both their connection and the means by which they, as structures, are constituted: in Wittgenstein's well-known formulation from the *Tractatus Logico-Philosophicus*: '*The limits of my language* mean the limits of my world' (his italics).[20] As Anthony Kenny observes in discussing Wittgenstein's theories of language:

> Language cannot be looked on, as a whole, as a means to some extra-linguistic end — 'the communication of thoughts' cannot be regarded as such an end, because there are so many thoughts which cannot even be thought without language.[21]

Identity is one such thought. The infant — *infans*: literally, unable to speak — can only distinguish itself from the rest of the world by the symbolising capacity that forms the foundation of language. The capacity for fantasy — another word for symbolisation — would seem to be innate. That fantasy constitutes the infant as the centre of the universe, which centrality is gradually deferred and decentred as reality impinges upon the imaginary, as when hallucinated satisfactions prove to be an 'empty' experience, leading to the recognition of the existence of the separate other. First there is the one, then there is the one and the other, as in 'Gemini', also from *Identi-kit*:

> GEMINI
> When all's said and spun,
> heads or tails?
> it's all two
> for I am a pun
> on someone unknown.
>
> My life's his uncracked code.
> Pleasure consists only in deflecting

the signals he transmits,
trying to flex his wit reflected
through my reflexes.

Thus we play a game
in which each day is a lost bet,
for how, when I must use his words,
can I communicate my paradox
to a distinctive third.

I'll never break true the mirror
that lies in each it and you,
in which I can see just me,
watching him,
watching me.

(*C* 206)

In 'Sagittarius' Forrest-Thomson deploys a self-centred view of the universe, in which everything revolves about the subject. 'Identi-kit' engages with an-other, but only instrumentally. In 'Gemini' there are textually two, and one is the mirror (impervious, reflexive) for the other: 'I'll never break true the mirror/that lies in each it and you'. A mirror which is 'true', of course, gives no distortion to the image reflected in it; and with that implied pun on 'true' and 'through', she implicitly calls into question the 'truth' of the reflection/reflecting surface.

This inevitably brings to mind the Mirror Stage as formulated by Jacques Lacan, and while Forrest-Thomson is unlikely to have been aware of this theory by the time of writing these poems – though she certainly did come into contact with Lacan by the early 1970s at the latest[22] – the essentials of this formulation have been in circulation for rather longer. Briefly, the Mirror Stage – a development of Freud's earlier theory of narcissism: 'love directed towards the image of oneself'[23] – is envisioned as a phase in development from around six to eighteen months, when:

> though still in a state of powerlessness and motor inco-ordination, the infant anticipates on an imaginary plane the apprehension and mastery of its bodily unity . . . it is exemplified concretely by the experience in which the child perceives its own reflection in a mirror.[24]

Prior to the actual development of motor co-ordination in its own body, the infant experiences an intensely pleasurable mastery of the movements of its reflection, and in this situation of the infant's love relation with the image of its unified body lies an alienation fundamental to Lacan's theorisation of the subject. The split in consciousness occasioned by the original misrecognition, as Lacan described it, of the subject itself as unified, and the concomitant alienation of the subject problematises the issue of identity.

What one knows – that is, the means by which an experience is known to consciousness – is necessarily partial and distorted. Both Freud and Lacan believed that the only units of meaning to escape from the unconscious into consciousness are those which obtrude from the unconscious in the forms of dreams, slips of the tongue, or jokes. In 'Gemini' as in 'Identi-kit' we see language-play, puns and wit, and perhaps something more: the construction of the poem as a net to catch the slippery and elusive unconscious processes, the restless metonymys of desire.

'Gemini' offers the metaphor that 'I am a pun/on someone unknown', and the poem moves from this playful evocation of a linguistic incursion from the unconscious, through an image of desire activated in imitation of the other (as in the mirror) where:

> Pleasure consists only in deflecting
> the signals he transmits,
> trying to flex his wit reflected
> through my reflexes.

The pleasure – and the identity – being that of reaction rather than action, for: 'My life's his uncracked code', the first line of this verse, also suggests living only through – and for – the beloved other; the relinquishing of individuation, the loss of identity and self. That loss of identity being part of the paradoxical pleasure of sexuality, the tantalising promise of blissful merging. And how impossible to register in language the nature of an identity which is already at least two removes from the subject, which is an other's 'uncracked code':

> for how, when I must use his words,
> can I communicate my paradox
> to a distinctive third.

This is a perfect description of the paradoxical nature of the psychoanalytic situation. The punctuation deliberately avoids the expected question mark:[25] this rhetorical question constructs its own answer, and reflects the impossibility of seeking the truth of the self in the other, the imaginary counterpart originated in the Mirror Stage. It is this imaginary counterpart through whom the desire of the subject – and thus the subject – is alienated, which is subsequently projected onto the inevitably narcissistically cathected love object:

> I'll never break true the mirror
> that lies in each it and you,

> in which I can see just me,
> watching him,
> watching me.

The subject's truth – and hence the subject's identity – according to Lacan, is not to be found in the ego, the place of the subject's alienated desires, but in the locus of the Other, which is that of the unconscious. This is not easily reached because of the essentially disturbing nature of truth, which only slips out in dreams, jokes and parapraxes. And perhaps too, as I have suggested, through the experience of poetry which is 'the record of a series of individual thresholds of the experience of being conscious'.[26]

Many of Forrest-Thomson's poems are clearly designed as language-games in the more common, ludic sense (one is even called 'Acrostic'), as well as the more precise sense used by Wittgenstein. As she described in *Solstice* magazine in 1969, 'his notion of language games suggests that basically what we do with our words is what we do with our experience of living'.[27] The nature of our discourse – 'what we do with our words' – dictates our experience of life and of our own subjectivity, and what we do with the special selection and arrangement of language that we call poetry does something more. To reiterate the opening quotation, the focus of my analysis: 'The question always is: how do poems work?' The poems are frequently constructed on three levels: 'narrative' or theme (and the special reading of that which she called the 'thematic synthesis'); linguistic experimentation; and a hidden or 'unconscious' of the text, which is not spoken or written, but can be detected through the play of the other two levels and by reading the silences or spaces. In *Poetic Artifice* Forrest-Thomson prescribed the kind of reading which she approved, where the impulse to naturalise, or rush to join words to world, is resisted by the reader. A resistance aided and guided by what she called the 'non-meaningful levels of poetic language, such as phonetic and prosodic patterns, and spatial organisation'.[28] At various times she called these levels of language non-meaningful, or non-verbal, or non-semantic. In a later discussion with the French poet Michel Couturier[29] she referred to a less intransigent formulation, a more accurate reflection of her practice: 'semi-meaningful' levels of language, or what Charles Bernstein calls 'anti-absorptive techniques'.[30]

Through the accumulation of 'image-complexes' that create the metaphorical level of the poem, it can be made to yield up both an unarticulated image, and a split-off emotional charge. The original split is sutured in the experience of the reader. One of the most intricate and complex of these verbal games which is as serious as it is playful is Forrest-Thomson's poem about metaphor itself, and the field of vision: 'Ducks & Rabbits'.

DUCKS & RABBITS

in the stream;[1]
look, the duck-rabbits swim between.
The Mill Race
at Granta Place
tosses them from form to form,
dissolving bodies in the spume.

Given A and see[2]
find be[3]
(look at you, don't look at me)[4]
Given B, see A and C
that's what metaphor[5]
is for.

Date and place
in the expression of a face[6]
provide the frame
for an instinct to rename,
to try to hold apart
Gestalt and Art.

(*C* 22)

[1] Of consciousness.

[2] The expression of a change of aspect is the expression of a new perception.

[3] And at the same time of the perception's being unchanged.

[4] Do not ask yourself "How does it work with me?" Ask "What do I know about someone else?"

[5] Here it is useful to introduce the idea of a picture-object.

[6] A child can talk to picture-men or picture-animals. It can treat them as it treats dolls.

[7] Hence the flashing of an aspect on us seems half visual experience, half thought.

This poem is a highly self-conscious attempt to articulate ideas about the structure of metaphor, and metaphor as a metaphor for psychic life. One of the most obvious formal features of this poem is the use of different registers of language. The language of the first verse is colloquial, conversational in tone, almost playful; that of verse two bears a resemblance to the language of mathematics or Aristotelian logic, and in fact refers to that form of metaphor which Aristotle identifies as analogy – on the model A:B as C:D. This has the formality of a proposition though retaining elements of colloquial speech: '(look at you, don't look at me)'. Verse three moves to a yet more formal diction, while the footnotes, for the most part quotations from Wittgenstein, give the appearance – if parodic – of a scholarly edition to the poem.

As Forrest-Thomson says in her 'Note' to the collection *Language-Games*:

> The poems attempt to set up a tension between the meaning of the statements which they steal from other contexts . . . and the structure of the poem itself . . . The process is a reflection of our constant attempt to integrate disparate levels of knowledge . . .[31]

Of knowledge and of consciousness. Those disparate levels of knowledge and the difficulty of their integration also find expression in the different registers of language within the poem. It is a problem to know how, literally, to read such a mixture of languages. Is it a duck (playful lyric), or rabbit (academic argument, poetry as knowledge – the subject of her doctoral thesis),[32] or a duck–rabbit? If we glance at the footnote at the end of the first line, and include that line of text in our reading, the even flow of the rhythm is upset, particularly where that rhythm is clearly marked by rhyme or assonance. The puzzle begins with the title: is this part of the poem? The syntax and punctuation indicate that it is, and that the poet has chosen this method, rather than repetition of the title as a first line, to indicate from the beginning that what is on the page belongs in the poem. It is for the reader to decide exactly how, or how to retain the plurality, shifting perspective, multiplicity of reference.

'Ducks & Rabbits' uses the quotations from Wittgenstein in the footnotes to much the same end as postmodern poets use the techniques of the cut-up, aleatory poem or collage: to disrupt the reader's absorption and narrative assimilation of the poem. ' "Do not forget", says Wittgenstein, "that a poem, even though it is composed in the language of information is not used in the language-game of giving information." '[33] Arguably all language is ultimately the language of information, even that which may appear, like an analysand's fragmentary communications, to lack reference or coherence, but some is not directly in the business of information-giving, and may represent the difficulty or as Forrest-Thomson put it, 'impossibility of expressing, or even of experiencing, a non-linguistic reality'.[34]

Forrest-Thomson uses the image-complex of the duck–rabbit – a trope of perception Wittgenstein also used – as a metaphor for her intention in the poem. It indicates that there is another way to see this arrangement of words on the page than that you immediately perceive – whatever the nature of your perception – and specifically makes the connection from the beginning of the poem with the reference to the theory of Gestalt which forms part of its conclusion. The relationship between Gestalt and the duck–rabbit figure, which also appears in Ernst Gombrich's classic *Art and Illusion*,[35] is concisely described by Raman Selden:

Gestalt psychology argues that the human mind does not perceive things in the world as unrelated bits and pieces, but as *configurations* of elements, themes, or meaningful, organised wholes. Individual items look different in different contexts, and even within a single field of vision they will be interpreted according to whether they are seen as 'figure' or 'ground'. These approaches have insisted that the perceiver is active and not passive in the act of perception. In the case of the famous duck-rabbit puzzle, only the perceiver can decide how to orient the configuration of lines. Is it a duck looking left, or a rabbit looking right?[36]

Like 'the perceiver' the reader of the poem is expected to be active in the construction of its meaning, rather than a passive consumer of the poet's 'vision'. References to theories of metaphor, to 'figure and ground', vehicle and tenor, are drawn from the reader in the search for the thematic synthesis of the poem, which is itself elaborated in the third and final verse.

Working diligently through the image-complexes from the duck–rabbits half dissolving in the stream of consciousness at a specific location (the Mill Race in Cambridge) and their analogue in ideas of metaphorical structure in verse two, we arrive at the enigma of the third stanza. This offers a reframing of metaphor, 'the instinct to rename', but also encapsulates a hidden message, past the memory of the first verse, its revision in the second, to the originary experience or image, which is not spoken, but informs the whole poem. The subject or thematic synthesis of this poem, for which the rest is a metaphorical transference, is revealed by the lines 'Date and place/in the expression of a face': it is a photograph.

The sense of intolerable loss and longing this perception releases is of the very essence of desire. This affect with which the image – literally the photographic image: of self or other – was cathected is split off by the techniques of artifice; the two are held apart until the final line, which joins what the poem tries with all its craft 'to hold apart/Gestalt and Art', being and representation, to maintain the perceptive split. A perceptive split engineered by language, which mimes the fissured subject, whose self-identity is fundamentally flawed.

Forrest-Thomson quotes Wittgenstein again in her poem 'Zettel':

> The concept of a living being
> has the same indeterminancy
> as that of a language.

> (C 24)

To which the conclusion of the poem offers this commentary:

> The *same* indeterminacy though,
> which could suggest a cast –
> list drawn up in language
> play, that speech commits
> to fantasy. And so it does
> at least in the first
> person singular, for:
> One's hand writes
> it does not write because one wills
> but one wills
> what it writes.

(C 25)

A subtle and precise description of the complex and paradoxical relationship between intentionality, consciousness, and the forces of the unconscious in the construction of subjectivity, in the performativity of poetry.

NOTES

1. Veronica Forrest-Thomson *Collected Poems and Translations*, ed. Anthony Barnett (London Allardyce, Barnett, 1990), p.61. Quotations from this edition reprinted by kind permission of Anthony Barnett.
2. Veronica Forrest-Thomson, *Poetic Artifice: A Theory of Twentieth-Century Poetry* (Manchester, Manchester University Press, 1978).
3. Forrest-Thomson, *Poetic Artifice*, p.x.
4. Veronica Forrest, *Identi-kit* (London, Outposts, 1967); Veronica Forrest, *Twelve Academic Questions* (Cambridge, The Author 1970); Veronica Forrest-Thomson, *Language-Games*, New Poets Award 2 (Leeds, School of English Press, University of Leeds, 1971). Elements of my discussion of 'Sagittarius' and 'Ducks & Rabbits' appeared in 'Hysteria and Poetic Language: A Reading of the Work of Veronica Forrest-Thomson', in *Women: A Cultural Review*, 5:3 (1994), published by Oxford University Press.
5. Suzanne Raitt, 'Veronica Forrest-Thomson: *Collected Poems and Translations*', in *Women: A Cultural Review* 1:3 (1990). pp.304–8 (p.305).
6. Forrest-Thomson, *Collected Poems*, p.227.
7. Ibid., p.31.
   Barnett notes: 'Manuscript dated 28/11/66, the author's nineteenth birthday.' (*C*, 281)
8. Raitt, 'Veronica Forrest-Thomson', p.305.
9. Forrest-Thomson, *Poetic Artifice*, pp.xi–xiii.
10. Jonathan Culler, *The Pursuit of Signs: Semiotics, Literature, Deconstruction* (London, Routledge & Kegan Paul, 1981), p.vi.
11. Ibid., p.33.
12. Alison Mark, *Reading Between the Lines: Language, Experience and Identity in the Work of Veronica Forrest-Thomson*, unpublished doctoral thesis, University of London, 1996.
13. Veronica Forrest-Thomson, *On the Periphery* (Cambridge, Street Editions, 1976).
14. Forrest-Thomson, *Collected Poems*, p.264.
15. Norman Bryson, *Vision and Painting: The Logic of the Gaze*, (Basingstoke, Macmillan, 1985), p.156
16. Ibid., p.155.
17. Forrest-Thomson, *Poetic Artifice*, p.20.
18. Raitt, 'Veronica Forrest-Thomson', p.307.
19. Forrest-Thomson, *Collected Poems*, p.263.
20. Ludwig Wittgenstein, *Tractatus Logico-Philosophicus* (London, Routledge & Kegan Paul, 1985), 5.6, p.149.
21. Anthony Kenny, *Wittgenstein* (Harmondsworth, Penguin, 1975), p.168.

22. Jonathan Culler has kindly sent me a copy of a page she annotated of volume one of the two volume Collection Points edition of *Écrits*, published in 1970 (though her interest in Lacan and psychoanalysis seems to have been limited).

23. J Laplanche and J-B Pontalis, *The Language of Psycho-Analysis*, trans. Donald Nicholson-Smith (London, Hogarth Press and Institute of Psycho-Analysis, 1983), p.255.

24. Ibid., pp.250–1.

25. That this is no oversight is reinforced by Forrest-Thomson's later deployment of punctuation and the rhetorical question in 'S/Z':

> What is true.
> I write no question mark
> after that question.
>
> (*C* 112)

26. Ibid, p.263.

27. Veronica Forrest, *Solstice*, 9 (1969), p.3, Contributor's Note; Forrest-Thomson, *Collected Poems*, p.262

28. Forrest-Thomson, *Poetic Artifice*, p.xi.

29. Michel Couturier and Veronica Forrest-Thomson, 'Poetry Forum: Unrealism and Death in Contemporary Poetry', Cambridge Poetry Festival, 18 April 1975, British Library National Sound Archive ref. T6023WR Spool.

30. Charles Bernstein, *Artifice of Absorption* (Philadelphia, Singing Horse Press/Paper Air, 1987), p.22.

31. Forrest-Thomson, *Collected Poems*, p.261.

32. Veronica Forrest-Thomson, *Poetry as Knowledge: The Use of Science by Twentieth-Century Poets* (unpublished doctoral thesis, University of Cambridge, 1971).

33. A quotation – unreferenced – from Ludwig Wittgenstein, *Zettel*, GEM Anscombe and GH von Wright (eds), trans. GEM Anscombe (Oxford, Blackwell, 1981) 160, p.27; Forrest-Thomson, *Poetic Artifice*, p.x.

34. Forrest-Thomson *Collected Poems*, p.261.

35. Ernst Gombrich, *Art and Illusion: A Study in the Psychology of Pictorial Representation* (New York, Pantheon, 1960), p.5, a work from which Forrest-Thomson quotes in 'Rational Artifice: Some Remarks on the Poetry of William Empson', *Yearbook of English Studies* 4 (1974), 225–38 (p.231).

36. Raman Selden, *A Reader's Guide to Contemporary Literary Theory* (Hemel Hempstead, Harvester Wheatsheaf, 1985), p.114.

FURTHER READING

Bernstein, Charles *Artifice of Absorption* (Philadelphia, Singing Horse Press/Paper Air, 1987).

Culler, Jonathan *Structuralist Poetics: Structuralism. Linguistics and the Study of Literature* (London, Routledge & Kegan Paul, 1975).

Culler, Jonathan *The Pursuit of Signs: Semiotics, Literature, Deconstruction* (London, Routledge & Kegan Paul, 1981).

Forrest-Thomson, Veronica *Poetic Artifice: A Theory of Twentieth-Century Poetry* (Manchester, Manchester University Press, 1978).

Forrest-Thomson, Veronica *Collected Poems and Translations*, ed. Anthony Barnett (London, Allardyce, Barnett, 1990).

Mark, Alison 'Hysteria and Poetic Language: A Reading of the Work of Veronica Forrest-Thomson', in *Women: A Cultural Review*, 5:3 (1994), 264–77.

Raitt, Suzanne 'Veronica Forrest-Thomson: *Collected Poems and Translations*', in *Women: A Cultural Review* 1:3 (1990), 304–8 (p.305).

15

Feminist Radicalism in (Relatively) Traditional Forms: An American's Investigations of British Poetics

Romana Huk

As a panel of poets and critics put it in a discussion several years ago at the ICA,[1] Americans know very little if anything at all about the 'New Generation' of British poets[2] (and much less about new writers working in experimental, small publishing circles). Quite reciprocally, little is read in the UK of current American work aside from that of, say, C.K. Williams or Sharon Olds, whose forms and temperaments mirror those in the New Generation, or in *The New Poetry*,[3] and therefore find publishers and distributors in Britain. Peter Forbes (editor of *Poetry Review*) remarked that other kinds of American poetry seem 'somehow not *real*'; Tom Paulin added later that poetry infected by the sort of abstruse theoretical thinking he associates with American universities' writing programmes is 'the most introverted and elitist writing you can get'. Jo Shapcott confirmed much of this by suggesting that British poetry appeals to a wider audience – a belief the panel defended by means of comparisons drawn in terms of sales. In America, the comments one is likely to hear about recent British poetry from those who have read anything of it can be equally dismissive. It appears to be too conventional in terms of form, many will offer as a first response; and speaking specifically about women's poetry, American critics will often offer some variant of the opinion – usually based on having seen one of the Penguin or Faber anthologies (or, more rarely, one of the Bloodaxe ones, – that the work seems, at a glance, quite traditional in its concerns, forms and attitudes towards language and empirical 'reality' (i.e., to return to Forbes' comment above, it is perhaps *too* real).

To what extent are readings such as these to be taken seriously, and to what extent do they demonstrate culturally-specific blindnesses to important new developments as they have taken place in these poetries? Certainly exclusionary practices in poetry publishing, especially in the UK, have made it difficult to assess the reception of the full range of experimental as opposed to mainstream work. But my speculative answers to the question begin with the assertion that the deeper problems in Anglo-American cross-cultural readings – in both mainstream and experimental circles – have everything to do with our unspoken and surprisingly outdated assumptions on either side of the water about poetic form itself, and particularly about what constitutes 'radical' form. For present purposes I will narrow the focus of my argument onto women's poetry, beginning with a brief transatlantic comparison of writers not usually compared – American poet Susan Howe and Irish poet Eavan Boland – in order to work towards a new American reading (or at least *one* American's reading) of 'radical feminist' forms in British women's poetry by examining the work of one poet in particular, Denise Riley, who I think succeeds in writing most 'radically' by (ironically) bridging the gap between mainstream and experimental modes. What I have learnt from exploring poetry circuits in the UK is that there are a number of good reasons why American feminist critics and writers should be interested in current formal/theoretical innovations in British women's work although (or perhaps because) they do not reflect the face of our own radicalism, and despite the fact that some of the most interesting poets remain excluded from the many anthologies of British women's poetry that have appeared in the last decade.[4]

I have too little space here to rehearse at any length the old arguments about form with which most readers will be familiar – those that assume, on the one hand, traditional forms' enslavement to patriarchal poetry, or those that fear, on the other, the abandonment of an essential and unifying feminine identity in radical/post-structuralist forms[5] – though these arguments come back with different values nearer the end of this chapter. Certainly it is true that in the UK mainstream (meaning 'available' because published and distributed by big publishers) women's poetry tends to retain the integrity of the line as well as of the speaking voice – so much so that Linda France could, in her introduction to *Sixty Women Poets*, write without compunction that her selection would only include poems that 'successfully order thought, emotion and imagination into a form that communicates itself effectively and *unequivocally* to the reader' (my emphasis).[6] This description insures the anthology against the appearance of any 'linguistically innovative' or experimental poems. Does this general tendency mean that British women's poetry is less informed by current theories of language, unrocked at its foundations by post-modern philosophy, and therefore less 'radical' in its political transgression than American work? Certainly it is also true that in

America our mainstream of autobiographically-inclined, 'unequivocal' writers has been increasingly upstaged by a much more visible avant-garde of women poets working in disruptive forms.[7] Most of these artists have taken at least somewhere near to heart the late-twentieth-century notion that structures long-informed by rigidified power relations control the formation of subjectivities and their expression; they also believe that creation of the seemingly 'natural' or 'commonsensical' world in which those structures operate depends upon 'speaking unequivocally' – buying into the 'transparency' or apparent naturalness of the operations of language. As feminists, their oppositional practice within phallogocentric discourse therefore might be said to involve, to varying degrees, the disjunction of language in order to emphasise it and disrupt its naturalised linkage of word to world – and again, to varying degrees, they employ that brand of diminished reference (including self-reference) and focus on operations of signs which loosely characterise the by-now-infamous $L=A=N=G=U=A=G=E$ poetries.[8] In their 'most radical' forms, they often therefore become *anti*-forms which break apart syntax, reference and reader expectations – sometimes with explosive results scattered all over the white space of the page. Does this mean that such work, liberated as it is from traditional communication, offers a more sophisticated critique of dominant discourse? And is it 'more radical' at the expense of locating a feminine voice? My answers to all of the above questions is 'no', or, at least, that it's not that simple, though my interest is not in the usual sorts of compromises made between these positions – that traditional forms *can* hold radical content, for example, or that radical or 'Language' poetry forms *can*, in the cases of women's and minorities' poetries, retain (self) reference and therefore remain viable venues for identity politics. Instead, I intend to argue, somewhat perversely, that neither of the models is capable of breaking fully with tradition; that both construct positions of (male) transcendent authority for the poet according to their own oxymoronically particular 'universalising' notions of how poetic discourse works in their respective cultures, British and American. Wholly or radically breaking with those traditions is, according to the very theories that inform experimental or Language poetry in both cultures, impossible; as impossible as it is to fully transcend what we might think of as linguistically-inscribed 'selves' in order to write a poetry unlinked to one's own discursive horizons. It seems that what we must redefine as 'radical poetry' or 'radical feminist poetry' would be a practice that works more self-reflexively from within as well as without the conventional/historical/discursive boundaries that locate its project to critique or explode those limits.

In America, our particular and potent mythos of revolution and progress, and of poets as pioneers of transcendent (or 'projective') proportions engaged in the discovery or remapping of history (in the Poundian/Olsonian tradition, from whence our 'radicalism' stems), still underwrites the contradictions that beset some of our most daring and successful new work. What I mean by this is that despite the important (and feminist) turn made by our newest poetries away from the 'Romantic' work of their forebears – meaning the latter's tendency toward 'lyric address to the human-eternal, to the Imagination, that seems to allow the poem to appear to transcend the partiality of its origin . . . [and] refus[e] markers that would pull against the universality of "his address" '[9] – other injunctions within the theory call for the erasure of all such gendered and locational 'markers' for the poet/speaker, emphasising 'the ambiguity of the speaking subject at the level of the sentence' or syntax.[10] A different kind of universality, rather than an undermining of the same, as well as a new myth of progress, has emerged in theorising that suggests that we have moved beyond 'Self-writing', or writing that uses any 'trace of [specific] consciousness', into work in which '[t]here are no terminal points (me – you)', only 'a sounding of language from the inside'.[11] By acknowledging the 'partiality of [the poem's] origin' I do understand that Language poetry theorists mean taking into account its origins in its medium; but does such acknowledgement then guarantee unlimited movement and freedoms through and against language irrespective of the poet's historical (as well as gendered) positioning within it? In many of the poems, readers are led by an unsituated hand that either powers words about the page or severs bits of 'found' historical texts and phrases as well as contemporary discursive strains and marshals them into the new sorts of (dis)orders that are said to reflect not the 'author's' associative processes but rather those of language itself. How can this be, unless the orchestrator of the words that appear on the page occupies some species of transcendent positioning? Although the disappearing of self-reference (along with the illusion of unitary consciousness) is meant to signal the overdetermination or entrapment of selfhood in linguistically produced subjectivity, Language poetry theory (and as a result, some of the practice) tends to elide the problem of historical situatedness in discourse that specifically and unequally constructs/entraps/oppresses language users.

The impact of such early contradictions in the theorising of Language and quasi-Language work has not been such that self-reference and its identity politics are pre-empted in poems by women. It has become commonplace to note that theoretical arguments about the erasure of the (female) subject in Language work ignore what actually happens in the poems themselves, which ever since the 1970s (when Lyn Hejinian was writing *My Life* (1980), to name one relatively early landmark) have often been engaged in exploring women's different entry into discursive frameworks for memory and self-construction. However, what the abutment of diminished self-referentiality in the theory and feminist practice in the poetry has at times inadvertently led to is, again, a universalization of experience in language, a phenomenon not unlike the 'essentialisations' objected to in earlier feminist work, although this time 'the feminine' is often retrieved as a force or an effect in discourse. Hejinian's *My Life* navigates the problem so valuably precisely because, I would argue, the specific memory/history of the speaker that to some extent delimits the poem's excursions through the larger linguistic landscape of her fluid autobiography also disallows universalisation of the gendered experience found there. When a poem ranges in formally radical fashion without subject-delimitation through a cultural 'textscape', invoking or encountering feminine workings upon it, the tendency is to produce these effects as though they exist, or have existed, objectively there in language when they reflect instead our current theoretical constructions – all of which quite ironically date the 'non-subject' to a specific juncture in philosophical time.

For an example of this uneasy collocation of theory and practice one might even look into the radical textscapes of Susan Howe's work – work that is without question among the most sophisticated and influential of the 1980s and 1990s in America, and rightfully acclaimed for being formally ground-breaking and revisionary in its exploration of textual history. She digs deep, as did Olson, into histories like that of their native New England, but with the radically different project of sounding out the silences (often gendered female) in its texts. Her disruptive form also derails monologic accumulations of texts into 'histories' by folding over competing tracks of available histories and writings, offering these to her readers as strategies of intervention. In, for example, the following sections from *Singularities*, 'Scattering as Behavior Toward Risk',[12] as material bits of the '[v]iolent order of a world' and contemporary 'counter-thought' (p.65) are '[l]oaded into' found historical discourse on 'the perfect commonwealth' – or indeed any 'idea' as it comes ashore – the lines become literally encumbered by other signs that disrupt the printed page's authority, or its march toward an unquestioned 'signified':

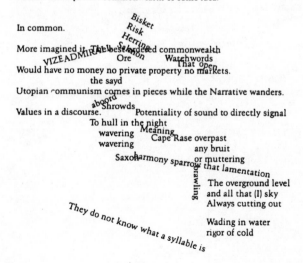

The disruptive signs are, in theory, guided into the poem by the *'Revealing traces/Regulating traces'* of language, as she identifies them in the previous section. The poem suggests that these traces enter into the work's 'Meditation of a world's vast Memory' through the random promptings of syllables – a strategy also famously employed by Olson, who excavated his Gloucester's 'understory' (p.50) as Howe does her New England's by letting the syllable lead him. However, it is suggested here that he (and all patriarchal authors of master narratives) did 'not know what a syllable is', as we see in a vector angling toward assertion at the bottom of Howe's page – did not know syllables for what they are, perhaps: regulators/revealers of a constructed history and selfhood, and not a sonic path to Romantic wholeness 'out there'. Howe's syllables and signs, quite importantly, act less as numinous markers to the past than as traces of cornerstones in mythologies that obscure it. Yet out of the wreck of these mythologies is retrieved a 'me' (p.67) which the 'Fathers dare[d] not name' – an unidentified feminine force that enters the poem via, it would seem, a kind of Kristevan semiotic chora, storming in syntactic scatterings the 'hatchet-heartedness' (p.68) 'of the Adversary' (or male) way of thinking toward linear destruction. On page 69 of the poem the latter is now forced to angle *itself* downward while the storm and its feminine properties of fluency and open-ended relationality move up 'on mum's arm' (a pun for their silence as well as their gender[13]):

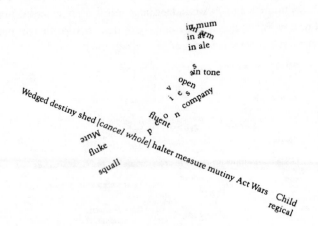

Like the earlier disruptive fragments, these would appear to arise out of the matrix of *'Revealing traces/Regulating traces'* mined in the textscape of the poem, though they are at the same time illustrative of a certain kind of current view of 'the feminine' as a disruptive principle in language – 'Yes, she, the Strange, excluded from formalism' (p.41), as it is referred to in an earlier section of *Singularities*. It would seem that though both the form of the poem and its vision of such gendered alterity are radically new, and as revisionary as the latest strains of psycholinguistic theory, their arrival as argument through the implied dissolution of the writing subject happens in what, by modern American standards, is an ultimately 'traditional' way: by creating for the poet a seemingly transhistorical positioning within language, though one that appears as a kind of photo-negative of Olson's projective persona 'Maximus' – a 'Maxima' that leaves tracks through the vulnerable spots in thetic structures (like the *'[cancel whole]'* above) but cannot herself be sighted or reconstructed. Yet 'she, the Strange' is of course a construction, with a specific and very important location in our current thoughts; my intention here is not to displace 'her' but to historicise her, and ask: is it possible simply to 'sound language from the inside' without arranging it into arguments that reflect the language wielder's specific positioning among its sines and cosines of entry and directionality? What I have been suggesting as an answer is that although most radical forms have been developed in acknowledgment or response to a post-modern awareness of our entrapment in textual inscriptions, the work of the erased subject is ironically 'bound' to effect the illusion of wholly exceeding them in order to take its place within an American inheritance of formally revolutionary but also, in some key respects, continuingly 'Romantic' and authoritatively visionary, explorer poems.

I want to shift my focus at this point to another kind of formal situation at the other end of the spectrum, though it might be seen here as a 'middle ground' of sorts, since it is found in the work of Irish poet Eavan Boland, whose poems are very well received in the UK and widely anthologised in collections such as the one edited by Linda France. The sequence I have in mind is 'Outside History', which I read as a response, much like Howe's to Olson, of Boland to Seamus Heaney, particularly to his explorations of Irish history and language in works such as *North* (1975). In Boland's sequence I find, as I did in Howe's, a work preoccupied with post-modern philosophical and linguistic predicaments involving the recovery of one's own construction in the discursive webs of history rather than myth – only Boland's poem is more traditional in form and therefore, we might suspect, in 'content' as well; the blurb on the back of the collection *Outside History* even suggests that readers might consider Boland a 'modern Romantic'.[14] Yet in this poem the form, given its situatedness of the speaking subject, effects a different rather than a less radical approach to the same dilemmas – by enacting the blockage, the limitations, that dissolved positionality and freer play in composition can at times seem to transcend. For example, in the section entitled 'Old Steel Engraving' (p.39), the speaker remains 'outside' but implicated in the slippage of past and present historical events into proliferating texts. She is also made speechless before those events that have slipped *out* of texts to become through their absence other sorts of inhibiting forces, like the one that in this section freezes the witness of battle's 'unfinished action' – a half-fallen patriot who 'cannot die' – in an Irish engraving. The speaker, like the passer-by etched in the metal of the engraving, 'cannot escape', 'cannot stop staring at/this hand which can barely raise/the patriot above the ground which is/the origin and reason for it all'. Not being privy to much of that subordinated history the speaker becomes a figure in a hall of mirrors, staring at her own 'hand' or writing in which she too is attempting to 'raise/the patriot' or Ireland above that cryptic ground of history; in the words of the poem she finds herself looking

More closely now:
At the stillness of unfinished action in
afternoon heat, at the spaces on the page. They widen
to include us:
we have found

the country of our malediction where
nothing can move until we find the word,
nothing can stir until we say this is

what happened and is happening and history
is one of us who turns away
while the other is
turning the page.

Is this river which
moments ago must have flashed the morse
of a bayonet thrust. And is moving on.

For Boland, as for Howe, the working recognition signalled by her line-breaks is that nothing, in a sense, *is* until it becomes textualised, until it enters our linguistic medium (according to the latter's rules), until it is articulated: 'nothing can move until we find the word'. History, therefore, though it holds a complex matrix of causality – 'the origin and reason for it all' – goes unrealised except as written, and lost altogether unless someone is able to say 'this is'. Therefore the limits of the 'story' as told in the engraving are reflected in the spaces that 'widen' following the longer line in the second stanza. Situated in that space, 'the country of our malediction' (read, subtextually, as 'male diction'), is also much of 'What We Lost' in terms of women's stories, as another poem's title in the sequence puts it. The feminine image from the past is also, like that of the precariously supported and undying warrior in the steel engraving, caught throughout the poem ('en-graved', entombed, represented) only through the inarticulate details that the speaker gathers, the conversations she half-remembers ('half-raises'), and the mythological images she awkwardly attempts to demythologise. But the very first poem challenges the forms available to the speaker for setting such images, bereft of verbal accounts, into motion; like the 'Court poems of the Silver Age' (p. 27) in the book which her younger self read without 'comprehend[ing]', the rest of the sequence employs

> the harmonies of servitude,
> the grace music gives to flattery
> and language borrows from ambition –

and is shown to be seemingly 'oblivious to', like the speaker was as a sleeping girl,

> the planets clouding over in the skies,
> the slow decline of the Spring moon,
> the songs crying out their ironies.

('The Achill Woman', p. 28)

In other words, Boland challenges her own form even as she works through it, admitting her unconscious formation by it and thus the impossibility of recovering all that was 'cloud[ed] over' or unlogged by 'Court poets' – as well as unlogged by the women whose experience may never have fitted or entered such 'grace'-ful forms. Though history 'is', as the section above asserts, also this lost life – 'this river which/moments ago must have flashed the morse/of a bayonet thrust. And is moving on' in unrecoverable process, its language is encoded now, or 'morse'; its causes of death, like those of the figure in the steel engraving, were perhaps briefly discernible in that flow but are now displaced by time. (And indeed Boland's half-formed interrogative in the last stanza of the first quote above casts even *this* proposition into doubt.) 'We are', as her last lines in the sequence put it, 'always too late'. We are, perhaps, 'always already' too late, in the Derridean sense, as Boland's unsuccessful struggle to unravel her own textual imagination might suggest, though like Howe, Boland seems to affirm the possibility of passages and inarticulate presences having been preserved somehow 'otherwise' if not in any fully-recoverable matrix of signs. However, in Boland's poem there is no mysterious force to be summoned out of the widening spaces located in the text, no 'Dear Unconscious [to] scatter syntax' upon (impossible, i.e. unconscious) invocation such as Howe's poem made use of in order to glimpse the 'Last fact dim outline', to 'Hear trace tidings' of the past she pursues. One might say that Boland is, contradictorily, too representational in a poem that displaces representations, and less self-reflexive in her medium than her own themes would call for; certainly her work and work like it in recent anthologies do little to question language *qua* language – in its fundamental operations – in the way that more formally disruptive work such as Howe's is able to do. Even more important, in my view, would be the criticism that the sequence moves from its local positioning to use of the plural pronoun too seamlessly, and thus ends up, like Howe's sequence, offering theoretical universalisms. Howe's and Boland's choices at either end of the formal–antiformal prosodic spectrum allow them *differing* but not necessarily *more* or *less* 'radical' insights into the changing relationships between history, identity and textuality. The judging of their poems' relative weights as radical texts/forms must take into account the fact that the very perception of radicality is mediated in either case by twentieth-century 'tradition' in their respective contexts. Howe's audience is more prepared to welcome the linguistic experiment and theoretical expansion into (anti)epic vision that her investigation of language and American history affords, and Boland's audience her project of communicating 'unequivocally' with readers – to the extent of speaking for them about commonly felt entrapments within language, and of testing complex theoretical ideas through the struggles of her own historically-situated (rather than erased) subjectivity, or 'real' life.

'Real'. This takes me back to Peter Forbes' remark, '[American poems] seem somehow not *real*', with which I began this chapter. There is nothing terribly new about the observation that British and Irish poetics in general have demonstrated a different relationship to changing concepts of 'reality' and perceived audiences in this century: in other words, relationships influenced by a long (primarily British) tradition of empiricism and/or definite location of common grounds. That tradition is still active in constructing not only the different approach to writing taken by a relatively formal writer like Boland as opposed to the experimental Howe, but also the different approach taken by a number of the key British experimental women poets as compared with their American counterparts.[15] In America, the compelling modern presences that have exerted what I would describe as their contradictory forces on post-modern poetry represent the more deconstructive and enigmatic strains in American literary history; among them – particularly for women poets – are Gertrude Stein, whose precocious dismembering of her verbal medium still makes some Language poetry look tame, and the quasi-mystical, quasi-psychoanalytic and lyrically subversive poet H.D., from whose gnomic *Trilogy* Susan Howe chose an epigraph for *Singularities*. The revolutionary/deconstructive and the Romantic/epic/discovery forces so uneasily twinned in this strain of American poetry rarely demonstrate themselves to be in the business of finding the usual sort of common ground with readers; instead, they are preoccupied with finding new enabling theories and of breaking new ground. In other words, American poetry's readiness for the L=A=N=G=U=A=G=E revolution can be understood historically, as can the particular kinds of radical formal choices and contradictions inherent in its practice; it also makes sense that experimental British poetry should have developed different ways of responding radically to the same ideas against the backdrop of its own tradition.

That tradition has evolved, I believe, out of empiricism proper into a post-modern rendition of the same. What I mean by this apparently oxymoronic remark is that it involves a distinctly non-romantic focus on social discourse and manners of speaking (especially important within a continuingly class-based society) as being constitutive of a common if artificial *linguistic* reality. Evidence of the beginnings of such evolution is everywhere discoverable; my own favourite instance is in the work of Stevie Smith who, while Stein was composing some of her most famous works in the 1920s, was concurrently beginning to write what I have argued elsewhere were her own equally effective subversions of language, but from an entirely different positioning and with an entirely different sense of audience.[16] Instead of creating Cubist verbal artefacts that demonstrate the difference between language and its objects, or issuing disjointed propositions to foil reference and narrative progression – strategies Stein employed with the effect of locating the author somewhere beyond the constraints of linguistic codes, in a place of meaning otherwise – Smith always positioned herself within the encircling discourses she set into motion in her work. 'I am', as she liked to write in her letters as well as her novels and poems, 'a desperate *character*' (my emphasis): a construction of the many authoritative registers that keep colliding and shifting in her writings, all of them presciently 'disunified' like our current model of the self. She worked with those current discourses and customary usages that were most familiar to her and to her audience, such as newspaper reports, nursery rhymes, best-loved lyrics (and even tunes) from sources like *Hymns Ancient and Modern*, old English and French ballads and their revivals, fairy tales, modern-day psychology, theological debates, literary criticism and philosophy. Such splicings, refracted as they are in her work through contemporary discourses of power just prior to and following the Second World War, account for the alarm as well as the comedy that her poems produce; their project is to display culture's occlusions and cruelties as they possessed and highlighted the darker regions of her own specific, historically situated consciousness. Smith's differences from Stein (whose prose work almost certainly provided a model for Smith's novel trilogy) are best revealed by comparing their formal choices for their poetry; Smith's attest to a more acute apprehension of her imagination's structural limitations, given her own specific cultural positioning within language and history, as well as to her desire to remain within the realm of 'practical' application of her apprehensions about language rather than move into arenas of linguistic abstraction and experiment with *ideas* about the word which these generate. In some ways, I have argued, such writing is at once more traditional and more radical than writing such as Stein's; and yet for decades we have assumed its greater conventionality due to our simplistic readings of radicalism and their circumscription within disjunctive or scattered syntax.

More recently, evidence of a differently radical, formal sensibility can be found in the important work of Veronica Forrest-Thomson, a young poet who died an untimely death in 1975 but not before writing her prose manifesto, *Poetic Artifice*, which has in many ways remained as illuminating a document for the study of British experimentalism as Marjorie Perloff's *Radical Artifice* has become for the study of American Language poetry.[17] Her understanding of 'artifice' as opposed to 'bad Naturalisation' predates and prefigures what Perloff and others like Charles Bernstein (in his 'Artifice of Absorption'[18]) refer to by the same term: the emphasis on a poem's construction by language's partisan referrals and Derridean deferrals, as well as its mediation of the lyric 'voice'. Her version, however, describes an experimental poetry that does not respond by becoming what she calls 'irrationally obscure', or non-referential, or wholly obfuscatory in its rearrangement of syntax, or prone to point toward forces or principles outside the reality of the discourse that is the poem through imagistic or linguistic gestures in the manner of Ezra Pound and Charles Olson (a romantic gesturing which she calls 'silly'). Instead, its maintenance of 'continuity', as she puts it (which we might see as a new type of 'common ground'), between the discursive ken of the reader and that of the poem facilitates the reader's perception not only of the latter's 'artificiality' but also that of her or his own linguistically-constructed 'world'. Forrest-Thomson is therefore able to embrace the use of conventional syntax and even poetic forms as artifice, as well as all other kinds of spoken and written traditions that have assembled her culture's seemingly 'natural' sensibility over time. Her own poems were disjunctively discursive and full of formal parodies – a combination of William Empson, J.H. Prynne and John Ashbery, with perhaps a dash of the peculiar irreverence of Kenneth Koch.

The attraction to America's 'New York School' of poets remains one of many important links between Forrest-Thomson and Denise Riley, one of the best regarded of the British experimentalists. Known for their anti-romantic focus on the voice, and playful discursivity – as opposed to the more disruptive and asyntactical work of the later L=A=N=G=U=A=G=E school – the New York poets (especially Frank O'Hara) are the first Americans a poet like Riley will cite as being important to her own development.[19] O'Hara's tongue-in-cheek advocacy of 'Personism', which lampoons both abstraction in poetry (particularly Olson's notion of 'projective verse') and showy confessionalism at the same time that it stresses communication, strikes a chord with another of Riley's favourites from the preceding generation, Scottish poet W.S. Graham. Graham's only slightly less comic art grapples more immediately with the problem of communication in a medium of signs he seemed to regard more and more suspiciously:

> I am learning to speak here in a way
> Which may be useful afterwards.
> Slops in hand we shuffle together,
> Something to look forward to
> Behind the spyhole. Here in our concrete
> Soundbox we slide the jargon across
> The watching air, a lipless language
> Necessarily squashed from the side
> To make its point against the rules.
> It is our poetry such as it is.[20]

It is the poet's austerity that Riley admires, 'an austerity which isn't melancholic or self-dramatising' in the manner of confessional/autobiographical work, nor too quick to leap beyond the pale of its specific linguistic boundaries to stake a claim in meaning otherwise. And yet it also formulates a potent post-modern critique of those governing boundaries which, in their 'lipless[ness]' or abstraction, marshal or 'squash' their speakers into margins with their 'rules'. Graham's seemingly simple, syntactical discursivity, which urgently seeks a common 'dialect for our purpose' (p.84), enacts from a limited perspective the struggle of the non-universalised subject in language – at work to identify itself there as produced by the latter's discourses and to communicate with others engaged in the same project. Exploring the very new locale of the 'real' (or experienced) subjecthood of the poet requires, in this form of radicalism, a focus on discursive construction and even a kind of semiosis of its attendant emotions. Though brief, this glimpse at the alternative tradition that informs Riley's work may help me to explain how it illuminates both her conception of the radical feminist project and the shape it takes in poetry.

Riley's own uncompromising anti-romanticism has been evident since the outset of her writing career, though its sources are not, like those of the American poetics that have influenced her, entangled in the Romantic objectivism of American modernism. Instead, since her involvement with radical poetics and feminism was not only informed by the tradition just described but also by the political left (as it was for many more women in Britain than in America at the time), her work maintains clearer connections to the severe attitude toward myths of self-discovery which became evident in the changing Marxisms of 1970s Britain and their Althusserian critique of language. Her critique of some early forms of romanticised feminist radicalism growing out of the women's movement and into poetry, much of which demonstrated the influence of the American poet Adrienne Rich, was already taking form in her first collection of poems, *Marxism for Infants* (1977). The best-known poem in it, for example, 'A note on sex and "the reclaiming of language"', dramatises with its disjunctive lyricism the impossibility of finding a 'herland' or essential 'she' in language – or of, as Rich recently described it again, expecting 'Poetry the Immigrant' to 'recall us to ourselves – to memory, association, forgotten or forbidden languages':[21]

> The Savage is flying back home from the New Country
> in native-style dress with a baggage of sensibility
> to gaze on the ancestral plains with the myths thought up
> and dreamed in her kitchen as guides
>
> She will be discovered
> as meaning is flocking densely around the words seeking a way
> any way in between the gaps, like a fertilisation
>
> The work is
> e.g. to write 'she' and for that to be a statement
> of fact only and not a strong image
> of everything which is not-you, which sees you
>
> The new land is colonised, though its prospects are empty
>
> The Savage weeps as landing at the airport
> she is asked to buy wood carvings, which represent herself[22]

On the simplest level one might say that Riley's emigrant finds that she cannot escape representations of herself; the appearance of her new image already commodified upon her arrival in the last stanza suggests not only this, but that her 'original' conception of it was based on her own representation of the 'primitive', 'thought up' in accordance with cheap images made available by the media and reductive forms of popular culture. More subtly, the second stanza suggests that 'she' *is* the words themselves – the child of a linguistic process that may as well be described in 'natural' terms, Riley seems to suggest (with satirical bite), if it is assumed that her re-representation as 'Savage' can be. Both are processes that involve language, with all of its long history of constructing meaning on the basis of eliding difference and preserving systems of subordination, rushing in like spermatozoa upon the gap caused by her departure from definition, 'coming' 'like a fertilisation' – uninvited, unwanted, like a rape, since it is gendered male in imitation of those forces dominant within it. This ironic naturalising metaphor extends to the next stanza's intimation that 'she', unaware, will be stamped in the hereditary image of the 'Father's' genes – his words, his descriptions, everything that is 'not [her]'. 'Sex' as gendered essence is thus *de*-naturalised by the poem's parodic naturalisation of the relentless and inevitable process of linguistic construction of selfhood – all of which issued, when the poem appeared twenty years ago, a potent early critique of romanticised projects in the female construction of identity.

The fact that Riley's forms have often remained within the realm of recognisable lyric (if distorted by other kinds of discourse) underscores her recognition that radical 'departures' such as the one attempted by the Savage in the poem above, or those attempted in theoretical or poetic/syntactical terms, are misleading, and that the only possible way out of discursive binds is to 'shuffle' through them, as Graham did, confronting all the seeming irreconcilables that inform our time. For women, the latter include: 1. the culturally mediated nature of language, and therefore the constructed and corrupted nature of any description of self, 'womanhood' or 'the feminine'; 2. a temperance of that recognition by the acknowledgement that one operates only *through* such constructions, being located in language by them, unable simply to abandon them; and 3. the need to 'maintain a politics of "as if [definable women] existed" – since the world behaves as if they unambiguously did" '. The last quote is from the final pages of Riley's well-known book, *'Am I that Name?' Feminism and the Category of 'Women' in History*,[23] in which she offers an argument whose project, as I understand it, is to reconcile an empirical tradition of working historically through observation and experience with needing to face post-modernism's deconstruction of all epistemologies, particularly the experiential, which includes 'women's ways of knowing', but also (if held to consistency) the theoretically 'anti-epistemological', which includes schemas that begin with the death of the subject or the location of the feminine as a disruptive force in language. In her poetry she has, since the 1970s, moved dialectically between such widening divergences of positionings (or 'non-positionings'), working slowly along within/against/through provisional descriptions of herself and her discursive *v.* concrete world, constantly testing the borders between traditional forms and radical breakage, in many ways bridging the gap between 'mainstream' and 'experimental' women's poetry even if neither camp, given their own frozen positions of opposition, has recognised the significance of her progress.

The fact that Riley, Wendy Mulford, Maggie O'Sullivan and a number of other experimental women writers are almost entirely ignored by mainstream publishers and editors of women's anthologies in Britain is well known and needs no evidencing here.[24] O'Sullivan's work no doubt conjures up – simply by virtue of its disjunctiveness, by which it is tagged – the spectre of American L=A=N=G=U=A=G=E experimentalism, whose abstruse theoretical play (as described by Forbes and Paulin) offers the threat that must inevitably reinforce lines drawn here between equivocal and non-equivocal writing. Given that Riley's poems incorporate many conventional devices, such as flights of narrative, for example, and generally syntactical usages, it seems odd that her work would be shunned as well, unless categorical dismissals of certain kinds of poetic projects are at work, regardless of overlaps with mainstream concerns and forms. On the opposite front, Riley's interest in mainstream usages wins her criticism from some of those in alternative camps for not playing by the rules set up through post-modern poetics – most particularly for her use of confessional tones and an all but obsessive self-referentiality. Instead of being read for their different – 'radical' – usages, such formal elements become shibboleths in the drawing of mainsteam/experimental lines.

It is very true that Riley almost invariably casts an 'I' into her poems: not the sort of stock figure that can appear in experimental work only to be stripped of flesh and lost in the word horde, but an 'I' that demonstrates historical, gendered, socio-economic and other particularities of positioning by which its linguistic construction is limited and *from* which it must negotiate some way along in its verbal medium. This is neither a transcendent non-positioning such as those assumed at times by Language-oriented poets, nor is it the conventional or 'natural' positioning that uses language to communicate unequivocal, essential or universal truths. Its relationship to its own 'lyric voice' and form runs the continuum between strained and tortured; it acknowledges its own infiltration by and identification with the lyric imagination while at the same time recognising that conventional 'lyric urge[s]' quite ironically separate it from anything approximating 'original' feelings. Markedly feminine in terms of socio-historical situation, Riley's 'I' nevertheless finds no alternative narrative by 'writing the body' or recovering unarticulated, unadulterated feminine experience. Instead, her depiction of the body, when it appears, is as of a war-zone – unrecuperable as it *was*, in some 'Savage' state of feminine power; tracked through, sutured and subsequently 'distorted by' culture's abortive operations upon it:

> All the connectives of right recall
> have grown askew. I know
> a child could have lived, that
> my body was cut. This cut
> my memory half-sealed but glued
> the edges together awry.
> The skin is distorted, the scar-tissue
> does damage, the accounts are wrong.
> And this is called 'the healing process'.
> Now nothing's aligned properly.
> It's a barbarous zone.
> The bad sutures
> thicken with loss and hope –
> brilliant, deliberate
> shaking patients in an anteroom
> refusing the years, ferocious to be called
> so I'll snip through the puckered skin
> to where they tug for re-aligning. Now
> steady me against inaccuracy, a lyric urge
> to showing-off. The easy knife
> is in my hand again. Protect me.[25]

Riley's description of the feminine body is not of a 'wild zone' of free play and 'being otherwise', as it has been described in some forms of feminist theory,[26] but of a 'barbarous zone' (meaning, from the Greek, full of 'incomprehensible voices'). 'Self-discovery' becomes a process of dissecting constitutive discourses and 'damage, the accounts' of oneself in order to see, in a sense, more clearly where one stands in the flux of *textual* time. 'This swaying motion', Riley writes, referring to the back-and-forth between various textual identifications without essentialised foothold,

> need not be a wonder, nor a cause for despair. If feminism is the voicing of 'women' from the side of 'women', then it cannot but act out the full ambiguities of that category. ... Instead of veering between deconstruction and transcendence, we could try another train of speculations: that 'women' is indeed an unstable category, that this instability has a historical foundation, and that feminism is the site of the

systematic fighting-out of that instability – which need not worry us. . . .
[A]n active scepticism about the integrity of the sacred category 'women'
would be no merely philosophical doubt to be stifled in the name of effective
political action in the world. On the contrary, it would be a condition *for*
the latter.[27]

Self-reference as practised in a textualised terrain is not a delusion but a necessity in
Riley's political philosophy; provisional descriptions of difference are prerequisites
in a world of representations which behaves 'as if [definable women] exist', while
constant recognition of these descriptions' non-essentiality or provisionality allow
for their dynamism and revision – i.e., allow more control over their political fate.
Translated into poetic terms, such self-referentiality constitutes a way of writing
which preserves local difference or historical/textual delimitations for each subject
while resisting illusions that one's words issue from romantically-constructed spaces
either within the body or across an abstracted, transhistoricised vision of language's
workings as a whole.

The dynamic that powers such a radical practice of 'self-expression' might be
best seen in those of Riley's poems that are even less distanced from their subject
than the two already quoted – in other words, those that are cast most deeply
into the 'confessionalism' and obsessive self-reference that supposedly deviate from
experimental forms. For examples, one might turn to poems such as 'Wherever You
Are, Be Somewhere Else', or 'Disintegrate Me', one section of a sequence entitled
'Seven Strangely Exciting Lies'.[28] In the former, Riley enacts in constricted tercets
the simultaneous lack of 'integrity' and yet discursively circumscribed ground
her speaking subject confronts in her attempt to express or define herself – to
communicate:

> I can try on these gothic riffs, they do make
> a black twitchy cloak to both ham up and so
> perversely dignify my usual fear of ends.
>
> To stare at nothing, just to get it right
> get nothing right, with some faint idea of
> this as a proper way to spend a life. No, what
>
> I really mean to say instead is, come back
> won't you, just all of you come back, and give
> me one more go at doing it all again but doing it
>
> far better this time round – the work, the love stuff –
> so I go to the wordprocessor longing for line cables
> to loop out of the machine straight to my head

and back, as I do want to be only transmission –
in sleep alone I get articulate to mouth the part of
anyone and reel off others' characters until the focus

of a day through one-eyed self sets in again: go into it.
I must. *The flower breaks open to its bell of sound*
that rings out through the woods. I eat my knuckles

hearing that. I've only earned a modern, what, a flatness.
Or no, I can earn nothing, but maybe
some right to stop now and to say to you, Tell me.

– That plea for mutuality's not true. It's more ordinary that
flying light should flap me away into a stream of specks
a million surfaces without a tongue and I never have wanted

'a voice' anyway, nor got it. Alright. . . .

The 'million surfaces' or poses available to the speaker reflect her position
in history as being beyond the possibility of gothic dramatics, or romantic
Chuvash lyric, but also not convinced by the 'mutuality' or self-erasure
demanded by modernism's flattening theories. And although feminism's demand
for an unadulterated 'voice' for women reverberates unsuccessfully in this hall
of mirrors, the voice which asserts at the end of the poem that 'I can't do this.
I can't talk like any of this./You hear me not do it' is nonetheless 'doing'
something identificatory as a specifically-located complex of historically-possible
self-descriptions and attendant emotions that casts off the illusion of its own
essentiality at the same time that it presents the 'experience' of struggling 'to
be' in language.

Even struggling *not* to be a limited 'one-eyed self' in language, as she puts
it in one of the latter stanzas quoted above, is suggested to be impossible
in 'Disintegrate Me', a poem that dissolves formal lineation in an experiment
with self-erasure. In this poem the very drive to escape self reveals it
and all of its operant assumptions; the form therefore takes, despite its
fluid enjambments, a block-like shape on the large square pages of *Mop
Mop Georgette*, leaving a rigid column of white space to the right of the
poem's line-ends. The form's wrap-around motion thus produces effects of
both fluidity and constricture, and causes the turn-abouts and changes of
discourse or direction within its four walls to give us the impression of reeling
in language, of weltering at sea, of working a way around and along familiar and
new representations of self:

There was such brilliance lifting off the sea, its aquamarine strip
blocked in behind white-dashed mimosas, that it stung my eyes
all morning as I stood in the old playground, pushing the swing
steadily, looking out across the water and longing to do without
these radio voices, and without my post as zealous secretary, as
transmitter of messages from the dead, who'd issue disclaimers
that they'd ever sent them – all the while a slow hot cut spreads
to baste me now with questions of my own complicity in harm
muttering thoughtfully about 'patterns' until I'm stamped out as
an old paisley shawl or worn kelim, do I look good as this one
or should I be less loud, or less repetitive? and on the top of my
wardrobe, familiar spirits cluster and hang to chatter, lean over
to peer down interestedly at me, vivaciously complaining about
the large amounts of fluff I've left up there, 'that's just as we'd
expect': meanwhile the out-to-kill person is not, or so she or he
shrugs, pulled at by voices, but dead at heart stands amnesiac
plumped out with the effective innocence of the untroubled –
This gloss is taking me on unconvincing dashes down blind
alleys I mistrust, since desperate to see things straight, I can't fit
apt blame in to self-damnation: could I believe instead in drained
abandon, in mild drift out over some creamy acre studded with
brick reds, to be lifted, eased above great sienna fields and born
onward to be an opened stem or a standing hollow, a flesh ring
through which all slips or a fluent cylinder washed through by
azure-tangled braid, trailing Stella Maris, fervent star of the sea . . .

The poem's line-ends break like a changing and uneasy but repetitive ocean to
underline both the tensions between 'swing[ing]/steadily' in the project to 'see
things straight' as well as the constant, reflexive recognition that such desire
for straightness 'can't fit'. This speaker, a mother 'pushing a swing' in 'the
old playground' that doubles as her own formative textual terrain, longs to do
without the voices that emanate from that 'dead' but still alive, interfering nexus
of language – 'radio voices' that she is bound to 'transmit' as both a speaker and in
her 'post as zealous secretary', or writer/recorder of their 'messages'. The languages
of kitchen and dressing room inform, delimit and distract her from her apprehension
that she is 'complicit[ous] in harm' all the while; their metaphorical linkage of her
to the domestic products she makes demonstrate her imagination's bondage to the
cultural text. Recognising that her desire for ameliorative 'disintegration' and the
colourful, sensual description and verbal play she uses to describe it (as well as
to escape from further struggle with self-reference) is only 'decoration of an old

self-magnifying wish' for self-destruction, the speaker later swings back to find a selfhood demanding interrogation even there, in her runaway words, and thus 'no "release from service to [the] hard master" ' of her more inscrutable employer, the larger cultural text. It is a hard thought that arrives as the poem nears 'closure': that her 'I', or 'drive of shame', which has been 'fighting to clear a name to itself' 'can't, because its motor runs on a conviction that if I understood/my own extent of blame then that would prove me agent: it doesn't/want to face a likely truth of helplessness'. The contradictions and self-delusions endemic within the very language she uses cast the speaker's voice into despair at the end; yet though the poem's conclusion sounds like a defeat – an admission of 'the humiliating lack of much control' and inability to 'get past this thought with any confidence' – it is ironically a triumph of sorts, given the poem's original desire for self-destruction. In other words, it is due to the particularised situating of unravelled historical representations that the speaker acknowledges herself to be locked within, even erased by, that she remains indelible; her view into the text *from* the text is what *is* hers, and from it she gleans whatever possibility there might be for intersecting speech and perspective.

Which brings me back, once again, to the idea of the 'real', though by this point it has changed to mean lived experience in language and inscribed selfhood. Riley contours theoretical universalisms by moving with them through time and space and from within her own subjective limits; she thereby resurrects the subject as an inescapable construct, albeit defined within its own particular discursive history. Her implicit critique of universals as they form in both the mainstream and experimental poetry worlds help me to round off my thoughts here, which have been ricocheting between two misconceptions, as I see them, operant not only transatlantically but also within the UK: first, on the part of experimentalists, that a use of traditional forms or a particular speaking-subject can only be seen as retrogressive; and second, on the part of more traditionally-based poets, that all experimental poetry that breaks with syntax or 'unequivocal' modes of communicating is off on theoretical/élitist tangents that have no connection with actual lives or politics. I would propose that 'form no longer equals meaning' in either camp: that the new shift in what 'meaning' means has not yet found a formal response that is not beset by contradictions (as is the writing of critical theory as well, given its mode of authority assumed in erasing authority, etc.). Some process, or rather some dialectic between provisional processes – empirical and theoretical – might stem the tendency for absolutisms to reproduce themselves as 'the new generation'. By recognising that despite the seeming impossibility of going on in language as an unequivocally-speaking, unified self there is also no way of renouncing one's 'I-view' – one's particular construction/experience within the same medium – Denise Riley does, I think, begin to disrupt the all-too-simple binary constructions erected between poetic camps in women's writing with poems that must therefore, in some new way perhaps, be described again as 'radical'.

NOTES

1. Institute of Contemporary Arts, London, Spring 1994; the discussion was one event in the Poetry Society's series 'Poets on Poets'.
2. The reference here is to the group of poets so named and celebrated in *Poetry Review* and elsewhere in 1994 and who have been marketed as a package through readings and television appearances; they are (with one or two possible exceptions) writers in the 'mainstream' or loosely lyrical, post-Movement mode, and in terms of popularity led by Carol Ann Duffy and Simon Armitage.
3. Michael Hulse, David Kennedy and David Morley (eds), (Newcastle-upon-Tyne, Bloodaxe Books, 1993).
4. An important new anthology appeared from Reality Street Editions at the end of 1995: *Out of Everywhere: An anthology of contemporary linguistically innovative poetry by women in North America and the UK.*, ed. Maggie O'Sullivan; it is the first British book dedicated to experimental women's poetry. (Its only precursor is to be found in Paladin's *The New British Poetry*, Gillian Allnutt, Fred D'Aguiar, Ken Edwards and the late Eric Mottram (eds), which appeared in 1988 and included work by a number of these poets.)
5. For a very helpful reconsideration of these arguments published in this country I would refer readers to an essay by the British experimental/performance poet Caroline Bergvall: 'No Margins to this Page: Female Experimental Poets and the Legacy of Modernism', *fragmente* 5 (1993), pp.30–8.
6. Linda France (ed.), *Sixty Women Poets* (Newcastle-upon-Tyne, Bloodaxe Books, 1993), p.16.
7. 'More visible' because they and other 'alternative' poets have found publishers as rich and reputable as Norton; see, for example, *Postmodern American Poetry*, ed. Paul Hoover (New York, Norton, 1994).
8. The term was coined as spelled by Bruce Andrews and Charles Bernstein in the 1970s for their magazine dedicated to language-oriented poetry (or poetry affected by post-modern linguistic theory), from which key excerpts were later drawn for their influential collection *The LANGUAGE Book* (Carbondale, Southern Illinois University Press, 1984). It seems that the term is still used when referring to strict adherents of the original agenda as mapped out in the magazine, and reversion to regular typography usually means that the idea of 'Language' poetry in its much broader sense is being invoked.
9. Charles Bernstein, 'Comedy and the Poetics of Political Form', in *The Politics of Poetic Form*, ed. Charles Bernstein (New York, Roof, 1990), p. 238.
10. Barrett Watten, *Total Syntax* (Carbondale and Edwardsville, Southern Illinois University Press, 1985), p.139. It is important to note here that Watten's important descriptions of work like Steve Benson's also conceptualise the subject of poems as being in 'continually reflexive encounter[s] with . . . language' (p.113), but it is his claim that the 'explo[sion]' of 'the structure of identity' at the border of self and non-self 'locates the writer on a new and expanded scale' (p.114) that becomes the focus of my concern.
11. Charles Bernstein, 'Writing and Method', first collected in *In the American Tree*, ed. Ron Silliman, (Orono, Maine, National Poetry Foundation, 1986), p.594, 'Language Sampler', *The Paris Review* 24/86 (Fall 1982) p.75.
12. Susan Howe, *Singularities* (Hanover, University of New England Press, 1990), p.67.
13. The pun also encompasses elements in one of the generative texts for this poem, Herman Melville's *Billy Budd*; readers of my own essay should note that my argument forces a focus on only one trajectory for the many ideas that arise from these lines.
14. Eavan Boland, *Outside History* (Manchester, Carcanet, 1990).
15. I cannot responsibly say 'experimental women poets in general' here because at least one major figure in the small group of them, Maggie O'Sullivan, demonstrates deep affinities with American experimentalists in terms of her scattered syntax and conjurings with words as materials and pure sounds. This is, of course, one explanation for the enthusiasm with which her work has been met by Language poets in the States.
16. 'Eccentric Concentrism: Traditional Poetic Forms and Refracted Discourse in Stevie Smith's Poetry', *Contemporary Literature* 34:2 (Summer 1993), pp.240–65; 'Poetic Subject and Voice as Sites of Struggle: Towards a 'Post-Revisionist' Reading of Stevie Smith's Fairy Tale Poems', in *Dwelling in Possibility: Essays on Gender and Genre*, Yopi Prins and Maeera Shreiber (eds), (Cornell University Press, forthcoming); *Stevie Smith* (Macmillan's *Women Writers* series, forthcoming).

17. Veronica Forrest-Thomson, *Poetic Artifice* (Manchester, Manchester University Press, 1978); Marjorie Perloff, *Radical Artifice* (Chicago, University of Chicago Press, 1992).
18. Collected in Bernstein's *A Poetics* (Cambridge, Massachusetts, Harvard University Press, 1992).
19. All quotes and my descriptions of Riley's ideas are drawn from my interview with her; see *PN Review* 103, 21:5 (May–June 1995), pp.17–22.
20. See Frank O'Hara's 'Personism: A Manifesto' and 'Personal Poem', in *The Collected Poems of Frank O'Hara*, Donald Allen, John Ashbery (eds), (New York, Alfred A. Knopf, 1972). The quote is from Graham's poem 'Clusters Travelling Out', which can be found in his *Collected Poems 1942–1977* (London, Faber and Faber, 1979), p.185.
21. Adrienne Rich, 'Passages from What is Found There: Notebooks on Poetry and Politics', *American Poetry Review* 22:1 (January/February 1993), p.64.
22. Denise Riley, *Dry Air* (London, Virago, 1985), p.7.
23. London, Macmillan, 1988.
24. See Claire Buck's and Vicki Bertram's essays on women's poetry in *Contemporary British Poetry: Essays in Theory and Criticism*, James Acheson and Romana Huk (eds), (Albany, State University of New York Press, 1996). *PN Review*'s publication of my interview with Riley and subsequent inclusion of her work in its 100th issue/anthology is one notable exception to the rule above.
25. Denise Riley, from 'A Shortened Set', in *Mop Mop Georgette* (London, Reality Street Editions, 1993), p.16.
26. I refer here of course to Elaine Showalter's now-famous description, constructed with the help of Oxford anthropologists Shirley and Edwin Ardener, of the wild zone of female difference outside overlappings with the male-dominated sphere; see Showalter's 'Feminist Criticism in the Wilderness', in *Contemporary Literary Criticism: Literary and Cultural Studies*, Robert Con Davis and Ronald Schleifer (eds), (New York, Longman, 1994, 3rd edn), pp.51–71. Also implicit in this sweeping reference are the many denominations of feminist 'body politics' arising out of writings such as those by Hélène Cixous and Luce Irigaray.
27. Riley, *Am I that Name*, pp.112, 5, 113.
28. *Mop Mop Georgette*, pp.28–9; 62–3.

FURTHER READING

Andrews, Bruce and Bernstein, Charles (eds), *The L=A=N=G=U=A=G=E Book* (Carbondale and Edwardsville, Southern Illinois University Press, 1984).

Barry, Peter and Hampson, Robert (eds), *The New British Poetries: The Scope of the Possible* (Manchester, Manchester University Press, 1993).

Bernstein, Charles (ed.), *The Politics of Poetic Form* (New York, Roof Books, 1990).

Bernstein Charles, *A Poetics* (Cambridge, Massachusetts, Harvard University Press, 1992).

Easthope, Antony and Thompson, John O. (eds), *Contemporary Poetry meets Modern Theory* (Toronto/Buffalo/London, University of Toronto Press, 1991).

Messerll, Douglas (ed.), *From the Other Side of the Century: A New American Poetry 1960–1990* (Los Angeles, Sun and Moon Press, 1994).

O'Sullivan, Maggie (ed.), *Out of Everywhere: An Anthology of contemporary linguistically innovative women in North America and the UK* (London, Reality Street Editions, 1996).

Perloff, Marjorie, *Radical Artifice* (Chicago, University of Chicago Press, 1992).

Silliman, Ron (ed.), *In the American Tree* (Orono, Maine, The National Poetry Foundation, 1986).

Watten, Barrett *Total Syntax* (Carbondale and Edwardsville, Southern Illinois University Press, 1985).

RELEVANT JOURNALS WITH TRANSATLANTIC EXCHANGE

Poetics Journal, Lyn Hejinian and Barrett Watten (eds) (USA).
Reality Studios, ed. Ken Edwards (UK).
Sulfur, ed. Clayton Eshleman (USA).
fragmente, ed. Anthony Mellors (UK).
Parataxis, ed. Drew Milne (UK).

Section Six: Woman/Poet: Reconfigurations

These chapters consider ways in which traditional ideas about poetry, and the role and status of the poet in Western culture, clash with accepted versions of female subjectivity. In particular they consider the problems women encounter in laying claim to poetic subjectivity. Their unifying theme is the discovery of new configurations of the idea of the poet, and their interest in poetry as a particular kind of discourse among many other, more frequently analysed, discourses.

Fiona Sampson uses her practical experience as a poet-in-residence within the National Health Service to explore these issues. She offers an original and surprising assessment of the value of poetry writing. Refuting claims that poetry can provide authentic accounts of the self, she proves that language is controlled by social systems of meaning, and thus can never offer unmediated subjective truth. However, through its position as one discourse, in competition – in a Foucauldian sense – with other, more powerful discourses, poetry can perhaps dislodge their pre-eminence, by laying bare the foundations of their suspect claims to authority. Dramatising its own instability and untruthfulness, it can contest the hegemony of scientific and medical discourse. Sampson suggests that health-care patients are disempowered by the dominance of such discourses; as a result, while her patients are not all female, she argues that they are in a position analogous to that of women: a position she labels 'discursive weakness'.

Deryn Rees-Jones, taking her cue from Freud's suggestion that the answer to the riddle of femininity might lie in poetry and in science, explores the use of science in the poetry of Elizabeth Bishop and Lavinia Greenlaw. She shows how both poets work to undo the association of science with dry objectivity and – by association – masculinity, and at the same time critique the methods of Western scientific exploration. Greenlaw, a contemporary poet, turns to Bishop's earlier reconfiguration of objectivity for aid. Using the discourse of science gives the woman poet access to an unfamiliar degree of detachment and authority. In a careful reading of Greenlaw's poem, 'Galileo's Wife', Rees-Jones shows how the poet reveals the limitations of masculine scientific method with subtle irony, and gestures towards the fuller potentials of a less inflexible and intransigent version of objectivity, one tempered by recognition of the fluidity and unfixable nature of experience and identity.

Nicole Ward Jouve's essay is a meditation on the relationship between mothering and poetry. Using insights gleaned from various psychological and philosophical theories, she investigates the apparent incompatibility of the two. Noting how all Western myths depict the poetic subject as male, she speculates as to whether Sappho stands as the lost Poet-Mother, still sought by today's women poets. Ward Jouve then splits open the category 'Mother' in order to show how various are the manifestations produced by the term, and suggests that the problem she set out to address can be overcome by recognising that neither Mother nor Poet are fixed, immutable identities. She quotes from the numerous poetic depictions of mothering that have appeared during the last twenty years, thus showing that these two roles are not, in fact, mutually exclusive, while also acknowledging the very real economic and emotional costs of mothering and their potential interference with poetic creativity. She concludes with the suggestion that we need to separate out the vast range of projections and archetypes surrounding motherhood from the real mothers; one way to do this, of course, is to listen to the real mothers who write.

16

Poetry and the Position of Weakness: Some Challenges of Writing in Health-Care

Fiona Sampson

Two contradictory claims are routinely made for my practice as a writer-in-residence in health-care, in which I facilitate the production of poetry and other texts by people who are receiving health-care and who have in most cases never written, as they would say, 'creatively' before. One claim is that through writing the client is able to individuate: to present their authentic self without the mediation of forms which have been supplied from an external source. The other is that the new writer, hitherto merely the ground on which discourses such as clinical diagnosis have acted to produce their own kind of picture of him or her, becomes a participant in the discursive field when they adopt a culturally sanctioned poetic voice.

In this chapter I am working with Foucault's definition of a discourse as the 'field' of each set of linguistic activities – naming, reading – and practices arising from them, such as judgements or procedures, which are carried out around a particular topic and *are defined by conventions which they follow*. For example, around the topic of ill-health the discursive field of clinical diagnosis includes the practices of 'reading' a client's symptoms as isolated occurrences of physiological pathology and of prescribing treatment accordingly. Were a diagnosis to begin to use terms from other approaches to the topic, such as 'soul-sickness' or 'humours', it would cease to be part of clinical discourse. Foucault's 'Archaeology of the Human Sciences' uncovers the way in which these conventions have grown up for historical reasons but are not generated by an extra-discursive 'Order of Things'.[1]

I will focus on the idea that in writing poetry the health-care client offers a challenge to the discursive status quo, around which those contradictory claims circle. I will use examples of writing by clients to ask whether poetry is subversive, either in the sense of winning greater authority than other accounts of experience through its greater authenticity, or in the sense of challenging a hegemonic process – of self-perpetuation – carried out by discursive claims of authority. If it were to do the latter we could argue with confidence that both individuating authenticity and authoritative participation were merely 'poetic' figures of speech.

By 'authority' I mean the power a discourse achieves when its own and other discursive conventions identify it as competent to speak. For example a discourse such as autobiography will assume the conventions within its own practices – such as 'accurate' remembering – and in the wider field of discursive competitiveness, for example through claiming a privileged 'inside' view of what it regards as authenticity.

In post-modernity my questions seem naive: surely poetry just plays? But consideration of poetry not as a set of artefacts with a culturally determined destination but as a discourse (that is, a perhaps culturally determined practice) indicates that poetry, at least in the initial and most basic selections it makes from among potential discursive forms and premises, does position itself in relation to other ways of thinking, talking and writing.

First, therefore, I'd like to survey some notions of discursive authenticity, as they can be applied to poetry, from Plato to Aldous Huxley. Such notions assure us that the health-care clients in my workshops are able to write directly out of their own experience. I would like to challenge these assurances; and, furthermore, to question the idea that any discursive claims of 'authority' can be founded on 'authenticity'. This challenges both empirical and confessional discourses, which rely on the narrator's status as (self-)observer to create some kind of guarantee of authenticity and hence of authority. One example of discursive authority is the discourse of scientific observation, in which therapeutic decisions affecting health-care clients are made. But is poetry simply an example of a discourse which relies for authority on 'authenticity', on what Jenny calls 'A transient feeling/Encapsulated into words./Set free from the mind'?[2] If poetry can be said to challenge the very notion of authoritative discourse, we can perhaps argue for the appropriateness of its use from a position of discursive weakness. In this chapter I do not wish to re-rehearse arguments that women could be said to occupy such positions, but rather to imply fruitful analogies with/-in the experiences of health-care.

Historically, texts have claimed to be authenticated in one of three ways, which it is useful to survey: by fidelity to the narrator's mental experience; by the presence of the supernatural – God, perhaps, or a Muse; or by proximity to experience of the material world.

'This is your subject speaking': Fidelity to Subjective Experience[3]

In Wordsworth's 1802 'Preface' to the *Lyrical Ballads* the poet's work is sentimental confession, inner perspective proposed as mapping both the general human condition, of which the poet is exemplar *par excellence*, and 'the goings-on of the universe', which revolves to the same super-human music as the poet's own 'soul'. The poet authenticates not only himself, through an apparently genetic predisposition to generate poetry, but also a (gender-specific) social hierarchy of sensibility naturalised by begging its own question: 'He must have a very faint perception of [the human mind's] beauty and dignity who does not know . . . that one being is elevated above another, in proportion as he possess this capability'.[4]

In English letters the influence of Wordsworth's Romanticism is seminal. But Wordsworth was a man of his peculiarly European time: his context that of the German Idealists – Kant, Fichte, Schelling, Hegel; the Neo-Platonism of Plotinus and Bonaventura; Platonic Idealism itself.

For Plato, the real entity exists as an Idea and not as any material instantiation of that Idea. It is the universal template or recipe by which we recognise the particular instance of, say, a chair. The Ideal chair isn't the plan of a particular 'best chair ever' – not even a bardic throne: rather, it perfectly encapsulates chairness. Texts which are to be the most precise, as well as of the most universal relevance, must be produced through recourse to these Ideas. The Philosopher Kings of Plato's Ideal *Republic* are qualified to rule by their reluctance to leave the 'upper' world of 'purely intellectual pursuits' in order to 'return again to the prisoners' in the earthly 'cave' of the material world.[5] Pure reasoning, unsullied by working opinions and beliefs acquired through living the contingencies of material and social circumstance, allows the potential Philosopher to reach Ideal understanding.[6]

Philosopher Kings gain their inner perspective on the real nature of things through intellectual effort: but only individuals who in the words of Plato's Foundation Myth 'have gold in their nature' will make it through the necessary training.[7] Wordsworth's poet, who finds the real nature of things mapped on his predisposed sensibilities, must nevertheless also 'have thought long and deeply'.

'My purpose,' wrote Rousseau in 1766, 'is to display to my kind a portrait in every way true to nature, and the man I shall portray will be myself.'[8] The *Confessions* represented autobiography as scientific observation. By examining the nature of one human individual – unique but like other scientific samples illustrative nevertheless of some general truths about such natures – Rousseau would 'display' human nature which, he argued in the *Social Contract*, was the foundation and end of all activity and authority, including the political.[9]

Successors in the genre have examined exceptional mental states: the pharmaceutical heavens and hells of Thomas de Quincey and Huxley, explorations of the experience of mental illness by William Styron or Janet Frame. Perhaps liberated by modernist diction, Sylvia Plath, Anne Sexton, Robert Lowell – the self-consuming confessional poets – peck like pelicans at their bleeding hearts to feed a public hungry to understand, though even such a diet may not offer the reader the experience of authenticity. As Sexton warns her 'Analyst': 'Your business is watching my words. But I/admit nothing'.[10]

But Beryl puts her finger on a more profound difficulty in the discourse of authentic individual experience than the risk of a tease:

> What goes through the mind of a poet while he or she is writing?
> I do not know and cannot fathom it out!
> A poet seems to feel very intense about things and just has this ability to put it down on paper.
> [But] the reader also has to have some comprehension of the poem to make it work.[2]

These texts work with the assumption that their reader can gain access to the writer's experience, but ignore a fundamental disjunction between the bounded subjectivity of the writer and that of the reader. Every donor card implies that it is merely the impossibility of my ever having your experience which stops me in fact *being* you. In *What is Literature?* Sartre argues that the writer is his own ideal reader, because only he experiences the language of his own or any other text *this* way.[11]

'For all good poets . . . are simply inspired to utter that to which the Muse impels them, and that only . . . by power divine.': The Presence of the Supernatural[12]

The Muse, characterised in Athens by 'honeyed fountains . . . gardens and dells',[13] breezes through English Romantic poetry in the bracing guise of a 'Wild West Wind'. By the time it reaches *The Stones of Venice* it is the very 'green fuse' of organic life. For Ruskin, as for Blake, 'Grecian is Mathematic Form: Gothic is Living Form'[14] and it is in the presencing of this 'olive branch, plucked off' that the Form is said to live.

Casting its perspective shadow behind the Christian symbolism of the living branch – present from the Anglo-Saxon 'Dream of the Rood' to nineteenth-century art history – is the Norse legend of Yggdrasil, the World-Tree. As the St Cross Writing Group, with whom I also worked, speculate,

> Perhaps the world isn't a round ball.
> Perhaps it's a tree.
> The roots go down to the underworld
> where anger and hate and criminals and murderers are;

and the branches go up to heaven
where God and the angels are.
That would mean that everything is joined
to everything else;
that the world is a place
where good and bad are joined.

If 'everything is joined to everything else', each of Ruskin's Gothic symbols brings with it a whole world of life. In *Le Texte du roman* Julia Kristeva also appropriates the ideal of a Gothic symbol: she locates it in the culture of 'the second half of the Middle Ages (thirteenth to fifteenth centuries)'. The symbol 'evoked' a 'transcendental foundation' and was unlike the 'strained' sign which succeeded it and has achieved currency through imitation.[15] The symbol thus relies on the authenticating presence of the supernatural.

However, the immanence of such a 'transcendental foundation' places its own strains on poetry:

Words strain,
Crack and sometimes break, under the burden,
Under the tension, slip, slide, perish,
Decay with imprecision, will not stay in place,
Will not stay still.[16]

This is an impersonal authenticity, 'Costing not less than everything'. In Jenny's helicon (the term comes from the mountain range where Greek myth located the spring sacred to the Muses) poetry comes up from the hitherto unknown and uncontrolled oracles of the unconscious:

The poet is like a bucket
Reaching deep down into the blackness, where
Echoes wait silently at first,
Waiting to be brought out of the deepest recesses
Of the well . . .[2]

Like Jenny's poet, Wordsworth's must cultivate a kind of poetic mania in order to 'produce an overflow of powerful feelings'. For a poem to be written an 'emotion is contemplated till by a species of reaction [. . .] tranquillity gradually disappears'.[17] In this picture the poet's work comes out of attention paid to what is at the very least private 'inspiration'; and does not arise from public or social stimuli.

But can poetry make these claims to use language in ways free of society's influence? Isn't language a necessarily social practice, a game whose authenticity resides in its rules of use? As Wittgenstein points out, though neologism may be 'carried' by the language in which it is embedded, a truly private language – not just a translation of one already in existence – would be unusable because there would be no way for the individual responsible for it to fix rules in place.[18] In Eden, apparently, Adam had God with him to help him into language practice; but language authentically free of societal influence would sound to us (and perhaps does) like the babble of Pentecost.

At another level, the use of vocabulary, grammar and such discursive tropes as genre and metaphor are influenced by social experience. For example, Ioan Davies records that prisoners' narratives are often autobiographical – 'prisoners ... are compelled by circumstances to try to come to terms with themselves and the world' – yet constructed in and valorised by a particular narrative climate: 'the story-teller lives in a limbo-world of the collective stories he would like us to believe in (even if he personalises them) and the hyper-real stories we have constructed about him'.[19] The appetite of the prisoner's audience for 'authentic' stories of experiences 'we' may not have had, leads directly to the self-confessed hyperbole of 'hyper-real' rumour and urban myth. Since a discourse is always a participatory practice, the prisoner is 'compelled' to use those that are available to him. These are the 'hyper-real stories' of popular perceptions and the 'collective' narrative culture used by prisoners as – and to identify themselves to each other as – a group. The limited nature of this choice makes narrative dependency on the availability of discursive fields especially clear.

'Poets love Nature': The Proximity of the Material World [20]

Discourses which make the third kind of claim to authenticity base that claim on the acknowledgement that writer's and speaker's experiences will present themselves in their texts. Sometime in the 1950s the Polish poet Andrzej Bursa was 'Talking to a Poet':

> How to convey scent in poetry ...
> certainly not through simple naming
> scent must permeate the whole
>
> both rhyme
> and rhythm
> must have the temperature of a honeyed glade
> each rhythmical leap
> resemble the swaying of a rose
> poised over a trellis
>
> we conversed in an atmosphere of the best symbiosis
> until I said:

'please remove this bucket
the piss-stench is intolerable'

maybe this was tactless
but I couldn't stand it any longer.[21]

This authenticity of what is close at hand rejects the poet's escape into the manic or the 'uncanny'. In 'The Thinker as Poet',[22] Heidegger says that 'singing and thinking are the stems/neighbour to poetry./They grow out of Being and reach into/its truth.' Heidegger's Being isn't the 'transcendental' Being of God which is presenced by Gothic symbol but Being-*there*: *Da*sein. It is the individual's own 'authentic' way of being in the world; that is, as what we might call a Subject. In a late essay '. . . Poetically Man Dwells . . .',[23] Heidegger argues that 'dwelling' (*'wohnen'*) is, as we might say, 'making oneself at home' in the world. Hence 'poetry, as the authentic gauging of the dimension of dwelling –' that is, as the 'authentic' Subjective version – 'is the primal form of building'.

Theodor Adorno's challenge to what he calls the *Jargon of Authenticity* is that Heidegger, in claiming some ways of living or of using language are 'authentic', uses language in an ideological way; in other words from a non-neutral stand-point.[24] However, Heidegger's claim that the realm of experience is laden with such values as 'in/authenticity' is not a claim for something 'ontologically queer' (that is, incompatible with what we know about the nature of things) unless we are sure we can claim that the realm of experience is not value laden at all: a claim it would be impossible to verify. Small wonder then that Adorno's challenge itself relies on the idea of an 'un-ideological' and dare we say 'authentic' way of using language.

In 'The Pipe' Raymond Carver has some fun with 'dwelling'. In the end it isn't material surroundings he slyly presences but, by situating his concrete images 'in the next poem' and narrator and text within the poem's metaphorical room, narrator and text themselves:

There'll be a lamp burning in the next poem;
and a fireplace where pitch-soaked
blocks of fir flame up, consuming one another.
Oh, the next poem will throw up sparks!
But there won't be any cigarettes in that poem.
I'll take up smoking the pipe.[25]

However, Heidegger himself challenges any notion of a discourse reproducing 'authentic' life experience. To name something is to introduce a system of naming between the Subject and subjective experience.[26] For Heidegger language is authentic when it reveals its own inability to reproduce the world of the writer's experience. This is telling for the ways in which, as we will see, poetry can be said to advertise its own distance from such 'reproductive' projects.

This challenge to the discursive authority of texts purporting to re-present authentic material experience is based on the disjunction between language and other material or social experience. However, some Marxisms and the feminist language politics of Dale Spender,[27] Annie Leclerc,[28] and Tillie Olsen[29] argue that, though language is undeniably not an atmospheric condition, say, or a piece of furniture, it *is* also a part of the existentially determining (though not perhaps over-determining) experiential situation of each individual. There are limits to the individual's autonomous use of language, since beyond certain boundaries he or she is in practice not speaking a given language or dialect, or even language at all. Language is material; and its use culturally material. This idea authorises the cultural specificity related by dialect, jargon and local detail. Meanwhile, Luce Irigaray and Hélène Cixous move to displace the centrality of cultural history; in theories of the writing body, they shift the pointer of authenticity from cultural materialism to the materiality of the body.[30]

The idea that language creates experience in its own image seems to exorcise the spirit of 'authenticity'. In psychoanalytic no less than in political narratives it is with the acquisition of the symbolic register that the Subject creates itself. We may define this acquisition as the ability to process experience by manipulating symbols – such as words or visual representations – of that experience. In the Kleinian account the infant realises its self is not co-extensive with the world when parts of that world – specifically, of its mother – fail to respond to its will. The anxiety that accompanies this discovery leads the child to make its own version of its experiences.[31] In the Kristevan account of the acquisition of the symbolic register, it is the infant's separation from its mother that first articulates the world of its experience as made up of bounded entities.[32]

John writes about this creative work of language: 'Most of all I want to purify and recycle the crap and the garbage I am set to work with, so that poetry or image-making eventually comes out. That makes me feel better'.[2] His comment indicates the importance he attaches to the sense of well-being his ability to transform experience within the symbolic register gives him.

Some Difficulties of Discursive Authority

I have challenged three claims of discursive authenticity. Can we also dismiss discursive claims to authority? Indeed are such claims being made? Tim, who has a learning difficulty, writes with discursive defensiveness:

> The poet builds a wall with words
> tells stories.
> He walks up the wall
> and falls down again.[2]

Gemma Corradi Fiumara prefaces her discussion of what she calls the 'discursive violence' of such a hegemony as clinical discourse with a quote from Elias Canetti: 'The sciences bite off pieces of life, and life shrouds itself in grief and pain'.[33] In Corradi Fiumura's thesis,

> everything that is sufficiently and suitably enunciated is in practice accepted as an enunciation of knowledge ... any knowledge that is sufficiently and suitably expressed (deployed) has a progressive tendency to establish itself as the only knowledge there is. And any discourse initiated outside the dominant body of knowledge turns out to be so very difficult to think and articulate that it almost seems unheard-of, simply because it is unhearable.[34]

The struggle between discourses is a struggle for discursive survival, as evinced in that way of processing experience we call 'common sense', whose prohibitions are sanctioned by the analytical-philosophical term 'counter-intuitive'. The appeal to 'common sense' is effective precisely because it is that to which appeal is commonly made.[35] Andrea Nye makes an analogous point about the operations of logic: 'The point of logic is to frame a way of speaking in which what another says does not have to be heard or understood, in which only the voice of a unitary authority is meaningful'.[36]

Clearly, a position of discursive weakness emerges between the high walls of this kind of power. But how does poetry situate itself in this field of discursive struggle?

' . . . *capable of being in uncertainties, Mysteries, doubts* . . .': Outside the Struggle for Authority[37]

It seems likely that an unusual proportion of mental-health-care clients writes poetry.[38] Some of this work is surreal, schizophrenic; some clipped into deeply traditional forms. What seems important to its writers is often apparently not what a health-care commitment to advocacy and the critical interest in autobiographical fiction unite in calling 'voice', but rather participation in the practice of writing. Seizing on a traditional trope of the poet as exceptional individual, certain individuals receiving health-care who feel themselves to be exceptional apparently adopt poetic discourse as part of that role. Analogously, poetic discourse – the whole discursive field which poetry founds, from critical studies to promotional blurb – characterises its narrative personae and aims, in relation to the prosaic, as figuring the 'negative capability' of such fictional poetic non-conformists as the *Sweeney Astray* of Seamus Heaney's translation,[39] or Edmond Rostand's *Cyrano de Bergerac*[40].

Almost from the outset of its life in modern academic criticism, poetry has positioned its ground in relation to that of other discourses. 'Our religion has materialised itself in the fact ... But for poetry the idea is everything', essays Matthew Arnold.[41] Poetry characterises its diction in relation to prose: 'the poetical gift ... [is] to utter a thing with the most limpid plainness and clearness'.[42]

Poetry positions itself on the page in ways which differentiate it from other kinds of texts. It marks out certain media, such as – among 'literary' practices – oral transmission, as almost peculiarly its own; and it marks out its territory within those media: for example in specific aural structures. In knowingly positioning itself in relation to other discourses in this way, poetry tenders that very recognition of the roles they have acquired which allows them to claim discursive authority. Yet in so doing poetry does not also reify a position of discursive weakness.

Kristeva situates poetry at the border of language, where it breaks down into involuntary aporia, the gaps caused by complete lack of connection. Poetry may gasp exclamation, fail to make it across the page's dangerous width. Involuntary connections may bubble up in pun and allusion. Moreover, for Kristeva the music of poetry is a psychotic return to the babble of the infant who does not yet differentiate between himself and the rest of the world: to the free play of un-significant pleasure.[43]

Things happen at the border, the 'strange space' – which 'does not exist, is not a present being in any form' – of productive *différance*.[44] Laura Riding says that 'The trouble of a book is', among other things, 'To speak its sermon, then look the other way./Arouse commotion in the margin '.[45] Gambling and gambolling with fragmentation on the brink of Jenny's aporetic well, poetry challenges the authority of self-grounding discourses, such as clinical diagnosis, which rely on the possibility of stability in the ways in which their language functions. (For what of Münchhausen's syndrome?) It further challenges discursive authority predicated on the stability of inter-discursive relationships, such as that between obituary and autobiography. (And what if one were to write one's own obituary?)

Here are some examples of such gambols. Poetry affords the chance for nonsense and obliquity. During an exercise in surreal juxtaposition, John writes:

> A hard-boiled egg in the tree-top nest
> It swings to and fro with the wind.
> To the sun and the cloud it shows its best;
> To the blue sky – everything.
>
> And I look down to sunlit pine-needles
> And see a foot set down.

> But I shall be quiet and secretive
> As a hard-boiled egg in the down.[2]

Poetry affords the chance to mix-up discourses, as in the fantasy 'Magic Forest' of the St Cross Writing Group:

> A brown camel
> decorated with branches.
> Sand.
>
> Trees.
> A big river
> sucking at the tree roots.
>
> The trees are green
> and brown
> light green like the green printed on towels
> dark brown like chocolate.
>
> Brown rats
> black rats
> water rats
> larger than life
> come out of the shadows.
>
> Great big white birds
> come from America.
> Their call is soft, low
> like thunder.
>
> They are warning of wet weather.[2]

Poetry affords the chance to don the liberating mask of metaphor. Andrew's self-portrait begins:

> I'm an elk, top heavy, awkwardly moving.
> An unpractised stilt walker
> Searching for lichen, other elks occasionally
> With a roaring bark like a breaking branch
> Made ponderously, with gravity . . .[2]

Paradoxically, in challenging discursive authority, poetry makes a return to effective participation in the discursive struggle. In the hands of health-care clients poetry can engage with and counter the hegemony of 'authoritative' discourses which position those individuals as discursive objects or at best as listeners. It does so by revealing, through its own non-conformity to such discursive functions, the ways in which discourses found their own claims to authority. Though the conventions of the practice of poetry include specific ·cultural expectations about its context and the identity of its practitioners, when these are destabilised – as in my practice and as when practitioners from unconventional groups including, historically, women emerge – the non-conformist role of poetry is not so much jeopardised as redoubled.

Used by health-care clients, poetry acquires a perverse quasi-Heideggerian 'authenticity' with resonances for other groups and individuals who find themselves positioned in discursive weakness. Women constitute one such group. These resonances represent another approach to the idea of playfulness and critique as significant feminist discursive strategies to that offered by psychoanalytic and essentialist feminists such as Cixous and Irigaray through the realms of *jouissance* and *écriture blanc*. Yet they complement each other.

As an unstable and destabilising discourse poetry presences the inauthenticity of many of language's other claims to authenticity. Moreover, and at this final margin, poetry may perhaps after all offer its writers and readers, through its very discursive obliquity, some soundings of what we might almost be tempted to call authentic experience. For to quote Jacques Derrida, 'It has been observed particularly in birds, that the precision of hearing is in direct proportion to the obliqueness of the tympanum. The tympanum squints. Consequently, to luxate the philosophical ear, to set the *locos* in *logos* to work, is to avoid frontal and symmetrical protest, opposition in all forms of the *anti*'.[46] Some obliquities can afford us certainties. By constantly eshewing ways of thinking and talking which claim authenticity or authority poetry may paradoxically provide us with a discursive field whose intra-discursive ways of functioning and whose inter-discursive relationships can be relied upon to exhibit consistency – of instability.

NOTES

1. Michel Foucault, *The Order of Things: An Archaelogy of the Human Sciences*, trans. Alan Sheridan-Smith (London, Tavistock Publications, 1966).
2. Copyright of this and all subsequent material by clients of the Healing Arts: Isle of Wight Writing Project remains with individual authors.
3. Andrew Motion, *Natural Causes* (London, Chatto & Windus, 1988), pp.49–57.
4. William Wordsworth, 'Preface to Lyrical Ballads', in *The Oxford Anthology of English Literature*, Vol. 2, Frank Kermode and John Hollander (eds), (New York, Oxford University Press, 1973), pp.597–8.
5. Plato, *The Republic* 514–521, trans. H.D.P. Lee (London, Penguin, 1955), pp.278–86.
6. Plato excludes poetry from his Republic as merely mimetic, a 'representation' of a material or behavioural flawed particular rather than an Ideal which militates against the development of that *inner* perspective which 'crowns' the exceptional individual.
7. Plato, *The Republic* 415, pp.160–1.
8. Jean-Jacques Rousseau, *The Confessions*, trans. J.M. Cohen (London, Penguin Books, 1953), p.17.

9. Such an individual's 'first law is to provide for his own preservation', and it is only 'natural' for him to enter into the Social Contract since and insofar as he needs to for his own preservation. Jean-Jacques Rousseau, 'The Social Contract', in *The Social Contract and Discourses*, trans. G.D.H. Cole (London, Dent & Sons, 1973), p.182.

10. *The Selected Poems of Anne Sexton*, Diane Wood Middlebrook and Diana Hume George (eds), (London, Virago, 1991), p.17.

11. Jean-Paul Sartre, *What is Literature?* (London, Methuen, 1966).

12. Plato, 'From *Ion* 532b–536b', trans. Benjamin Jowett, in *Philosophies of Art and Beauty*, Albert Hofstadter and Richard Kuhns (eds), (Chicago, University of Chicago Press, 1976), p.55.

13. William Blake, 'On Homer's Poetry and On Virgil', in *The Portable Blake*, ed. Alfred Kazim (London, Penguin Books, 1976), p.552.

14. John Ruskin, 'From *The Stones of Venice*', in *Unto This Last and Other Writings*, ed. Clive Wilmer (London, Penguin Books, 1985), p.105.

15. Julia Kristeva, *Le Texte du roman* (The Hague, Mouton, 1970), pp.1–11.

16. T.S. Eliot, 'Burnt Norton', in *Collected Poems 1909–1962* (London, Faber and Faber, 1963), p.194.

17. Wordsworth, 'Preface to Lyrical Ballads', in *Oxford Anthology of English Literature*, p.608.

18. Ludwig Wittgenstein, *Philosophical Investigations 258* (Oxford, Blackwell, 1953), p.92e.

19. Ioan Davies, *Writers in Prison* (Oxford, Blackwell, 1990).

20. John Clare, 'Poets Love Nature', in *Oxford Anthology of English Literature*, p.577.

21. Andrzej Bursa, 'Talking to a poet', in *The Burning Forest*, translated and edited by Adam Czerniawski (Newcastle-upon-Tyne, Bloodaxe Books, 1988), p.140.

22. Martin Heidegger, *Poetry, Language, Thought*, trans. Albert Hofstadter (New York, Harper & Row, 1975), p.11.

23. Ibid., p.227.

24. Theodor W. Adorno, *The Jargon of Authenticity*, trans. Knut Tarnowski and Frederic Will (London, Routledge & Kegan Paul, 1973).

25. Raymond Carver, 'The Pipe', in *Where Water Comes Together With Other Water* (New York, Random House, 1986), p.67.

26. See for example Martin Heidegger, 'Language', in *Poetry, Language, Thought*, pp.187–210.

27. Dale Spender, *Man Made Language* (London, Routledge & Kegan Paul, 1980).

28. Annie Leclerc, *Parole de femme* (Paris, Grasset, 1974).

29. Tillie Olsen, *Silences* (London, Virago, 1980).

30. For an introduction to these ideas, see for example Betsy Wing's useful 'Glossary', in *The Newly Born Woman* by Hélène Cixous and Catherine Clément, trans. Betsy Wing (Manchester, Manchester University Press, 1986), pp.163–8; and Luce Irigaray, 'Speculum', in *Speculum of the Other Woman*, trans. Gillian C. Gill (Ithaca, Cornell University Press, 1985), pp.133–240.

31. Melanie Klein, 'The Importance of Symbol Formation in the Development of the Ego', in *The Selected Melanie Klein*, ed. Juliet Mitchell (London, Penguin Books, 1986), pp.95–111.

32. Julia Kristeva, *Pouvoirs de l'horreur* (Paris, Editions du Seuil, 1980).

33. Gemma Corradi Fiumara, *The Other Side of Language: A Philosophy of Listening*, trans. Charles Lambert (London, Routledge, 1990), p.53.

34. Ibid., p.55.

35. For a discussion of the relationship between common sense and ideology, see also Catherine Belsey, *Critical Practice* (London, Methuen, 1980).

36. Andrea Nye, *Words of Power: A Feminist Reading of the History of Logic* (London, Routledge, Chapman and Hall, 1990), p.179.

37. John Keats, 'To George and Tom Keats, December 21, 27 (?), 1817', in *Oxford Anthology of English Literature*, p.768.

38. No quantitative research into this area of the NHS health-care context has yet been carried out, but a programme of qualitative research is being undertaken with the Department of Social Medicine, University of Bristol, by Dr Robin Philipp and Fiona Sampson.

39. Seamus Heaney, *Sweeney Astray* (London, Faber and Faber, 1984).

40. Edmond Rostand, *Cyrano de Bergerac*, (Paris, Bibliotheque de la Pleiade, rev. edn, 1974).

41. Matthew Arnold, 'From *Essays in Criticism: Second Series*', in *Selected Prose*, ed. P.J. Keating (London, Penguin, 1970), p.340.

42. 'On Translating Homer: Last Words', ibid., pp.91–3.

43. Susan Sellers, 'Julia Kristeva: A Question of Subjectivity', *Women's Review*, 12 (1988), pp.19–21.

44. Jacques Derrida, 'Différance', in *Margins of Philosophy*, trans. Alan Bass (London, Harvester Press, 1982), pp.5–6.
45. Laura Riding, *The Poems of Laura Riding* (Manchester, Carcanet, rev. edn, 1986), p.90.
46. Jacques Derrida, 'Tympan', in *Margins of Philosophy*, p.xi.

FURTHER READING

Adorno, Theodor W., *The Jargon of Authenticity*, trans. Knut Tarnowski and Frederic Will (London, Routledge & Kegan Paul, 1973).
Arnold, Matthew, *Selected Prose*, ed. P.J. Keating (London, Penguin, 1970).
Davies, Ioan, *Writers in Prison* (Oxford, Blackwell, 1990).
Derrida, Jacques, *Margins of Philosophy*, trans. Alan Bass (London, Harvester Press, 1982).
Fiumara, Gemma Corradi, *The Other Side of Language: A Philosophy of Listening*, trans. Charles Lambert (London, Routledge, 1990).
Foucault, Michel, *The Order of Things: An Archaeology of the Human Sciences*, trans. Alan Sheridan-Smith (London, Tavistock Publications, 1966).
Heidegger, Martin, *Poetry, Language, Thought*, trans. Albert Hofstadter (New York, Harper & Row, 1975)
Hill, Selima, *The Accumulation of Small Acts of Kindness* (London, Chatto & Windus, 1989).
Irigaray, Luce, *Speculum of the Other Woman*, trans. Gillian C. Gill (Ithaca, Cornell University Press, 1985).
Jackson, Laura (Riding), *The Poems of Laura Riding*, (Manchester, Carcanet, rev. edn, 1986).
Moi, Toril (ed.), *The Kristeva Reader* (Oxford, Blackwell, 1986).
Nye, Andrea, *Words of Power: A Feminist Reading of the History of Logic* (London, Routledge, Chapman and Hall, 1990).
Plath, Sylvia, *Collected Poems* (London, Faber and Faber, 1981).
Plato, *The Republic*, trans. H.D.P. Lee (London, Penguin, 1955).
Rousseau, Jean-Jacques, *The Confessions*, trans. J.M. Cohn (London, Penguin, 1953).
Ruskin, John, *Unto This Last and Other Writings*, ed. Clive Wilmer (London, Penguin, 1985).
Sampson, Fiona, *Writing in Healthcare* (Winchester, Hospital Arts, 1989).
Sexton, Anne, *The Selected Poems of Anne Sexton*, Diane Wood Middlebrook and Diana Hume George (eds) (London, Virago, 1991).
Wordsworth, William, 'Preface to Lyrical Ballads', in *The Oxford Anthology of English Literature* Vol. 2, Frank Kermode and John Hollander (eds), (New York, Oxford University Press, 1973), pp.594–611.

17

Objecting to the Subject: Science, Femininity and Poetic Process in the Work of Elizabeth Bishop and Lavinia Greenlaw

Deryn Rees-Jones

Concluding his 1933 lecture, 'Femininity', Freud begs his reader, in a disclaimer of typical archness:

> If you want to know more about femininity, enquire from your own experiences of life, or turn to the poets, or wait until science can give you deeper and more coherent information.[1]

The 'key to the riddle of femininity' is placed within a matrix of three distinct categories of knowledge: the experiential, which is to offer the empirical evidence against which to test his theoretical model; the literary tradition, as represented in its 'highest' (and perhaps most metaphysical) form, poetry; and science, a systematised form of knowledge, and the discourse of 'objective' truth, to which psychoanalysis itself was laying a large claim. Although all three categories have a history of a particularly problematic construction of femininity and have been guilty of representing a distorted, damaged, objectified or deified female subjectivity, what is interesting about Freud's hedging, and refusal to be pinned down on the matter of femininity, is the way in which in the process of unravelling femininity's riddle, science, poetry and femininity thus become somewhat incongruously connected. If science and poetry are meant to give us an answer to the elusive nature of femininity, the question is begged as to what, if anything, the connection between these categories of knowledge are. How *can* science or poetry help us to understand femininity? And more specifically to the concerns of this chapter, does the idea that science and poetry can somehow explain femininity have any useful bearing on the use of science in the work of women poets?

As Lisa Steinman has shown, developments in science and technology had an important influence on Modernist poetics in America in the 1920s and 1930s, and in particular on the work of William Carlos Williams, Wallace Stevens and Marianne Moore[2]. Yet the fêting of the scientific as a new aesthetic also became part of an elision which equated science with a hard, dry objective voice, which in its turn became equated with masculinity. Such codings, which are infamously and repeatedly to be found in the work of Ezra Pound, and which are, as Marilyn L. Brownstein points out, gleefully deconstructed by Moore, present themselves as a hallmark of canonical modernism.[3]

My interest here will be in the relationship of the work of the American poet Elizabeth Bishop (1911–79), whose work might be seen as acting as a bridge between modernist and post-modernist concerns, and the contemporary British poet, Lavinia Greenlaw (b. 1962). Throughout her work, Greenlaw makes use of scientific discourse to address multiple anxieties about the way in which to construct a poetic voice and articulate her femininity. Admiring Bishop for 'her use of distance, geographical poetic and emotional which she somehow manages to employ without any lack of commitment or involvement from herself',[4] Greenlaw simultaneously makes recourse to a female poetic precursor and her doctrine of objectivity, while using science as a discourse of authority: Greenlaw can 'take on' science, with all the ambiguities that the idea of 'taking on' entails. For in exploiting scientific discourse as both subject matter and poetic idiom, Greenlaw offers a critique of patriarchy through an examination of scientific methods and the history of science, while also using science as a strategy which gives her, as a woman poet, a special and uncompromised sense of authority and detachment not usually associated – even in the 1990s – with a female poetic voice.

As a precursor to Greenlaw, Bishop's notorious sense of privacy and her refusal to gender herself as a poet – her insistence on never appearing in any women-only anthologies – are of obvious importance. In interview, Greenlaw has spoken of her use of science in her poems in terms of averting her anxieties about the way she is constructed as a woman poet. She explains:

> In the past, quite naturally I have used what has been described as the controlled, detached 'scientific' voice and I think partly I was concerned about allowing myself too much emotional space within my work.[5]

Yet writing against a stereotype of the feminine voice (what Vernon Shatley describes as writing 'from the heart, from nature . . . to pour forth from the heart in the manner of the sentimental women poets popular in Bishop's youth: Millay, Wylie, Teasdale, Ella Wheeler Wilcox . . . a writing emotive and overflowing'[6]) doesn't lead either

Bishop or Greenlaw into a position by which they embrace masculinist models of subjectivity that compromise the expression of self. Instead both evolve a position which freely acknowledges indeterminacy and flux, but which is simultaneously desirous of an exploration of the world in terms of series of interrogations which may yield a response of no more than a corresponding set of momentary truths.

In the poem 'The Monument', which was included in Bishop's first collection, *North and South* (1946)[7], Bishop draws from T.S. Eliot's 1919 essay 'Tradition and the Individual Talent' in which he famously describes his theory of a poetics of impersonality.[8] 'The progress of an artist is a continual self-sacrifice, a continual extinction of personality':

> It is in this depersonalization that art may be said to approach the condition of science. . . . consider as a suggestive analogy, the action which takes place when a bit of finely filiated platinum is introduced into a chamber containing oxygen and sulphur dioxide.[9]

Continuing, Eliot defines the relationship between the poet and the poem through the scientific analogy of the 'catalyst':

> When the two gases previously mentioned are mixed in the presence of a filament of platinum, they form sulphurous acid. This combination takes place only if the platinum is present; nevertheless the newly formed acid contains no trace of platinum, and the platinum itself is apparently unaffected: has remained inert, neutral, and unchanged. The mind of the poet is the shred of platinum. It may partly or exclusively operate upon the experience of the man himself; but, the more perfect the artist, the more completely separate in him will be the man who suffers and the mind which creates; the more perfectly will the mind digest and transmute the passions which are its material.[10]

Eliot uses the metaphor of science not only as an objective method of distancing the reader from more Romantic conceptions of the artist, but to validate poetry (and it's interesting that we find in Freud a similar anxiety when he seeks to validate psychoanalysis by calling it a science[11]) by allying it with an authoritative, universal, and powerful, modern discourse. Although Bishop is obviously drawing on the essay, her relationship to the objective voice is an ambiguous one. While Eliot's essay reads in some ways like an hysterical attempt to cut off emotion and then re-member it in the body of a poem[12], Bishop's intersection with the essay shows how she will interrogate the relationship between poem and poet, subject and object, personal and literary history, rather than severing it.

'The Monument' ends with an instruction that it 'is the beginning of a painting, or poem, or monument' and that we must '[w]atch it closely'. In a frequently cited letter to Anne Stevenson, Bishop writes:

reading Darwin one admired the beautiful solid case being built up out of his endless, heroic, observations, almost unconscious or automatic – and then comes a sudden relaxation, a forgetful phrase, and one feels that strangeness of his undertaking, sees the lonely young man, his eyes fixed on facts and minute details, sinking or sliding giddily off into the unknown. What one seems to want in art, in experiencing it, is the same thing that is necessary for its creation, a self-forgetful, perfectly useless concentration.[13]

Here the poet's concentration on the object becomes an examination of the perceiver as well as the object perceived. If the poet is constructed as observer, the poem, for Bishop, comes into being as the *process* of observation. Not only does the subject construct the object under its scrutiny, but the construction of the object in its turn contributes to the construction of the subject describing it, and this dialogue between self and other, poem and poet, establishes a dynamic relationship which breaks down hierarchical positions between the subject and the object. Thus the objective voice becomes a medium not for the fixing of experience, but for interrogating and renegotiating its multi-facetedness.

At the same time as relating intertextually with Eliot's essay, Bishop's poem is also based on Max Ernst's series of thirty-four frottages, *Histoire Naturelle* (1925).[14] Bishop's interest in surrealism, and her early use of surrealistic imagery, accord well with the aesthetic principles which evolve in 'The Monument' in that one of surrealism's main aims is to break down the relationship between subject and object.[15] As a poetic model for 'The Monument', *Histoire Naturelle* demands an interrogation of perception. As Werner Spies elaborates, frottage is:

> bound up with a new objectivity. It creates this objectivity in that the structure that Ernst rubs through is subordinate to a pictorial element that has nothing to do with that structure. Two planes of reality coincide. A structure that refers a priori to something unrelated to the pictorial object, that at first glance does not seem adequate, encounters the pictorial object that has hitherto never been expressed in extrapictorial structural elements. . . . This apparent illogic creates the curious state of suspension in which Ernst's figures live. . . . Ernst's *Histoire Naturelle* . . . calls into question the rational and the explicable, which is the aim of natural history; through a slight stroke of the hand he again renders inexplicable and indescribable the world as explained and described. . . . To the artist frottage is not only a technique in which two object-planes overlap and penetrate each other; it is also a means by which he frees himself from his inhibitions.[16]

Such disorientation of the self in relation to the objects it perceives offers Bishop an emancipatory model which presents her with an opportunity, through an interrogation of the concept of 'the natural', to reconstruct herself in relation to subject and object, history and literary tradition.[17]

It is this model of objectivity to which Greenlaw turns in her first full-length collection. *Night Photograph* (1993)[18] examines the ethics of science in a socio-historic context as well as the ethics of replacing an unquestioning faith in religious structures by our relatively new but often strangely parallel 'blind faith in technology and science'.[19] In many poems science is used as a metaphor for human relationships. In 'Electricity' Greenlaw exploits this fully by using circuitry as a metaphor for power in a relationship. Self and other merge and become indistinguishable:

> I was thinking about electricity –
> how at no point on a circuit
> can power diminish or accumulate
> how you also need a lack of balance
> for energy to be released. *Trust it.*
> Once, being held like that,
> no edge, no end and no beginning
> I could not tell our actions apart:
> if it was you who lifted my head to the light,
> if it was I who said how much I wanted
> to look at your face. *Your beautiful face.*

> (*NP*, p.27)

But this trust in science is also one which Greenlaw believes must be regarded with a degree of scepticism, as she writes to 'a Russian mongrel bitch' in 'For the First Dog in Space':

> Laika, do not let yourself be fooled
> by the absolute stillness
> that comes only with not knowing
> how fast you are going. As you fall
> in orbit around the earth, remember
> your language. Listen to star dust
> Trust your fear.

> (*NP*, p.52)

Persistently Greenlaw asks us to relate science to the human scale, with poems about plastic surgery ('The Man Whose Smile Made Medical History', *NP*, pp.24–5), artificial insemination ('The Gift of Life', *NP*, p.21), Marie Curie ('A Letter From Marie Curie', *NP*, p.45), and radium poisoning ('The Innocence of

Radium', *NP*, pp.46–7) which look at scientific developments from a personal and historical perspective.

But it is in her long poem, 'Galileo's Wife' (*NP* pp.29–31) – an attempt at 'revisionary mythmaking'[20] which is the only poem in the collection which engages directly with a recognisable feminist politics – that Greenlaw engages with a key point in the history of science to explore perceptions and constructions of reality. In doing this she reconstructs a female subject by engaging with, and questioning, the authority of experience, poetry, and science as ways of formulating knowledge and 'truth'.

Although the issue is not addressed directly in the poem, in her use of Galileo Greenlaw is also entering into a debate which dramatises the struggle between science and religion. Galileo's imprisonment by the Inquisition for his anti-Catholic endorsement of the Copernican theory that the earth rotates on its axis and revolves around the sun once a year, raises a series of crucial philosophical questions. As the historian Maurice Finocchiaro has commented, the 'Galileo affair':

> involved *scientific issues* about physical facts, natural phenomena, and astronomical and cosmological matters; and it also involved methodological and *epistemological questions* about what truth is and the proper way to search for it.[21]

Galileo was made Professor of Mathematics at the University of Pisa at the age of twenty-five, and included in his achievements are the development of the modern telescope and the thermometer, the discovery of four satellites of Jupiter, the ring of Saturn and the spots on the sun, as well as his foreshadowing of Newton's law of motion. In her poem, Greenlaw deconstructs the myth of the isolated male genius, and offers to tell us the 'whole' story about the so-called Father of Modern Science. The unnamed wife of the poem, who is shown to be deeply involved in and perhaps even responsible for the generation of ideas that have contributed to her husband's status in the modern world, is publicly (and privately) unacknowledged.

In the first three stanzas which make up the first section of the poem, we are given a portrait of Galileo which subtly undermines the importance of detailed scientific enquiry when it is unaccompanied by sensitivity to human surroundings and conditions. The stars are 'brought down' and the riddles of the universe are demystified as Galileo's wife is left with the stars trapped between the pages of Galileo's cosmological studies – his *The Starry Messenger* (1610) and the *Sunspot Letters* (1613). As such, the stars have lost their dimension: their power and their mystery are only paper in the hands of Galileo's wife. Femininity, however, is a riddle which Galileo, despite his appetite for knowledge, is not even remotely interested in solving. Femininity is a category which Galileo's wife holds up as something which, if subjected to any kind of experimental testing, would fail to reveal a conclusive result, the kind of result which Galileo might be capable of understanding: 'If only he could measure me and find my secrets', she says. Galileo's wife, however, measures the secrets of the world in terms of her own body and its rhythms. 'I have dropped pebbles into water/six hundred times this morning', she says, and '[t]he average speed of descent//was three pulsebeats with a half-beat variable,/allowing for the different angle and force/with which each pebble hit the water.' The female body here is not used as a guarantor of a gendered authority, but it is perceived as a method of discovery, demonstrating the way Galileo's wife is able to humanise objective ways of perceiving. Greenlaw offers a critique of the rational which denies feeling or any kind of moral responsibility, as we see Galileo ordering that his dead children are cruelly and surreally subjected to his experiments.

The contrast between Galileo and his wife – and their approach to the value of scientific evaluation – is made metaphorical in a joke about their respective footwear. Galileo wears a pair of velvet slippers, while his wife wears boots: it is a sturdy moral framework which allows her to keep her perspective, to keep her feet on the ground. In section four of the poem Galileo's wife is sent off to find the edges of the world. This magic realist fabularisation of a journey from west to east, in which Galileo's wife is carried and supported by the natural world, dramatises an evolution of the self which, with its fish and tidal imagery, portrays her in Christ-like terms. She sees the world in terms dependent on immediate sensory responses to the world, and as such seems to counterbalance the Copernican world view, which was typically opposed in its time because of the way it so obviously deceived immediate sensory perception. Galileo's wife's perceptions act poetically in their reliance on metaphor to communicate emotion: a cloud over Dalmatia is the colour of her wedding dress, the 'desert is a sea of orchids', a 'powder' 'turns the sky to thunder and gold'. It is showing – rather than testing or explaining – that is Galileo's wife's prime concern; and yet paradoxically in the process of her experimentation to find out the shape of the world she also offers empirical proof about its physical construction, disproving Galileo's theory – as it is fictionalised in the poem – that the world is flat.

In presenting a search for truth, 'Galileo's Wife' offers a dialogue between subjective and objective ways of knowing while dramatising a series of binary divisions: between male and female, public and private, rational and emotional, showing and explaining, speech and writing. Similarly, a tension between subjective and objective ways of understanding is seen in Greenlaw's use of free-verse. Acting not only in rhythmic terms, free-verse is, of course, a highly artificial way of pluralising meaning through a self-conscious juxtaposition of semantic and syntactic structures. Greenlaw is deliberately undermining such aesthetics of uncertainty in her recurrent use of the end-stopped line that results in a pattern of assertion and objectivity, juxtaposed by a simultaneous conveyance of constraint and restriction. We see this particularly in the fourth section of the poem when it is the movements of Galileo's wife in the natural world which are mirrored by enjambment: 'I fall / and frozen air catches me'; '[a] tidal wave / carries me up into the mountains'. In such a way the end-stopped lines of the poem act to conjure up the edges of the world; likewise in carrying the line forward the use of enjambment attempts to emphasise and represent the circularity of that world. Having been asked to find the edge of the world, Galileo's wife returns, making her answer by drawing a circle. Edge and limit, themselves equated symbolically with masculinity, are countered by an equally symbolic feminised curve. Galileo is portrayed as incapable of representing knowledge in a way which can be shared with future generations – his students sleep – as history is left in the hands of Galileo's wife who must 'leave the truth' amongst her husband's papers while thanking 'the bears of Natolia' that she 'never taught him how to write'.

In seeking to assume an ungendered identity as poets it might be easy to accuse Bishop and Greenlaw of denying the many difficulties which present themselves for the woman poet – not least in the appropriation of a subjectivity traditionally denied them. But both Bishop and Greenlaw, in their suspicion of certainty and fixity, do not seem to be seeking to transcend gender, but rather to interrogate and destabilise it through their use of the objective voice. In suggesting that scientific idioms can be a fund of radical creativity, however, it is not my intention to disregard critiques of the patriarchal stranglehold there is on science and technology, its institutions and its ideologies and its methodologies, as feminist critics as diverse as and Dorothy Dinnerstein, Luce Irigaray and Evelyn Fox Keller have variously argued.[22] Such terms as 'authoritative' and 'objective' are of course problematic when left unqualified or seen in isolation, particularly when objectivity is elided with a commonsense notion of the natural, and subsumed into stubborn or rigid patriarchal constructions of reality; as we have seen, Greenlaw is herself keen to point this out. In her *Simians, Cyborgs and Women*, Donna Haraway argues for 'a doctrine of objectivity' which, rather than relying on rigid or absolutist assumptions, instead:

> privileges contestation, deconstruction, passionate construction, webbed connections, and hope for transformation of systems of knowledge and ways of seeing.[23]

And like Haraway, I'd like to see science and objectivity as forms of knowledge which allow, at their best, a redefinition of the universal through the necessary creation of a new language which creates new metaphors and new mythologies, promoting a perceptual bifurcation whereby everyday realist assumptions about the world are juxtaposed against narratives of alternative truths – a way of seeing to which Bishop and Greenlaw's poetry can surely be compared.

NOTES

1. 'Femininity', *New Introductory Lectures on Psychoanalysis*, Penguin Freud Library, Vol. 2 (Harmondsworth, Penguin, 1991), p.169.
2. Lisa M. Steinman, *Made in America: Science, Technology and American Modernist Poets* (New Haven and London, Yale University Press, 1987).
3. *The Gender of Modernism: A Critical Anthology*, ed. Bonnie Kime Scott (Bloomington and Indianapolis, Indiana University Press, 1990), p. 331. Brownstein shows how

> Subversion of binarisms ... typically takes three forms. First, Moore takes conventionally negative words in contexts that make them positive. ... Second, 'masculine' and 'feminine' words ... lose their gender distinct and biased functions without losing meaning; 'strong' women write 'erect' poems, 'violent' ones. ... Third, Moore employs paired oppositions, wittily exposing individual meanings based on difference ('controlled ardor', 'clean violence') and operating anterior to their oppositional judgement-weighted relations. As a consequence meaning is made more precise – and closer to Moore's goal of 'depersonalised' usage.

4. Ibid., p.78.
5. Interview with Raymond Friel, London, 1994, in *Talking Verse: Interviews With Poets* (St Andrews and Williamsburg, Verse, 1995), pp.78–81 (p.79).
6. *After the Death of Poetry: Poet and Audience in Contemporary America* (Durham and London, Duke University Press, 1993), p.44.
7. Elizabeth Bishop, *Collected Poems* (London, Chatto & Windus, 1991), pp.23–5.
8. Vernon Shatley makes this point in his reading of 'The Monument', in *After the Death of Poetry*, p.41.
9. 'Tradition and the Individual Talent', *Selected Prose of T.S. Eliot*, ed. with an introduction by Frank Kermode (London, Faber and Faber, 1975), pp.37–44 (p.40).
10. *Selected Prose of T.S. Eliot*, p.41.
11. See Jane Flax, *Thinking Fragments: Psychoanalysis, Feminism, and Postmodernism in the Contemporary West* (Oxford, University of California Press, 1990), p.74.
12. See Alison Mark's brilliant readings of Veronica Forrest-Thomson, hysteria and poetic language in 'Hysteria and Poetic Language', in *Women: A Cultural Review*, 5:3 (1994).
13. Anne Stevenson, *Elizabeth Bishop* (New York, Twayne, 1966), p.66.
14. See *Max Ernst Frottages*, trans. Joseph M. Bernstein (London, Thames and Hudson, 1986).
15. See 'Surrealist Situation of the Object', *Manifestoes of Surrealism*, trans. Richard Seaver and Helen R. Lane (London and New York, Ann Arbor, 1972), pp.255–78 (p.260). Here André Breton, outlining surrealism's debt to Hegel, defines surrealism in both poetry and the plastic arts as being a process which '[l]iberated from the need to reproduce forms essentially taken from the outer world' depends on 'inner representation'. Surrealism:

> confronts this inner representation with that of the concrete forms of the real world, seeks in turn ... to seize the object in its generality, and as soon as it has succeeded in so doing, tries to take that supreme step par excellence: excluding (relatively) the external object as such and considering nature only in its relationship with the inner world of consciousness.

16. *Max Ernst Frottages*, p.9.
17. Jo Shapcott's first collection, *Electroplating the Baby* (Newcastle, Bloodaxe Books, 1988), is strongly influenced by Bishop in both its adoption of an 'objective' narratorial voice and her use of surrealistic imagery. 'Electroplating the Baby' (pp.48–51), after which the collection takes its title, makes reference to Victorian popular science magazines and describes in intricate detail the process of mummification as figured in the experiments of a French scientist in the nineteenth century. Obviously indebted to Bishop's 'The Monument', as well as T.S. Eliot's chemical analogy of the poet as a piece of platinum, Shapcott writes with precise, realist description:

> He metallises our entire cadaver.
> He encloses it in an envelope

of bronze, copper, nickel, silver or gold
according to the wealth or caprice

of those who survive.
Does this waken your curiosity?

Do you wish to know
how Dr Variot proceeds?

In a double frame with four uprights
connected top and bottom by four square plates

is the body of a child which has been
perforated with a metal rod.

It is the bizarre and surreal elements of scientific exploration which are at the root of Shapcott's aesthetic, and, as an exercise in a literally morbid fascination 'Electroplating the Baby' is a self-reflexive critique of objectivity. It also depicts an obsession with technology which denies or marginalises any sense of the human scale. The ethos of the poem *is* double-edged because it does, despite our better instincts, awaken both Shapcott's and the reader's interest. Objectively detailing, examining, interrogating becomes a grotesque act. 'What is the future in store/for this process of mummification?' the narrator asks, replying that:

It would be impossible to say.
It is infinitely probable

that metallised cadavers
will never figure

except in small numbers
for a long, long time to come.

Because of its echoes of Mary Shelley's *Frankenstein* it is difficult to read the poem as a positive proposal for an aesthetic, yet in its intersection with Bishop's poem, it seems to demand that we read it as such. Is Shapcott making a point about women's relationship to the ethics of scientific experimentation? The levels of irony evident in Shapcott's narratorial voice are difficult to discern – perhaps the poem works as an overdetermined critique of her own poetic process? It remains as a kind of curate's egg which stands apart from the rest of the poems in the collection, asking us to re-examine both the method and motivation of our relationship to the world.

18. Lavinia Greenlaw, *Night Photograph* (London, Faber and Faber, 1993). Henceforth all references will appear in the body of the text.
19. *Talking Verse*, p.80.
20. See Alicia Ostriker, *Stealing the Language: The Emergence of Women's Poetry in America* (London, The Women's Press, 1987), pp.210–40.
21. *The Galileo Affair: A Documentary* (London, University of California Press, 1989), p.6.
22. See Dorothy Dinnerstein, *The Mermaid and the Minotaur: Sexual Arrangements and Human Malaise* (New York, Harper Row, 1977); Luce Irigaray, 'A Chance for Life: Limits to the Concept of the Neuter and the Universal in Science and Other Disciplines' (1986), in *Sexes and Genealogies* (New York, Columbia, University Press, UP, 1993) pp.185–206; and Evelyn Fox Keller, *Reflections on Gender and Science* (New Haven, Yale University Press, 1985).
23. Donna Haraway, *Simians, Cyborgs and Women: The Reinvention of Nature* (London, Free Association Books, 1991), pp.191–2.

FURTHER READING

Bishop, Elizabeth, *One Art: The Selected Letters*, selected and edited by Robert Giroux (London, Chatto & Windus, 1994).
Bloom, Harold, (ed.) and with an introduction, *Modern Critical Views: Elizabeth Bishop* (New York, Chelsea House, 1985).
Kennedy, David, 'The Poetry Lab.', *Poetry Review*, Vol.83, No.2 (Summer 1993), pp.26–9.
Miller, Arthur I., *Imagery in Scientific Thought: Creating Twentieth Century Physics* (Cambridge, Massachusetts and London, MIT Press, 1987).

18

'No-one's Mother': Can the Mother Write Poetry?

Nicole Ward Jouve

> For me, poetry was where I lived as
> no-one's mother, where I existed as
> myself.[1]

Let me suppose that the paradise of poetry is gendered. And Greek. I find two myths: one male, the other female.

The Male Myth: Homer stands on its Olympus. Singing *The Iliad*. Of human deeds strong and simple as the passions they stem from. Words that speak the heart. Hit like blows. Invite our marvelling eyes to plunge into the wine-dark sea. Song effective as deeds. Human beings who are one. From Homer on, it's all the way downwards for those who, like Marx, dream the Homer dream: down through tragedy, through Christianity, eventually down to Hegel's 'wretched consciousness'. The Shadow falls: between feelings and consciousness, desire and act, words and deeds. Doubt and guilt cloud the scene. The hallmarks of Western Modernity.

The Female Myth: It's an early myth. Its traces are almost gone. In the human re-membering we call history, it surfaces here and there, becomes erased, re-surfaces. It's much around in our century, charged with resentment, angry at erasure. We relate to tradition through our mothers if we're female, Virginia Woolf claims. Resentfully: why – she also asks – why did our mothers so mismanage our affairs? She is talking about finance; but does she imply, 'why weren't they poets'? 'Why did they leave us such a patchy tradition, barely a tradition really'? In that myth of the mother-who-would-be-a-poet-and-think-she-had-every-right-to-be, Sappho is the dream. Sappho who wrote for her daughter Cleis:

> There is no place for grief, [Cleis]
> in a house which serves the Muse;
> our own is no exception[2]

In Sappho's house, through service to the Muse, to which everyone is entitled, everyone is also entitled: to joy, to love, to making poetry. The mother sings to her daughter.

Is there a women's fall in the West, a fall from the mother's house, the house that served the Muse, and knew no grief? A fall so complete that the very memory that such a house existed became destroyed, along with most of Sappho's poems? A separation so savage that (Emily Dickinson is eloquent on this, as in her 'My Life Closed Twice Before Its Close') only the memory of the separation remains?

> Parting is all we know of Heaven
> And all we need of Hell.[3]

Is it because this loss has disempowered 'the second sex' that Simone de Beauvoir claims that 'humanity' has gone over not to the sex that gives life, but to the sex that kills? Gone, that is, to Homer's *Iliad* warriors, and their descendants. Not to Sappho's. Isn't it out of nostalgia for the lost Mother–Poet figure that many women poets this century have fantasised about Greece, gone to live on Greek islands (Renée Vivien, H.D. . . .)? Why else the fascination for Mother Goddesses, Demeter – or Colette's Sido: for the poetic prose writers have been searching too . . .

Men fall from oneness with themselves. Women, from oneness with the Mother.

The banned, the denied, the patchy, the suppressed, the suffocated Mother makes an uncanny return. *Unheimlich*, to use Freud's word. The Erynnies, the avengers of blood-right, driven underground by Athena, tamed to become the benevolent guardians of the home in the new city, return, summoned by Night their mother, as in Hélène Cixous' play *La Ville parjure, ou le retour des Erynnies*[4]. The Mother becomes she whose haunting presence estranges women from themselves. In Simone de Beauvoir, the Mother estranges women from humanity. For Adrienne Rich, poetry can only be written by the part of the self that is no mother. Evoking her difficulties as a young mother, her struggle with words, she explains: 'For me, poetry was where I lived as no-one's mother, where I existed as myself.'[5] Mme Ponteillier, in Kate Chopin's *The Awakening*, had already said, 'I would give my life for my children, I would not give myself'.[6] But there was no tug-of-war for Sappho, was there?

Can the Mother *no longer* write poetry then?

Never again?

Must a woman poet kill the mother in herself, at least whilst she is writing?

Do women write out of different selves? (Do men? Proust certainly thought there was nothing in common between the man who lives and the man who writes. He did not say that the man who writes has to kill the man who lives. Though he eventually did, closeted in his cork-lined room writing *A La Recherche du Temps perdu*. But that was not so as to kill part of himself. That was to find himself. To become one.)

But the woman poet: must she cut off part of herself, must she renounce motherhood if she wants to become a great poet?

Sappho did not have to choose. Descend the course of ages. Who are the women poets? Isn't Camille Paglia right when she claims that creativity is male, that 'Man, the sexual conceptualizer and projector, has ruled art because art is his Apollonian response towards and away from woman', and that females only create when their male side wins over?[7] Androgynes. 'Male' women. Athenas, fierce unmothered virgins, smouldering under constraints. Wild and deadly Artemises. The Emilys, Brontë and Dickinson. True, there are the passionate lovers, Louise Labbé, Marguerite de Navarre, Elizabeth Barrett Browning, H.D. . . . But look at Sylvia Plath. Is it accident that she is a young mother, alone to deal with the children, when she succeeds at last in what she's always made into an art: dying? Look at Marina Tsvetaeva, and that terrible suicide . . .

Is motherhood, being bodily 'occupied' by the other, is mothering, caring for others, compatible with lyric flight and freedom? Can you for that matter imagine Dante changing nappies, Milton getting up in the middle of the night to bottle-feed, Rochester helping with the maths homework, Byron knitting booties, Valéry making soup, T.S. Eliot on a Monday morning searching for the gym kit under the bed?

Am I mixing things up? Gender with sexual difference? Mixing economics, practicalities, societal roles, with sense of self? I am certainly mixing gender and class: sure, as Elizabeth Badinter has shown, motherhood has changed enormously over the ages[8] and sure, an aristocratic woman would have had everything that could be required to make writing possible: the literacy, the congenial cultural milieu, the servants to do the housework, the leisure time – which the peasant woman would not. Being able to be a poet should have been a question of class. But there would have been other constraints for the aristocratic or well-to-do woman despite all her privileges: upbringing, expectations, role-models, duties, all that Mary Wollstonecraft and her group deplored . . . how many of them became poets, *and* mothers? As for the current run of literate females . . . In *Silences*, Tillie Olsen described the sheer physical and emotional absorption, the hard work, of mothering, whose demands over the ages have debarred so many women from writing.[9] She puts together a (slender) list of mothers who have been writers also: but how many of those are poets?

In motherhood, Olsen urges, it is neither the capacity nor the need to create that are lacking, but:

> the need cannot come first. It can have at best only part self, part time. . . . Motherhood means being instantly interruptible, responsive, responsible. Children need one *now* (and remember, in our society, the family must often try to be the center for love and health the outside world is not). The very facts that these are needs of love, not duty, that one feels them as one's self; *that there is no one else to be responsible for these needs*, gives them primacy. It is distraction, not meditation, that becomes habitual; interruption, not continuity; spasmodic, not constant, toil. Work interrupted, deferred, postponed makes blockage – at best, lesser accomplishment. Unused capacities atrophy, cease to be.

Even today, unless a new race of superwomen has sprung up, an income equivalent to Woolf's £500 a year (however earned, but leaving leisure time) and a room of one's own, with a good nanny and supportive companionship thrown in, remain the basic ingredients for any mother to be a poet. Even so, what of the interruptions, the illnesses, the sleepless nights? Somehow I feel that the steadiness of prose is more compatible with motherhood: I think of Mrs Gaskell and her four daughters, of immensely productive George Sand and her two children (she *was* a phenomenon). What mother could afford to roam the roads of exile, composing *The Divine Comedy*, or the five years' total, ascetic immersion in music that enabled Rimsky-Korsakoff to develop as a composer? The work is a needy infant. The Muse is a demanding mistress. She loves celibates. Commands that her devotees choose which offspring they best love: of the body, or of the mind? There only are twenty-four hours to each day. Can you give your all to both?

And what of the incompatibility between the caring, the considerateness, the nurturing that mothering demands, and tends to develop in its practitioners, and the cruelty that creation requires? Can humans serenely suckle their young and write Lady Macbeth's speech about braining their babe rather than not murder Duncan? Watch over a sick child whilst composing the 'Ode on the West Wind'? Georges Bataille wrote of the bond between literature and evil. Camille Paglia harps on how goodness never produced good art. Angela Carter, that free spirit, edited the book *Wayward Girls and Wicked Women*.[10] Isn't it Plath's *savagery* that moves us? But 'Be nice', 'Godfathers'' voices urge Carol Ann Duffy's invisible poet-listener. You will get 'immortality at cost-effective price' if you remember that it is not 'the business of poetry/To stop the rot or rock the boat/or change anything': 'have a care/to keep emotion down to Gas Mark 2.'[11] The underlying message that emerges from the anger this poem exudes is that it is precisely through doing the reverse of what the 'Godfathers' advise that the ('Gas Mark 2': hence, I feel, female) listener-poet has a chance to write good poetry: by not being nice. By rocking the boat, not the cradle. Isn't it even more imperative for the woman poet than for the woman novelist to kill the Angel in the House? Can you be a poet and not draw upon your darkest, your most destructive self – since you must draw upon your deepest, your whole self – that which dares wrestle with sexuality and death?

Troubled, I tested friends with these questions: can you be a mother, and want to be a bad one? And not want to be 'good enough'? Can you be a poet, and be good? Does Mother imply good, and Poet bad? (Romantic, daemonic . . .) Can you think of great poets that were 'good' men – or women?

Adrienne Rich commented:

> I do know that for years I believed I should never have been anyone's mother, that because I felt my own needs acutely and often expressed them violently, I was Kali, Medea, the sow that devours her farrow, the unwomanly woman in flight from womanhood, a Nietzschean monster.'[12]

I got some interesting answers and a lot of jokes. 'Mallarmé asked the identical male question', a (male) French friend said. ' "Can you be a Father, and be a poet?" Are the demands of good fathering compatible with the demands of poetry?' Another (also male) named a woman poet who'd said that if her marriage broke down she would leave her children with her husband because she couldn't cope with both demands (creating, mothering) and creating was the more important for her. Another (ironic, female) said, to be a good poet you've got to suffer a lot; mothers are supposed to suffer a lot; therefore mothers are eminently destined to be poets. A necessary but not a sufficient condition, another replied. Then I got jokes: there was (as Jacques Lacan points out) a 'père-verse' (perverse), but not a 'mère-verse': or could we invent one?

But it got me thinking. What did I mean when I said poet? or when I said 'mother'? Had I created false questions by naming 'mother' and 'poet' as if they were identities? Was I working with the notion that each thing we are, or might be, is part and parcel of the whole, that (as Edmund Husserl would have it) the yellow of the lemon is continuous with, expressive of, its tartness and juiciness? 'Motherhood, in the sense of an intense personal relationship with a particular child, or children, is *one part* of female process; it is not an identity for all time', Rich points out.[13] Might it not be the case that the tug-of-war between motherhood and poetry was at its most intense when the children were small, most dependent? That the way Western societies organise mothering (virtually no support for the mother, in the UK few creches or nurseries) had created material and emotional incompatibilities between the two occupations? That the problem was, whatever might be claimed about myths, wholly historical and cultural? There have been, over the ages in Europe, countless Judith Shakespeares and Elizabeth Smarts – countless women with remarkable gifts with language, whose genius was swallowed up by material impossibilities, child-care first among them. Times are changing: the era of technological reproduction may be coming . . .

But in that Brave New World, who would do the mothering?

Can you for years strive for, as Rich again says, 'the qualities that are supposed to be "innate" in us: patience, self-sacrifice, the willingness to repeat endlessly the small, routine chores of socializing a human being'[14] *and* write *Les Fleurs du Mal?*

So then, what do I mean by Poetry? Lyricism. The lyre. The impulse to sing. And dance. Move to rhythm. Make music with words. Patterns with words. Numbers. To alternate one and two; and three. And five and six and eight and ten and twelve. The even, and the odd.

To celebrate, vent, state, soothe, rock, explore, express, in words that sing and dance. Surrender and concentration, at once. As in the story of the young man who had to learn both to admire the beauties of the surrounding world and not to spill the two drops of oil that were in the spoon he was holding.

The Aeolian Harp. The tree in whose leaves and boughs the wind makes sound. The Drunken Boat, abandoned to the elements, yet still one, still afloat, suffering and riding the sea-swell.

As in the Catholic Church there are three series of mysteries in the telling of the rosary: joy, pain and glory, so there are three realms of poetry. 1. Innocence: one of its Blakeian names is 'Infant Joy'. Soul that 'clap[s] its hands and sing[s]',[15] children in the foliage, 'hidden excitedly, containing laughter', as in T.S. Eliot's *Four Quartets.*[16] 2. Experience, with all its shades of knowledge, and of pain: its epics and tragedies and its lyrics. 3. And Glory: Pindaric Odes, celebrating the victor at Olympus. Horatian Odes, Renaissance Odes, and closer to us, Walt Whitman and Paul Claudel and St John Perse. Gerard Manley Hopkins and H.D. at one quiet end of the spectrum, Ezra Pound at the noisiest.

Poetry I also see as transformation. As metaphor, that is as voyage, as change. From the most lapidary (Emily Dickinson) to the most ample (Wordsworth's *The Prelude, or Growth of the Poet's Mind*). Poetry is metamorphosis. Binding by means of symbol. Discovering the hidden face of reality. Transforming pain into pleasure by means of cadence. Transmutation of frustrated desire, of ever-renewed longing, into song. Losing Syrinx whom he's pursued and lusted for and who, at her prayer to the river-god, has been changed into a reed to escape him, Pan picks a reed and makes music.

Are women debarred from any of these, except through power of tradition, rule or circumstance? I don't think so. You could imagine Phaedra, frustrated in her love for Hippolytus, lover of horses, making music out of horsehair: isn't that what the bow of violins is strung with? Or Echo, instead of pining to death for love, hewing down the sycamore at whose foot Narcissus bends over his watery image, and making a violin out of its wood. Eurydice, killing the snake whose bite has despatched her to Hades, and making strings for her lyre out of its guts to call to her beloved Orpheus ... Why don't we have any of these myths? We do have Renaissance French poet Louise Labbé, wishing herself the ivy that winds round her lover's body. Do women have to cling? (And to the lost Mother under the guise of a lover?)

Perhaps the difficulty is only there when I think of the Poet rather than of Poetry. The writing of Poetry. The obduracy and imaginary hold is in the gender roles, not the act.

Indeed, the poets that have been floating in my mind as I have been trying to say what poetry was for me have been the canonical ones, the high priests and the castaways, the Orphic ones, the damned and the exiles, from Dante to the Romantics and the French Symbolists. Or Establishment figures. Or groups of devotees, the Pléiade French Renaissance poets, the Surrealists, the Black Mountain poets (have there ever been schools of women poets?). Detach the persona from the act, poetry from traditional images of the poet, and the impossibility ceases.

The Mother, certainly, fits none of the above. Unless she is in an alternative world: Sappho in Lesbos.

Where does the Mother fit in, then?

As an object of desire. The object of desire. What the poet's language attempts to recapture. The Mother is a sort of universal Syrinx, forever lost, and by everyone, forever sought by means of the poem. Sought by women, as well as men. Julia Kristeva lists male writers only in her famous passage on the semiotic, but couldn't what she says also apply to women poets? I quote at length because it is such a compact and evocative statement. The 'semiotic activity, which introduces wandering or fuzziness into language and, *a fortiori*, into poetic language', Kristeva explains, is 'a mark of the workings of the drives (appropriation/rejection, orality/anality, love/hate, life/death)' and 'stems from the archaisms of the semiotic body', which is that of the infant, preceding the entry into the symbolic, into language:

> Language as symbolic function constitutes itself at the cost of repressing instinctual drive and continuous relation to the mother. On the contrary, the unsettled and questionable subject of poetic language (for whom the word is never uniquely sign) maintains itself at the cost of reactivating this repressed instinctual maternal element. If it is true that the prohibition of incest constitutes, at the same time, language as communicative code and women as exchange objects in order for society to be established, *poetic language would be* for its questionable subject-in-process the *equivalent of incest*: it is within the economy of signification itself that the questionable subject-in-process appropriates to itself this archaic, instinctual, and maternal territory; thus it simultaneously prevents the world from becoming mere sign and the mother from becoming an object like any other – forbidden. This passage into and through the forbidden, which constitutes the sign and is correlative to the prohibition of incest, is often explicit as such (Sade: 'Unless he becomes his mother's lover from the day she has brought him into the world, let him not bother to write, for we shall not read him,' – *Idée sur les romans*) . . .[17]

I prefaced this by saying it could apply to women writers as well, but could it? Kristeva goes on to add the names of Artaud, Joyce and Céline to that of Sade. No woman is mentioned. I am struck on reflection by her very Lévi-Straussian sentence about the prohibition of incest (a contract established between male subjects) both establishing language as communicative code and women as exchange objects. This has long been debated in feminism, and I myself have discussed it elsewhere.[18] But what this illuminates is why the myths I have mentioned (Narcissus, Orpheus, Syrinx) don't have their counterparts: we do live in a culture in which the poetic subject, the subject-in-process, is imagined as male. No wonder, then, Paglia's gut reaction: I say gut reaction, because she does not seem to be aware of what she is really saying, of her denial (of femininity? motherhood?). As *Sexual Personae* powerfully imagines them, it is insofar as they are androgynous, as there is maleness in them, that both Brontë and Dickinson can be poets. The same unconscious assumption applies to Bataille's essay on Emily Brontë. He imagines her as positioned in relation to the death that is in the reproductive act itself *as if she were a male subject-in-process*.

But female subjects-in-process also desire the mother. Is it then insofar as they unconsciously position themselves as male subjects, as both using women as an object of exchange in using language as communication, and as preventing the word from being only sign, and the mother from being forbidden through introducing semiotic disruption into language (word-play, word mutations, archaic sounds, rhythms, repetitions), that women can write poetry? And if then women have to, as it were, play an unconscious male part in order to write poetry, then what hope in hell can the mother have to write poetry? It follows that when a woman writes, it never can be the mother in her who writes. QED. But a sad QED.

Can we do better out of another French writer, Hélène Cixous, interested in what she calls 'feminine' writing? Though elsewhere she argues that it is found in men as in women, here she relates it to women writers, and links it specifically with the mother. Feminine writing, 'Castration or Decapitation' suggests, is

> very close to the voice, very close to the flesh of language . . . perhaps because there's something in [the women writers she is discussing] that's freely given, perhaps because they don't rush into meaning, but are straightaway at the threshold of feeling. . . . Writing in the feminine is passing on what is cut out by the Symbolic, the voice of the mother, passing on what is most archaic. The most archaic force that touches a body is one that enters by the ear and reaches the most intimate point.[19]

This is more hopeful in relation to the mother. What strikes me is the phrase 'passing on what is cut out by the Symbolic'. What passes on goes through the ear and reaches 'the most intimate point'. For this is about the daughter not having had to separate from the mother's body: oneness with the mother, which is exactly what I started from, using Sappho's fragment as a mythic image of a women's paradise of poetry. I am struck by the fact that the myths of poetry I have evoked – Orpheus and Eurydice, Pan and Syrinx – are all about losing the beloved's body and making poetry out of that loss. Is it the case then that the woman poet, if she wants to remain 'womanly' rather than 'androgynous' or 'male', can somehow hang on in and through words to the mother's body without having to go through the cruel loss that the male poet has to deal with? This would tally with a lot of contemporary ideas about women having less need to detach from the mother than men. Is this why Louise Labbé expresses her longing and love through the image of the ivy *clinging* to the trunk of the tree? Yet, in Kristeva as in Cixous, the focus is on the daughter who writes. Not the mother.

Still no answer to my question: can the mother write poetry? And it matters. Why else would a combination of workshops and symposium in Cardiff have called itself 'the mothers of invention', stating in its prospectus, 'The dignity of mothering is often undermined by a cultural ethos that intimates that the acts of creation and procreation are *incompatible*. The Mothers of Invention challenges the assumption that motherhood somehow interferes with rather than enhances creativity.' And it resourcefully threw down the gauntlet.[20]

Which returns me to Sappho. Extraordinary Sappho. Able to write as both daughter and mother. To write of continuity and separation. Of tradition and individuation. Of binding and of fire. Of loss and searching. Able to love both mother and daughter, and recognise that they are distinct from her, unreachable. According to an ancient biography, both her mother and her daughter were called Cleis:

> . . . my mother [used to say that]
> in her youth it was thought to be
> very fine to bind up your hair
>
> with a dark purple [headband] – yes,
> extremely fine indeed, although
> for a girl whose hair is golden
>
> like a torch flame [better] to wreathe
> in it garlands of fresh flowers;
> recently [I saw] a headband,
>
> brightly coloured, from Sardis . . .
>
> But for you, Cleis, I do not have
> a brightly coloured headband nor
> do I know where I may find one . . .[21]

And what of the Mother?

I have been writing as if she were one. But as I try to reflect what the Mother is, both inside and outside me, she multiplies. A veritable cast of characters, in which the unconscious, the dream-like, insists on mixing with reality. And the 'real' women, who are mothers, don't they write out of those Mothers!

1. First there is Darkness. Night. The mystery I come from. Which seizes me when, faced with images of what the Hubble telescope has photographed of galaxies in formation, I seem to be seeking for my own origins as I wonder at the origins of the world – the power that 'rolls through all things'. I became formed in my mother's womb: it is that womb, not the tiny snaky tadpole that, clever little chap, one among millions, found its way to my mother's egg in its white surge of spawn, that is for me the place of wonder.

But, having had children of my own, I know the eerie reality of those labour pains which one of Plath's *Three Women* experiences as an overwhelming sea:

> Far off, far off, I feel the first wave tug
> Its cargo of agony toward me, inescapable, tidal,
> And I, a shell, echoing on this white beach
> Face the voices that overwhelm, the terrible element.[22]

2. Mother Number 2: she is what I have used Cixous earlier to suggest: the source of food – the source of care – the source of language: the first speaker – the first voice I hear. I drink from her with all the force of my bare gums. She is what Melanie Klein has called the Breast. Good. Bad. I project my first love, my first hate, onto her. She is my first mirror. If she is cold, indifferent, lacking, I shall carry coldness, indifference, lack, inside me all the days of my life. Unless other people come to my help . . .

And the 'real' mother? The lacking, the needy, the bewildered flesh-and-blood mother, herself possessed by her own dream of the Mother? Plath again:

> Here is my son . . .
> He is turning to me like a little, blind, bright plant.
> One cry. It is the hook I hang on.
> And I am a river of milk,
> I am a warm hill.[23]

Whose desolation, whose rage at the hugeness of need – the mother's, the baby's? – speaks in 'I Want, I Want'?

> Open-mouthed, the baby god
> Immense, bald, though baby-headed,
> Cried out for the mother's dug.[24]

3. Then there's the Mother Kristeva invokes, the Mother from whom the Oedipal child must learn to separate, the Mother who is the object of desire, who surfaces as semiotic incest in poetic language. But does the desire have to be expressed as the semiotic? Can it not form itself into a clear new-born image, a bold little language explorer, searching for a new, a phantasy mother?

> The Language Issue
>
> I place my hope on the water
> in this little boat
> of the language, the way a body might put
> an infant
>
> in a basket of intertwined
> iris leaves
> its underside proofed
> with bitumen and pitch,
>
> then set the whole thing down amidst
> the sedge
> and bulrushes by the edge
> of a river

only to have it borne hither and thither,
not knowing where it might end up;
in the lap, perhaps,
of some Pharaoh's daughter.[25]

4. Archetypal then, the Mother? Ready to surface everywhere, whenever I speak,
paint, draw – but above all whenever I allow images to take over?

The Mother is my strength. Through her I bond with the earth, the sea. She
is the under-world also, the spaces before memory. She is the life in things, the
life in words. She frees me from intellect, from the distance of sight:

> My mind felt white and bloodless. I was trying to write an academic piece on
> Katherine Mansfield in the few hours a day I had free from domestic chores
> . . . and then, suddenly, I found that as soon as I tried to find words for the
> black shine of black trees in the rain, say, or the noise of heels knocking
> on a pavement at night, I could respond quite sharply to everything. . . .
> It was like coming back to life.[26]

The Mother is archaic: is powerful. She allows me to be naked. She
strokes and eases me. The sweet water of her creeks receives me. Her
caves and shades give me shelter. In her recesses I hibernate. She feeds
me honey, berries. Like Antaeus, I am re-born whenever I touch her. I
accept myself:

> Patience
>
> In water nothing is mean. The fugitive
> enters the river, she is washed free;
> her thoughts unravel like weeds of
> green silk: she moves downstream
> as easily as any cold-water creature
>
> can swim between furred stones, brown
> fronds, boots and tins the river holds equally.
> The trees hiss overhead. She feels their shadows.
> She imagines herself clean as a fish,
> evasive, solitary,. dumb. Her prayer:
> to make peace with her own monstrous nature.[27]

The Mother makes the sun and the seasons return, the moon and tides swell.
My bond to her is my dream of fusion: of omnipotence. I call her Ghea. I find
her in my body: easily. She makes metaphor easy:

Who speaks of the strong currents
streaming through the legs, the breasts
of a pregnant woman . . .?
. . .
Who speaks of the green coconut uterus
the muscles sliding, a deeper undertow
and the green coconut milk that seals
her well, yet flows so she is wet
from his softest touch?[28]

In My Name

Heavy with child

belly
an arc
of black moon

I squat over
dry plantain leaves

and command the earth
to receive you

in my name
in my blood . . .

my tainted

perfect child
my bastard fruit
my seedling
my sea grape
my strange mulatto
my little bloodling

Let the snake slipping in deep grass
be dumb before you.[29]

Yes, I know: I blanket so much by simply seeking for the distant rumble of
some archetypal voice in poems so charged with other dimensions: the (raped or
seduced?) (slave?) mother in her solitude and deprivation in Nichols' poem turning
anger, mixed blood, powerlessness, bastardy around through the power of her love:
in whose name is this done, the name of love, the naming power of language, the

mother daring to name outside patriarchal naming? Does the snake cease to be symbolic, the sign of the (sexual, Christian) fall, the sign also of a powerful value system, to re-become a dumb beast, a real snake that can no more tempt Eve than bite Eurydice, or threaten the child? In Sujata Bhatt's poem, here speaks that wonder of wonders whom Kristeva and others seek like salvation: the desiring mother. No, I will not invoke the blunt concepts of race and colour, nor the hardly less blunt ones of culture or ethnicity to distinguish these poems from others in which I try to hear mothers' voices. It would be glib, and probably untrue, to contrast the easier, earthier relation to coconut or plantain leaves or moon of these two poems with the anguish in Plath, the hospital context of Elaine Feinstein's 'Calliope in the labour ward' in which women, 'as little squeamish as/men in the great war', 'grunting in gas and air' 'give birth/bleak as a goddess'.[30] It's not a matter of the happier, more sensuous and loving non-Western women poets versus their more technology or depression-ruled Western counterparts. Bhatt and Nichols write in English and in England, for one thing. I'm not trying, as the phrase goes, to do justice to the poems, so full of specifics and complexities. I'm listening for something. Ghea. Her echoes.

Ghea is life. Is death. The twin and opposite mother figures in Michèle Roberts' 'After my grandmother's death': mother, grandmother, spinners, weavers. In and out of death, of life:

> ... my mother's womb spun me a fine cocoon
> spun me round and out, death tugged
> my umbilical cord, she grinned
> and tied me into her weaving
>
> the moon who eats babies on winter nights
> has her dark face, and rubbery hands
> but grandmother rescued me
> and held me close, she shone
> steady for me, then I felt so blessed
>
> then death strode out
> trawling, trawling
> and grandmother was mackerel to her silver net
>
> the womb is the house of death
> and each woman
> spins in death's web; as I inch
> back to the light
> death pays out the bright thread[31]

5. Enter Madonna, pensive and patient. The wise virgin, with oil in her lamp. Come the Angel, wind and wings, she is ready: 'I am the servant of the Lord'.

She is the sign that the lowly will be exalted, and the powerful brought down. That the world's values will be overturned. I picture her as a very young girl. Now she has her child. She holds him gently. Unpossessively: she knows he is not for her.

She crushes the dragon's head. She is spotless. She can keep me from sin. She knows no sex, but is infinitely available: to me. She is thousands of Western images: haloed in gold, painted in bright colours, the colours of dream. She is mercy incarnate: on the western side of cathedrals, her rose contains the fire of judgement. But oh how easily she slides into her more ambiguous predecessors, the protective, the fertility-making goddesses of the cross-roads, the hidden springs, the secret places. Forms of Ghea linger.

But look at the Pietà. Absolute suffering, the worst: yet accepted. The fainting Pietà, the fainting St Theresa: how easily they become eroticised. Female Masochism, Kristeva's 'Stabat Mater' would remind me:

> Feminine perversion [père-version] . . . promotes feminine masochism to the rank of structure stabilizer . . . by assuring the mother that she may thus enter into an order that is above that of human will it gives her her reward of pleasure.[32]

Darts pierce the mother's heart: as if the heart were the womb's deepest recess. Sex only known, only allowed, through pain. Ecstasy through self-extinction: Plath all over again, is it?

But what of the young Mary, the mother with child? Who writes her?
6. 'And what about', asked Suniti Namjoshi who heard a first version of this chapter, 'what about the Amazon mother? the Lion Mother, Stevie Smith's lion aunt? the Unlicensed Mother? the Two-Headed Mother? the servant Mother? the Knight-Mother, in shining armour?'
7. Oh yes. And then there is the Bad Mother. The castrating Mother, the Destroyer. Her name is Kali. Her name is Medea. She wants me dead. She gives me poison to drink, a bitter pink draught that is all dregs and that I call the Mother of Vinegar. Hysterically I suffocate, and this is called the Suffocation of the Mother. Or else she is fragile, and her brittleness threatens me:

> I am always aware of my mother
> ominous, threatening . . .
> She prevents freedom of movement
> if I move she quickly breaks
> and the splinters stab me.[33]

> Her eyes mirrored no clear-edged branches
> but countless garrottes.[34]

292   *Nicole Ward Jouve*

The bad Mother persecutes me. She sabotages everything I do. She wants my youth. She wants my cunt, now that nobody wants hers. She wants to subdue me, make me into her thing. She punishes me: I hide from her. If I want to live, I'll have to kill her.

8. And then there is real mother. A human being, who had her mother too, and that mother her mother. To whom things were passed down. Qualities and faults. Gifts and traumas. The fallible human being on whom we project the archetypes of the unconscious, Jung argues:

> Up till now everybody has been convinced that the idea 'my father', 'my mother', etc. is nothing but a faithful reflection of the real parent, corresponding in every detail to the original . . . [A] supposition of identity by no means brings that identity about. This is where the fallacy of the . . . 'veiled one' comes in. . . . X's idea of [her mother] is a complex quantity for which the real [mother] is only in part responsible, an indefinitely larger share falling to the [daughter]. So true is this that every time [she] criticizes or praises [her mother] [she] is unconsciously hitting back at [her]self . . .[35]

I have substituted 'she' for 'he', 'mother' for 'father' and 'daughter' for 'son' in this passage: it still makes a lot of sense. Those we imagine to be our fathers and mothers are complex projections of anima and animus. It is important, according to Jung, to dig them out of the webs in which they are caught, or else tragic results may ensue:

> They are quite literally the father and mother of all the disastrous entanglements of fate. . . . Together they form a divine pair. . . . Those who do not see them are in their hands, just as a typhus epidemic flourishes best when its source is undiscovered.[36]

The Mother is the figure of the emotional investment I make in people, in things. Look after me, love me, care for me, approve of me, protect me, work things out for me. Admire me, desire me. Save me from fear, of life, of death, of the future, of myself. I cling to the Mother–Father, institutions, the police, pension schemes, hospitals, the dream socialist state. I want to be able to say to the Mother, 'I hate you', hurl stones at shop windows, and she won't bash me on the head, she'll answer, 'I love you'.

> You gave me these lips
> Mother
> and I wanted to use them

> to say it was your fault —
>   so that nothing I could do would hurt.
>
>   . . .
>
> I wanted to blame you with my mouth
> so you could use yours
> to kiss away the tears.[37]

The Mother is she whose fault it endlessly is that things go wrong. It's her fault I am lonely, frustrated, plain, unsuccessful, unknown, unloved. If only she took me in her arms and loved me better everything would be alright. But she won't, the bitch. Right then. I'll batter and punish her till she gives me what I want. She still won't? OK. I'll hurt myself and make myself into pure pain and *that* will be her punishment:

> And now I
> Foam to wheat, a glitter of seas.
> The child's cry
>
> Melts in the wall.
> And I
> Am the arrow,
>
> The dew that flies
> Suicidal, at one with the drive
> Into the red
>
> Eye, the cauldron of morning.[38]

Oi, oi. I have been bad. I haven't done the right thing. I'll be good, Mother, I swear: then you'll make everything right. Anne Halley's speaker is the 'bearded mother' who has discovered 'twelve hairs on [her]/formerly smooth, virgin round chin'. In mock terror at having turned into one of Neumann's monstrosities of the primordial archetype through neglect of all the Mother-Goddess pieties (vegetarian, ritualistic and witch-like), she comically begs the 'Great Moon Mother' like a guilty little girl:

> It must be the red meat I've been eating.
> That I abandoned
> the sweet sisterhood of weavers . . .
>
> I neglected likewise
> the prescribed ritual baths, came at the wrong
> moon and other times, refused. . . .
> [D]idn't look in the oven for days

> but swept away the cobweb
> and my true friend, the spider, unregarded. . . .
>
> Holy Mother
>   I am most sorely distressed . . .
> when I contemplate these fruits
> sprung from the Great Unconscious
> these – who would not say, on the evidence –
> willed but unwished-for
> bristling projections.

The speaker ends with a prayer, 'by the hairs of my chinny-chin-chin', that 'we' may not 'be punished too cruelly', 'made into myth', 'turned into stone' – into Medusa.[39]

One reason why the Mother is such a big chunk for women is that the primary human being who bears us, the figure that embodies motherhood and generally does the mothering, is also the figure we, potentially at least, are as women meant to become. 'Mothering . . . involves a double identification for women, both as mother *and* as child', Nancy Chodorow points out. 'The whole preoedipal relationship has been internalized and perpetuated in a more ongoing way for women than for men.'[40] This is a source of greater inner contradictions:

> The *wants and needs* which lead women to become mothers put them in situations where their mothering *capacities* can be expressed. At the same time, women remain in conflict with their internal mother [I would add, *and* with the archetypal figures of the Mothers] and often their real mother as well.[41]

'*Wants and needs*': Chodorow italicises. As Kristeva maintains in 'Stabat Mater', it is those same wants and needs, especially the need for power, often denied women in the patriarchal system, that drives women to seek the realm of the maternal as especially privileged.

When I mother, I am pulled apart by the Mothers. The ideal ones, Ghea the fusional, the sensuous, the all-powerful, Mary the virginal, the kind, the both humble and powerful. The real one, in 'my' mother and in myself, easily exhausted, short-tempered, resentful of demands: how easily she becomes Medea, or the martyred Pietà!

Generations

Know this mother by her three smiles.

One grey one drawn over her mouth by frail hooks.
One hurt smile under each eye.

Know this mother by the frames she makes.
By the silence in which she suffers each child
to scratch out the aquatints in her mind.

Know this mother by the way she says
'darling' with her teeth clenched.
By the fabulous lies she cooks.[42]

And behind these mothers there's the Ideal Mother, whom I want to be because I do want to love: and I want her approval. But I am a real mother. The Ideal Mother in my head punishes me. It's the real mother's fault. I'll punish her: my mother, myself.

And so it goes.

And which of these mothers writes poetry?

Don't they all? Haven't I just shown it?

Women write: not the Mother, but mothers, plural: about mothers, about motherhood, about mothering. About themselves. Like Diogenes demonstrating to the Sophists that movement existed by getting up and crossing the room, women poets stage the conflicts of the Mothers, in mothers. A great many answers to Rich have been found in the last twenty years, through mothers writing poems.

The question, 'can the Mother write Poetry?' thus begins to dissolve. It was a false question. It came from making identities of 'Mother' and of 'Poetry': not acts and experiences in a continuous process of change and reinvention. It came from being invested by archetypes, projections. Answers came of themselves once I began to search within myself for what the Mother was, and found mothers. Once I began to listen to real mothers writing real poems.

In the 1970s, with Rich, many questioned Motherhood as an institution. The 1980s worked at separating motherhood from mothering. I want to argue for further types of separation, for distinguishing the archetypes and projections from the real mother, and the real self. In *Mothers Who Leave*, Rosie Jackson attacks the mythology of the perfect Mother. She agrees with Dorothy Dinnerstein's view that *'the problem is that woman has been constantly apprehended as a fantasy Mother and not as a separated being in her own right.'*[43] Jackson argues that our nostalgia for the imagined body of the Mother is a search for a wholeness which our secular culture does not allow:

the desire to merge with something beyond the personalised separated self, to move into a non-linguistic, oceanic state, need be neither unconscious nor regressive. It is the bliss of union consciously sought as the height of mature mystical experience.

Fantasies of the Mother take on such power and numinosity precisely because we are locked in a materialistic and secular society, where desire for another realm has nowhere else to locate itself.[44]

There is truth in that statement. And mothers do write poems. But I would bet that the question of the Mother and Poetry will not go away. For three reasons: 1. Every time a child is born, there is a need, a long-lasting need: who will fulfil that need? Realities haven't changed much since Tillie Olsen wrote: economic and social and political realities. 2. The Mothers will continue to do battle inside us, and more especially in mothers-who-write, until humanity has become very much wiser. 3. Ethics and Poetry don't necessarily match. If human beings become wiser or more fulfilled the world will be a great deal better but individuals might well not produce better poetry as a result. The worst mother may be the best poet . . .

NOTES

1. Adrienne Rich, *Of Woman Born* (London, Virago, 1977), p.36.
2. Sappho, *Poems and Fragments*, trans. Josephine Balmer (London, Brilliance Books, 1984), p.75
3. *The Complete Poems* ed. Thomas H. Johnson (London, Faber & Faber, 1970), p.703.
4. Hélène Cixous, *La Ville parjure, ou le retour des Erynies* (Paris, Théâtre du Soleil, 1994).
5. Rich, *Of Woman Born* p.31.
6. Kate Chopin, *The Awakening* (London, The Women's Press, 1978), p.80
7. Camille Paglia, *Sexual Personae: Art and Decadence From Nefertiti to Emily Dickinson* (New Haven, Yale University Press, 1990; Harmondsworth, Penguin, 1991).
8. Elizabeth Badinter, *L'Amour en plus: Histoire de l'amour maternel (XIIe–XXe s.)* (Paris, Editions Odile Jacob, 1992).
9. Tillie Olsen, *Silences* (London, Virago, 1980), p.33.
10. Angela Carter (ed.), *Wayward Girls and Wicked Women* (London, Virago, 1986).
11. Carol Ann Duffy, *Purple and Green: Poems by 33 Women Poets* (London, Rivelin Grapheme Press, 1985), p.22.
12. Rich, *Of Woman Born*, p.32.
13. Ibid., p.37.
14. Ibid.
15. Yeats, 'Sailing to Byzantium' in *Collected Poems* (London, Macmillan, 1982), p.217.
16. T.S. Eliot, 'Burnt Norton' in *The Four Quartets* in *The Complete Poems and Plays of T.S. Eliot* (Faber & Faber, 1969).
17. Julia Kristeva *Desire and Language* (Oxford, Blackwell, 1980), p.136.
18. Nicole Ward Jouve, *White Woman Speaks with Forked Tongue: Criticism as Autobiography* (London and New York, Routledge 1991), Chapters 4 and 5.
19. Hélène Cixous, 'Castration or Decapitation?', *Signs*, No.1 (1981).
20. 'the mothers of invention', The Point, Cardiff, Wales, 28 August – 3 September 1995, Workshops and Symposium.
21. Sappho, *Poems and Fragments*, trans. Josephine Balmer (London, Brilliance Books, 1984) p.74.
22. Sylvia Plath, *Collected Poems*, ed. Ted Hughes (London and Boston, Faber and Faber, 1981), p.179.
23. Ibid., p.183.
24. Ibid., p.89.
25. Nuala Ní Dhomhnaill, *Pharaoh's Daughter*, trans. Paul Muldoon (Dublin, The Gallery Press, 1990).
26. Elaine Feinstein, in *The Bloodaxe Book of Contemporary Women Poets: Eleven British Writers* ed. Jeni Couzyn, (Newcastle-upon-Tyne, Bloodaxe Books, 1985), p.115.
27. Ibid, p.119.
28. Sujata Bhatt, 'White Asparagus', in *Brunizem* (Manchester, Carcanet, 1988).
29. Grace Nichols, *i is a long memoried woman* (London, Karnak House, 1983).

30. Elaine Feinstein, *Some Unease and Angels: Selected Poems* (London, Hutchinson and University Center, Michtgan Green River Press, 1977), p.117.

31. Michèle Roberts, *Touch Papers* (London, Allison & Busby, 1982), p.51.

32. Julia Kristeva, 'Stabat Mater', in Toril Moi (ed.), *The Kristeva Reader* (Oxford, Blackwell, 1986), p.183.

33. Nagase Kiyoko, 'Mother', trans. Kenneth Rexwroth and Ikuko Atsumi, in Linthwaite, Illona, *Ain't I A Woman! Poems by Black and White Women* (London, Virago, 1987), p.96.

37. Nancy Morejon, 'Mother', trans. Kathleen Weaver, ibid., p.97.

35. Carl Jung, *Aion: Researches into the Phenomenology of the self.* (London and New York, Routledge, 1959), p.18.

36. Ibid., p.21.

37. Cheryl Moskowitz, 'Mother', in *Purple and Green: Poems by 33 Women Poets* (London, Rivelin Grapheme Press, 1985), p.115.

38. Plath, 'Ariel', in *Collected Poems*, pp.239–40.

39. Anne Halley, *The Bearded Mother* (Amherst, University of Massachusetts Press, 1979), pp.4–6.

40. Nancy Chodorow, *The Reproduction of Mothering* (Berkeley, University of California Press, 1978), p.204.

41. Ibid., p.205.

42. Anne Stevenson, in *The Bloodaxe Book of Contemporary Women Poets*, ed. Jeni Couzyn, pp.191–2.

43. Rosie Jackson, *Mothers Who Leave* (London, Pandora, 1994), p.283.

44. Ibid., p.285.

FURTHER READING

Badinter, Elizabeth, *L'Amour en plus: Histoire de l'amour maternel (XIIe–XXe s.)* (Paris, Editions Odile Jacob, 1992).

Bataille, Georges, *Literature and Evil*, tr. Alastair Hamilton (New York and London, Marion Boyars, 1985), pp.15–31.

Bhatt, Sujata, *Brunizem* (Manchester, Carcanet Press, 1988).

Carter, Angela (ed.), *Wayward Girls and Wicked Women* (London, Virago, 1986).

Chodorow, Nancy, *The Reproduction of Mothering* (Berkeley, University of California Press, 1978).

Chopin, Kate, *The Awakening* (London, The Women's Press, 1978), p.80.

Cixous, Hélène, 'Castration or Decapitation?', *Signs*, 1 (1981).

Cixous, Hélène, *La Ville parjure, ou le retour des Erynies* (Paris, Theatre du Soleil, 1994).

Couzyn, Jeni (ed.), *The Bloodaxe Book of Contemporary Women Poets: Eleven British Writers* (Newcastle, Bloodaxe Books, 1985).

Dhomhnaill, Nuala Ní, *Pharaoh's Daughter* (Dublin, The Gallery Press, 1990).

Duffy, Carol Anne, *Standing Female Nude* (London, Anvil Poetry Press, 1985).

Feinstein, Elaine, *Some Unease and Angels: Selected Poems* (London, Hutchinson; and University Center, Michigan: Green River Press, 1977).

Halley, Anne, *The Bearded Mother* (Amherst, University of Massachusetts Press, 1979).

Hulse, Peter, David Kennedy and David Morley (eds), *The New Poetry* (Newcastle, Bloodaxe Books, 1993).

Jackson, Rosie, *Mothers Who Leave* (London, Pandora, 1994).

Jung, Carl, *Aion: Researches into the Phenomenology of the Self* (London and New York, Routledge, 1959).

Kristeva, Julia, *Desire and Language* (Oxford, Blackwell, 1980).

Kristeva, Julia, 'Stabat Mater', in Toril Moi (ed.), *The Kristeva Reader* (Oxford, Blackwell, 1986).

Linthwaite, Illona (ed.), *Ain't I a Woman! Poems by Black and White Women* (London, Virago, 1987).

Nichols, Grace, *i is a long memoried woman* (London, Karnak House, 1983).

Olsen, Tillie, *Silences* (London, Virago, 1980).

Paglia, Camille, *Sexual Personae: Art and Decadence from Nefertiti to Emily Dickinson* (New Haven, Yale University Press, 1990; and Harmondsworth, Penguin, 1991).

Plath, Sylvia, *Collected Poems*, ed. Ted Hughes (London and Boston, Massachusetts, Faber & Faber, 1981).

Purple and Green: Poems by 33 Women Poets (London, Rivelin Grapheme Press, 1985).

Rich, Adrienne, *Of Woman Born* (London, Virago, 1977).

Roberts, Michèle, *Touch Papers* (London, Allison & Busby, 1982).

Sappho, *Poems and Fragments*, tr. Josephine Balmer (London, Brilliance Books, 1984).

Stevenson, Anne, *Travelling Behind Glass: Selected Poems 1963–73* (Oxford, Oxford University Press, 1974).

Woolf, Virginia, *A Room of One's Own* (Penguin, 1979).

Notes on Contributors

KATHLEEN BELL is a lecturer in English at De Montfort University where she teaches courses on poetry and nineteenth- and twentieth-century literature. She is the author of a number of articles, chiefly on twentieth-century poetry and popular fiction.

VICKI BERTRAM is Senior Lecturer in English Studies at Oxford Brookes University. She has published several essays on contemporary women's poetry and feminist theory, and is working on a book on poetry and gender. Together with colleagues at Brookes, she is currently organising the second 'Kicking Daffodils' conference.

PAULA BURNETT lectures at Brunel University College, London. In 1986 she compiled and edited the anthology *Caribbean Verse in English* (Penguin), after living in Jamaica in the late 1970s. She began as a Renaissance specialist but from the early 1980s has concentrated on the post-colonial. She is close to completing a study of Derek Walcott's work, and is working on a book to be published by Manchester University Press, *The Dark Heart of Empire: Sexuality and Colonialism in Contemporary Culture*, a study of Conrad's *Heart of Darkness* against a wide range of literary and film intertexts.

MEGAN LLOYD DAVIES gained her BA from the University of York, and is intending to do postgraduate study on the Sexual Dissidence and Cultural Change programme at the University of Brighton.

ALISON DONNELL lectures in post-colonial literatures at the Nottingham Trent University. She has published articles and contributed works on Caribbean women's writing and on the intersections and tensions between post-colonial and feminist literary theories. She is co-editor of *The Routledge Reader in Caribbean Literature* (1996).

GABRIELE GRIFFIN is Professor of Women's Studies at Leeds Metropolitan University. Her most recent publications include *Feminist Activism in the 1990s* (ed., Taylor and Francis, 1995); *Difference in View: Women and Modernism* (ed., Taylor and Francis, 1994); *Outwrite: Lesbianism and Popular Culture* (ed., Pluto, 1993). She is author of *Heavenly Love? Lesbian Images in 20th Century Women's Writing* (Manchester University Press, 1993) and is currently working on a book on AIDS and representation.

KARIN VOTH HARMAN is researching recent writing on motherhood at Sussex University. She teaches courses on writing and motherhood in Brighton.

ROMANA HUK is an Associate Professor of English at the University of New Hampshire (USA). Her publications include *Contemporary British Poetry: Essays in Theory and Criticism*, co-edited with James Acheson (State University of New York Press, 1996), *Stevie Smith* (Macmillan *Women Writers* series, forthcoming), and essays on intersections between poetic form and contemporary political and linguistic philosophy. In 1996 she hosted the first international conference/festival for 'alternative' poetries, and will be collecting essays and videographic footage from that event for publication.

HELEN KIDD is a poet and editor, and teaches English Studies at Oxford Brookes University. She co-edited *The Virago Book of Love Poetry* and *New Poetry from Oxford*, and also works with ITHACA Community Arts Group running writing groups. She has just finished a project with Katherine House Hospice in Adderbury. She has contributed to *Diverse Voices* (ed. Harriet Jump), *Contemporary Poetry meets Modern Theory* (Antony Easthope and John Thompson) and *The Scope of the Possible* (ed. Robert Hampson), and she is currently working on Scots, Irish and Caribbean women poets.

DECLAN LONG was born in Larne, Co. Antrim, and educated at Queen's University, Belfast, and Lancaster University. Currently living in Dublin, he is researching 'city spaces' in twentieth-century Irish poetry at Trinity College.

ALISON MARK is Research Fellow and Lecturer in English at Brunel University. She is also Assistant Editor of *Women: A Cultural Review*.

PARASKEVI PAPALEONIDA received her BA in English Language and Literature from the Aristotle University of Thessaloniki, Greece, and her MA in Women's Studies from the University of York, UK. She is currently working on a Ph.D thesis on late-Victorian women's poetry and the role of the auditor, in the English Department at Aristotle University. Her research interests include performance poetry, contemporary theories of genre, feminist theory and psychoanalysis. She earns a living by teaching English in a Merchant Marine Academy.

GILL PLAIN is a lecturer in English and Women's Studies at the University of Glamorgan. Her research interests include World War II, representations of sexuality, and detective fiction. She is the author of *Women's Fiction of the Second World War* (Edinburgh University Press, 1996), and is currently working on a study of gender in twentieth-century detective fiction.

DERYN REES-JONES is a freelance writer, editor and lecturer. In 1993 she received an Eric Gregory Award, and her first collection of poems, *The Memory Tray*, was published by Seren in 1994, and shortlisted for a Forward Prize. In 1996 she received an Arts Council of England Writer's Award. A collection of essays, *Consorting With Angels: Modern Women Poets*, will be published by Bloodaxe Books in 1997.

FIONA SAMPSON lives near Aberystwyth. She has pioneered the development of writing in health-care in the UK. Awards for her poetry include the Newdigate Prize, a Southern Arts Writer's Award and a Residency at the Millay Colony in New York State. Her first collection, *Picasso's Men*, was published in 1994, and commissions include *BirthChart* (1992) with printmaker Meg Campbell and *Stone Dials* (1995) with stonecarver Alec Peever. She co-curated the artists' books exhibition *My Grandmother* in 1994, and directs Aberystwyth International Poetryfest.

AILBHE SMYTH is a feminist activist, writer and critic, and Director of the Women's Education, Research and Resource Centre (WERRC) at University College Dublin. She has worked in feminist publishing and is co-editor of *Women's Studies International Forum*. She has written/edited several books, including *Wildish Things: An Anthology of New Irish Women's Writing* (Attic Press, 1989). Her research focuses mainly on feminist politics, culture and the state.

CATH STOWERS is a D. Phil. student and part-time lecturer at the Centre for Women's Studies, York University. She runs the York Women's Writing group and also set up the international Network on contemporary women's writing. She has had articles published on Jeanette Winterson and Michèle Roberts, and writes poetry.

HARRIET TARLO teaches English and Creative Writing at Bretton Hall College, a college of the University of Leeds. Her Ph.D was on H.D.'s long poem, *Helen in Egypt*, and she writes on H.D., Lorine Niedecker and other twentieth-century poets. She also publishes poetry and reviews.

NICOLE WARD JOUVE was born and bred in Provence and has lived her adult life in Britain.

She tends to write fiction/autobiography/family history in French, and essays in English, but this neat bi-lingual pattern is evidently changing. She has written books on Baudelaire, Colette, criticism as autobiography (*White Woman Speaks With Forked Tongue*, Routledge, 1991), a study of the Yorkshire Ripper case (*The Streetcleaner: The Yorkshire Ripper Case on Trial*, Marion Boyars, 1986) thoughts on her own writing and gender (*The Semi-Transparent envelope*, co-authored with S. Roe and S. Sellers, Marion Boyars, 1994), stories in various collections including her own *Shades of Grey* (Virago Press, 1981: from *Le Spectre du gris*, Editions des femmes, 1977) and *The House Where Salmon Perched* (1994), and one novel in French, *L'Entremise*. Her *Male and Female Created (S)he Them: Gender and Creativity* is forthcoming from Polity Press. She is Professor of Literature and Women's Studies at York University, UK.

Index